D1569899

HOMELESS,
FRIENDLESS,
AND PENNILESS

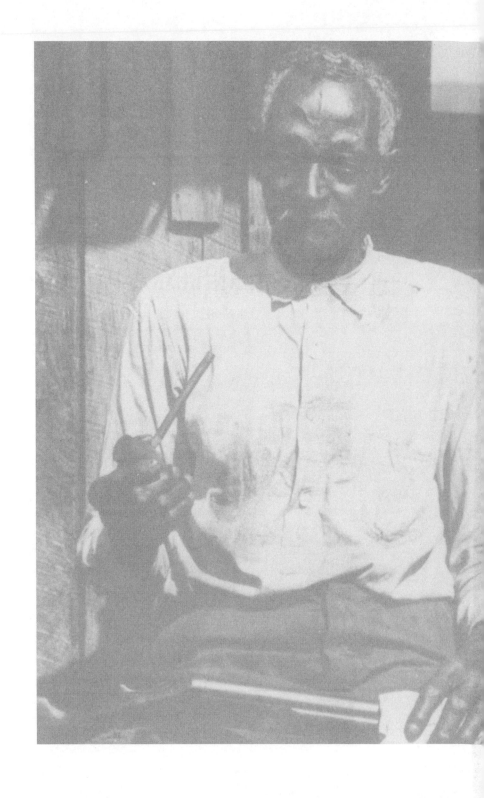

HOMELESS, FRIENDLESS, AND PENNILESS

THE WPA INTERVIEWS WITH FORMER SLAVES LIVING IN INDIANA

RONALD L. BAKER

INDIANA UNIVERSITY PRESS
Bloomington and Indianapolis

Publication of this book is made possible in part with the assistance of a Challenge Grant from the National Endowment for the Humanities, a federal agency that supports research, education, and public programming in the humanities.

This book is a publication of

Indiana University Press
601 North Morton Street
Bloomington, IN 47404-3797 USA

http://www.indiana.edu/~iupress

Telephone orders 800-842-6796
Fax orders 812-855-7931
Orders by e-mail iuporder@indiana.edu

The paper used in this publication meets the minimum requirements of American National Standard for Information Sciences—Permanence of Paper for Printed Library Materials, ANSI Z39.48-1984.

Manufactured in the United States of America

Library of Congress Cataloging-in-Publication Data

Homeless, friendless, and penniless : the WPA interviews with former slaves living in Indiana / [compiled by] Ronald L. Baker.
p.   cm.
From interviews conducted in the 1930s by fieldworkers of the Federal Writers' Project of the Works Progress Administration.
Includes bibliographical references and index.
ISBN 0-253-33803-4 (alk. paper)
1. Slaves—Indiana—Interviews. 2. Slaves—Southern States—Social conditions—Sources. 3. Plantation life—Southern States—History—Sources.   I. Baker, Ronald L., date.   II. Federal Writers' Project.

E444 .H66 2000
975—dc21
00-032004

1 2 3 4 5   05 04 03 02 01 00

TO
JILL

Nowhere do American history and
folklore intersect more closely than in
the "peculiar institution."

—RICHARD M. DORSON

CONTENTS

Acknowledgments xix

PART ONE: A FOLK HISTORY OF SLAVERY

Background of the WPA Interviews 3

Presentation of Materials 10

Living and Working on the Plantation 14

The Treatment of Slaves 20

Escaping from Slavery 25

Education 27

Religion 31

Folklore 35

Recollections of the Civil War 45

Living and Working after the Civil War 49

Value of the WPA Interviews 56

PART TWO: THE WPA INTERVIEWS WITH FORMER SLAVES

1. JOSEPH ALLEN
I'll Eat You Up Like a Dog 59

2. GEORGE W. ARNOLD
The Life of a Roustabout Is the Life of a Dog 60

3. THOMAS ASH
I Have No Way of Knowing Exactly How Old I Am 64

4. ROSA BARBER
Slaves Were Not Taught the Three Rs 64

5. LEWIS BARNETT
That Was the Way He Went When He Was Trying to Get Away 65

6. ROBERT BARTON
That's How Some Escaped to Canada 66

7. ANTHONY BATTLE
Runaway Slaves Would Kill the Dogs Chasing Them
and Never Be Caught 67

8. GEORGE BEATTY
Many Blacks with Only Their Clothing Crossed the River 67

9. SAMUEL BELL
Religion Is Worth the Greatest Fortune 68

10. MITTIE BLAKELEY
They Were Whipped Often and Hard 70

11. PATSY JANE BLAND
Free? Is Anybody Ever Free? 70

12. LIZZIE BOLDEN
A Much Easier Time Before She Was Free 72

13. CARL BOONE
Our Lives, Though Happy, Have Been Continuously
Ones of Hard Work 73

14. WALTER BORLAND
If Anyone Said Anything against the Negroes,
There Was a Fuss 75

15. JULIA BOWMAN
Living in the Big House 76

16. ANGIE MOORE BOYCE
Arrested in Indiana, Jailed in Louisville 76

17. EDNA BOYSAW
When Lincoln Freed Us, We Rejoiced 77

18. CALLIE BRACEY
Women Had to Split Rails All Day Long Just Like the Men 79

19. TOLBERT BRAGG
He Had a Great Desire to Go Up North
and See the Country 80

20. GEORGE WASHINGTON BUCKNER
Yes, the Road Has Been Long 81

21. GEORGE TAYLOR BURNS
Yes, I Know a Lot about Boats 86

22. BELLE BUTLER
A Mean Old Devil 94

23. JOSEPH WILLIAM CARTER
I Wish the Whole World Would Be Decent 95

24. ELLEN CAVE
Her Owner Was a Mean Man   98

25. HARRIET CHEATAM
And Did We Eat!   100

26. ROBERT J. CHEATHAM
Educated Slaves Forged Passes and Escaped to Northern States   101

27. JAMES CHILDRESS
Slaves Always Prayed to God for Freedom   108

28. SARAH COLBERT
The Village Witch   109

29. FRANK COOPER
Misery Days   110

30. JOHN COOPER
I Got Religion   111

31. MARY CRANE
Almost Sold down the River   113

32. CORNELIUS CROSS
Auctioned Off More Times Than He Had Fingers and Toes   114

33. ETHEL DAUGHERTY
A Slaveholder Kept Many Black Women in His House   116

34. JOHN DAUGHERTY
Ignorance of the Bible Caused All the Trouble   118

35. LIZZIE DAUGHERTY
One of the Saddest Events That Could Happen to a Mother   118

36. RACHAEL DUNCAN
Some of the Folks Was Mean to Me   119

37. H. H. EDMUNDS
They Poured Out Their Religious Feelings in Their Spirituals   120

38. JOHN EUBANKS
Most the Time We's Hungry, but We Win The War   121

39. JOHN W. FIELDS
Twelve Children Were Taken from My Mother in One Day   125

40. GEORGE FORTMAN
Indian Slaves   129

41. ALEX FOWLER
The First Black in Lake County 135

42. MATTIE FULLER
I Have Sang Myself to Death 136

43. FRANCIS GAMMONS
Slaves Were Treated as Well as Could Be Expected 138

44. JOHN HENRY GIBSON
He Liked Indianapolis So Well That He Decided to Stay 138

45. PETER GOHAGEN
We Used to Have Some Fine Times 141

46. SIDNEY GRAHAM
Escaping from Ku Kluxers 144

47. Ms. L. GREEN
If Anyone Got Paid for Her Family's History, She Wanted the Money 144

48. BETTY GUWN
Discipline Was Quite Stern 145

49. JOSIE HARRELL
Buried Treasure on the Old Stephen Lee Place 146

50. MASTON HARRIS
Valued at $1,200, He Was Permitted to Buy His Freedom 147

51. NEALY HARVEY
Many Times She Had Nothing to Eat 148

52. JOSEPHINE HICKS
Her Master Was Also Her Father, so She Was Always Well Treated 148

53. DR. SOLOMON HICKS
All He Was Given Was a Three-Legged Horse to Start Life Anew 149

54. MRS. HOCKADAY
Northerners Would Not Trust Them 151

55. SAMANTHA HOUGH
I Believe a Little in Dreams 152

56. ROBERT HOWARD
A Very Kind Old Man 153

57. MATTHEW HUME
They Came to Indiana Homeless, Friendless, and Penniless 153

58. LILLIAN HUNTER
Punishment Sent Direct from God   156

59. HENRIETTA JACKSON
Ironing White Folks' Collars and Cuffs   156

60. MATTIE JENKINS
Pins Were Stuck through Their Tongues   157

61. LIZZIE JOHNSON
They Wanted Most for Their Children to Learn to Read and Write   158

62. PETE JOHNSON
That's a Whipping House for the Likes of You   159

63. ELIZABETH (BETTIE) JONES
Yes, Honey, I Was a Slave   160

64. IRA JONES
Ira's Family Was Mistreated by White People   162

65. NATHAN JONES
A Very Cruel Way to Treat Human Beings   163

66. RALPH KATES
I Came to the World a Year Too Late to Be Born a Slave   164

67. ALEXANDER KELLEY
A Mature Man-Slave of Good Physique Was Worth as High as $3,000   165

68. BELL DEAM KELLEY
Bell's Parents Lived Together but Worked on Different Plantations   166

69. ELVIRA LEE
God Washed Out Her Insides with Milk, Which Killed All Her Sins   167

70. ADELINE ROSE LENNOX
I've Seen and Done a Lot of Things That Most Folks Have Missed   170

71. THOMAS LEWIS
There Was No Such Thing as Being Good to Slaves   172

72. LEVI LINZY
Salt and Pepper Put in Raw Wounds   174

73. SARAH H. LOCKE
An Intelligent Old Lady   175

74. MARIA LOVE
Her Mother Had to Work Very Hard, Just Like a Man   176

75. THOMAS MAGRUDER
A Possible Prototype for Harriet Beecher Stowe's Uncle Tom 177

76. HETTIE MCCLAIN
Slaves Were Held in Kentucky after the Civil War 179

77. ROBERT MCKINLEY
Considered Rich, for They Could Eat Meat without Stealing It 181

78. RICHARD MILLER
His Early Life Was a Nightmare 181

79. BEN MOORE
Ben Was a Hoss 184

80. JOHN MOORE
At the Wedding Both Bride and Groom Jumped over a Broom Handle 186

81. HENRY CLAY MOORMAN
Slaves Seldom Married among Themselves on the Same Plantation 188

82. AMERICA MORGAN
She Believed Firmly in Haunts 190

83. GEORGE MORRISON
I Don't Really Believe in Ghosts, but You Know How It Is 192

84. JOSEPH MOSLEY
Sometimes They Had Nothing but Garbage to Eat 194

85. HENRY NEAL
You Are Just as Free as I or Anyone Else in This United States 195

86. REVEREND OLIVER NELSON
Speak Those Greasy Words Again, Brother 196

87. SARAH O'DONNELL
It Is Tiresome, but I Am Patiently Waiting the Call 197

88. RUDOLPH D. O'HARA
Just Like the Ground Had Swallowed Him Up 198

89. W. F. PARROTT
Slaveholders Showed a Different Face to Union Troops 199

90. AMY ELIZABETH PATTERSON
She Became a Firm Believer in Communication with Departed Ones 201

91. SPEAR PITMAN
Some Overseers Liked to See Blood and Whipped for Nothin' at All 203

92. Nelson Polk
Dogs Couldn't Trail Runaway Slaves on a Stream Bed   204

93. Nettie Pompey
The Slave Children Were Treated as Well as the White Children   206

94. Mrs. Preston
Her Father's Farm Was Burned Out by the Ku Klux Klan   206

95. William M. Quinn
Gift Slaves   207

96. Candies Richardson
Jim Scott Beat Her Husband for Praying   208

97. Joe Robinson
Rube Black Beat His Slaves Severely for the Least Offense   211

98. Rosaline Rogers
Slaves Couldn't Even Mix with Poor Whites   211

99. Parthenia Rollins
Treated So Cruelly That It Would Make Your Hair Stand on Ends   212

100. Katie Rose
The Hant Began Coming to Our Cabin   214

101. John Rudd
The Cries and Prayers of the Whipped Slaves Were Ignored   217

102. Elizabeth Russell
I Hadn't Only Seen President Lincoln but Had Sat on His Knee   219

103. Amanda Elizabeth (Lizzie) Samuels
Forced to Eat Chicken Heads, Fish Heads, Pig Tails, and Parsnips   223

104. Mary Elizabeth Scarber
Blacks Who Worked on the Donnell Farm Were Treated Kindly   224

105. Lulu Scott
'Course I Can See Spirits   225

106. Arthur Shaffer
They Moved at Least Two Hundred Slaves over the Mason-Dixon Line   227

107. Jack Simms
He Regretted Very Much That He Had Been Denied an Education   228

108. Billy Slaughter
There Must Be Someone Left to Tell about Old Times   229

109. Moses Slaughter
A Cause That Had Both God and President Lincoln on Its Side 231

110. Alex and Elizabeth (Betty) Smith
I Like to Talk and Meet People 235

111. Mattie Brown Smith
There Was Lots of Colored Folks Crossed the River at This Point 237

112. Mrs. Robert Smith
They Were Sorry to Leave Their Owners and Shift for Themselves 239

113. Susan Smith
The Presence of White People Still Seemed to Annoy Her 239

114. Sylvester Smith
They Said the Civil War Would Be Only a "Breakfast Spell" 240

115. Mary Ann Stewart
Eat Plain Foods, Take Reasonable Exercise, Refrain from Worry,
and Read the Bible 240

116. Barney Stone
Sixteen Years of Hell as a Slave on a Plantation 241

117. Mary Stonestreet
They Had to Have Freedom Papers Before They Could Settle in Indiana 244

118. Adah Isabelle Suggs
One Night in a Dream Her Mother Received Directions for Escaping 244

119. Katie Sutton
Yes, Ma'am, I Believe in Evil Spirits 246

120. Mary Emily (Mollie) Eaton Tate
These Are Scenes of My Childhood That I Can Never Forget 248

121. Preston Tate
It Was Not Unusual for Boys and Girls to Dress Alike 252

122. George Thomas
Pioneer Industries and Amusements in Clark County 253

123. George Thompson
I Have No Education; I Can Neither Read nor Write 255

124. Joe Wade
His Mother's Master Was Very Cruel to Her 256

125. Reverend Wamble
His Mother Died from a Miscarriage Caused by a Whipping 257

126. LOUIS WATKINS
They Were Taught to Read, Write, and Figure 260

127. SAMUEL WATSON
Samuel Was Sent to the Poor House 261

128. HENRY WEBB
Plans for the Escapes Were Hatched in a Black Masonic Lodge 263

129. NANCY WHALLEN
Preaching and Shouting Sometimes Lasted All Day Sunday 263

130. ANDERSON WHITTED
They Often Took Babies from Their Mothers and Sold Them 264

131. ALFRED (PETE) WILSON
Ol' Boss Was Ordinarily Good to Us 266

132. GEORGE WINLOCK
The Entire War Was a Mistake 267

133. ALEX WOODSON
I Don't Believe in Ghosts, but I Do in Spirits 270

134. ANTHONY YOUNG
He Doesn't Dare Touch You; You're a Free Man 272

Appendixes
Appendix I. Informants 275
Appendix II. Slave States of Informants 286
Appendix III. Indiana Towns of Residence of Informants 290
Appendix IV. Indiana Counties of Residence of Informants 295
Appendix V. Unaltered Versions of Previously Unpublished Indiana
Interviews with Former Slaves 300
Appendix VI. Thematic Index 313

Living and Working on the Plantation 313
The Treatment of Slaves 314
Escaping from Slavery 316
Education 317
Religion 318
Folklore 318
Recollections of the Civil War 319
Living and Working after the Civil War 320

Works Consulted 323
Index 325

ILLUSTRATIONS

George Washington Buckner   81

John W. Fields   125

Peter Dunn (Peter Gohagen?)   141

Anderson Whitted   264

ACKNOWLEDGMENTS

I thank Robert L. Carter and David E. Vancil of the Rare Books and Special Collections Department of the Cunningham Memorial Library at Indiana State University for making the WPA manuscripts available. Under their supervision, the Indiana WPA files have been carefully organized and indexed, and a microfilm edition and a guide to the collection have been prepared (see Carter and Vancil 1992). A number of other libraries, historical societies, and genealogical societies assisted in locating and providing newspaper articles, obituaries, and photographs. Among those especially helpful in providing materials were the following:

Allen County Public Library

Clay County Genealogical Society

Elkhart County Historical Society

Evansville Museum of Arts and Science

Evansville-Vanderburgh County Public Library

Gary Public Library

Indiana State Library (Newspaper Section, Indiana Division)

Jay County Genealogy Society

Johnson County Historical Society

Library of Congress (Manuscript Division)

Madison-Jefferson County Public Library

Monroe County Historical Museum

Monroe County Library

Noblesville Southeastern Public Library

Ohio County Public Library

Randolph County Historical and Genealogical Society

Saint Joseph County Public Library

Scott County Public Library

Southern Indiana Genealogical Society

Tippecanoe County Historical Association

Vigo County Public Library

I also thank Father Anthony Spicuzza, pastor of the Annunciation of the Blessed Virgin Mary Church in Brazil, Indiana, for ushering my family through a rite of passage while I was working on this book. Father Spicuzza, a family friend for years, claims that he is glad he does not have the talent to write books. Though he has the intellect, wit, compassion, and experience to write a shelf of books, he—like Socrates, Jesus, and the former slaves who told the stories in this book—deals more immediately with the fundamental reality of life.

I am appreciative, too, of the sabbatical I was awarded during the spring semester of 1998. Without a semester's leave from teaching and administrative duties in the Department of English at Indiana State University, I could not have completed this book.

PART ONE

A FOLK HISTORY OF SLAVERY

BACKGROUND OF THE WPA INTERVIEWS

This book is based on a collection of interviews with former slaves who were living in Indiana in the late 1930s. The interviews were conducted as part of Indiana's contribution to a federal project undertaken in seventeen states during the Great Depression. Over a three-year period, former slaves and, in some cases, descendants of former slaves shared their memories with field-workers of the Federal Writers' Project (FWP) of the Works Progress Administration (WPA), renamed the Work Projects Administration in 1939. As a result of this early fieldwork in folklore and oral history, today we have an invaluable record of the lives and thoughts of former slaves who moved to Indiana after the Civil War and made significant contributions to the evolving patchwork of Hoosier culture. The Indiana interviews are especially notable because they were collected from freed slaves living in a state that was free during the Civil War. Most of the other former slaves interviewed for the national project still lived in the South. In fact, according to John W. Blassingame, most of the WPA informants interviewed in southern states "had spent all of their lives in the same locale as their former master's plantation" (Blassingame 1985: 89).

The Indiana slave narratives provide a glimpse of slavery through the memories of those who experienced it; thus, they preserve insiders' views of a deplorable chapter in American history. Though the former slaves represented in the Indiana collection lived in Indiana at the time of the interviews, they had, of course, been held in slavery in other states; therefore, the interviews reveal experiences of African Americans enslaved not in a single state but in eleven different states from the Carolinas to Louisiana, though most of them were slaves in Kentucky (see Appendix II). Just as important, the interviews reveal how former slaves fared in Indiana after the Civil War and during the Depression. Some became ministers, a few became educators, and one became a physician; but many lived in poverty and survived on Christian faith and small government pensions.

The interviews on which this book is based are located in the Cunningham Memorial Library at Indiana State University in Terre Haute, Indiana. Since the Department of Public Relations at Indiana State Teachers College, now Indiana State University, was the state sponsor of the Indiana Federal Writers' Project, the manuscript files of the Indiana Federal Writers' Project were deposited in the library at Indiana State, where they remain. The 36-cubic-foot collection, housed in the Department of Rare Books and Special Collections of the Cunningham Memorial Library, contains around 60,000 pages of material on, among other things, the oral history and folklore of all of Indiana's ninety-two counties (see Carter and Vancil 1992). In addition to the interviews with former slaves living in Indiana at that time, the collection is a storehouse of traditional foodways, songs, beliefs, customs, sayings, cures, legends, jokes, and place-name anecdotes, as well as other accounts of Hoosier folklife and local history. Material related to the slave narrative project includes papers about the Underground Railroad in Indiana, a summary of slave laws in Indiana, records of indentures in Indiana, and an account of the Roberts Settlement, a black community in Hamilton County. The slave narrative project represented here was simply a small, albeit important, part of a larger project funded by the federal government during the Depression to provide jobs for unemployed white-collar workers. A major goal of the Federal Writers' Project was the preparation and publication of a guidebook for each state; Indiana's guide, *Indiana: A Guide to the Hoosier State,* was published in September 1941.

The WPA's slave narrative collection project grew indirectly out of earlier efforts to preserve the personal-experience stories of former slaves. Even before the Civil War, slave autobiographies and epistolary slave testimonies were published, but probably the first systematic attempt to collect the dictated experiences of former slaves began around 1927. Andrew P. Watson, then a graduate student in anthropology at Fisk University, spent two years interviewing 100 older African Americans, mainly former slaves, and eventually, in 1945, the Social Sciences Institute at Fisk University published six autobiographical narratives and fifty accounts of conversion experiences in *God Struck Me Dead: Religious Conversion Experiences and Autobiographies of Negro Ex-Slaves* (Fisk University 1945a), later reprinted in part by Johnson (Johnson 1969) and in full by Rawick (Rawick 1972, vol. 19).

A year or two after Watson began his fieldwork, Charles S. Johnson, founder of the Social Science Institute at Fisk University, organized a community study, and in 1929 a member of his research staff, Ophelia Settle, interviewed a number of former slaves living near Fisk. Encouraged by Johnson, Settle broadened the scope of her project and began collecting the life histories of other former slaves then living in rural Tennessee and Kentucky (Yetman 1967: 540–541). In 1945, thirty-seven of her one hundred interviews were published as *Unwritten History of Slavery: Autobiographical Account of Negro Ex-Slaves* (Fisk University 1945b), also reprinted by Rawick (Rawick 1972, vol. 18).

Also in 1929, John B. Cade—who chaired the Extension Department of Southern University in Scotlandville, Louisiana—asked students in his U.S. history class to collect recollections of slavery from former slaveholders as well as from former slaves. During the 1929–1930 academic year, thirty-six of his students turned in eighty-two interviews as class assignments. In 1935 Cade published some of this material in "Out of the Mouths of Ex-Slaves," an article in the *Journal of Negro History*. From 1935 to 1938, Cade directed a similar project at Prairie View State College, collecting more than four hundred additional unpublished interviews with former slaves (Yetman 1967: 540; Perdue, Barden, and Phillips 1980: xii).

Lawrence D. Reddick studied under Charles S. Johnson at Fisk University and interviewed former slaves as part of Johnson's community study project (Yetman 1967: 541). Reddick later joined the faculty at Kentucky State University (then Kentucky State Industrial College) in Frankfort, and on June 14, 1934, he proposed a collection of testimonies of former slaves to Harry L. Hopkins, director of the Federal Emergency Relief Administration (Botkin 1944: 37). Since the Federal Emergency Relief Administration supported programs that put unemployed Americans to work, Reddick received federal funding to initiate the collecting project (Perdue, Barden, and Phillips 1980: xiii). Reddick first proposed a pilot study conducted by a dozen African American students who would interview former slaves in the Ohio River Valley, and then he planned a broader project that would put as many as five hundred white-collar African Americans to work interviewing surviving slaves throughout the South. Although nothing came of Reddick's large-scale project, his pilot project resulted in nearly 250 interviews, which are apparently still unpublished, in Kentucky and Indiana from September 1934 through July 1935. What is more, Reddick was the first to get federal funding to support the collecting of interviews with former slaves (Yetman 1967: 542–543; Perdue, Barden, and Phillips 1980: xiii).

In April 1935, Congress passed the Emergency Relief Appropriations Act, which provided authority for the establishment of the Works Progress Administration, and Harry L. Hopkins, director of the Federal Emergency Relief Administration, was appointed to a similar position with the WPA. In August 1935, when the WPA announced that it would sponsor projects to employ out-of-work artists, musicians, dramatists, and writers, Hopkins created the Federal Writers' Project, appointing Henry G. Alsberg—former newspaperman, writer, and theater director—to direct the WPA's writing program. Among its significant accomplishments, the Federal Writers' Project collected local folklore and oral history, including life histories of former slaves, and produced the American Guide Series (Mangione 1972: 53–56). In 1936 Alsberg had the foresight to appoint Sterling A. Brown to the Federal Writers' Project's Washington office as National Editor of Negro Affairs. Brown, a member of Howard University's English Department, was a poet of some stature and a pioneer in the study of African American literature, so at the time he was the right person to oversee the development of the Writers' Program's projects dealing with African American culture (Yetman 1967: 546).

The first WPA testimonies of former slaves were collected in 1936 by the Georgia Writers' Project under the direction of Carolyn P. Dillard (Perdue, Barden, and Phillips 1980: xv). Later in 1936, fieldworkers also began interviewing former slaves in South Carolina, Virginia, and Florida. Significantly, in the middle of the same year, folklorist John Lomax, already well known for his collections of American folksongs, was appointed National Advisor on Folklore and Folkways for the Federal Writers' Project, a position he held for more than a year. Reviewing some of the Florida interviews with former slaves that had been sent to the national office, Lomax liked what he read and proposed a large-scale program directed by the national office to collect slave testimonies in other states; consequently, on April 1, 1937, instructions were sent to FWP directors in other southern and border states charging workers to begin collecting the experiences of former slaves living in their states (Yetman 1967: 549–550; Perdue, Barden, and Phillips 1980: xv–xvi). Though the Florida interviews were not the first, they persuaded Lomax, who apparently was unaware of the Georgia and Virginia interviews, to initiate a national slave narrative collecting project. As Yetman notes, "Lomax's tenure with the Writers' Project was relatively brief, but his impact upon its program and especially upon the formation of the Slave Narrative Collection was enduring" (Yetman 1967: 545).

On August 31, 1939, the states assumed control of the WPA, and the Federal Writers' Program became simply the Writers' Program. Earlier the same year, most of the interviewing of former slaves already had stopped, but from late 1936 through early 1939, seventeen states turned in around 2,300 interviews to the Washington office. Arkansas turned in the most interviews, 677, and Kansas submitted the fewest, only 3 (Perdue, Barden, and Phillips 1980: xvi).

State fieldworkers in the Slave Narrative Project followed a standard set of suggestions and questions provided by the national office, so the interviews share common textual and stylistic features. Although the fieldworkers' questions do not appear in the edited texts, using the list as an interview guide enabled inexperienced fieldworkers to gather information on a variety of subjects. In many cases, however, following the list did not allow an informant the opportunity to "talk freely," "to say what he pleases without reference to the questions," as the instructions prescribed.

After the fieldworkers had interviewed their informants, their field notes usually went through several drafts to meet the guidelines of the Washington office. Sometimes the notes were rewritten to read as if they were in response to a fieldworker's questions, and sometimes editors contributed their notions of African American dialect in their revisions. Once the interviews were reworked and typed with manual typewriters on 8½" x 11" paper, some of the them, at least, were forwarded to the national office (Baker and Baker 1996: 6, 9).

Today professional fieldworkers in folklore and oral history use portable audio and video tape recorders to preserve the words and behavior of their informants, but these electronic tools were not available to WPA fieldworkers in the 1930s. Although in some states some of the WPA interviews with former slaves were recorded on aluminum disks and then transcribed, the amateur fieldworkers in Indiana apparently took notes with pencil and paper, simply jotting down the main ideas at the time of the interview. Later, either the fieldworkers or their editors fleshed out the material in preparation for the federal Slave Narrative Project.

Although the WPA fieldworkers did not provide the contextual information that contemporary folklorists and oral historians prefer, what we know about the social and physical contexts of the interviews must be considered when reading the Indiana interviews with former slaves. First, although most of the texts were collected from African Americans who had experienced slavery firsthand and probably regularly told their children and grandchildren personal-experience tales, the informants were quite old in the 1930s when the tales were collected by the WPA fieldworkers, and over the years their memories had probably become selective. In addition, a good many of the informants had still been children at the end of the Civil War and had had limited experience with slave life. Adults who had spent long, hard lives in servitude before experiencing freedom probably would have told even grimmer stories of life on the plantations (Blassingame 1985: 88). Moreover, all but one (Anna Pritchett) of the eighteen fieldworkers who interviewed former slaves living in Indiana were white, which probably had some influence on the interviews. Blassingame points out, "Not only did most of the whites lack empathy with the former slaves, they often phrased their questions in ways that indicated the kinds of answers they wanted" (Blassingame 1985: 86); and Woodward observes, "The distinctiveness of interviews where the interviewer and the interviewed were of the same race is readily apparent. The whole atmosphere changes. The thick dialect diminishes and so do deference and evasiveness and tributes to planter benevolence" (Woodward 1985: 52).

Some of the informants were probably cautious about providing information because the fieldworkers were government workers, and they either did not trust or did not want to offend the WPA interviewers. White fieldworker Richard M. Dorson recalls how difficult it was for him to establish rapport with African American informants in Calvin, Michigan, in the 1950s. After several "strenuous unrewarding days in the field," one black female resident finally confessed why they mistrusted him and had not given him any folktales: "We didn't know what to make of you when you first came here; there had been two federal detectives around not long ago, to break up a marijuana ring, and some thought you were from the FBI" (Dorson 1967: 21–22).

On October 17, 1939, the WPA established the Writers' Unit of the Library of Congress Project to edit and prepare the slave narrative collection for deposit in the Library of Congress. Another folklorist, Benjamin A. Botkin, who had joined the FWP as folklore editor in 1938, was appointed chief editor of the project. Organizing the interviews first by state and then alphabetically by informant within each state, Botkin had them bound in seventeen volumes and deposited in the Rare Book Room of the Library of Congress. The sixty-one Indiana typescripts are bound in Volume V, "Indiana Narratives" as "Prepared by the Federal Writers' Project of the Works Progress Administration for the State of Indiana." Botkin's introduction to the collection stresses the value and limitations of the interviews with former slaves:

> Set beside the work of formal historians, social scientists, and novelists, slave autobiographies, and contemporary records of abolitionists and planters, these life histories, taken down as far as possible in the narrators' words, constitute an invaluable body of unconscious evidence or indirect source material, which scholars and writers dealing with the South, especially, social psychologists and cultural anthropologists, cannot afford to reckon without. For the first and last time, a large number of surviving slaves (many of whom have since died) have been permitted to tell their own story, in their own way. In spite of obvious limitations—bias and fallibility of both informants and interviewers, the use of leading questions, unskilled techniques, and insufficient controls and checks—this saga must remain the most authentic and colorful source of our knowledge of the lives and thoughts of thousands of slaves, of their attitudes toward one another, toward their masters, mistresses, and overseers, toward poor whites, North and South, the Civil War, Emancipation, Reconstruction, religion, education, and virtually every phase of Negro life in the South. (Reprinted in Rawick 1972: I, 171)

In 1945 Botkin introduced scholars as well as general readers to the slave narrative collection when he published a one-volume selection of edited excerpts and some complete narratives from the collection as *Lay My Burden Down: A Folk History of Slavery.* Botkin viewed the book "not as a collection of source material for the scholar but as a finished product for the general reader" (Botkin 1989: xxxiii). That meant using mainly edited excerpts rather than whole narratives, abandoning the original attempts at dialect writing, and focusing on narratives that reflected broad "human and imaginative aspects" as well as "on those oral, literary, and narrative folk values for which in 1928 I coined the word 'folk-say'" (Botkin 1989: xxxiii). To give the book unity and coherence, Botkin organized the material in five sections, dealing with folklore, life histories, the slave's world, the Civil War, and Reconstruction; so the book generally moves from antebellum slavery through the war and Reconstruction to the 1930s.

In 1970, Norman R. Yetman published another work based on the WPA slave narratives, *Voices from Slavery: Selections from the Slave Narrative Collection of the Library of Congress,* which consists of an introduction and around a hundred texts. Like Botkin, Yetman edited the texts. As Rawick points out,

> Professor Yetman's selections in this volume of 100 of the WPA narratives, while excellent, also have been edited. At times, in order "to improve readabil-

ity and continuity," he has rewritten sentences and deleted others; he has eliminated the different "dialect" spellings in "an attempt to achieve some uniformity"; he has eliminated "those comments . . . that concerned the informant's situation when interviewed"; and he has usually deleted all the material included in the interviews that deal with events that occurred after the Civil War. (Rawick 1972: I, xvii)

In 1972 George P. Rawick published photographic reproductions of all of the interviews in the seventeen bound volumes in the Library of Congress as the first part of *The American Slave: A Composite Autobiography,* accompanied by an introductory volume, *From Sundown to Sunup: The Making of the Black Community.* As volumes 18, *Unwritten History of Slavery,* and 19, *God Struck Me Dead,* he also included the slave narratives recorded in the 1920s and 1930s by fieldworkers from Fisk University. The sixty-one Indiana narratives, along with the Alabama narratives, appear in volume 6.

Subsequently, in state depositories Rawick uncovered many other WPA interviews with ex-slaves that for some reason had not been sent to Washington. With the publication of this material in two separate supplemental series in 1977 and 1979, Rawick's monumental project eventually expanded from nineteen to forty-one volumes. The Indiana narratives that he found in the Cunningham Memorial Library at Indiana State University appear with the Ohio narratives in the first supplement, Series 1, Volume 5. Rawick includes three narratives collected in Indiana in the 1979 supplement (Rawick 1979: I, 275–283), but they had previously appeared in the 1977 supplement (Rawick 1977: IV, 82–83, 89–91, 230–231). The narratives in the two supplemental series are photographic reproductions of retyped narratives instead of photographic reproductions of the original typescripts, as in the earlier volumes. Rawick explained that he "left the interviews exactly as they were recorded, thus permitting future scholars to handle the narratives as they see fit" (Rawick 1972: I, xvii). In 1976 the Scholarly Press issued a seventeen-volume edition of the bound narratives in the Library of Congress. Like Rawick's volumes, this edition was intended for scholarly purposes and marketed mainly to libraries.

PRESENTATION OF MATERIALS

While the worthy aim of some collections of WPA interviews with former slaves is to present the material in its "original form" as far as possible (see, for example, Perdue, Barden, and Phillips 1980: xi), the WPA texts were never verbatim. Since the so-called "original texts" were retold in the words of the fieldworkers and their editors, and since most of the unaltered texts are readily available to professionals, I feel justified in rewriting the Indiana interviews for a general reading audience. In working with the Indiana interviews, I have assumed the role of final editor, receiving the material in 1998.

Though at first I attempted to present the interviews under thematic headings, there was so much overlapping of topics in most of the interviews that I finally decided to follow most earlier collections of WPA interviews and arrange the interviews alphabetically by name of the former slave or informant; as a compromise, however, I have provided a thematic index in Appendix VI. Thus, readers interested mainly in life and work on the plantation, the treatment of slaves, escaping from slavery, education, religion, folklore, recollections of the Civil War, or life and work after the Civil War can follow the order of the interviews under these headings in Appendix VI. I also have supplied titles reflecting main ideas in the interviews to guide readers to particular topics. Appendix I gives as much of the following information as is available for each interview: name of former slave (with informant, if different), dates of birth and death, city and county of residence in Indiana, slave state, name of fieldworker, date of the interview or date the text was deposited, and references to Rawick's volumes for the convenience of those who would like to read or compare unaltered texts.

In reworking the interviews, I have generally followed the models of Botkin and Yetman, rewriting and organizing the interviews to improve readability, unity, and coherence. In rewriting the texts, I have corrected typographical errors, misspellings, grammatical errors, errors in capitalization, and errors in punctuation without notation, though in alleged direct quotes of the infomants I have retained some usages that are considered grammatically and politically incorrect. If there was more than one interview with an informant, I combined the information in these interviews into a single text. If I found obituaries or newspaper articles about the informants, I incorporated and internally documented information from those sources in the interviews, too. Since slaves generally took the surnames of their holders, I refer throughout Part Two to the informants or former slaves by their first names to avoid confusing the slaves with their masters, though I realize that some readers may consider this practice patronizing.

I have eliminated most of the fieldworkers' and editors' attempts at recording dialect. Recording dialect in standard orthography is a problem, especially for amateur fieldworkers such as those employed by the WPA. While a Joel Chandler Harris or Rowland E. Robinson can do a reasonably good job of representing regional or ethnic dialects, most attempts by lay people have been unsuccessful. Even when literary artists render dialects in phonetic spellings, their efforts are not always appreciated or understood. For example, most critics agree that Rowland Robinson faithfully depicted the dialect from his area of Vermont; however, in an otherwise enthusiastic review of *Danvis Folks* in the *Atlantic Monthly* (June 1885: 819), the reviewer wrote:

> Mr. Robinson probably had no deliberate intention of writing for posterity. Still, if given a chance, good work will survive, and there certainly seems no need for burdening it with the hideous phonetic spelling, unpronounceable by any one [sic] not acquainted with the dialect represented. . . . Mr. Robinson's subtle accuracy in dialect . . . quite needlessly restricts the enjoyment of his human and very appealing work to those people to whom the vanishing dialect he writes offers the fewest difficulties, and cuts it off entirely from popular appreciation by the future but not far-distant generations to whom its gnarled idiom will be utterly unknown. (Quoted in Baker 1973: 221–222)

From the beginning of the slave narrative project, recording African American dialect presented a problem for the FWP fieldworkers and those in the Washington office. On May 1, 1937, John Lomax wrote to the acting director of the Virginia Writers' Project:

> I have read with intense interest all of the ex-slave stories that you have sent in. Your workers are doing a splendid job in this field and I hesitate to make any suggestions that may be interpreted as unfavorable. However, I wish to make a few suggestions:
> The story of Charles Grandy, as written out by Mr. David Hoggard, contains interesting material, but unfortunately it is told in the language of Mr. Hoggard. In every case, so far as possible, the speech of the ex-slave should be recorded.
> I suggest further that your workers get together and agree on the commonly used dialect words. There is no use in putting into dialect words that are pronounced just the same after they are dialectized. . . .
> My own strong feeling is that all the dialects should be simplified. . . .
> Of course I understand that there is no norm for Negro dialect. Our efforts

will be to preserve as nearly as possible the flavor of this speech and at the same time make it easy for those unacquainted with Negro speech to read the stories. (Quoted in Perdue, Barden, and Phillips 1980: 377)

Lomax enumerated dialect spellings that should not be used. For example, he said that fieldworkers should not write "yuh" for "you," "datter" for "daughter," "tuh" for "to," and "nevah" for "never."

The following month, on June 20, 1937, Sterling Brown sent written instructions about recording dialect to all the states participating in the national slave narrative project.

> Simplicity in recording the dialect is to be desired in order to hold the interest and attention of the readers. It seems to me that readers are repelled by pages sprinkled with misspellings, commas and apostrophes. The value of exact phonetic transcription is, of course, a great one. But few artists attempt this completely. Thomas Nelson Page was meticulous in his dialect; Joel Chandler Harris less meticulous but in my opinion even more accurate. But the values they sought are different from the values that I believe this book of slave narratives should have. Present day readers are less ready for the over-stress of phonetic spelling than in the days of local color. Authors realize this: Julia Peterkin uses a modified Gullah instead of Gonzales' carefully spelled out Gullah. Howard Odum has questioned the use of goin' for going since the g is seldom pronounced even by the educated.
>
> Truth to idiom is more important, I believe, than truth to pronunciation. Erskine Caldwell in his stories of Georgia, Ruth Suckow in stories of Iowa, and Zora Neale Hurston in stories of Florida Negroes get a truth to the manner of speaking without excessive misspellings. In order to make this volume of slave narratives more appealing and less difficult for the average reader, I recommend that truth to idiom be paramount, and exact truth to pronunciation secondary. . . .
>
> Finally, I should like to recommend that the words darky and nigger and such expressions as "a comical little old black woman" be omitted from the editorial writing. Where the ex-slave himself uses these, they should be retained. (Quoted in Perdue, Barden, and Phillips 1980: 380–381)

Brown sprinkled the middle of his memo with plenty of examples of the kinds of dialect features that could be used and the kinds that should not be used (see Perdue, Barden, and Phillips 1980: 380–381), but unfortunately his sensible instructions were not followed by many Indiana fieldworkers, or perhaps in some cases the instructions arrived too late. In simplifying the dialect and eliminating those racial epithets not used by the informants in the Indiana interviews, I have followed the professional advice of Lomax and Brown.

None of the earlier publications included all of the slave narratives collected in Indiana, though Rawick's massive collection of unaltered texts includes all but seven of the Indiana texts. The present book makes available for the first time in a single volume all the WPA interviews with former slaves living in Indiana during the Depression in a language and format appropriate for the general reader interested in the experience of slavery in the United States, or more specifically in Indiana folklore, genealogy, and history. Professional historians, linguists, folklorists, and other scholars with their own special interests in this material should consult, as well, the original typescripts in the Cunningham Memorial Library at Indiana State University and the Library of Congress or as most of them have been reproduced in their "original form" by Rawick. Unaltered versions of the few interviews from Indiana that are not in Rawick's volumes are included in Appendix V of this book.

Though not verbatim oral-historical or folkloric documents, the Indiana WPA interviews nevertheless tell us much about slave life on the plantation; how slaves were treated; escapes and attempted escapes from slavery; education, religion, and folklore of slaves and former slaves; memories of the Civil War; and the fate of former slaves after the Civil War. However, the folk history preserved in the WPA narratives does not reflect a single vision of slavery. As Robin D. G. Kelley observes in the "Foreword" to *Remembering Slavery*:

> Those ex-slaves who lived to tell their stories do not all speak in one voice, nor do they share one big collective memory. The interviews do represent one of the few bodies of slave thought in which black slaves described the conditions they faced, their oppressions, their resistance. But some of the passages will frustrate readers interested only in dramatic cases of brutality or heroic acts of defiance. Alongside the tragic we find stories of "happy darkies" who virtually pine for the days of slavery, as well as detailed, moving descriptions of the day-to-day violence inflicted on the very young and very old. (Kelley 1998: vii–viii)

Yet, as Kelley concludes, "If all of these disparate stories and diverse voices embody one single theme, it is humanity. Together the narratives reinforce the incredible ability of African Americans to maintain their dignity and self worth, to offer the rest of the world a model of humanity. . . . It is our recognition of the ex-slaves' humanity that enables us to discard the false dichotomies of 'Sambo' and 'rebel' and see these amazing black survivors as complicated human beings" (Kelley 1998: viii).

LIVING AND WORKING ON THE PLANTATION

The interviews with former slaves living in Indiana remind us that slaves worked on southern farms and plantations of various sizes. Reverend Wamble's owner, for example, usually had two hundred or more slaves, who worked under the supervision of overseers, who sometimes were slaves themselves. Candies Richardson said that her master had about fifty slaves, who raised crops, cotton, tobacco, and hogs. Sylvester Smith, his sister, and her husband, on the other hand, were the only slaves on Richard Newsom's farm. Newsom lived in a log house for a time, though later he built a frame house. Then quite young, Smith lived with the Newsoms, but his sister and her husband lived in a shack that was no better than a coal shed. On another plantation, according to Rosaline Rogers, both male and female slaves lived in a single cabin, no matter how many there were. She recalled that at one time twenty slaves lived in a small cabin, which had holes between the logs big enough for cats and dogs to crawl through. The cabin was heated by a wood-burning fireplace, which also was used for cooking food.

Adeline Rose Lennox reported that slaves on the plantations where she was held lived in small but comfortable log houses a distance from the owner's house: "Our quarters, both on the Reuben Rose plantation and then later on the Henry Rose place, were in log cabins. The floors were dirt, and there were fireplaces built of mud and sticks." Reverend Wamble said the slaves' living quarters were made of logs covered with mud. Roofs were made of coarse boards covered with about a foot of dirt, and the floors also were dirt. Their furniture included a small stove and board beds attached to corner walls. Slaves slept without blankets on these board beds or directly on the dirt floor. George Washington Buckner said that his crude slave cabin in Kentucky had only holes in the walls for windows, with bark shutters to keep out the rain and snow. His parents slept on a wooden bed covered with a straw mattress and patchwork quilts, and the children slept on a straw bed that was pushed under the bed during the day and pulled into the middle of the cabin at night. Patsy Jane Bland recalled sleeping on a straw pallet on the floor and in a trundle bed shoved back under the big bed. John W. Fields said that his "life as a slave was a repetition of hard work, poor quarters and board. We had no beds at that time; we just bunked on the floor. I had one blanket, and many's the night I sat by the fireplace during the long cold nights in the winter."

Apparently some slaves ate well, but others had barely enough to eat. This varied not only from plantation to plantation but also on the same plantation. Candies Richardson, for instance, said that the slaves who worked in her owner's house ate the same food that the owner and his family ate; those working on other parts of the plantation, however, did not fare so well. They ate fat meat and parts of the hog that people in the big house would not eat. A week's ration of food was given each slave, but if it was eaten before the week was up, the slave had only salt pork to eat until the next ration. A person could not eat much of that, though, because it was too salty.

Ellen Cave said that on her plantation slaves lived mainly on bran-bread, but the owner's children often slipped them meat and other food. Sylvester Smith said that slaves on his plantation ate corn cakes, side pork, and beans. Seldom did they have anything sweet except molasses. Patsy Jane Bland baked corn dodger on a hot brick fireplace, hanging the kettle over the crane to cook "pawn hoss," which was made from meal and bacon. She roasted sweet potatoes and sweet corn and baked ash cake. Mollie Tate indicated that even some slaves living in slave quarters fared pretty well: "Our meals at the cabin were cooked in the fireplace. Mother would make cakes of meal and water, sometimes a little salt, and cover them with ashes. Potatoes were baked likewise. With our menu of hoecakes and molasses, we thrived and grew stout and healthier than most children do today with all kinds of food and luxuries."

In general, though, it seems that slaves living in the big house were better off than those living in slave quarters. As Harriet Cheatam explains, "When I was a child, I didn't have it as hard as some of the children in the quarters. I always stayed in the big house and slept on the floor, right near the fireplace, with one quilt for my bed and one quilt to cover me. Then when I growed up, I was in the quarters." Mittie Blakeley's mother died when Mittie was a baby, so she was taken into the "big house," raised with the white children, and assigned only light chores, such as gathering eggs with the white children. She said the child who brought in the most eggs got a ginger cake, and she nearly always won the cake. When she was older, she spun wool and knitted. At first Henrietta Jackson was a plow hand in the cotton fields, but later she was taken into the big house to work as a maid.

It appears that "gift slaves"—slaves given as presents, generally to family members—also had a better life than most slaves. William M. Quinn said that gift slaves were never sold from the plantation on which he worked. Another gift slave, Robert McKinley, said that his master was extremely cruel in general but was always kind to Robert because he had been the master's present to his favorite daughter. McKinley worked in the owner's blacksmith shop, because the master's daughter did not want him working on the farm. According to George Washington Buckner, some slave children were given to the slaveholder's young children and became their property. As a child, Buckner served the master's son—taking care of his clothing, polishing his boots, and putting away his toys—though the two children were about the same age.

Several former slaves reported that children were not worked as hard as adults. For instance, Adeline Rose Lennox said she "was put to work when I was six years old, just like other slave children. We were never worked hard because of our age. We worked in the fields and in the houses." At the age of fourteen, though, Lennox plowed, harrowed, and seeded the fields. Still, she maintained that she was "treated tol'able" well when she was a slave, and that "I've worked a heap harder since I was freed than I did before." Henry Clay Moorman said that as a boy he did small jobs around the plantation, such as planting tobacco and going to the mill. George Thomas, who was only about nine years old when freed, said that as a slave he had helped turn the spinning wheel and knitted stockings. Ellen Cave worked as a maid in the "big house" until she grew up. Then she had to do most kinds of outdoor labor. In the winter she sawed logs in the snow all day, and in the summer she pitched hay and did other work in the fields. Other slaves apparently enjoyed an easier life because they were related to the owner. The master of Josephine Hicks's grandmother "was also her father, so she was always well treated. It was her work to do the spinning, so she had no outside work at all."

Some female slaves served as wet nurses in the big house and also received better treatment. Moses Slaughter's mother had ten children of her own and also was wet nurse to ten of her master's children. She kept house for the owner and slept in a room in the big house so that she could take care of his children at night. Peter Gohagen told the WPA fieldworker, Iris Cook, that back in Kentucky he had known her grandfather and her father's wet nurse: "Yes, ma'am, ol' Aunt Barbara, what nursed your pa, was shore a mighty fine colored woman. She was low and heavyset and light-skinned. She nursed the Gohagen boys, too." Since Anderson Whitted's mother took care of the white children on the plantation, her own nine children were well treated, too.

The former slaves interviewed in Indiana had performed a variety of jobs on southern farms and plantations. Sarah Locke's father cradled grain, and the female slaves milked ten or twelve cows a day, knitted socks, and wove linsey-woolsey for their dresses. Locke's master sheared sheep with the slaves. Susan Smith had to pick cotton, shear sheep, spin, thread looms, weave cloth, take the wool to the carding machine, mold candles, and go to the mill. Maria Love's mother, Elmira Polk, had to work very hard, "just like a man," plowing and working in the fields from morning until night. Patsy Jane Bland also reported that she "worked like a man." In addition to her household duties, she plowed and helped raise tobacco. She said she had always worked and would not have it any other way. Mattie Jenkins pointed out that on her plantation the slaves' main job was raising cotton, but they also washed, ironed, milked, tended stock, and raised feed for the stock. Callie Bracey's mother, Louise Terrell, worked hard in the fields from early morning until late in the evening, when it was too dark to see. When she returned from the fields, she cooked and packed lunches for the field hands for the next day. She, too, said that women had to split rails all day long just like the men. John Daugherty's mother cut corn, chopped wood, and drove oxen in the field. He said that many times his mother's toenails were mashed off by oxen stepping on her bare feet.

Some slaves were paid, some were given garden space or stock, and some moonlighted. Solomon Hicks's father "was allowed a very small pittance" for all the hemp over a hundred pounds that he could cut in a day. He also made baskets at night and sold them to make extra money. William M. Quinn said it was unusual for a slave to receive money for working, but his owner paid his brother and him ten cents a day for cutting and shucking corn. Quinn's master also paid his own son ten cents a day for working in the fields. Mrs. Hockaday reported that many slaveholders gave their slaves small tracts of land to tend after working hours. Anything raised belonged to them, and they could even sell the products and keep the money. Many slaves were able to save enough from these tracts to purchase their freedom long before Emancipation. Matthew Hume's father was allowed to raise an acre of tobacco, an acre of corn, garden vegetables, and chickens for himself. He also was given milk and butter from one cow. His overseer advised him to save his money, but Hume said his father always drank it up. Slaves were given a little of everything that was raised on the large farm on which Julia Bowman worked.

Shoes and clothing were scarce on the plantations. Candies Richardson said, "We had to make our own clothes out of a cloth, like you use, called canvas. We walked to church with our shoes on our arms to keep from wearing them out." Mollie Tate observed, "It would seem peculiar nowadays to see children wearing tow sacks for clothing. But that was what the children on the plantation often wore, or at least that was the resemblance, just a hole on each side for the arms and one for the head." Preston Tate reported that since the boys in a family were not fortunate enough to each have a Sunday suit, one homespun suit and a pair of homemade shoes were rotated among them. The other boys in the family wore their everyday clothing, long tow shirts, to church. He said that if you took a sack, cut an opening in the bottom for the head, and split each side for the arms, you would have something like a tow shirt. Sometimes it was difficult to distinguish boys from girls by their clothing, as it was common for them to dress alike. Callie Bracey's mother was given two dresses a year and wore her oldest dress as an underskirt. She never had a hat, so she always wore a rag tied over her head.

As a child, Anthony Young never had any shoes, and in the winter he had to run to keep his feet from freezing. He said that he would chase hogs from their beds and stand on the warm straw to warm his feet. Likewise, Mrs. Preston often warmed her bare feet in cattle bedding, but she claimed that slaves did not always go barefoot; they sometimes wore old shoes or wrapped their feet in rags. Joseph Mosley's father served as the shoemaker for all the adults and farmhands on the plantation. In September he began making shoes for the year. First he made shoes for the people in the big house, and then for the workers. Summer or winter, though, the slave children never wore shoes, according to Mosley. Rosaline Rogers said that slaves on her first owner's plantation generally were given a pair of shoes at Christmas, but if the shoes were worn out before summer, they had to go barefoot. Her second owner, however, would not buy shoes for his slaves. When they plowed, their feet would crack and bleed from walking on the hard clods. If they complained, they were whipped, so very few complained. Patsy Jane Bland said, "I never wore anything but wool underwear in the wintertime, and none of my younguns did either. I used to sit and knit wool up for their stockings. Indeed, I've worked hard."

Frequently slave families were separated. When John Rudd was a small boy, his master died, and the slaves were auctioned to the highest bidders. "If you want to know what unhappiness means," Rudd said, "just you stand on the slave block and hear the auctioneer's voice selling you away from the folks you love." According to Rudd, mothers and fathers often were separated from their children at the auction block. As Amy Patterson explained, "Our sorrow began when slave traders came to Cadiz and bought any slaves they took a fancy to and separated us from our families." Separation from her mother and sisters at a slave auction was among her earliest memories. When Adeline Rose Lennox was seven years old, she "was carried away from my parents to the farm of the master's son, Henry Rose, and there I stayed until after the war." She recalled that she cried when she had to leave her parents, but she was told that she had to go to a new home. Solomon Hicks said his "mother was a partial slave. By that I mean she was taken from her mother, who was a slave, while an infant and given to a family to raise. . . . She was given away in order that my grandmother would be of more value to her master if not burdened with the care of a baby." Hicks also said that "When the slaves became too numerous the old ones were sold down south in order to make room for the younger ones." Mary Crane explained how slaves were sold down the river:

> In those days, there were men who made a business of buying up Negroes at auction sales and shipping them down to New Orleans to be sold to owners of cotton and sugar cane plantations, just as men today buy and ship cattle. These men were called "nigger-traders," and they would ship whole boatloads at a time, buying them up, two or three here, two or three there, and holding them in a jail until they had a boatload. This practice gave rise to the expression "sold down the river."

Henrietta Jackson could not remember her father, who was sold soon after her birth, and when still a child she was taken from her mother and sold. She remembered the auction block and said that she had brought a good price, for she was strong and healthy. John W. Fields also was separated from his parents as a child: "I can't describe the heartbreak and horror of that separation. I was only six years old, and it was the last time I ever saw my mother for longer than one night. Twelve children were taken from my mother in one day!"

George Fortman said that his master did not sell slaves or separate slave families, but he recalled slave auctions where blacks were stripped of their clothing so that their bodies could be examined. He also saw boats loaded with slaves on the way to slave markets. Sarah Locke said that her owner was kind to his slaves and never sold them to slave traders. His family was very large, so they bought and sold slaves within the family or to neighbors. Locke's father, brothers, and grandmother belonged to the same slaveholder, but her mother and two sisters belonged to another branch of the family, who lived about seven miles away. Her father visited them on Wednesday and Saturday nights, and they would have big dinners on these nights in their cabin.

Although gift slaves sometimes enjoyed a better lifestyle than other slaves, the practice of giving slaves to members of the slaveholder's family as wedding gifts also separated slave families. As Mary Crane explained, "In those days, slaveholders, whenever one of their daughters would get married, would give her and her husband a slave as a wedding present, usually allowing the girl to pick the one she wished to accompany her to her new home."

THE TREATMENT OF SLAVES

Two-thirds of the former slaves interviewed in Indiana tell how they or others were treated as slaves. As Spear Pitman recalled, "They was all sorts [of slaveholders], some good and some mean as they could be." According to Reverend Wamble, families with only moderate incomes usually were kind to their slaves; because they could afford only a few, they had to take good care of them, just as a small farmer had to take good care of his few horses. Wealthy slaveholders, however, had a lot of slaves, and a slave or two did not matter to them.

Many former slaves living in Indiana reported gruesome tales of mistreatment on the plantation. Susan Smith still held bitter feelings toward her former owners because of the hard work she had had to do as a slave, and according to the fieldworker, white people still seemed to annoy her. Parthenia Rollins could hardly speak on the subject because of the cruel treatment many slaves had endured. She said that slaves were beaten until their backs were blistered, and then overseers would open the blisters and sprinkle salt and pepper in the wounds. According to Rollins, slaves were beaten to death, thrown into sinkholes, and left there for buzzard food. She said that many slaves were only half-fed and half-clothed, and they were treated so cruelly that it "would make your hair stand on ends." John Rudd said that slaveholder Henry Moore employed several white men just to whip slaves. The hired floggers used a large barrel near the slave quarters as a whipping post. The slaves were strapped across one side of the barrel and whipped until the floggers were worn out.

Ellen Cave's master had twenty slaves, whom he fed only now and then. Belle Butler's mother, Chancy Mayer, told her that slaves scarcely had enough to eat unless they stole it. If they were caught stealing food, though, they generally got a severe beating. Lizzie Samuels reported that her young mistress forced her to eat chicken heads, fish heads, pig tails, and parsnips. Ethel Daugherty maintained that field slaves, who were treated worse than house slaves, were lined up and slopped like hogs in wooden troughs. Alex Smith went hungry many times on the Robert Stubblefield plantation. "Often," he said, "I would see a dog with a bit of bread, and I would have been willing to take it from him if I had not been afraid the dog would bite me."

Belle Butler's mother contended that slaveholder Coffer whipped his slaves for the slightest offense. Often he whipped them for nothing at all; he just enjoyed seeing them suffer. Many times Coffer would whip a slave, then throw him down and gouge out his eyes. If slaves relaxed while hoeing corn, whether they were ill or just plain worn out, their backs were lashed and salted. One slave woman was caught leaving the plantation without a pass, and the overseer whipped her to death. Frank Cooper's mother told him that "three white women beat me from anger because they had no butter for their biscuits and cornbread." One woman whipped Cooper's mother, and another broke her back with a big board.

Mattie Jenkins described heartless torture of slaves. She said that pins were stuck through their tongues, which also were burned. Ira Jones said that whites made his aunt put her hands palms down on a barrel and then drove nails into them. As a result, she got lockjaw and died. Joe Wade reported that his mother's owner tied her to a tree and beat her for anything that aggravated him. If she could not work, he locked her in a guardhouse with nothing to eat. Slaves marched in a line on their way to work in the fields, and any slave who got out of line was tied to a tree and beaten. According to the fieldworker, Wade still loathed the slaveholders and wished that he could get even with the overseers for mistreating his mother.

As a matter of fact, several former slaves did get even. Levi Linzy's owner was always cruel to him; one day Linzy had had enough, so he retaliated by hitting his master on the head. The owner then lashed Linzy two hundred times and put salt and pepper in his raw wounds. After Linzy recovered from the whipping, he hit the slaveholder on the head again and escaped to Canada. Joseph Carter recalled how a muscular blacksmith knifed to death two professional slave whippers and an overseer before stabbing himself and bleeding to death. Joseph Allen related how he tried to break his mistress's habit of beating him: "I was gettin' too big, and I studied how I'd break her. Next time I bit her like a dog and held on with my teeth to her leg. Ol' Missus was lame for a spell; I broke her. I says, 'I'll eat you up like a dog.' After that, she buckled me up on the ground and lashed me." Joe Robinson's father was owned by a Kentuckian, Rube Black, who beat his slaves severely for the least offense. Once he tried to beat Robinson's father—a large, strong man—and the slave nearly killed him. Slaveholder Black never attempted to whip Robinson's father again, but soon after that Black sold him to a Louisiana slaveholder.

A number of former slaves interviewed in Indiana said that they were not mistreated on the plantations, though they saw or knew of others who were mistreated. Spear Pitman saw a slave named Alex tortured for fighting. He said, "They whipped him, and then turned the dogs loose on him. They tore him pretty near to pieces, and I don't know but what the dogs ate some of what they pulled off. Then they took the dogs off Alex and poured raw alcohol on him." Robert McKinley's master, Parker, was a cruel man, though he was kind to Robert because he had given him to his favorite daughter as a gift. Before whipping his slaves, Parker always drank a big glass of whiskey for strength. Once Parker beat McKinley's mother until she collapsed. He tied other slaves to trees and whipped them until he was exhausted, then put salt and pepper on their backs.

Mittie Blakeley recalled that once an elderly female slave upset her owner about something, so he had her beaten until blood gushed from her body. Carl Boone's father gained his freedom in 1829, so Boone was born a free man and was not mistreated. His father was "a picked slave" and was never mistreated either, though his mother was treated cruelly until she married his father in 1825. Boone, in fact, told several stories of mistreatment, including one his father had told him about a slave who was severely beaten and then tied behind a horse and dragged to death.

Reverend Wamble acknowledged that except for the whippings they received, slaves were well treated. He claimed that they were well fed, and if injured or ill, they were attended by a doctor, just as an injured horse or sick cow would be cared for, since the slaveholder earned more money if his slaves could work. Slaves, according to Wamble, generally were given plenty of meat, potatoes, and whatever else was raised. If the master had plenty to eat, his slaves did, too; if the master didn't have much to eat, neither did his slaves.

Other former slaves reported that slaves were treated well on the southern plantations. Mrs. Robert Smith said that all her relatives were treated so well in slavery that they did not want to leave their masters after the war. Ira Jones said that one of his cousins had difficulty taking care of himself after receiving his freedom because his master had done so much for him during slavery. Mary Elizabeth Scarber's mother lived in middle Tennessee with a family who did not believe in slavery, so all the blacks who worked on that farm were treated very well. Josephine Hicks said, "My grandmother, Mrs. Myers, was a slave near Danville, Kentucky. Her owner was also her father, so she was always well treated.... My grandmother was one of the fortunate ones, if we can call anyone fortunate to be held in slavery." Samuel Bell said that he was well taken care of at a contraband camp as well as on the plantation. His owner, John Bell, "was a good and a just man and fed his slaves well. He only used the lash when it was absolutely necessary.... A good slave was seldom punished, but mean ones had to be punished to prevent their taking advantage of their master and the other slaves."

Francis Gammons agreed that "on the average" slaves were treated as well as could be expected on the plantation. James Childress could not recall any occasion when his owner was cruel to him or other slaves, but still he said the slaves always prayed for freedom, and that black preachers always preached about the day when the slaves would be free and happy. Bettie Jones did not recall any unkind treatment, either. "Our only sorrow," she said, "was when a crowd of our slave friends would be sold off; then the mothers, brothers, sisters, and friends always cried a lot, and we children would grieve to see the grief of our parents."

Several slaves tell of the horrors of the auction block. Ethel Daugherty said that at slave auctions, women had to stand half-dressed for hours while a crowd of rough, drunken men bargained for them. Frequently, she said, the men examined their teeth, heads, hands, and other body parts to determine if they were strong and healthy. Frank Cooper's mother told him that she was put on the auction block after her back was broken and it was thought that she might not be able to work again. She recalled that "One man bid $1,700, after puttin' two dirty fingers in my mouth to see my teeth. I bit him, and his face showed anger. He then wanted to own me so he could punish me. . . . but my master saved me."

Throughout his narrative, Barney Stone emphasized "sixteen years of hell as a slave on a plantation." The fieldworker commented that Stone's story "will convince the reader that, even though much blood was shed in our Civil War, the war was a Godsend to the American nation." Stone explained how slaves were sold at private sales as well as at public auctions: "Slaves were sold in two ways, sometimes at a private sale to a man who went about the Southland buying slaves until he had many in his possession. Then he would have a big auction sale and would re-sell them to the highest bidder, much in the same manner as our livestock are sold now in auction sales. Professional slave buyers in those days were called 'nigger buyers.'"

Robert McKinley said that slaves on the Parker farm were not allowed to associate with slaves on the Hayden plantation, who were considered rich because Hayden's slaves were given meat to eat and did not have to steal it. When slave traders came to the Parker farm, old Mrs. Parker greased the slave children's mouths with meat skins so that the slave traders would think she had fed her slaves well.

Some slaves welcomed the auction block as a way of escaping a cruel master. For example, Nathan Jones's stepfather, Willis Jones, got tired of his master's cruel treatment and ran off into the woods. His master's searchers looked for him for days but couldn't find him. On a sale day, however, Willis Jones showed up and was the first slave to be put on the auction block. His new owner was good to him, and Jones said it was a pleasure to work for him.

Several former slaves reported cruel treatment from the patrollers during slavery, and from members of the Klan after slavery. Spear Pitman explained, "There was county officers that was called 'paddle rollers' [patrollers] that rode around the county all the time stopping niggers and making them show their passes. Any slave that left his quarters had to have a pass from his overseer or the paddle rollers would catch him. If they caught a fellow, they whipped him before they took him back home." Ellen Cave was caught and whipped by patrollers as she tried to sneak out to a black religious meeting. According to Frank Cooper,

"These paddy-rollers were a constant dread to the Negroes. They would whip the poor darkies unmercifully without any cause." John Rudd recalled his fear of the Klan and remembered seeing seven former slaves hanging from a tree just after the close of the Civil War.

ESCAPING FROM SLAVERY

Some former slaves reported escapes or attempted escapes from slavery. Arthur Shaffer gave a long account of his grandfather, Hillery Chavious, freeborn in 1833, who with his two older brothers moved from plantation to plantation helping slaves escape. The Chavious brothers estimated that they moved at least two hundred slaves over the Mason-Dixon Line to freedom. Mattie Brown Smith told the fieldworker, "Yes, ma'am, I can tell you something interesting about the escape of slaves across the river," and she gave a detailed account of her Uncle Charlie's escape to California by way of Canada. William M. Quinn said that sometimes slaves from neighboring plantations ran away during the night, and "we would give them something to eat."

Reverend J. B. Polk also described in detail how slaves helped other slaves escape. Polk explained that runaway slaves would run loops among the field hands in an attempt to lose their scent and confuse the dogs chasing them, and the field hands would shout "Step long, jump high!" to distract the dogs. Polk also said that slaves hid pots along rivers, which runaways would put over their heads when they waded across. Air in the pots provided breathing space when the water rose over the slaves' heads.

Henry Webb reported that his father, a slave, told him that runaway slaves came across the Ohio River from Portland, now a part of Louisville. Plans for the escapes were concocted in a black Masonic lodge, and slaves crossed the river in a boat operated by men posing as fishermen. If the coast was not clear on the Indiana side, they went up the river, sometimes past Louisville, and crossed the Ohio around Utica. On the Indiana side, slaves hid with friends in the hills back of New Albany. When they felt it was safe, they traveled north by way of Salem.

Sarah Emery Merrill said that her great-uncle, Lewis Barnett, and twelve other slaves were hidden in a wagon full of corn and crossed the Ohio, also at Portland. In New Albany, however, they were betrayed by a black family for a reward and taken back to Louisville, where they were punished or sold. George Morrison affirmed that slaves hid in wagons under provisions and crossed the Ohio on ferryboats. "That's the way lots of 'em got across here," he said.

Robert Barton never attempted to escape, but he had a sister who successfully escaped from slavery. Barton told how slaves were helped to escape by means of the Underground Railroad. Runaway slaves frequently put pepper in their shoes, so they could not be traced by bloodhounds, and escaped to Canada. Those who were caught were returned to their owners, who usually punished them. According to Anthony Battle, sometimes a slaveholder helped a slave escape on the Underground Railroad: "Sometimes when a slave man was being chased for doing something that they would kill him for, his owner would help get him away over what we called the 'underground railway' and would sell him away off from home, where he wouldn't be found. They did that because they couldn't afford to lose the money they would lose if the slave was killed by those who were after him."

Adah Isabelle Suggs escaped with her mother, who knew what would happen to Adah if she stayed on the plantation. According to Suggs, it was customary throughout the South for the master to father the first child of each female slave as soon as she reached puberty, so Adah's mother took her to Henderson, Kentucky, where they hid under a house until Federal soldiers took them across the Ohio River to Evansville, where they were befriended by free blacks.

When Rudolph O'Hara's grandfather ran away from the plantation, slaveholder O'Hara threatened to change his will: "If my slaves don't show a more helpful spirit hereafter, I'm going to change my will and not let Louisa [his wife] free them at her death." Although the slaveholder gathered a large number of men to search for the runaway slave, they never found him. O'Hara's grandmother, left to care for three small sons and a daughter, said it was "just like the ground had swallowed him up."

At least one former slave did not think it was right to escape. According to Robert Cheatham, his owner was not treated fairly. After being allowed to learn to read and write, his educated slaves forged passes, which they were required to carry, and escaped to northern states. Cheatham said they got away with it because "so few slaves were good penmen." Apparently a number of slaves did not attempt to escape. As John W. Fields pointed out, "We knew we could run away, but what then? An offender guilty of this crime was subjected to very harsh punishment." Others escaped but returned to their masters. Pete Johnson ran away when he was "about ten or thirteen years" old and "boarded the old ferryboat headed for Madison." After a year or so, however, Johnson returned to the plantation. He realized that "My old mistress and master were so nice to me I don't see how I could have been misled into leaving them."

Other slaves could earn money to buy their freedom. Maston Harris reported that his father was a slave in Harrodsburg, Kentucky. Valued at $1,200, his father was permitted to work at an inn to buy his freedom, and all the money he made over $13 a month was credited toward his freedom bill. His freedom papers, bearing the date 1833, were still in possession of the Harris family.

EDUCATION

Quite a few WPA informants pointed out that slaves were forbidden to learn how to read and write, and some slaves were even punished for trying to learn basic skills. As Joseph Allen pointed out, "Flat Rock church an' schoolhouse was near the plantation, but it was for the whites." After slavery, when he was past eighteen, Allen went to school for two three-month terms and learned to read print; on the plantation, however, he was punished when he was caught studying: "A white man teached us in their slave room. I learned my A, B, Cs quick, and Ol' Missus catched me studying and learning. I hain't forgot it. When she whipped, she stuck my head between her knees and clamped me tight. She slipped my garment aside and fanned me plenty with a shingle on my bare self."

Rosa Barber agreed that slaves were not taught the three Rs and were forbidden to even look in a book. Belle Butler confirmed that slaves were not allowed to look at books for fear they might learn to read. One day when a slave boy's mistress caught him with a book, she cursed him and asked him what he thought he could do with a book. She said he looked like "a black dog with a breast pin on" and forbade him to ever look at a book again. George Taylor Burns also pointed out that slaves "were not allowed an education. It was dangerous for any person to be caught teaching a Negro, and several Negroes were put to death because they could read."

Reverend J. B. Polk reported, too, that "No slave on the Collins plantation was permitted to pick up or open a book or get curious or anxious about any kind of education. A violation of these rules was certain to result in a whipping." John W. Fields maintained that it was illegal to educate slaves: "It was the law that if a white man was caught trying to educate a Negro slave, he was liable to prosecution entailing a fine of fifty dollars and a jail sentence."

Since many slaveholders did not want their slaves to know how to read and write, many slaves were not educated. For instance, the WPA fieldworker noted that Adeline Rose Lennox did not know how to read or write, that she had never talked on a telephone, and that she had never seen a movie. Lennox contended, however, "I've seen and done a lot of things that most folks have missed." She was not apologetic for not having learned to read and write, because "none of us slaves was given any education." Lizzie Johnson proffered that many slaves who were caught trying to learn to write had their thumbs smashed so that they could not hold a pencil.

Other former slaves corroborated these testimonies. Susan Smith vouched that there were no schools for slaves; Sarah O'Donnell said she "never had any education"; Jack Simms regretted very much that he had been denied an education; and Rosaline Rogers's children "were not allowed to go to school; they were taught only to work." George Thompson never learned to read and write, though he tried: "Our master wouldn't allow us to have any books, and when we were lucky enough to own a book we would have to keep it hid, for if our master would find us with a book he would whip us and take the book from us. After receiving three severe whippings I gave up and never again tried for any learning, and to this day I can neither read nor write."

In spite of the fact that a number of former slaves reported a lack of opportunities for education and even threats of punishment for attempts to acquire basic skills of reading and writing, some former slaves interviewed in Indiana were literate, and a few were highly educated. Some were educated on the plantation, and others went to school after slavery. For example, James Childress reported that "The slaves at Mr. Childress's place were allowed to learn as much as they could. Several of the young men could read and write." After slavery, Mollie Tate walked six to ten miles to school. She explained, "What education I received in those days from my speller, reader, geography, arithmetic, and dictionary has never been regretted. My parents weren't able to continue my education, so the fourth grade was the end of my school days."

The best-educated of the former slaves was George Washington Buckner, who became a schoolteacher, physician, and minister to Liberia under Woodrow Wilson. Buckner recollected that his earliest educational experience was reciting the ABCs from McGuffey's blue speller to his sister, his first teacher. Later he attended a school conducted by the Freedmen's Bureau. By the time he was sixteen, he was teaching other black children. When Buckner arrived in Indianapolis, he became acquainted with Robert Bruce Bagby, then principal of the only school for blacks in Indianapolis. When he left Bagby's school, he worked as a houseman in a private residence and waited tables in hotels and restaurants. While waiting tables, he met Colonel Albert Johnson and his wife, who advised him to enter Indiana State Normal School (now Indiana State University) in Terre Haute. After studying two years at Indiana State, Buckner taught for a time at schools in Vincennes, Washington, and other Indiana communities before studying medicine at the Indiana Eclectic Medical College, from which he was graduated in 1890.

Other former slaves, though not so well educated, were taught to read and write by various individuals and institutions. Some were taught by family members. Anderson Whitted's family had a Bible and an elementary spelling book. Whitted's father, owned by Whitted's master's half-brother, lived fourteen miles away, but every two weeks he visited his family. His father could read and spell very well, and he taught his family on these visits. Whitted learned to read the Bible first and later learned to read other things.

Somehow Reverend Wamble's grandmother, who was brought from Africa as a slave when she was seventeen, learned to read and write, and Wamble recalled that during the Civil War she secretly read to him late at night. Wamble continued his education after slavery, but he said he was twenty-seven years old before he read his first newspaper. Lulu Scott said her "father could read and write; don't know how he learn nor who teach him, but he know."

Robert J. Cheatham was educated by his owner, who maintained, "You colored boys and girls must learn to read and write no matter what powers object. Your parents and your grandparents were taught to read and write when they belonged to my forefathers, and you young children have to learn as much." Robert Barton often was sent after the mail, which he said made him want to learn to read and write. Through the help of his mother and his owner, he received enough education to enable him to teach school for a few years after gaining his freedom. Louis Watkins had a white tutor who came on Sunday afternoons and taught the slaves in a room in the big house. Watkins said they were taught to read, write, and figure, and they could "go as far as they were capable." A white man also taught Lizzie Johnson's father to read and write. Many nights he studied by the light from a blazing wood fire in the fireplace.

Adah Isabelle Suggs was taken into the big house to work and borrowed books from the master's library. She recalled receiving "words of praise and encouragement" for her efforts. As the slaveholder's daughter practiced reading, Moses Slaughter's mother followed each line of text with her; she became a fluent reader and taught her own children how to read. Robert McKinley was taught to read and write by his master's daughter, to whom he had been given as a gift. Reverend Oliver Nelson credited his mistress with giving him a good education: "She had graduated from a university up east, and by paying strict attention to what she said, I had a better education than most of the slaves; therefore, I started on my ministerial life as soon as I was free."

Elvira Lee's master was well educated, and each night he taught his children their lessons. Lee worked in the big house and studied along with the white children; by the time the master's children were old enough to go off to school, she had received a pretty good education in basic subjects. After the war, Lee's master gave his slaves an acre of ground for a school and another acre for a church and cemetery. Lee, one of the first black teachers, taught school in a cabin until the new school was built. There was so much prejudice against the black school, however, that it was burned after a few weeks. The government intervened, and Lee "lived to see the Negroes getting an education as well as the white children."

Mary Ann Stewart said that late in her life a rural carrier working out of Greencastle taught her to read, stopping at her house each day to hear her recite her lessons. Barney Stone learned to read and write while serving in the Union Army and taught black children after the Civil War. Then for three years he studied in a lawyer's home. In 1857 Sarah Locke and her sister went to Cincinnati for a year to study, since at that time there were not any Kentucky schools they could attend. That was the longest time the sisters went to school. John Moore, like George Washington Buckner, attended a school operated by the Freedmen's Bureau. The teacher always kept his pistol on his desk, because whites objected to blacks' being educated. Teaching blacks was a dangerous occupation, according to Moore.

America Morgan, according to the fieldworker, could read and write and was "rather intelligent." In 1865, when Morgan's father took her to Paducah, Kentucky, she was thirteen years old, and she "didn't know A from B," but "glory to God," a white man from the North opened a school for black children. Morgan attended school there for a short time. After that, the white people for whom she worked continued to educate her after her work was done. They gave her an old-fashioned spelling book and a first reader, and she said she was "taught much and began to know life." At the time of his interview, Joe Robinson was learning to read and write in a class sponsored by the WPA.

After the Civil War, according to Mrs. Hockaday, slaves who were uneducated and unskilled found it very difficult to adjust to freedom and a different lifestyle. She said that some slaveholders had schools for their slaves, and former slaves who could read and write were more successful in finding employment after the war. Apparently, however, some slaves did not take advantage of their owners' attempts to teach them to read and write. Pete Johnson, for example, confessed that he was not a willing student: "My mistress tried to teach me to read on rainy days. I can still see the little yellow-backed reader. As soon as I learned my letters I wouldn't pay any more attention to her, as I then felt so big I thought there was nothing more for me to learn. I wish now I weren't so ignorant."

RELIGION

Former slaves interviewed in Indiana generally were religious during and after slavery. Robert J. Cheatham said, "We read the Bible until the pages became dog-eared and the leaves fell from their binding." Rosaline Rogers reported that slaves were allowed to go to their master's church, though they had to sit on one of seven benches at the back of the church. Rogers said, "I am 110 years old; my birth is recorded in the slave book. I have good health, fairly good eyesight, and a good memory, all of which I say is because of my love for God." According to Callie Bracey, on special occasions older slaves were allowed to go to their master's church, but they had to sit in the back of the church and could not take part in the service. Susan Smith agreed that slaves attended the same church as whites, and Louis Watkins was permitted to go to church with his parents on Sunday, a day of rest for the slaves.

Candies Richardson corroborated that slaves on her plantation attended a Baptist church with their owner and had to sit at the rear of the church, but she said the sermon was never preached to the slaves: "They never preached the Lord to us. They would just tell us not to steal. Don't steal from your master!" She said slaves walked six miles and waded a stream to get to church just to hear the minister tell them, "Don't steal from your master!" Richardson was "so happy to know that I have lived to see the day when you young people can serve God without slipping around to serve him like we old folks had to do. . . . But I lived to see both him and Miss Elizabeth [her owners] die a hard death. They both hated to die, although they belonged to church. Thank God for his mercy! Thank God!"

Richardson also claimed that her master beat her husband many times when he caught him praying, but she said the "beatings didn't stop my husband from praying. He just kept on praying. He'd steal off to the woods and pray, but he prayed so loud that anybody close around could hear 'cause he had such a loud voice. I prayed too, but I always prayed to myself." She believed that it was her husband's prayers and "a whole lot of other slaves' [prayers] that caused you young folks to be free today." She said, too, that slaves on her plantation did not have a Bible because it meant a beating or even "a killing if you'd be caught with one. But there were a lot of good slaves who knew how to pray, and some of the white folks loved to hear them pray 'cause there was no put-on about it. That's why we folks know how to sing and pray 'cause we have gone through so much, but the Lord's with us. The Lord's with us, he is."

According to John Moore, slaves were religious and always prayed for freedom, and emancipation was a major theme of the sermons of black preachers. Slaves preferred the sermons of black preachers because they preached from experience, not from the Bible. He said that slaves praised and worshiped God because they believed that God would deliver them from bondage. About religion and freedom, Robert Cheatham said, "The Negro preachers preached freedom into our ears, and our old men and women prophesied about it. We prayed, and our forefathers offered prayers for 275 [sic] years in American bondage that we might be given freedom." James Childress, too, remembered that the slaves always prayed for freedom, and that black preachers always preached about the day when the slaves would be free and happy. He sang a stanza of "Swing Low Sweet Chariot" and said it related to God's setting the blacks free. "My people loved God; they sang sacred songs. 'Swing Low Sweet Chariot' was one of the best songs they knew."

Slaves sometimes held religious services in their quarters. Harriet Cheatam said, "We often had prayer meeting out in the quarters, and to keep the folks in the big house from hearing us, we would take pots, turn them down, and put something under them. That let the sound go in the pots. We put them in a row by the door. Then our voices would not go out, and we could sing and pray to our hearts' content." Nelson Polk similarly described religious services in the slave quarters: "When the slaves held a religious service in their quarters, they were required to turn a tub against the door to catch the sound and absorb it before it reached the mansion of the plantation owner. If they couldn't find a tub, they used a pot."

Slaves and former slaves also had camp meetings and revivals. Nancy Whallen said that blacks held revivals in the woods. Sometimes they held services in a brush shelter with leaves for a roof, and the preaching and shouting lasted all day Sunday. Services usually were held away from white people, and blacks from miles around attended. Rachael Duncan agreed: "Camp meetings? Yes, ma'am. They used to have some grand ones down in Breckinridge County. They was always held out in the woods in a clear space, away off to ourselves, under a big tree. And they was preachin' and singin' and folks got religion right." Samuel Bell was converted at a revival meeting in Evansville. He said the happiest time of his life was "when Jesus saved my soul and gave me the hope of eternal life." Mollie Tate also was converted at a revival meeting, when she was about ten years old. John Cooper, a member of the Baptist Church, told a good personal-experience tale about how he reluctantly got religion at a meeting in Evansville and then the following day was baptized in a frozen river. Cooper allowed, "I ain't never been nowhere only in the flock of the Lord since."

Mrs. Hockaday said that slaves were mainly Methodists and Baptists, that most slaves belonged to the same church the slaveholder belonged to, and that generally they continued to attend the same church after the war. At the time of her death, Candies Richardson was a member of the West 10th Street Free Church of God in Indianapolis. Elizabeth Russell had been a member of the Methodist Church since childhood. Moses Slaughter was baptized in the Cumberland River when he was a slave, and was baptized again in the Ohio River when he joined a Baptist church in Evansville.

Several former slaves living in Indiana were Roman Catholics. Sarah O'Donnell was baptized, confirmed, and married in the Catholic Church. John Rudd was a devout Catholic who believed that religion and freedom were the two richest blessings ever given to human beings. Carl Boone stressed that "I became connected with the Colored Catholic Church and have tried to live a Christian life. I have only missed church service twice in twenty years." Matthew Hume pointed out that the slaveowner's wife on a neighboring plantation was a devout Catholic who gathered all the slave children each Sunday afternoon to study the catechism and repeat the Lord's Prayer. After the service, she always served candy or a cup of sugar. Hume said although she led them to Christ, she was not very successful in converting them to Catholicism, for when they grew up, most of them became either Baptists or Methodists. He said he did not learn much of the catechism; he attended only for the candy and sugar.

After the war, many former slaves living in Indiana remained active in church work, several becoming Protestant ministers. For instance, in 1903 Henry Clay Moorman moved to Franklin to become pastor of the African Methodist Episcopal Church, which he served for twelve years. When interviewed, Barney Stone had been a Baptist preacher for sixty-nine years and had been instrumental in building seven churches. Elvira Lee helped organize one of the first black churches in New Albany and outlived all the other charter members. Edna Boysaw was an active church worker in Brazil and often was asked to speak at white churches as well as black churches. One of her daughters was a talented singer, and Boysaw appeared on many church programs with her. According to Boysaw's obituary in the *Brazil Daily Times* (January 8, 1942), this was the fulfillment of a childhood dream: "When Mrs. Boysaw was a small slave girl she had a dream in which she had a vision that she would some day go from city to city, county to county and state to state spreading the gospel."

H. H. Edmunds, who served as a minister for many years, was very religious, but he felt that religion had greatly changed from the "old time religion." He believed that in slavery days, blacks were so suppressed and uneducated that they were especially susceptible to religion, and they poured out their religious feelings in their spirituals. Be that as it may, Christianity offered slaves some comfort in the present and some hope for the future. Bettie Jones said, "What God wills must happen to us, and we do not save ourselves by trying to run away. Just as well stay and face it as to try to get away. Of course, I'm a Christian. I'm a religious woman and hope to meet my friends in heaven." Adeline Rose Lennox said her "one ambition in life is to live so that I may claim heaven as my home when I die."

Christianity also helped slaves and former slaves understand their situations. John Daugherty thought that slaveholders behaved as well as they could with the little knowledge of the Bible they had. Slaveholders, he felt, had not read enough of the Scriptures to know that it was wrong to hold human beings in bondage. Samuel Bell concluded, "Religion is worth the greatest fortune. It explains why man must labor and suffer, and his trying experiences make him more worthy of the great reward promised by the kind Father. When his years of sorrow are fulfilled, he will understand and appreciate the reward, which is heaven." Billy Slaughter sometimes wondered why he was still left on earth when all his brothers, sisters, and friends were gone; however, he read the Bible often, and "the Bible," he said, "says that two shall be working in the field together, and one shall be taken, and the other left. I am the one who is left." Slaughter believed he was still living because somebody had to be around to tell stories about the old days.

FOLKLORE

Two eminent folklorists, John Lomax and Ben Botkin, were selected to administer the Slave Narrative Project, indicating that initially the collection was considered part of the study of folklore. Indeed, the Indiana slave narratives for the most part are folklore; they are orally collected legends and memorates (personal-experience narratives) relating the experiences of African American Hoosiers who lived under slavery. As Botkin points out, the WPA slave narratives belong to folk history:

> The narratives belong to folk history—history recovered from the memories and lips of participants or eye-witnesses, who mingle group with individual experience and both with observation, hearsay, and tradition. Whether the narrators relate what they actually saw and thought and felt, what they imagine, or what they have thought and felt about slavery since, now we know *why* they thought and felt as they did. To the white myth of slavery must be added the slaves' own folklore and folk-say of slavery. The patterns they reveal are folk and regional patterns—the patterns of field hand, house and body servant, and artisan; the patterns of kind and cruel master or mistress; the patterns of Southeast and Southwest, lowland and upland, tidewater and inland, smaller and larger plantations, and racial mixture (including Creole and Indian). (Quoted in Rawick 1972: I, 171)

As Botkin stresses here as well as in the subtitle of *Lay My Burden Down,* the WPA slave narratives represent a folk history of slavery, but he also notes that the interviews with former slaves are folk literature:

> The narratives belong also to folk literature. Rich not only in folk songs, folk tales, and folk speech but also in folk humor and poetry, crude or skillful in dialect, uneven in tone and treatment, they constantly reward one with earthy imagery, salty phrase, and sensitive detail. In their own unconscious art, exhibited in many a fine and powerful short story, they are a contribution to the realistic writing of the Negro. Beneath all the surface contradictions and exaggerations, the fantasy and flattery, they possess an essential truth and humanity which surpasses as it supplements history and literature. (Quoted in Rawick 1972: I, 171)

While the slave narratives themselves may be considered folk history, within the narratives other genres of folklore abound. Many of the interviews incorporate family legends. For instance, Henry Clay Moorman related his own personal-experience stories as well as family legends handed down by his mother. Robert J. Cheatham said that his father often told tales of his journey from Virginia, and Cheatham retold these tales. Cheatham also passed on tales about his father's experiences as plantation overseer and stories his parents had told him about the night of his birth. Dr. Solomon Hicks told a family story about his Uncle Jerry, who broke one of his mother's prized forks while eating a coon at a family reunion: "Knowing a battle would be staged, he hid the fork under the tablecloth. Mother didn't find it until after he left and, of course, couldn't say anything to him."

Folk beliefs, most corroborated in Puckett's *The Magic and Folk Beliefs of the Southern Negro,* and belief stories can be found throughout the interviews, though these were not universally believed. For example, Ralph Kates, according to the fieldworker, was not "a believer in ghosts, haunts, or spiritual visitations, and in his youth scoffed when other blacks told stories of goblins. He has no fear of graveyards, cats, nor rats and harbors no superstitions. His parents always told him that those things were only believed by ignorant persons." Bettie Jones likewise said that she did not believe in evil spirits, ghosts, or charms, though she remembered hearing friends pass along superstitions about black cats. Jones said some former slaves thought that building a new kitchen always was followed by a death in the immediate family, and a bird flying into a window also meant someone in the family would die.

John W. Fields, however, maintained that slaves were ardent believers in ghosts, supernatural powers, tokens, and signs; and he related several folk beliefs, including a tale illustrating that "A turkey gobbler sitting on a nest of green peaches is a bad omen." Fields also said that throughout the South, possessing a horseshoe was considered good luck, hitting someone with a broom was bad luck, and carrying a buckeye in a pocket relieved "the rheumatics." George W. Arnold, who worked as a roustabout, advised that one should "Always heed the warnings of nature. If you see rats leaving a ship or a house, prepare for a fire." George Taylor Burns recalled similar superstitions of river men, but he had little faith in them: "It was bad luck for a white cat to come aboard the boat. Horseshoes were carried for good luck. If rats left the boat, the crew was uneasy, for fear of a wreck." George Fortman said that he "never believed in witchcraft or spells," but he recalled several weather beliefs and omens from family and friends. According to Fortman, "More than any other superstition entertained by the slave Negroes, the most harmful was the belief in conjurers. One old Negro woman boiled a bunch of leaves in an iron pot, boiled it with a curse, and scattered the tea made from the leaves, and she firmly believed she was bringing destruction to her enemies. The old woman said, 'Wherever that tea is poured there will be toil and troubles.'"

Lulu Scott was full of familiar folk beliefs. She said that a child born with a veil over its face can see spirits, and people who are not born with a veil can see spirits by looking over the left shoulder of someone who was born with a veil. Scott said that a copper ring worn on the left ankle will ward off rheumatism, and a bag of asafetida worn on a string around the neck will ward off other diseases. She believed that a string tied to an ankle or wrist will keep a person from cramping in water. She pointed out that they did not have almanacs in the old days, but they "could just go out and look up and tell just what the weather goin' be, tell by the elements." Scott also related several death omens: a dog howling, rats gnawing, mysterious knocking, and sick people wanting to eat a lot all predict death.

Katie Sutton also was a reservoir of familiar folk beliefs. She said that the seventh son of a seventh son or the seventh daughter of a seventh daughter can heal diseases, and that a child born after its father's death possesses "a strange and unknown power." Sutton had some kind of power, too. She claimed that she once planted a tree and cursed her worst enemy, who then died the same year. She believed that a rabbit's foot brought good luck, but only if the rabbit had been killed by a cross-eyed black person in a country graveyard in the dark of the moon, though that kind of rabbit's foot could be found only once in a lifetime or maybe once in a hundred years. Sutton also scrubbed her back steps with chamber lye each day to ward off evil spirits and death, and she sprinkled salt in the footprints of departing guests "so they can leave no ill will behind 'em and can never come again without an invitation." During the interview, Sutton refused to lend a neighbor a shovel, explaining to the fieldworker that "She just wanted that shovel so she could hex me. A woman borrowed a poker from my mama and hexed Mama by bending the poker, and Mama got all twisted up with rheumatism until her uncle straightened the poker, and then Mama got as straight as anybody. No, ma'am, nobody's going take anything of mine out'n this house." Sutton also recalled that the slaveholder's wife and daughter told the slave children that although white babies were brought by a stork, slave children were hatched from buzzards' eggs, "and we believed it was true." Sutton was indeed an active bearer of superstitions. She told the fieldworker, "Yes, ma'am, I believe in evil spirits and that there are many folks that can put spells on you, and if'n you don't believe it, you had better be careful, for there are folks right here in this town that have the power to bewitch you, and then you will never be happy again."

Several of the FWP informants related beliefs about dreams. Adah Isabelle Suggs said that her mother received directions for escaping from slavery in a dream, and Samantha Hough, one of the white informants interviewed by FWP fieldworkers, said, "I believe a little in dreams. . . . One time I dreamed my husband got his pension rejected, and everyone said that was impossible when I told it, but he did. Again I dreamed of a lost knife being in a certain place, and, sure enough, there it was."

John Moore recollected that his grandfather had told his father that "It rained blood one day." The slaves feared God's wrath because their owner forced them to work in the fields on the Sabbath. Considering this sinful, they prayed that they might be excused, and a storm broke out and rained blood. After that, the frightened slaveowner always allowed his slaves to rest and worship on Sundays. Moore also related a few folk beliefs that were handed down from parent to child: "If you don't want a visitor to come again, sprinkle salt in his tracks, and he won't come again. If a black cat crosses your path, go back home and start again; if he crosses your path again, go home and stay awhile and don't try to go where you had started out to go." Moore also recalled that slaves sprinkled chamber lye on their cabin steps at four o'clock in the morning to keep away evil spirits. Many slaves, he said, believed in the power to hex. If your enemy wanted to hex you, all he or she had to do was borrow or steal some object of yours and give it your name.

Sarah Colbert told three tales of witchcraft, including one about Jane Garmon, the village witch. Garmon, she said, tormented the slaves with her cat. The cat always showed up at milking time, and at night it would go from cabin to cabin putting out all the grease lamps with its paw. They tried to kill the cat but couldn't until an old witch doctor told them to melt a dime, form a bullet with the silver, and shoot the cat with the silver bullet. Jane Garmon also bewitched the slaves' chickens. The chickens were dying fast, and nothing the slaves tried could save them until they broke the spell by building a big fire and throwing the dead chickens into it.

Examples of both supernatural and natural folk medicine also show up in the slave narratives and in an ancillary text that FWP fieldworker Anna Pritchett collected from Lark Jones, son of John Jones, 2835 Boulevard Place in Indianapolis (also in Rawick 1977: V, 89–91, and Rawick 1979: I, 275–277). Pritchett said, "This story of the Hoodoo Doctor was told me by a man who knows all persons concerned and remembers perfectly, although just a boy, of having taken part in the ceremony":

> There was an old man who had been very sick, and no one seemed to be able to help him. The family decided someone had put a spell on him. They became alarmed about him and sent for the hoodoo doctor. The sick man was not to know of the hoodoo doctor's coming, as he did not believe in him.
>
> When the doctor came, he asked the wife of the sick man to give him a piece of clothing her husband had worn. She gave him a piece of his coat. The doctor took this piece and formed a little man, put the form in a bottle, poured a clear liquid over it, gave it to the wife, and told her to put it under the doorstep. The old man coming and going over the step many times during the day would cause the charm to work faster.
>
> The time limit was nine days to break the spell. At the end of the nine days, instead of the spell being broken, the old man got worse. This excited the

family very much, and someone told the wife if she would take the charm to a stream of running water, throw it in the water, and not look back, that would cast the spell back to the person who had put it on her husband. The son was sent with the charm to a nearby stream. He cast it in the water and did not look back, as he, too, was very anxious about his father's health.

After nine more days, the old man was entirely well, but the hoodoo doctor had died. The family firmly believed the current of the stream was too strong for the hoodoo doctor to combat, throwing the spell back to himself, and the spell killed him.

One FWP informant, Robert McKinley, claimed that he was an herb doctor, and Elizabeth Russell told how her leg was crushed when a wagon she was riding in turned over and how "One of the old slaves gathered herbs and made what they called an ooze, and some of the men cut down a hickory tree and made splints for my crushed leg." Joseph William Carter said that he did not believe in witchcraft but had once helped his cousin, who feigned that he was a folk healer, cure a woman of rheumatism: "He sent me into the woods to dig up poke roots to boil. He then took the brew to the house where the sick woman lived and had her to put both feet in a tub filled with warm water, into which he had placed the poke root brew. He told the woman she had lizards in her body, and he was going to wring them out of her."

Many of the former slaves believed in ghosts and wandering spirits. Katie Rose, for instance maintained that she saw jack-o'-lanterns, also known as will-o'-the-wisps: "We often saw lights off in the woods, near the river. We called them jack-o'-my-lanterns, and we always tried to see how fast we could run home when we saw them. I was always afraid to even try." The slave narratives teem with ghostlore. Lulu Scott contended that she could see spirits: "'Course I can see spirits. Seed one just before Christmas. I seed this'n and knowed they was something I done forgot to do, something *she* want me to do before she died. Like as not I done forgot to do it, and she done come back to see."

Elizabeth Russell saw two headless ghosts. Thomas Lewis told of a place haunted by the cries of the spirits of black people who were beaten to death. America Morgan was haunted by the ghost of the slaveholder's mean wife knocking on the wall with her cane, and she maintained that after the old slave-holder's death, his ghost returned once a week to ride his favorite horse, old Pomp, all night long. Morgan also contended that she had lived in several haunted houses since coming up north. Katie Rose said, "When I was a very young girl my stepfather died, and then I saw my first hant, or ghost."

George Morrison told the fieldworker that he did not "really believe in ghosts, but you know how it is. I live by myself, and I don't like to talk about them, for you never can tell what they might do." Nevertheless, Morrison related an eerie experience that he "never could figure out." He swore that "A man I knew saw a ghost once, and he hit at it. He always said he wasn't afraid of no ghost, but that ghost hit him and hit him so hard it knocked his face to one side, and the last time I saw him it was still that way." Amy Elizabeth Patterson recalled that many slaves were afraid of ghosts and evil spirits, but she did not believe in them until three years before the interview, when through a medium she received a message "from the spirit land." She said she still did not believe in "ghosts and evil visitations," but after that experience she became a firm believer in communication with departed ones "who still love and long to protect those who remain on earth."

There also are several religious legends in the Indiana slave narrative collection. Elvira Lee told her daughter, Sarah Emery Merrill, that Sister Ridley, an aged black woman, believed that God had split her open, scraped her just like a hog, and washed out her insides with milk, which killed all her sins. Then God healed her, and she was all pure and white inside. Lillian Hunter related a family legend that her mother had often told her, about how her great-great-grandfather, a Scottish slaveholder who hated blacks, was punished by God. Hunter said that on a day when there was not a cloud in the sky, "my great-great-grandfather was standing by his dining room window when one of his slaves passed through the room. He immediately began cursing the man unmercifully, when a bolt of lightning struck him, killing him instantly."

Other informants relate historical legends. For instance, Josie Harrell related a legend about buried treasure, and to illustrate a point, George Washington Buckner told a story about Andrew Jackson's faithful slave, Sammy. Fieldworker Merton Knowles gives an account of Ben Moore, allegedly Davy Crockett's servant, who escaped the Mexicans at the Alamo and finally wound up in Indiana. Knowles's account of Moore includes familiar folklore motifs of strong men, including Motifs F631, "Strong man carries giant load," and F615.0.1, "Death of strong man" (Thompson 1966). Suggestive of strong man Barney Beal, who strained and killed himself hauling in a dory, a job for four men (Dorson 1964: 53–57), late in his life, strong man Ben Moore lifted a clay mixer from a wagon, a job for several men, and died soon after from the strain.

Besides legends, there are plenty of humorous folktales in the Indiana slave narratives. George Beatty's interview includes one of the most popular tall tale motifs in American folklore. Beatty said that between Hanover and Lexington there was a dense forest. In the fall, pigeons flew in such large flocks that the sun was hidden from view (Baughman 1966: X1119.1[c], "Thick pigeons darken sky"). John Moore told a trickster tale that appears frequently in collections of African American folklore, including Botkin's *Lay My Burden Down* and Dorson's *American Negro Folktales* (Dorson 1967: 143–145, 168). Moore said that the other slaves and the slaveholder often heard a slave named Isam praying to the Lord to take him to heaven from his awful situation. The slaveowner enjoyed tormenting his slaves, so one night he climbed to the roof and heard the prayer, "Oh, Lord, please come take poor Isam to heaven." "Who's there?" asked old Isam, hearing the owner on the shingles. "It is the Lord, come for Isam," said the owner. "That nigger ain't home tonight," replied Isam, and that ended his prayers for deliverance for a long time (Baughman 1966: J217.0.1.1, "Trickster overhears man praying for death to take him"). Sarah Emery Merrill reported a version of the same tale that she had learned from her mother, Elvira Lee.

There are two other humorous tales of answered prayers in the Indiana slave narratives. In a story told by John W. Fields, two slaves apparently steal the slaveowner's 250-pound hog, and one of the slaves hides in the attic when the owner shows up to inquire about his pig. The other slave confronts the owner, telling him, "Massa, I know nothing of any hog. I never seed him. The Good Man up above knows I never seed him. He knows everything, and He knows I didn't steal him!" The terrified slave in the attic yells, "He's a liar, Massa; he knows just as much about it as I do!" Another trickster tale that Elvira Lee told her daughter, Sarah Emery Merrill, has similar motifs.

In his narrative, Reverend Oliver Nelson draws on two anecdotes involving laymen taking a preacher's metaphors literally (Motif J2470, "Metaphors literally interpreted"; cf. Motifs J1738.5ff [Thompson 1966]), including, in part, this one: "I was exhorting an older colored lady about heaven, reading to her from Revelations. 'Aunt Sarah,' I says, 'when we leave this world we'll go to a better world, one where there isn't work, and our food will be milk and honey.' 'Brother Nelson, is that all we're going to have to eat in heaven? Milk gives me a pain in the stomach. Honey makes me sick, so I don't know whether I want to go to heaven or not.'"

Folksongs also appear throughout the WPA interviews. Adah Isabelle Suggs recalled slaves singing and dancing together in the slave quarters after a day's hard work. Their voices were strong and their songs sweet, she observed. Katie Rose mentioned that "The slaves sang songs when the moon was bright, and the young slaves danced and played games." Rosa Barber said that slaves found consolation mainly in their field songs, and George W. Arnold recalled that roustabouts sang songs while loading boats with freight and provisions. Asked if he knew any boatmen's songs from earlier days, George Taylor Burns replied that boatmen sang versions of the same songs to different tunes. Burns remarked that many boat songs were sung to the tune of "Dixie," and a number of songs mentioned the name of a captain of some craft. To illustrate, he sang a version of "Dixie" that was sung on a boat captained by W. H. Daniels. George Fortman said that "Whistling Coon" was another popular song that boatmen sang to the tune of "Dixie," and he provided a text of another song they often sang when nearing a port.

Lizzie Samuels sang "Old Saul Crawford Is Dead," a song she had learned from soldiers, and Katie Sutton sang a lullaby for the fieldworker, who reported that Sutton's voice "was thin and wavering, but she recalled an old song she had heard in slavery days." Sarah Emery Merrill said that her mother, Elvira Lee, had taught her a couple of songs, of which she gave examples, and to her knowledge neither had ever been written down. Songs of blacks, she said, are different from songs of whites, as they are songs of experience. For example, slaves working in the plantation fields, often for a cruel slaveholder, sang for the Lord to take their souls to heaven or to give them courage to continue. Sarah said that the "notes of our music are peculiarly shaped because the rhythm is not perfect." The songs were created "not according to a fixed rule but according to the rhythmical nature of our race."

Sometimes a FWP fieldworker volunteered an item of folklore. For example, Merton Knowles, Fountain County fieldworker, recalled a version of "Run Nigger Run" (White 1965: 168), which he calls a "Negro Folk Song," from his own memory (see Ben Moore's narrative for the text). He suggests that either immigrants from the South or returning soldiers brought the song to Indiana.

Many former slaves had still been children when they were held in slavery, and they remembered examples of slave children's folklore, including folk toys and folk games. As a child in North Carolina, Rosa Barber said that she played with rag dolls or a ball of yarn, if she had enough old string to make one. She claimed that any toy considered educational was forbidden. Katie Rose described a game, "Rock Candy," that young blacks played at parties. She said the game was popular among both whites and blacks, but "The preachers and church-going people hated for us to rock candy. They called it dancing, but that only made us more determined to play it."

A children's fict—a genre of folklore told to children to frighten them into behaving—appears in both of Candies Richardson's obituaries, though not in her WPA interview. The *Indianapolis Star* (October 12, 1955) reported that Richardson recollected that during the Civil War children who misbehaved were told that Abraham Lincoln would get them: "They told us he was 'a hairy man' and we would run and hide in fear of him." This was an interesting threat, since Lincoln became a folk hero. Elizabeth Russell, for example, said that one of the greatest events of her life was meeting Abraham Lincoln on one of his trips through the South. She related two versions of this family legend in her WPA interviews. In one account, she refers to a children's traditional knee-riding game (cf. Opie and Opie 1955: 12–14): "the president sat Mima on one knee and me on the other, then trotted each of us on his foot with the nursery rhyme of 'Trot, Trot to Boston.' I will never forget how proud I felt to think I hadn't only seen President Lincoln but had sat on his knee."

The Indiana slave narratives include a number of references to popular entertainments and folk customs, both during and after slavery. Henry Clay Moorman reported that slaves gathered from various plantations and held parties and dances that sometimes lasted all night. Peter Gohagen described barbecues and beef shoots, and Alex Woodson also talked about the good times at barbecues: "Barbecues! My, we sure used to have 'em. Yes, ma'am, we did!

Folks would come for miles around, would roast whole hogs and cows; and folks would sing, and eat, and drink whiskey. The white folks had 'em, but we helped and had fun, too. Sometimes we would have one ourselves."

George Morrison provided detailed information about square dances, which, he said, like play parties, were more popular in the country than in towns. After slavery, whole families attended these affairs, which lasted from early evening until midnight in someone's home. The playing of "Old Dan Tucker" usually signaled the last dance. Morrison said that he attended a square dance that was held near Saint Joseph, Indiana, one summer afternoon and was invited to perform a dance recalling plantation days. The fiddler played a hoe-down, and George performed a dance from slave days to an appreciative audience. "Yes, ma'am," he told the fieldworker, "I had everybody laughin'. You could hear them for four miles." He emphasized that he was better at it in the old days, though: "Lady, you ought to hear me rattle bones when I was young. I can't do it much now, for my wrists are too stiff."

Sarah H. Locke said that Christmas was a joyous time on her plantation, for slaves had a whole week to celebrate—eating, dancing, and generally having a good time. Lulu Scott added that at "Christmas time we'd hang up our stockin's and get a glass-headed doll. And we'd have black cake and plum puddin'. Black cake was like fruitcake except it didn't have no raisins or nothin' in it. We had turkey, chitlins and everything—cook enough to last a week. And we'd go to church—the children in front and ol' folks behind."

Henry Clay Moorman recalled a slave wedding on a southern plantation just before the end of slavery. He said that slaves on the same plantation seldom married among themselves, that male slaves generally courted and married women from other plantations. He said a male slave had to get the consent of three people before he could get married: the woman's mother, the woman's owner, and his own owner. If he could not get consent from all three people, sometimes a couple eloped, but Moorman said that caused problems. Generally, though, slaveholders encouraged couples to marry, and if the couple got consent from everyone, the wedding usually took place on Saturday night. Slaves from other plantations brought food and took part in the music and dancing. After the wedding, the groom returned to his master, but every week he was allowed to visit his wife from Saturday night until Monday morning. Only if one of the two owners bought the husband or wife could the couple live together. Children born in slavery became the property of the mother's master, according to Moorman.

John Moore described the traditional wedding ceremony of his father and mother in the slave quarters of a Tennessee plantation. Both the bride and the groom had to jump over a broom handle held by two wedding guests. After jumping the broom, they were considered married, though later they remarried in a legal ceremony.

Details of slave funerals are lacking in the Indiana FWP interviews, but George Fortman provided a detailed account of a white funeral. Henry Clay Moorman recalled that there were two graveyards on the plantation—one for whites and one for blacks. Moorman could not remember any deaths among the whites living on the plantation, though.

George Thomas contributed a full account of folklife in Clark County, Indiana, after the war. He described house raisings, log rollings, food preservation and preparation, play parties, square dances, singing, games, and maple syrup making. Alex Woodson mentioned work bees, too, saying that they "Used to have rail splittin's and wood choppin's. The men would work all day and get a pile of wood as big as a house. At noon they'd stop and eat a big meal that the women folks had fixed up for 'em. Them was some times. I've went to many a one." Lulu Scott offered material on folklife, too, including food preservation: "Potatoes and carrots and cabbage and apples'd be buried in the ground, but the apples'd sometime have a groun'y taste, so sometimes we wouldn't bury them. And we'd make a keg of sauerkraut; many's the hour I spent makin' sauerkraut. Why, just makin' it, like you make all sauerkraut."

RECOLLECTIONS OF THE CIVIL WAR

Some former slaves interviewed in Indiana were too young to have fought in the Civil War. George Fortman, for instance, stayed home during the war, so he was able to report on changes that took place on the plantation at the beginning of the Civil War. Many slaves, he said, left the plantation and enlisted in the Union Army, believing it their duty to fight for freedom. His mother, too, took her family off the plantation to work in the broom cane; however, soon "she discovered she couldn't make enough to rear her children, and we were turned over to the court to be bound out." According to Henry Clay Moorman, slaveholders poisoned the minds of their slaves, and the slaves were in constant fear of Union soldiers. Once when some slaves saw around two hundred Union soldiers approaching, they hid in the woods and covered their small children with leaves.

Katie Rose said, "Everything was happy and lovely at the Holloway home until the Civil War started. Then some of the slaves enlisted to fight, and Young Marse John went to the war. Old Missus and Young Missus never seemed happy again. Things went from worse to worse, and soon the young marse was brought home in a coffin." Elizabeth Russell noted that when the Civil War broke out, many slaveowners left their plantations to join the fight. Elizabeth's owner, however, loaded his slaves in wagons and, with other slaveholders, headed for San Antonio, Texas, attempting to escape the Yankees.

Some plantation owners who fought in the war left their slaves in charge of their family, money, and livestock. Mollie Tate's relatives, for instance, looked after their master's wife and children: "A short time before the war closed, the master, Dave Tate, was conscripted and had to go. Before leaving he charged Uncle Isom and Aunt Nancy to care for his wife, two sons, David and William, and daughter, Tennessee. He never returned alive." Alex Woodson's mother's owner gave her a large roll of bills, "greenbacks as big as your arm," to keep for him when he was forced to leave his plantation. After the war, the Woodsons returned all the money. Figuring that Union soldiers would kill him if he stayed on his farm but would spare his wife, Mrs. Preston's owner took his best horses and hogs to Frankfort during the war and left his farm and family in the care of an overseer. Ira Jones contended that when Union soldiers marched through Kentucky, slaveholder Tandy was so frightened that he hid in a thicket. W. F.

Parrott said that slaves on his plantation supported the North and befriended Union soldiers, and toward the end of the war, when plantation owners knew that the South had lost, slaveholders themselves assisted Union troops. In fact, one slaveholder, apparently a Union sympathizer, was drafted as a picket in the Union Army.

Former slaves served in both the Southern and Northern armies. Betty Guwn recollected that "When the Civil War came on there was great excitement among us slaves. We were watched sharply, especially for soldier timber for either army." Moses Slaughter contended that General Lee wanted to offer immediate freedom to all slaves who enlisted in the Southern army, but his proposal was rejected because large slave dealers opposed it. Slaughter claimed that after the U.S. Congress allowed slaves to enlist, many slaves joined the Union Army. George Washington Buckner noted, however, that whites were indignant because blacks were allowed to enlist.

According to Billy Slaughter, some slaves who wanted to join the Union Army were not allowed to because they were still under their masters' control, and some slaves, he reported, were forced to join the Southern army. John Eubanks, however, said that when the North appeared to be losing the war, black regiments were formed, and slaves joining the Union Army were granted freedom. He joined the Union Army at the beginning of the Civil War, when he was twenty-one. Eubanks's master told him that if he wished, he could join the army instead of running away, as some slaves were doing, so Eubanks joined a black regiment located at Bowling Green, Kentucky.

The wives and unmarried children of black men who enlisted in the Union Army were given freedom, too. Billy Slaughter's father joined the Union Army, so Slaughter's father and mother and their unmarried children were freed. Slaughter maintained that black soldiers never fought in any decisive battles. Someone, he reflected, had to polish harnesses, care for horses, dig ditches, and build parapets. Slaughter's father, however, was at Memphis during a battle there. George Morrison's father also fought for the North. "Yes, ma'am," he told the fieldworker, "the war sure did affect my family. My father, he fought for the North. He got shot in his side, but it finally got all right." Francis Gammons's husband ran away from the plantation and joined the Union Army during the Civil War because "He wanted to be free and declared that he was willing to take his share in securing this freedom, which he did by fighting for the Union." Likewise, Betty Guwn's husband "ran away early and helped Grant to take Fort Donaldson [Donelson?]. He said he would free himself, which he did." Anderson Whitted's uncle also ran away; he broke through the lines and joined the Northern army.

Thomas Ash recalled "how the grown-up Negroes on the place left to join the Union Army as soon as they learned of Lincoln's proclamation making them free men." When asked if he had served in the Civil War, Joseph Carter responded, "Of course, I did. When I got old enough, I entered the service and barbecued meat until the war closed." Barbecuing was Carter's specialty as a slave, so he did the same work as a Union soldier. Barney Stone was a soldier in the Union Army for nearly two years. He remarked that "After those experiences of sixteen long years in hell as a slave, I was very bitter against the white man, until after I ran away and joined the Union Army." Stone swore that "hundreds of male slaves were shot down by the rebels, rather than see them join with the Yankees." Moses Slaughter, who gave a long account of his Civil War adventures as a Union soldier, reflected that "Army life is a hard life no matter how well the men are trained. It seems you are always meeting with some unexpected occurrence." Maybe that's why George Beatty's father chose to run off to Canada rather than serve in the Union Army.

Several former slaves served in the Southern army. George Morrison "saw them fellows from the South take my uncle. They put his clothes on him right in the yard and took him with them to fight. And even the white folks, they all cried." Candies Richardson said that her husband went off to war to be "what you call a valet for Marse Jim's son, Sam." Ira Jones said that one time some of the slaves were to be taken away to join the rebel army. His father was among the group, but he escaped and ran barefoot over frozen ground. When he returned home, his feet were so sore that he could hardly walk.

Former slaves who did not serve in one of the armies during the Civil War related personal-experience tales about the war, especially encounters with troops. Sylvester Smith recollected that soldiers leaving for the Civil War said that it would be only a "breakfast spell." He was not old enough to serve in the war but saw a few skirmishes. Nancy Whallen remembered soldiers coming to the farm for food, camping on the farm, and teasing her. Mollie Tate gave a good account of both Union and Confederate troops pilfering food: "Every day spies were making their rounds, and often soldiers, both Yankee and Rebel, visited our cabin, taking what they could find—bacon, molasses, meal, anything they wanted. They'd fill their canteens with water and be off."

Elvira Lee, who was about sixteen when the Civil War began, told about soldiers drilling in a large field belonging to her master. She said that during the war it was sometimes dangerous for officers to visit their families, and she related how on one visit she hid her master, a captain in the Confederacy, in her cabin most of the night. On another visit her owner was safeguarded by his wife, who kept the soldiers looking for him out of the house by telling them that her child had smallpox. Adeline Rose Lennox recalled hearing the distant roar of cannons, but admitted that at the time she "didn't know what it was about." She also recalled that Southern soldiers often came to the farm with wagons and carried off all the food they could find to feed the Southern army. Thomas Lewis said that his mother told Union soldiers "where the stillhouse was. Her master didn't want her to tell where the stillhouse was because some of his rebel friends were hiding there. Spies had reported them to the Yankee soldiers. They went to the stillhouse and captured the rebels."

Sarah O'Donnell remembered cooking a meal for General Jefferson C. Davis and his troops, but she was not quite sure whether they were Union or Confederate soldiers. She explained, "I hadn't much time to look and see who all they were. They were in a hurry and hungry, and you know it didn't pay to ask questions of soldiers, especially not of generals, as to who they were." Preston Tate recalled a battle near Mossy Creek, Tennessee. He and other children were playing when they discovered that they were surrounded by soldiers. Frightened by "shells flying thick and fast," they crawled unharmed behind trees and through thickets to escape the battlefield.

Confederate general John Hunt Morgan shows up in several of the WPA interviews with former slaves. When General Morgan, the famous Southern raider, crossed the Ohio and raided southern Indiana, John Eubanks was one of the black soldiers who, after heavy fighting, forced Morgan to retreat back across the river. Alex Woodson remembered hiding all night in the woods with his mother and other children when Morgan's soldiers came. The raiders took all the horses and cattle and combed the woods for Yankees. Alex said that he saw Morgan from a distance riding a big horse, and he "was shore a mighty fine looker." George Winlock noted that "General John H. Morgan made two raids through Kentucky. His trail could be followed from Glasgow to Elizabethtown. He was routed at Elizabethtown and hurried out of the state by way of New Haven and Burkesville by infuriated Kentuckians led by General E. H. Hobson." Robert Barton recalled that Morgan once stayed all night on his master's farm.

George Winlock thought that "the entire war was a mistake. The fight was not altogether over the emancipation of the Negroes, but resulted from the political quarrels and misrepresented facts. Many Negroes were happy while they were slaves." Still, Winlock conceded that when Lincoln was assassinated, every Union soldier grieved, for Lincoln "had given his life for the cause of freedom." Billy Slaughter agreed that "Freeing the slaves was brought about during the Civil War, but it was not the reason that the war was fought." He said that the real reason for the war was that the South withdrew from the Union and elected Jefferson Davis president of the Confederacy. While Slaughter respected the federal government, he regarded John Brown as a hero, and among his prized possessions was a book about John Brown's raid.

LIVING AND WORKING AFTER THE CIVIL WAR

According to Hettie McClain's narrative, Lee's surrender did not end slavery in Kentucky. Although 72,000 African Americans who served in the Union Army were freed, half the slaves in Kentucky belonged to Confederate sympathizers and were not given their freedom immediately at the end of the Civil War. When the Thirteenth Amendment was presented to the states for ratification, only a fraction of Kentuckians favored unconditional ratification. Some favored rejecting the amendment completely, and some, including the governor of Kentucky, favored the amendment only if Kentuckians were compensated for their loss of slaves. Consequently, the freedom of many slaves living in Kentucky was delayed while this debate was going on.

Mattie Jenkins said that slaves on her plantation were so deprived of news that they were not set free until a year after the Emancipation Proclamation was passed. Anthony Young was not told when the slaves were freed, either. One day his overseer was going to whip him, so Young hid in the home of a white neighbor, who informed him, "You're a free man. If he whips you, you can have him arrested for assault and battery." George Thompson stated that at the age of twelve he was too immature to leave the plantation: "I was so young and inexperienced when freed that I remained on the Thompson plantation for four years after the war and worked for my board and clothes as coach boy and any other odd jobs around the plantation."

Some slaves were given a choice of leaving the plantation or staying and working for wages. Louis Watkins said that when his master told the slaves they could leave if they wanted to or stay on the plantation and work for wages, no one left right away. Peter Neal and his family were given the same choice, according to his son, Henry Neal, and decided to stay: "We remained for several years in the employ of this kind friend, and my mother was also employed as cook. While here my father was permitted to tend some ground for himself, and he raised chickens for market instead of stealing them, as so many do now." Sylvester Smith also claimed that he was treated well as a slave, which encouraged him to stay with his master for a year without pay after the war, though on gaining her freedom his sister left immediately.

H. H. Edmunds recollected that the slaves were very happy when they heard they were free. Those who had been mistreated by slaveholders left the plantations right away, but many, not knowing what else to do, remained with their former owners. Some had no money and no place to go. As William M. Quinn explained, "We didn't know that we were slaves, hardly. Well, my brother and I didn't know anyhow 'cause we were too young to know, but we knew that we had been when we got older. After emancipation we stayed at the Stone family for some time 'cause they were good to us and we had no place to go." Betty Smith, too, stayed on the plantation for a while, first working in the fields for food and clothes. A few years later she nursed children for twenty-five cents a week and food, though eventually she got fifty cents a week, board, and two dresses.

Some former slaves stayed on the plantations simply to keep their families together. When the slaves were freed, Sarah Parrott's master ordered her off his plantation, but Parrott refused to go without her five children, since she knew that as soon as she was gone, her master would bind her children to work for him until they were twenty-one. At that time he would have to give her sons only $100 and a horse. When her husband returned from the war, Parrott left the plantation with her family and moved to Mitchell, where the Parrotts were married under civil law to protect their children from being considered orphans and indentured to their former slaveholder. Rosaline Rogers explained that she stayed on the plantation to keep her fourteen children with her, too: "I decided to stay on; that way, I could have my children with me. They were not allowed to go to school; they were taught only to work."

When Samuel Watson's mother learned that she was free, her former master ordered her and her three children off the plantation. They went to another plantation, hoping to find work so they could remain together; their wages would not support them, however, so they left that plantation, too, and worked from place to place for starvation wages. Two of the older children returned to their former owner, who had an article of indenture drawn up binding them to his service. Watson remained with his mother, who took him to a third plantation, where the owner had him indentured for eighteen years. Watson explained that an indentured person was supposed to be given a fair education, a good horse with bridle and saddle, and a suit of clothes after bondage, but the plantation owner said that Watson did not deserve them. Watson finally ended up with $95 after hiring a lawyer friend to sue the plantation owner.

George Arnold acknowledged that some slaves reluctantly left the plantations because freedom "broke up a lot of real friendships and scattered many families." One former slave who was reluctant to leave was Adeline Rose Lennox, who maintained that she did not know she was a slave until the close of the Civil War. After the war, Lennox did not want to leave the plantation when the master's wife told her that she was free to return to her father's home.

Mrs. Hockaday summarized the situation very well. She pointed out that after the Civil War, many slaves were unskilled and uneducated and, as during the Depression, found it difficult to find jobs. Thinking they might not find employment elsewhere, many former slaves never left the plantations. In fact, some who left eventually returned to their former plantations, where they continued to live much as they had during slavery. Mrs. Hockaday also said that in the North, as during the Depression, relief stations were established where former slaves who could not find jobs could get food and shelter. According to Anderson Whitted, however, the government provided former slaves with only hardtack and pickled beef. Whitted said his family was satisfied with the hardtack but believed that the strange-looking pickled beef was really horse meat.

Some slaves, such as Samuel Bell, were sent to contraband camps—camps within Union lines where slaves escaped to or were brought to during the Civil War. Bell said he was well cared for at the camp but soon grew tired of camp life and was granted permission to leave. He farmed for a while before settling in Evansville, where he worked as a janitor in a local bank for a number of years.

Matthew Hume could not understand why so many former slaves remained on the plantations. He thought the Emancipation Proclamation was Lincoln's greatest contribution, though the slaves on his plantation did not hear about it until the following August. His master offered to let the former slaves remain on the plantation as sharecroppers, but Hume's family chose to leave. Their only possession, a cow, was taken from them, so Hume said they came to Indiana homeless, friendless, and penniless. At the close of the war, Ethel Daugherty's family, too, was simply turned off the plantation without any help from their master. When Solomon Hicks's father was released after forty-seven years of servitude, he was given only a three-legged horse with which to begin a new life. Betty Guwn's master "begged us to stay and offered us five pounds of meal and two pounds of pork jowl each week if we would stay and work," but her family left the plantation, too.

Candies Richardson said that "old Marse Jim told us everyone was free, and that was almost a year after the other slaves on the other plantations around were freed." The slaveholder told them "he didn't have to give us anything to eat and that he didn't have to give us a place to stay, but we could stay and work for him and he would pay us. But we left that night and walked for miles through the rain to my husband's brother and then told them that they all were free." After the war, Joseph Allen's master told his slaves with tears in his eyes, "Boys, do you know what is up this morning?" They answered, "No, sir." "Well, you are as free as I am; Abe Lincoln set you free," he told them. Allen said, "Well, if I'm free, I guess I'll get out."

Nelson Polk's family wanted to remain together on the plantation and work for shares or wages, but the planter did not want Polk around, so, leaving his wife and family in Mississippi with his former owner, Polk went to Tennessee, where he married another woman. James Childress said that the slaves on his plantation rejoiced when they got their freedom but "still depended on old Marse John for food and bed. . . . They hated to leave their homes, but Mr. Childress told them to go out and make homes for themselves."

The mistreatment of blacks did not stop with the end of slavery. Mattie Jenkins said that some slaves were deprived of news and knew nothing of the Emancipation Proclamation until a year after it was passed. Many slaves, she said, were not freed when they should have been. Pete Johnson said that after the war he took a job with a terrible woman near Louisville. He said he "complained about the poor quarters, only to be told that 'anything was good enough for niggers.' This was a terrible woman who kept pistols, guns, and other firearms around in all rooms." Angie Moore Boyce reported that she and her baby were not treated very well on arriving in Indiana, where they were arrested and returned to Kentucky. They were placed in the Louisville jail, where they shared a cell with a big, rough, drunken Irish woman, who got upset by the baby's crying and threatened to "bash its brains out against the wall if it didn't stop crying." Richard Miller recounted that when slavery ended, some former slaves decided to leave Kentucky and head farther south to buy farms. When they got to Madison County, Kentucky, however, they were told that in the Deep South they would be forced into slavery again. Thinking that might be true, they remained on Madison County farms and worked for low wages. After the war, Sidney Graham worked in a powder mill in Tennessee. When he accidentally splashed some hot water on someone working near him, he was warned that Klansmen would visit him that night for burning a white man. The Klan arrived as promised, and broke through Graham's barricaded rear door. Graham shot and killed the first man who tried to enter his house, and the Klansmen took the body and left. Graham slipped off to Nashville, Tennessee, where he was later joined by his family.

Thomas Lewis also related an encounter with a white gang who went "to my grandmother's place and ordered the colored people out to work. The colored people had worked before for white men on shares. When the wheat was all in and the corn laid by, the white farmers would tell the colored people to get out and would give them nothing. . . . Our family left because we didn't want to work that way." Edna Boysaw told a grim tale about how former slaves coming from Virginia to work in Clay County mines were met by whites at the train station in Harmony: "When they arrived about four miles east of Brazil, or what was known as Harmony, the train was stopped, and a crowd of white miners ordered them not to come any nearer Brazil. Then the trouble began. . . . Mr. Masten took some of them south of Brazil about three miles, where he had a number of company houses, and they tried to work in his mine there. But many were shot at from the bushes and killed."

Several former slaves and their families fared better than others in Indiana. George Washington Buckner got a medical degree, practiced medicine in

Evansville for many years, and was appointed minister to Liberia during Woodrow Wilson's presidency in 1913. Henry Clay Moorman's family remained on the plantation for a year after slavery was abolished, moved to Evansville for a while, and in 1903 settled in Franklin, where he served as pastor of the African Methodist Episcopal Church for twelve years. J. B. Polk also was a minister. Rudolph D. O'Hara became an attorney and served the black population of Vanderburgh County. W. F. Parrott graduated from Mitchell High School and Indiana University. He taught at Spencer for ten years as well as at schools at Ghent and Carrollton, Kentucky.

After settling in Bloomington, Mattie Fuller took a course in hair dressing, took music lessons from some of the best music teachers in Bloomington, and became well-known in the community as owner and operator of Bloomington's earliest beauty shop and as a church organist and singer. Until a year before the WPA interview, Ralph Kates worked as a paperhanger and interior decorator. His father "was a smart man, working as a stonecutter or stone mason and interior decorator. He was also a good accountant and bookkeeper. He helped to build the new Vanderburgh County courthouse, working in stone and mortar." Bell Deam Kelley worked as a housekeeper and Alexander Kelley as a cook in Indianapolis and Muncie.

John Rudd labored on farms for several years before serving for fifteen years as a porter in an Owensboro hotel. For eight years he worked as a janitor in a hospital. Mary Elizabeth Scarber quilted for a number of people, and Lulu Scott was a cook for years. Alex Fowler, the first African American in Lake County, operated a barber shop. Anderson Whitted worked at the brickyards in Rockville, and he claimed that to make a decent living, he often did the work of two men. Pete Wilson was a furniture worker for Showers Brothers in Bloomington.

For thirty years, Preston Tate was a fireman in a sawmill; after the mill burned, he worked in a stone quarry. Then for a dozen or so years he worked in a greenhouse. Joseph Allen pushed a wheelbarrow and helped keep the fires burning at the Muncie Foundry until he was eighty-three years old. At that time he supposedly was the oldest manual laborer working in an Indiana factory.

Several former slaves, including Carl Boone and John Henry Gibson, farmed. Gibson farmed a section of the bottomlands where the James Whitcomb Riley Hospital now stands in Indianapolis. He raised corn and wheat, tended hogs and cattle, and traded horses. Another group of former slaves worked on boats. Moses Slaughter said, "After the war ended I took to the river trade, steamboating on the *R. C. Gray* from Cincinnati to Fort Smith, Arkansas." When the Missouri woman who brought George Taylor Burns to Troy, Indiana, found out she could not own a slave in Indiana, for $15 a month she indentured Burns to a flatboat captain to wash dishes and wait on the crew. After gaining experience on the flatboats, Burns was hired as a cabin boy on a steamboat and spent most of his active days steamboating. Burns claimed to "know steamboats from woodbox to sternwheel." George W. Arnold worked as a roustabout on a sternwheeler. He claimed that food was always plentiful on the boats but confessed, "In spite of these few pleasures, the life of a roustabout is the life of a dog." After coming to Indiana, Cornelius Cross worked on a canal boat on the Wabash and Erie Canal and traveled between Evansville and Terre Haute. He reflected that "The [Wabash and Erie] canal was a pretty sight." In his earlier days, Billy Slaughter worked on a steamboat that traveled from Louisville to New Orleans.

As Henrietta Jackson noted, after the war some slaveholding families lost their wealth. Their households were broken up by the war, and their farms were destroyed by the armies. Jackson, nevertheless, remained with her former owner for a while. Then she found a job in a laundry "ironing white folks' collars and cuffs." Several years after the Civil War, Susan Smith came to Jeffersonville, where she worked in several homes. When she could not work anymore, she was put in the Clark County Poor Farm. At the time of the WPA interview, she still was not fond of her former owners, recalling how hard they had made her work.

Some former slaves living in Indiana survived on pensions. Alex Woodson and his second wife ran a sparsely stocked grocery store in the front room of their small house in New Albany and got along with the help of Woodson's pension. After working two years in a coke plant in Gary, Reverend Wamble was laid off during the Depression. Though he had been a preacher for thirty-seven years, he was living on a small pension when interviewed. John Rudd and his second wife were living in Evansville on an old-age pension of $14 a month, and Nettie Pompey was living in Indianapolis on an old-age pension of $20 a month. Joe Robinson, also living in Indianapolis, said the pension he and his wife received was barely enough to live on, and he hoped it would be increased.

Alex and Betty Smith were living in a shack patched with tarpaper, tin, and wood, and their only income was a government old-age pension of about $14 a month. Joseph Mosley said it was not easy to get along on his small pension of $18 a month, and he wondered if the government was going to increase it. Samuel Watson was entitled to an old-age pension, which he received from 1934 through 1935, but on January 15, 1936, the money was withheld for some reason, and Watson was sent to the poorhouse. In 1936 he again applied for a pension and received $17 a month to pay for his upkeep.

Other former slaves were living in poverty in Indiana when they were interviewed during the Depression. The fieldworker described Maria Love's house as "a little old worn shack, not very neat." Robert J. Cheatham was an invalid, and his ill health had contributed to his poverty. He and his wife had lost their house and were living in a small apartment in a day nursery for black children. He had faith, though, that he and his wife would not be left to suffer from either hunger or cold.

In fact, some former slaves stressed that times were harder during the Depression than in slavery. Cynthia O'Hara contended that in Evansville she worked harder to support her children than she had ever worked as a slave on the plantation. Julia Bowman stated that she never knew deprivation in slavery as she knew it during the Depression. According to Adeline Rose Lennox, slaves on her plantation were well taken care of and had plenty of corn, peas, beans, and pork to eat. She claimed she had more pork as a slave than during the Depression.

Several former slaves interviewed in Indiana had visited or longed to visit the southern plantations on which they had been held. For instance, in her old age Sarah Parrott visited her former slaveholder in Kentucky. Much more feeble than Parrott, he greeted her cordially, and she said they enjoyed talking about the old days. Alex Woodson allowed that "I like to go back down in Kentucky on visits, as the folks there won't take a thing for bed and vittles. Here they are so selfish that they won't even give a drink of water away." Elizabeth (Bettie) Jones regretted that she could not return to Kentucky: "I would like to go back to Henderson, Kentucky, once more, for I have not been there for more than twenty years. I'd like to walk the old plank walk again up to Mr. Alvis's home, but I'm afraid I'll never get to go. It costs too much." Henrietta Jackson said that she sometimes longed for her old home in Alabama, where her friends lived, but for the most part she was happy in Fort Wayne.

VALUE OF THE WPA INTERVIEWS

As Dorson stresses, slavery, the "peculiar institution," "imparts a special character" to both American history and American folklore (Dorson 1983: 330). In fact, he argues that "Nowhere do American history and folklore intersect more closely than in the 'peculiar institution'" (Dorson 1971: 71). Rawick suggests, however, that the WPA interviews with former slaves may be of more value to the local historian or folklorist than to the general historian of slavery. He claims that the interviews are of value not because they describe great historical events but because they "reveal the day-to-day life of people, their customs, their values, their ideas, hopes, aspirations, and fears. We can derive from them a picture of slave society and social structure and of the interaction between black and white" (Rawick 1972: I, xvii). In one of the supplemental volumes, he reiterates that the Indiana interviews "are not particularly significant for the general historian of slavery, although they may be of considerable interest to students of particular aspects of local Indiana history and for genealogical purposes" (Rawick 1977: lx).

For readers interested in a folk history of slavery from the point of view of those who suffered through it, however, the WPA narratives are essential reading, as Escott notes: "For all who want to understand slavery in North America, the WPA slave narratives are an indispensable source. Along with other types of slave narratives, they open a window on a side of slavery that was largely hidden from white observers" (Escott 1985b: 40). Levine, too, shows that although folk documents such as the WPA slave narratives may not provide the kind of chronology and precise details that intrigue professional historians, folklore can assist in re-creating a people's thought and culture (Levine 1977: xii–xiii). In essence, the WPA interviews with former slaves are folklore, since they are recorded oral traditions, and I approach these narratives as a folklorist, a traditional humanist, and not as a scientific historian, a quantifier. As Escott argues, "both methodologies can and should be used in examining the WPA narratives" (Escott 1985b: 40). Indeed, as Botkin suggests above, the WPA slave narratives, considered folklore, "possess an essential truth and humanity" and surpass as they supplement both history and literature.

PART TWO
THE WPA INTERVIEWS WITH FORMER SLAVES

1. JOSEPH ALLEN

I'll Eat You Up Like a Dog

Joseph Allen was interviewed on separate occasions by two fieldworkers, Martha Freeman and William W. Tuttle, and some of the details of their interviews vary. Joseph was born May 4, 1851, three miles from Birchfield in the southeastern part of Cumberland County, Kentucky, on the plantation of Matt (or Met) and Eliza Allen. His father, Joe Smiley, lived on a different plantation and thus took the name of another slaveholder. Joseph told fieldworker Freeman that he remembered his birthday very well because Eliza Allen whipped him severely when he could not remember his age or his birthday. She cut switches and lashed him under his arms to make him remember. Sometimes she woke him at night and asked him when his birthday was, but he said he never forgot his birthday after that whipping. Joseph told of other times that Eliza Allen whipped him and said that she "sure was bad, but I expect I was bad, too."

Joseph also told Freeman that he did guard duty for the rebels, and when he was about thirteen years old, Union soldiers came by the plantation and wanted him to go with them as a drummer boy. But he did not go. According to Freeman, after the war, Matt Allen told his slaves with tears in his eyes, "Boys, do you know what is up this morning?" They answered, "No, sir." "Well, you are as free as I am; Abe Lincoln set you free," he told them. Joseph said, "Well, if I'm free, I guess I'll get out." According to fieldworker Freeman, Joseph left the plantation around Christmas before he was thirteen years old. Freeman claims that Joseph went to Metcalfe County, Kentucky, and worked at whatever job he could get for about a year. Then for about five years he worked for a man named John Durr.

Joseph went to school for two three-month terms after he was eighteen years old. He said he could read print, though he had difficulty reading longhand. He told Freeman that he always had plenty to eat when he was a slave and that he never forgot it. After he was set free, though, he "scratched like a hen with one chick" to get enough to eat.

Fieldworker Tuttle reports, however, that though Joseph was freed in 1865, he did not leave the plantation until two years later. The first year Allen offered him $40 to stay, but never paid him. Toward the end of the second year, Joseph was offered $150 and a horse; however, he no longer trusted Allen, so according to Tuttle, Joseph left the plantation and made his way to Glasgow, a town about forty-five miles away. He married and lived there and in the adjoining county about fifteen years. After his wife died, he married a second time in Carroll County, Kentucky. When Teddy Roosevelt was elected the second time, he came to Muncie. In Muncie, according to Freeman, Joseph pushed a wheelbarrow and helped keep up the fires at the Muncie Foundry until he was eighty-three years old. He was said to be the oldest man doing manual labor in a factory in the state at that time.

When Joseph was interviewed, his second wife also had died, and he lived with his daughter, Celia Million, and her husband on East Kirk Street. Tuttle reports that Joseph, then in his late eighties, walked without a cane and seemed in excellent health. Freeman says that about ten years before the interview, Joseph was hit by an automobile, and thereafter his memory was no longer as good as it had once been. Here is Joseph's story, according to Tuttle's field report:

> I was born on May 4th, exactly at 4 o'clock in the year 1851. This here happened on the plantation of Met Allen, but they called me Joe Allen instead of Met Allen. The plantation growed corn, tobacco, oats, and a little wheat. Maybe rye. My father's name was Joe Smiley; he's born somewhere on a Joe Smiley plantation. My mother, she's brought in from Virginia. Boss didn't put me into the field till I come seven years of age. 'Fore this I run errands coverin' their plantation. Ol' Missus was cross and whipped us children a-plenty. A white man teached us in their slave room. I learned my A, B, Cs quick, and Ol' Missus catched me studying and learning. I hain't forgot it. When she whipped, she stuck my head between her knees and clamped me tight. She slipped my garment aside and fanned me plenty with a shingle on my bare self. I was gettin' too big, and I studied how I'd break her. Next time I bit her like a dog and held on with my teeth to her leg. Ol' Missus was lame for a spell; I broke her. I says, "I'll eat you up like a dog." After that, she buckled me up on the ground and lashed me.

> When I get seven years old, I go to the field. I suckered the tobacco and wormed it. My boss was Bill Stiltz. We was glad when he joined the Union Army. We never saw him again. The plantation was nigh the Cumberland River, and slaves passed through runnin' away. I run away two times. Older slaves caused me. Both times I come back. My mammy lay sick in bed. I get forty miles away and walked back. Flat Rock church an' schoolhouse was near the plantation, but it was for the whites.

2. GEORGE W. ARNOLD

The Life of a Roustabout Is the Life of a Dog

George W. Arnold was born on April 7, 1861, in Bedford County, Tennessee. He was held by Oliver P. Arnold, owner of a large plantation in Bedford County. His mother was a native of Rome, Georgia. When she was twelve, Oliver Arnold bought her, her three brothers, and an uncle at auction. The four of them, along with other slaves, were taken from Georgia to Tennessee to work on the Arnold plantation, where George was born. As a child, he was allowed to live in a cabin with his relatives.

George said that Evansville, a steamboat port, was a very nice place in the early days when he worked as a roustabout on a sternwheeler, so in 1880 he decided to make his home there. He said that food was always plentiful when he worked on the boats. Passengers and freight were crowded together on the decks. At night they sang, danced, and played fiddle music. On May 10, 1880, he got a job as porter in a wholesale feed store, John Hubbard and Company; he worked for this firm for thirty-seven years. George married an Evansville woman.

George remembered when "The courthouse was located at Third and Main Streets [in Evansville]. Streetcars were mule drawn, and people thought it great fun to ride them." He also recalled that when the new courthouse was being built, two men finishing the slate roof fell to their deaths in the courthouse yard. His memory of Civil War days, though, was limited to a few events.

George offered the interviewer the following advice: "Never do anything to hurt any other person; the hurt always comes back to you. Beware of strong drink; it causes trouble." Here is George's story:

Mother, my young brother, my sister, and I were walking along one day. I don't remember where we had started, but we passed under the fort at Wartrace. A battle was in progress, and a large cannon was fired above us, and we watched the huge ball sail through the air and saw the smoke of the cannon pass over our heads. We poor children were almost scared to death, but our mother held us close to her and tried to comfort us. The next morning, after we were safely at home, we were proud we had seen that much of the great battle, and our mother told us the war was to give us freedom.

I cannot say that they [members of his family] were happy [when they were set free], as it broke up a lot of real friendships and scattered many families. Mother had a great many pretty quilts and a lot of bedding. After the slaves were set free, Marse Arnold told us we could all go and make ourselves homes, so we started out, each of the grown persons loaded with great bundles of bedding, clothing, and personal belongings. We walked all the way to Wartrace to try to find a home and some way to make a living.

Long lines of tired men passed through Guys Gap on their way to Murfreesboro. Older people said that they were sent out to pick up the dead from the battlefields after the bloody battle of Stones River that had lately been fought at Murfreesboro. They took their comrades to bury them at the Union Cemetery near the town of Murfreesboro.

Wartrace was a very nice place to make our home. It was located on the Nashville and Chattanooga and St. Louis Railroad, just fifty-one miles from Nashville, not many miles from our old home. Mother found work, and we got along very well, but as soon as we children were old enough to work, she went back to her old home in Georgia, where a few years later she died. I believe she lived to be seventy-five or seventy-six years of age, but I never saw her after she went back to Georgia.

My first work was done on a farm. There are many fine farms in Tennessee. Although farm labor was not very profitable, we were always fed wherever we worked and got some wages. Then I got a job on the railroad. Our car got sidetracked at a place called Silver Springs, and right at that place came trouble that took the happiness out of my life forever. It was like this: Three of us boys worked together. We were like three brothers, always sharing our fortunes with each other. We should never have done it, but we had made a habit of sending to Nashville after each payday and having a keg of Holland rum sent in by freight. This liquor was handed out among our friends, and sometimes we drank too much and were unfit for work for a day or two. Our boss was a big, strong Irishman, red-haired and friendly. He always got drunk with us, and all of us would become sober enough to soon return to our tasks.

The time I'm telling you about, we had all been invited to a candy pulling in town and could hardly wait till time to go, as all the young people of the valley would be there to pull candy, talk, play games, and eat the goodies served to us. The keg of Holland rum had been brought in that morning, and my chum, John Sims, had been drinking too much. About that time our boss came up and said, "John, it's time for you to get the supper ready!" John was our cook, and our meals were served on the caboose, where we lived whenever we were sidetracked.

All the time Johnny was preparing the food, he was drinking the rum. When we went in, he had many drinks inside of him and a quart bottle filled to take to the candy pull. "Hurry up, boys, and let's finish up and go," he said impatiently. "Don't take him," said the other boy. "Don't you see he's drunk?" So I put my arms about his shoulders and tried to tell him he had better sleep awhile before we started. The poor boy was a breed. His mother was almost white, and his father was a thoroughbred Indian, and the son had a most aggravating temper. He made me no answer, but ramming his hand into his pocket, he drew out his knife and with one thrust cut a deep gash in my neck. A terrible fight followed. I remember being knocked over and my head striking something. I reached out my hand and discovered it was the ax. With this awful weapon I struck my friend, my more than brother. The thud of the ax brought me to my senses as our blood mingled. We were both almost mortally wounded. The boss came in and tried to do something for our relief, but John said, "Oh, George, what an awful thing we have done. We have never said a cross word to each other, and now look at us both."

I watched poor John walk away. Darkness was falling, but early in the morning my boss and I followed a trail of blood down by the side of the tracks. From there he had turned into the woods. We could follow him no farther. We went to all the nearby towns and villages, but we found no person who had ever seen him. We supposed he had died in the woods and watched for the buzzards, thinking they would lead us to his body, but he was never seen again.

For two years I never sat down to look inside a book or to eat my food that John Sims was not beside me. He haunted my pillow and went beside me night and day. His blood was on my hands; his presence haunted me beyond endurance. What could I do? How could I escape this awful presence? An old friend told me to put water between myself and the place where the awful scene occurred. So I quit working on the railroad and started working on the river. People believed at that time that the ghost of a person you had wronged would not cross water to haunt you.

My first job on the river was as a roustabout on the Rolliver H. Cook sternwheel packet, which carried freight and passengers from Nashville, Tennessee, to Evansville, Indiana. I worked a round trip on her, then went from Nashville to Cairo, Illinois, on the B. S. Rhea. I soon decided to go to Cairo and take a place on the Eldorado, a St. Louis and Cincinnati packet, which cruised from Cairo to Cincinnati. On that boat I worked as a roustabout for nearly three years.

The roustabout is no better than the mate that rules him. If the mate is kindly disposed, the roustabout has an easy enough life. The Negroes had only a few years of freedom and resented cruelty. If the mate became too mean, a regular fight would follow, and perhaps several roustabouts would be hurt before it was finished. We roustabouts would get together and shoot craps, dance, or play cards until the call came to shuffle freight. Then we would all get busy, and the mate's voice giving orders could be heard for a long distance.

In spite of these few pleasures, the life of a roustabout is the life of a dog. I do not recall any unkindnesses of slavery days. I was too young to realize what it was all about, but it could never have equaled the cruelty shown the laborers on the riverboats by cruel mates and overseers.

When I was a roustabout on the Gold Dust, we were sailing out from New Orleans, and as soon as we got well out on the broad stream, the rats commenced jumping overboard. "See these rats," said an old river man. "This boat will never make a return trip!" At every port some of our crew left the boat, but the mate and the captain said they were all fools and begged us to stay. So a few of us stayed to do the necessary work, but the rats kept leaving as fast as they could.

When the boat was nearing Hickman, Kentucky, we smelled fire, and by the time we were in the hopper, passengers were being held to keep them *from jumping overboard. Then the captain told us boys to jump into the water and save ourselves. Two of us launched a bale of cotton overboard and jumped onto it. As we paddled away we had to often go under to put out the fires, as our clothing would blaze up under the flying brands that fell upon our bodies.*

The burning boat was docked at Hickman. The passengers were put a-shore, but none of the freight was saved; and from a nearby willow thicket my mate and I watched the Gold Dust *burn to the water's edge. Always heed the warnings of nature. If you see rats leaving a ship or a house, pre-pare for a fire.*

3. THOMAS ASH

I Have No Way of Knowing Exactly How Old I Am

Thomas Ash was sick when he was interviewed, so his narrative is brief. In the WPA files his story precedes that of Mary Crane (q.v.), in a single text entitled "Reminiscences of Two Ex-Slaves."

I have no way of knowing exactly how old I am, as the old Bible contain-ing a record of my birth was destroyed by fire many years ago; but I believe I am about eighty-one years old. If so, I must have been born sometime during the year 1856, four years before the outbreak of the war between the states. My mother was a slave on the plantation, or farm, of Charles Ash in Anderson County, Kentucky; and it was there that I grew up.

I remember playing with Ol' Marse's (as he was called) boys—Charley, Jim, and Bill. I also have an unpleasant memory of having seen other slaves on the place tied up to the whipping post and flogged for disobeying some order, although I have no recollection of ever having been whipped myself, as I was only a boy. I can also remember how the grown-up Negroes on the place left to join the Union Army as soon as they learned of Lincoln's procla-mation making them free men.

4. ROSA BARBER

Slaves Were Not Taught the Three Rs

The fieldworker provided only a summary of Rosa Barber's narrative. Rosa Barber was born into slavery on the Fox Ellison plantation at North Carden, North Carolina, in 1861. She was four years old when she was freed, so her memory of slavery was confined to the short period of her childhood in North

Carolina. Her recollection of the days before and immediately following the Civil War came mainly from stories related to her by her parents.

Her maiden name—taken from her master, as was the custom—was Rosa Fox Ellison. When they were freed, her parents took her from the plantation, and they lived in different places. When she was quite young, her parents died, and she later married another ex-slave from the Fox Ellison plantation, whose name, Fox Ellison, also was taken from the plantation owner. She and her husband lived together forty-three years until his death, and they had nine children. After the death of Fox Ellison, Rosa married again; she also outlived her second husband. She was a seventy-six-year-old widow when she was interviewed.

Rosa recalled that her parents spoke of no extreme discipline on the Fox Ellison plantation; however, slaves were not taught the three Rs, and they were forbidden to even look in a book or at any other printed material. She had no pictures. Even traditional rhymes and tales were forbidden if they were thought to convey any direct or indirect knowledge or in any other way enlighten or uplift the spirits of the slaves. The slaves found consolation mainly in their field songs. As a child in North Carolina, Rosa played with rag dolls or a ball of yarn, if she had enough old string to make one. Any toy considered educational was forbidden.

5. LEWIS BARNETT

That Was the Way He Went When He Was Trying to Get Away

The informant, Sarah Emery Merrill, told two close versions of the following narrative about her great-uncle Lewis Barnett to the fieldworker, Iris Cook. Another fieldworker, Velsie Tyler, collected three texts of songs and tales that Sarah Emery Merrill had learned from her mother, Elvira Lee (q.v.).

I have heard my mother and father tell this story more times than I can remember. My great-uncle, Lewis Barnett, was a slave, and he was brought to Louisville from the south to be sold at auction. He escaped and crossed the Ohio River at about where Portland is. He came to New Albany with twelve other Negroes.

He came out State Street and down where Cherry Street is now and went west on Cherry Street till he hit the knobs west of the town. The slaves were covered up in a wagon full of corn.

When they hit the knobs, west of town, a colored family by the name of Balley took the fugitives in and kept them awhile. But these Balleys betrayed them—for a reward, no doubt—and in the meantime had gotten word to Louisville.

Men came from Louisville and took all of the twelve Negroes back to Louisville to be punished and sold. In Louisville, my uncle Lewis denied knowing his master: "I never seen you before in all my life," he says. Therefore, he had to be sold again and was sold on the block for $1,500 and taken to New Orleans.

He came back three times to see us after that when the war was over. And we children have heard him tell this story many times and point down Cherry Street and tell us that was the way he went when he was trying to get away. We lived on State Street near Cherry.

We came from near Munfordville, Kentucky. My father and mother were slaves.

6. ROBERT BARTON

That's How Some Escaped to Canada

When interviewed, Robert Barton lived at 317 South 2nd Street in Terre Haute. Held as a slave during his early life, he was born in 1849 at Lancaster, Kentucky, the last year of President Polk's administration. That is how Robert's mother said he could always figure his age.

Robert had two owners, Albert Huntington and a family named Dunlap, but he primarily remembered being held by the Dunlaps. With them, he often was sent after the mail, which he said made him want to learn to read and write. With the help of his mother and his master, he received enough education to enable him to teach school a few years after gaining his freedom.

An officer named Morgan once stayed all night at the home of the Dunlaps. News that soldiers were near always caused considerable fear. Robert remembered several times when he and other children were hidden in the basement. Some ammunition for cannons and rifles was kept on the estate. He said he always wanted to examine the ammunition until it was moved near a beehive.

Robert never attempted to escape, but he had a sister who successfully escaped from slavery. He explained how slaves were helped to escape by way of the Underground Railroad. Runaway slaves frequently put pepper in their shoes so they could not be traced by bloodhounds. That's how some escaped to Canada. Some were caught, returned to their owners, and generally punished. Robert said that a number of times he was whipped for various offenses.

Seeing cattle brought to market to be sold reminded Robert of the way slaves were sold at auctions. Though he could not clearly recall Emancipation Day, he remembered more about Abraham Lincoln. He said newspapers telling of Lincoln's death sold for twenty-five cents.

7. ANTHONY BATTLE

*Runaway Slaves Would Kill the Dogs Chasing Them
and Never Be Caught*

The source of the narratives of Anthony Battle and Spear Pitman (q.v.) seems to be an article in the April 11, 1929, *Rockville Republican,* in which former slaves in Greencastle related their experiences. According to the fieldworker, there were not many former slaves still living in the area in the 1930s, though Greencastle had a few, and G. E. Black interviewed them for the *Greencastle Banner.* These elderly blacks were part of a large group of six hundred former slaves who had left the South in 1880. Once in the north, they scattered over several states, and those living in this area said they "just happened" to come here.

Anthony Battle, who had been a slave in Battleboro, North Carolina, said that he was seventy-eight years old, but the reporter said he appeared to be older, because rheumatism had crippled him. Still, according to the reporter, "it is easy to see how that in his prime he was a fine specimen of manhood, which was much admired by slave buyers." Here is Anthony's narrative:

> There was about three hundred of us slaves on old Marse Turner Battle's plantation—little and big. He bought me when I was a little fellow. When old Marse Turner died, his boys, Jake and Joe, divided the place. We had to work terrible hard.
>
> Sometimes when a slave man was being chased for doing something that they would kill him for, his owner would help get him away over what we called the "underground railway" and would sell him away off from home, where he wouldn't be found. They did that because they couldn't afford to lose the money they would lose if the slave was killed by those who were after him.
>
> Lots of slaves ran away, and when the dogs got after them, some would kill the dogs and never be caught. I never knew how they could kill one of those big dogs, but lots of dogs got killed that way.

8. GEORGE BEATTY

Many Blacks with Only Their Clothing Crossed the Ohio River

George Beatty was born in 1862 near Hanover, Indiana, and lived on Sixth Street in Madison until six months before his death on March 7, 1951, at the home of his son, Carl, in Muncie. According to his obituary in the *Madison*

Courier (March 8, 1951), he was the only African American who had attended the former Leutherian College at Lancaster, Indiana. George said that between Hanover and Lexington there was a dense forest. In the fall, pigeons flew in such large flocks that the sun was hidden from view (Baughman 1966: X1119.1[c], "Thick pigeons darken sky"). Wild game was very plentiful, especially turkeys, rabbits, and squirrels.

During the Civil War, blacks were numerous in Jefferson County, Indiana. At least thirty families owned farms and lived north of the Kent Road as far as Volga. In Hanover there were twenty black families. At the close of the Civil War, many blacks with only their clothing crossed the Ohio River from Kentucky to Indiana. Several located in or near Hanover. Whites were very good to them. Some blacks worked on farms, and others found employment in village boarding houses.

George's father owned his farm. The only fault George found with his father was that when the government called for volunteers and began to draft men during the Civil War, his father went to Canada. His mother remained on the farm, and since George could only crawl, he stayed with her.

His father had not been gone long when a man forced his way into their home at midnight, grabbed George's mother, choked her, and threatened to kill her if she did not give him her money. She managed to escape and ran to the neighbors, who had heard her screams and come to meet her. The neighbors telegraphed George's father, who returned and hired Wright Ray, considered one of the best detectives at that time. Ray soon caught the man, who was tried at Madison and received a year's sentence in the state prison.

George walked a mile and a half to school and often broke a path when the snow was to his knees. At school the benches were about nine feet long. He said that when the benches were replaced with double seats, the students felt like they were in college.

9. SAMUEL BELL

Religion Is Worth the Greatest Fortune

Samuel Bell was born a slave in 1853. His master, whom Samuel served for twelve years, was John Bell, who owned a plantation in Kentucky. At the age of twelve, Samuel was taken—along with his parents, brothers, and sisters—to a contraband camp [a camp within Union lines where slaves escaped to or were brought to during the Civil War] at Clarksville, Tennessee. Samuel said that he was well taken care of at the camp, where he was taught to read and write. After his father died at the camp, his mother asked to be allowed to return to

Kentucky, and her request was granted. She found a job in Hopkinsville and later returned to the camp to reclaim her children, whom she continued to support while their grandparents looked after them. After her death a few years later, her children were returned to the camp in Clarksville, Tennessee. Samuel, however, soon became tired of camp life and asked permission to leave to earn his own living. After leaving the camp, he farmed for a while and worked on a large cotton farm on the Cumberland River. He recalled that the cotton farm included 100 cabins and two cotton gins. After working in the cotton fields for twelve months, he traveled twenty miles to Brenton, located ten miles from Ashville, and for two years worked there as a houseman with the Newland family. Finally settling in Evansville, he worked as a janitor in a local bank for a number of years, joined the Masons, and became a highly respected citizen. Samuel's narrative follows:

[John Bell] . . . was a good and a just man and fed his slaves well. He only used the lash when it was absolutely necessary. You know how it is in the court! Well, it was the same way on the plantations in slavery days. A good slave was seldom punished, but mean ones had to be punished to prevent their taking advantage of their master and the other slaves. Slaves were not subject to the laws of the land, and this punishment had to be governed by a slave's deeds and errors. The master's will was the only law he was compelled to obey. When a slave refused to work, he was flogged until he was willing to work. The master had to feed and clothe him and expected him to repay with work.

The government was not well founded, and the Freedmen's Aid Society cared for the Negroes [in the contraband camps]. Colonel Eaton was in charge of the Freedmen's Aid Society in Tennessee, and the contraband Negroes were well treated in camp. I have never been misused by the white man of America. He has always been my friend. The Newland family wanted to give me an education and make me fit for a lawyer, but I worked against my own interest and refused to obey their wishes. I have been in bondage and orphaned by the death of my parents. I have lived in the contraband camps and toiled for both rich and poor, but I have never been given abuse.

[The happiest time of my life was] when Jesus saved my soul and gave me the hope of eternal life. I was given the promise at a revival conducted by the Reverend W. H. Anderson in the Old McFarland Church at Evansville. Green McFarland baptized me, and I have lived a Christian life since that day. Religion is worth the greatest fortune. It explains why man must labor and suffer, and his trying experiences make him more worthy of the great reward promised by the kind Father. When his years of sorrow are fulfilled, he will understand and appreciate the reward, which is heaven.

10. MITTIE BLAKELEY

They Were Whipped Often and Hard

The fieldworker provided only a summary of Mittie Blakeley's narrative. Mittie was born in Oxford, Mississippi, in 1858. Her mother died when she was a baby, so she was taken into the "big house" and raised with the white children. She was always treated kindly and assigned only light chores, which had to be done well or she was chided, just as the white children were. Every evening the children collected eggs. The child who brought in the most eggs got a ginger cake, and Mittie almost always got the cake. When she was old enough, she had to spin wool for her mistress, who wove it into cloth to make the family clothes. She also learned to knit, and after supper she knitted until bedtime.

Her older brothers and sisters were not treated as well as she was. They were whipped often and hard. She said she hated to think, much less to talk, about their awful treatment. She also recalled that once an elderly female slave had displeased her master about something. He had a pit dug and boards placed over the hole. The woman was made to lie face down on the boards, and she was beaten until the blood gushed from her body. Then she was left there to bleed to death. Mittie remembered, too, that the slaves gathered in a cabin at night to dance. If they went without a pass, which they often did, and were caught, they were severely beaten. If the slaves heard the overseers riding toward the cabin, those without a pass would take the boards up from the cabin floor and hide under the floor until the overseers had gone. Mittie, a very serious woman, said she felt sorry for those who were treated much worse than any human would treat a beast.

11. PATSY JANE BLAND

Free? Is Anybody Ever Free?

When interviewed, Patsy Jane Bland was nearly 107 years old and had outlived most of her seven children. According to her obituary in the *Terre Haute Tribune* (June 29, 1938), she died at the age of 107 in Terre Haute and was buried in Rockport, Indiana. At the time of the interview, she was living at 1519 North 27th Street in Terre Haute with her next-to-youngest son, Johnny Wilson, who himself was up in years. Patsy said her oldest daughter lived in Dayton, Ohio, and "looks as old as her ma." She came to Terre Haute in 1919 because some of her relatives already were living there. She still cooked and kept house, but she told the fieldworker that "I ain't seen a well day for three years."

Nevertheless, with the help of a hickory cane, which she called her "wooden leg," she got around fairly well. She was living on benefits from her late husband, a Civil War veteran.

Patsy said her religion was deep, and whenever she could she attended a Baptist church near her home. She was preparing to celebrate her birthday at home on August 8, 1937, and said she hoped everyone she knew would send her a birthday present. Sitting in an old armchair, smoking a pipe, and looking out the door, she reflected on her past. On the south side of her house was a patch of tobacco raised by her son and her, but Patsy said she was "too delicate to smoke that old Tennessee red now." Instead, she smoked "sack tobacco" in her corncob pipe, claiming she could not do without it.

One of a large family, Patsy was born on August 8, 1830, in a cabin on the plantation of William Kettering in Shelby County, Kentucky. She was sold twice, first to Charles Morgan and then to John Boyle. Patsy recalled that as a child she was a "reggler limb" [regular lamb], though there was nothing she would not do to have fun, and "many was the lickin'" she got. Although she claimed that at her age her mind did not "work in a straight line," the interviewer reported that "her mental faculties are in excellent condition" and she remembered plantation life well. She was one of only a few people then living who could recall so many years before the Civil War.

Along with her owner's daughter, she learned to "spell out her letters" until the white child's mother decided that Patsy was getting too smart, so her education ended until she was married to her fourth and last husband, who taught her some more. Patsy said she could read "for a long time by spelling it out," but recently her eyes "ain't so good."

On the plantation, Patsy did all kinds of work, even plowing: "I worked like a man. I've spun flax, cut wool off sheep, washed it, carded and spun it for stockings and underwear. I never wore anything but wool underwear in the wintertime, and none of my younguns did either. I used to sit and knit wool up for their stockings. Indeed, I've worked hard." Patsy also recalled that her clothes were made of tow. Besides carding and spinning, Patsy helped raise tobacco—two crops some years, when she would cut the leaves off the old stalks to let another crop grow. She said she had always worked and would not have had it any other way.

Patsy remembered sleeping on a straw pallet on the floor and in a trundle bed shoved back under the big bed. She remembered baking corn dodger on a hot brick fireplace; hanging the kettle over the crane to cook "pawn hoss," which was made from meal and bacon; roasting sweet potatoes and sweet corn; and baking ash cake in hot ashes. She said blacks sang jubilee songs and even made up songs down on the old plantation in Kentucky.

Patsy also recalled observing the wedding of the master's daughter in the big house. The wedding preparations began days in advance with the saving of chickens, eggs, and butter. She said the preparations included the liveliest egg-beating, butter-creaming, raisin-stoning, sugar-pounding, cake-icing, coconut-scraping and -grating, jelly-straining, silver-cleaning, egg-frothing, floor-rubbing, pastry-making, ruffle-crimping, tarlatan-smoothing, and trunk-moving time you ever saw. All the slaves turned out to help. She also recalled peeping at the bride with her long veil and train and at the guests. The night before the wedding, the slaves all gathered in their quarters to sing, over and over, every song they knew to celebrate the bride's marriage and her departure to Virginia. Patsy also remembered that the young bride died soon after the big wedding and that she was buried in her bridal dress. She recalled, too, the deaths of some other whites and the burial of some of her black friends.

Already the mother of four when the Civil War began, Patsy remembered seeing soldiers, and "because they were scared," the slaves ran from them and hid out. She remembered the day all the blacks on her plantation were set free. There was shouting and crying; there was joy and sadness. She said many blacks did not want to leave the plantation to go out into a world of which they knew nothing. Patsy, though, gathered her four children around her and with her husband, who was named Wilson, left the plantation. When the fieldworker asked if she was happier free, Patsy looked off into the distance and said, "Free? Is anybody ever free? Ain't everybody you know a slave to someone or something or other?"

12. LIZZIE BOLDEN

A Much Easier Time Before She Was Free

Lizzie Bolden's story was told by her daughter, Mrs. William D. Perry, who at the time of the interview lived on Poplar Street in Madison. Mrs. Perry did not think her father was ever in slavery. She remembered seeing him come to their cabin dressed in a long blue coat with a cape and brass buttons and a cap to match. She said her mother had a much easier time with Harris, her master, than she did after she was free. She said her mother worked especially hard while her husband was off fighting in the war. This is what Mrs. Perry recalled about her mother:

My mother was a slave somewhere in Kentucky. She belonged to a very kind old man by the name of Harris. Mr. Harris was a cripple, with several sons who liked to torment my mother.

One day Mr. Harris was out in his yard standing with a crutch and cane watching his boys at work some distance from the house. He said, "Lizzie, you go to the field and call the men-folks to dinner." As it happened, they had just killed a large blacksnake and threw it, touching my mother, who ran screaming back to the house. She never forgot how her master looked as he stood there shading his eyes watching, too crippled to go to her aid; but he called, "Never you mind, Lizzie, child; they'll come in to eat." When they arrived, their father saw that they were severely whipped for their cruel joke.

13. CARL BOONE

Our Lives, Though Happy, Have Been Continuously Ones of Hard Work

Carl Boone, the youngest of eighteen children of Stephen and Rachel Boone, was born in Marion County, Kentucky, on September 15, 1850. His father was born in the slave state of Maryland in 1800 and died in 1897. His mother was born in Marion County, Kentucky, in 1802 and died at the age of 115 in 1917. Like his father, Carl also was the father of eighteen children. He was a religious man, having missed church services only twice in twenty years. Interviewed in Anderson when he was eighty-seven, Carl still had a keen memory and still could do a hard day's work. Since Carl's father gained his freedom from slavery in 1829, Carl was born a free man and was not mistreated during the time of slavery; however, in his narrative he remembers very well the wrongs done to slaves on neighboring plantations in Kentucky. Carl's narrative follows:

My name is Carl Boone, son of Stephen and Rachel Boone, born in Marion County, Kentucky, in 1850. I am father of eighteen children. Sixteen are still living, and I am grandfather of thirty-seven and great-grandfather of one child. I came with my wife, now deceased, to Indiana in 1891, and now reside at 801 West 13th Street in Anderson, Indiana. I was born a free man, fifteen years before the close of the Civil War. All the colored folks on plantations and farms around our plantation were slaves, and most of them were terribly mistreated by their masters.

After coming to Indiana, I farmed for a few years, then moved to Anderson. I became connected with the Colored Catholic Church and have tried to live a Christian life. I have only missed church service twice in twenty years. I lost my dear wife thirteen years ago, and I now live with my son.

My father, Stephen Boone, was born in Maryland in 1800. He was bought by a nigger-buyer while a boy and was sold to Miley [or John] Boone in Marion County, Kentucky. Father was what they used to call "a picked slave," was a good worker, and was never mistreated by his master. He married my mother in 1825, and they had eighteen children. Marse Boone gave Pappy and Mammy their freedom in 1829, and he gave them forty acres of land to tend as their own. He paid Pappy for all the work he did for him after that and was always very kind to them.

My mother was born in slavery in Marion County, Kentucky, in 1802. She was treated very mean until she married my father in 1825. With him she gained her freedom in 1829. I was the last born of her eighteen children. She was a good woman and joined church after coming to Indiana and died in 1917, living to be 115 years old.

I have heard my mother tell of a girl slave who worked in the kitchen of my mother's master. The girl was told to cook twelve eggs for breakfast. When the eggs were served, it was discovered there were eleven eggs on the table, and after being questioned, she admitted that she had eaten one. For this, she was beaten mercilessly, which was a common sight on that plantation.

The most terrible treatment of any slave is told by my father in a story of a slave on a neighboring plantation owned by Daniel Thompson. After the slave committed a small wrong, Marse Thompson became angry, tied his slave to a whipping post, and beat him terribly. Mrs. Thompson begged him to quit whipping the slave, saying, "You might kill him," but the master replied that he aimed to kill him. Then he tied the slave behind a horse and dragged him over a fifty-acre [or thirty-acre] field until the slave was dead. As a punishment for this terrible deed, Marse Thompson was compelled to witness the execution of his own son one year [or a few years] later.

The story is as follows: A neighbor to Mr. Thompson, a slave owner by the name of Kay Van Cleve, had been having some trouble with one of his young male slaves and had promised the slave a whipping. The slave was a powerful man, and Mr. Van Cleve was afraid to undertake the job of whipping him alone. He called for help from his neighbors, Daniel Thompson and his son Donald. The slave, while the Thompsons were coming, concealed himself in a horse stall in the barn and hid a large knife in the manger. After the arrival of the Thompsons, they and Mr. Van Cleve entered the stall in the barn. Together, the three white men made a grab for the slave, when the slave suddenly made a lunge at the elder Mr. Thompson with the knife, but missed him and stabbed Donald Thompson. The slave was overpowered and tied, but too late; young Donald was dead.

The slave was tried for murder and sentenced to be hanged. At the time of the hanging, the first and second ropes used broke when the trap was sprung. For a while the executioner considered freeing the slave because of his second failure to hang him, but the law said "He shall hang by the neck until dead," and the third attempt was successful.

After coming to Indiana, our lives, though happy, have been continuously ones of hard work. The task of raising a large family has kept me busy, but I've done a good job of it and am happy for the privilege.

14. WALTER BORLAND

If Anyone Said Anything against the Negroes, There Was a Fuss

Walter Borland, who was born in Monroe County, Indiana, was not a former slave. He was a white retired carpenter-contractor and farmer living at Rural Route 6, Bloomington, when his reminiscences of blacks after the Civil War were collected. His obituary appeared in the *Bloomington Daily Telephone* on February 25, 1941. He is buried in the Rose Hill Cemetery in Bloomington.

I was born right after the Civil War in 1867. I was raised in a neighborhood of Presbyterians, United Brethren, Campbellites, Covenanters, and a few Methodists. Everyone in the neighborhood was in sympathy with the Negro. They took southern Negroes as hired hands in that neighborhood, and a Rebel had no business there whatever. A good many soldiers who had served in the war lived there. I don't know how many, but a good many. The Wylies, the Strongs, and some of the Hathaways and Hights were in the army. And they were all firm believers that Negroes had the same rights as a white person to live and labor. The Underground Railroad ran right through the neighborhood, which is right west of the present location of the Country Club, southwest of Bloomington. People who were in on the Underground Railroad were the Gordons, the Wylies, the Roddys, the Ervins, and the McCaughans. The people were mostly Irish, Scotch, and Scotch-Irish. Everybody in the neighborhood was strictly loyal to the government. There were no secessionists.

Just after the Civil War and up into the '70s, if anyone said anything against the Negroes, there was a fuss right then. The Negroes were good hands with horses, and that's what people liked.

I remember one Negro who came into the neighborhood with his wife. His name was Dick Hutchinson. He studied and made a Methodist preacher of himself. The last I heard of him he had charge of a church in Louisville.

During the latter part of the Civil War, at one time there were a lot of soldiers in Bloomington on a furlough. A man from north of town, a southern sympathizer, made several remarks. He finally said something that touched them off, and they grabbed a rope and were going to hang him on the northwest corner of the square. W. O. Free ran a general store there, and he got the man away from the mob and took him through the store, put him on his horse, and sent him home. He didn't come back to town for a number of years.

Another Negro family lived in the neighborhood. One son was named George Brown. He had twelve brothers and sisters. Six of them were black, and six were yellow. George was yellow. I think he was the best man that ever drew a line over a four-horse team. He had been a teamster in the South. It was all he ever did. His mother lived to be almost one hundred and did washings. The Negroes were good citizens.

15. JULIA BOWMAN

Living in the Big House

The interviewer provided only a summary of Julia Bowman's narrative. Julia was born in Woodford County, Kentucky, in 1859. She said that her owner, Joel W. Twyman, had many slaves and was kind and generous to all of them. All of his slaves worked hard on a large farm, on which all kinds of crops were raised. The slaves were given some of everything that was raised on the farm. Julia said she never knew want in slave times as she had known it during the Depression.

Twyman had his own slaves, and his wife had her own slaves. At the age of six, Julia was taken into the Twyman "big house" to help Mrs. Twyman in any way she could. She stayed in the house until slavery was abolished.

The Twyman slaves were always referred to as Twyman "kinfolks." After the slaves were freed, old Twyman was taken very sick, and some of the former slaves were sent for, as he wanted some of his "kinfolks" around him when he died. Julia was given the Twyman family Bible, in which her birth was recorded with the rest of the Twyman family. She showed it with pride to the fieldworker.

16. ANGIE MOORE BOYCE

Arrested in Indiana, Jailed in Louisville

The fieldworker deposited only a summary of Angie Boyce's narrative. Most of Angie's information came from her mother, Margaret Breeding King.

Angie was born into slavery on March 14, 1861, on the Breeding plantation in Adair County, Kentucky. Her parents were Henry and Margaret King, who were held by James Breeding, a Methodist minister who reportedly was kind to his slaves. Angie's mother told her that the slaves were in constant dread of the rebel soldiers, and when they heard they were coming, they would hide the infant Angie under leaves.

Angie's mother was married twice; her first husband was a man named Stines, and her second husband was Henry King, who bought his and his wife's freedom. He sent his wife and baby, Angie, to Indiana, but upon their arrival they were arrested and returned to Kentucky. They were placed in the Louisville jail, where they had to share a cell with a large, brutal, drunken Irish woman. The jail was so infested with bugs and fleas that Angie cried all night. The drunken white woman became enraged at the cries of the child and threatened to "bash its brains out against the wall if it didn't stop crying." Mrs. King was forced to stay awake all night to keep the white woman from carrying out her threat.

The next morning when Mrs. King was tried in court, she produced her free papers. When she was asked why she had not shown those papers to the arresting officers, she replied that she was afraid that they would steal them from her. She was exonerated of all charges and with Angie was sent back to Indiana.

17. EDNA BOYSAW

When Lincoln Freed Us, We Rejoiced

At the time of the interview, Edna Boysaw had lived near Brazil for about sixty-five years—forty of these years on a small farm two miles east of Brazil on the Pinkley Street Road. Her husband had been dead for thirty-five years, and most of her twelve children had relocated to other places throughout the United States. Only her youngest son and the son of one of her daughters lived with her. Edna was not certain about her age, but thought she was around eighty-seven. She was very active and alert, though, as she still did her own housework and performed other chores about the farm.

Because of her long residence in the community, Edna was looked upon as one of Brazil's pioneers. According to her many friends, including a number of prominent citizens of Brazil, she was very kind and intelligent, and her family was well liked and respected in the community. Edna was an active church worker and often was asked to speak at white churches as well as black churches. One of her daughters was a talented singer, and Edna appeared on many church programs with her. According to her obituary in the *Brazil Daily Times* (January 8, 1942), she died at the home of her daughter, Mrs. Frances Foulkes Gaines, in Chicago in 1942, but her body was returned to Brazil for burial in Cottage Hill Cemetery. Her obituary stresses that she was a very religious person:

> When Mrs. Boysaw was a small slave girl she had a dream in which she had a vision that she would some day go from city to city, county to county and state to state spreading the gospel. As she had been doing this lately telling groups what a Christian life has meant for her, she said she felt this vision had been fulfilled. Part of her daily prayer for many years was, "Make my last days my best days and heaven my resting place." She declared her last days were her

happiest and her friends and neighbors are confident she has received her heavenly reward. . . .

When in mature age she attended night school and learned to read. Her best tutor was Marie Knapp, then a little child living across the road. As Marie learned her letters and primary subjects she would sit on the porch with Mrs. Boysaw and teach her what she had learned that day in school. Mrs. Boysaw learned to write fairly well and to read. It was a happy day when she learned to read her Bible.

After coming to Brazil she organized a prayer band which met in her home and through this she established the First [Second] Baptist Church, which is active today at east Jackson and south Alabama streets.

Edna's narrative, which follows, is one of the best in the Indiana collection:

When the Civil War ended, I was living near Richmond, Virginia. I am not sure just how old I was, but I was a big, flat-footed woman and had worked as a slave on a plantation. My master was a good one, but many of them were not. In a way, we were happy and contented, working from sunup to sundown. But when Lincoln freed us, we rejoiced, yet we knew we had to seek employment now and make our own way. Wages were low. You worked from morning until night for a dollar, but we didn't complain. About 1870 a Mr. Masten, who was a coal operator, came to Richmond seeking laborers for his mines in Clay County. He told us that men could make four to five dollars a day working in the mines, going to work at seven and quitting at three-thirty each day. That sounded like a paradise to our menfolks. Big money, and you could get rich in little time! But he didn't tell all because he wanted the menfolk to come with him to Indiana. Three or four hundred came with Mr. Masten. They were brought in boxcars. Mr. Masten paid their transportation, but was to keep it out of their wages. My husband was in that bunch, and the womenfolk stayed behind until their men could earn enough for their transportation to Indiana.

When they arrived about four miles east of Brazil, or what was known as Harmony, the train was stopped, and a crowd of white miners ordered them not to come any nearer Brazil. Then the trouble began. Our men didn't know of the labor trouble, as they were not told of that part. Here they were, fifteen hundred miles from home, no money. It was terrible. Many walked back to Virginia. Some went on foot to Illinois. Mr. Masten took some of them south of Brazil about three miles, where he had a number of company houses, and they tried to work in his mine there. But many were shot at from the bushes and killed. Guards were placed about the mine by the owner, but still there was trouble all the time. The men didn't make what Mr. Masten told them they could make; yet they had to stay, for they had no place to go. After about six months, my husband, who had been working in that mine, fell into the shaft and was injured. He was unable to work for over a year. I came with my two children to take care of him. We had only a little furniture, slept in what was called "box beds." I walked to Brazil each morning and worked at whatever I could get to do. Often I did three washings a day and then walked home each evening, a distance of two miles, and got a dollar a day.

Many of the white folks I worked for were well-to-do, and often I would ask the mistress for small amounts of food, which they would throw out if left over from a meal. They didn't know what a hard time we were having, but they told me to take home any of such food that I cared to. I was sure glad to get it, for it helped to feed our family. Often the white folks would give me other articles, which I appreciated. I managed in this way to get the children enough to eat, and later when my husband was able to work, we got along very well and were thankful. After the strike was settled, things were better. My husband was not afraid to go out after dark. But the coal operators didn't treat the colored folks very good. We had to trade at the company store and often pay a big price for it. But I worked hard and am still alive today, while all the others are gone who lived around here about that time.

There has sure been a change in the country. The country was almost a wilderness, and where my home is today, there were very few roads, just what we called a pig path through the woods. We used lots of cornmeal, cooked beans, and raised all the food we could during them days. But we had many white friends and sure was thankful for them. Here I am, and still thankful for the many friends I have.

18. CALLIE BRACEY

Women Had to Split Rails All Day Long Just Like the Men

When interviewed in 1937, Callie Bracey was a widow with a grandchild living with her. She felt that she was doing very well, since her parents had had so little and she owned her own home. The interviewer provided only a summary of Callie's narrative. Callie's information about slavery came from her mother. Callie said that when her mother, Louise Terrell, was a child, she was bought by Andy Ramblet, a farmer near Jackson, Mississippi. Louise had to work very hard in the fields from early morning until late in the evening when it became too dark to see. Then when she returned from working all day in the fields, she had to cook and pack lunch buckets for the field hands for the next day. It made no difference how tired she was; when the horn blew at 4:00 A.M., she had to go into the fields for another day of hard work.

Women had to split rails all day long just like the men. Once Louise got so cold that her feet seemed to be frozen. When they warmed a little, they had swollen so much that she could not wear her shoes. She had to wrap her feet in burlap so she could go into the field the next day. Louise was given two dresses a year and wore her oldest dress as an underskirt. She never had a hat, so instead she always wore a rag tied over her head.

The Ramblets were known for their good butter, and they always had more than they could use. The owner wanted the slaves to have some, but his wife wanted to sell it. She did not believe in giving good butter to slaves, so she always let it get strong before she would let them have any. Slaves from neighboring farms were not allowed on the Ramblet farm. If any showed up, they got whipped and chased off, as Mr. Ramblet did not want anyone to put ideas in his slaves' heads. On special occasions the older slaves were allowed to go to the church of their master, but they had to sit in the back of the church and could not take part in the service.

19. TOLBERT BRAGG

He Had a Great Desire to Go Up North and See the Country

On April 18, 1836, Tolbert Bragg was born on the Bill Tate plantation near Mossy Creek, Grainger County, Tennessee. He was a slave for several years and was sold on the block. When he lived in the South his surname was Tate, after his master, but after coming north he changed his name to Bragg. For years he was known in Portland as Daddy Bragg, especially to his fellow workers at the Butter Tub factory. Tolbert died on November 9, 1922, at his home on West 2nd Street in Portland, Indiana.

Tolbert had heard a lot of talk about the North, and after gaining his freedom he had a great desire to "go up north and see the country." By this time his wife had died, leaving him to care for three sons. One spring morning in about 1881, he and his sons loaded their few belongings into a two-horse wagon and started north. After a long, tedious journey of several days over mountains, they reached Cincinnati, Ohio, were they left their wagon and traveled the rest of the way by rail.

In Portland Tolbert found work with the Richard Hammonds family, who at that time lived near the fairgrounds. He sent his sons—Mack, Herd, and Ramsey—to the East Ward School. Eventually, he bought land from Jonas Votaw south of the Lake Erie and Western Railroad and west of Middle Street on West 2nd Street. At that time there were only about two or three houses there, and on a small lot located in a swampy area of underbrush and trees, Tolbert built a one-room house. Later, as his sons grew, he added another room. When interviewed, he was planning another addition.

After establishing his home in Portland, Tolbert returned to the South only once—a visit of about three weeks to Tennessee in 1895.

20. GEORGE WASHINGTON BUCKNER

Yes, the Road Has Been Long

George Washington Buckner
(Collection of the Evansville Museum of Arts and Sciences)

The fieldworker had several interviews with George Washington Buckner but provided mainly a summary of George's narrative, with only a few quotes. She also talked to Rudolph D. O'Hara (q.v.), a black attorney in Evansville, about George. Since George was a practicing physician at the time, the interviews with him often were interrupted by the ringing of the doorbell or telephone. The fieldworker described George as tall, lean, white-headed, genial, and alert.

George was born December 1, 1852, "in fox hunting time." One brother, George said, was born in "persimmon time," one in "sweet potato time," and another in "planting time." His parents were slaves held by a man named Buckner, who was not wealthy enough to provide adequately for them. Slaveholder Buckner, along with several of his relatives, had purchased a large tract of land in Green County, Kentucky. George said that at that time landowners who owned no slaves were considered "poor white trash" and scarcely were recognized as citizens of Kentucky.

George's first recollections were of a slave cabin in Kentucky. The cabin was the home of his stepfather, his invalid mother, and several children. His mother had become disabled from bearing children each year without proper medical attention. The crude cabin had no real windows, only holes in the walls with bark shutters to keep out the rain and snow. His parents slept on a wooden bedstead covered with a straw mattress and patchwork quilts. The children slept on a straw bed that was pushed under the bedstead during the day and pulled into the middle of the cabin at night.

According to George, some slave children were given to the slaveholder's young sons and daughters and, even in childhood, became their property. Thus, young George served Dickie Buckner, although the two children were nearly the same age. George cared for Dickie's clothing, polished his boots, and put away his toys. George became Dickie's friend and playmate, though, as well as his slave, and was grief-stricken at Dickie's untimely death. George said that after Dickie's death, he could not bear the sight of Dickie's toys, books, and clothing.

George recalled an eerie experience after the death of Dickie. George's grandmother, a housekeeper and kitchen maid for the Buckner family, was in the kitchen one late afternoon preparing the evening meal, while the slaveholder and his family were visiting a neighbor. From the veranda where he was sitting, George looked through a window into the bedroom where Dickie had lain in bed just before his death. When he placed his face near the window pane, he thought he saw Dickie's face looking out at him. He ran to his grandmother, screaming that he had seen Dickie's ghost. George firmly believed he had seen a ghost and never really convinced himself otherwise until he reached adulthood, when he speculated that he had mistaken evening shadows of trees and vines for Dickie's ghost. He recalled how the story reached the ears of the other slaves and how they were terrorized at the suggestion of a ghost being in the slaveholder's home. George reflected, "That is the way superstitions always started. Some nervous person received a wrong impression, and there were always others ready to embrace the error."

George remembered that when one of the slaveholder's daughters married, George's sister was given to her as a bridal gift and had to leave her family to live in the young bride's new home. George said, "It always filled us with sorrow when we were separated either by circumstances of marriage or death. Although we were not properly housed, properly nourished, or properly clothed, we loved each other and loved our cabin homes and were unhappy when compelled to part."

George retained fond memories of his boyhood home: "Yes, the road has been long. Memory brings back those days, and the love of my mother is still real to me, God bless her! There are many beautiful spots near the Green River, and our home was situated near Greensburg, the county seat of Green County. The area occupied by Mr. Buckner and his relatives is located near the river, and the meanderings of the stream almost formed a peninsula covered with rich soil. Buckner's Hill relieved the landscape, and clear springs bubbled through crevices, affording much water for household use; and near those springs, white and Negro children met to enjoy themselves. Forty years after I left Greensburg, I went back to visit the springs and try to meet my old friends. The friends had passed away. Only a few merchants and salespeople remembered my ancestors."

George remembered very little about the Civil War, but did recall an evening at the beginning of the war: "I had heard my parents talk of the war, but it did not seem real to me until one night when Mother came to the pallet where we slept and called to us to get up and tell our uncles good-bye. Then four startled little children arose. Mother was standing in the room with a candle, or a sort of torch made from grease drippings and old pieces of cloth. These rude candles were in common use and afforded but poor light. And there stood her four brothers—Jacob, John, Bill, and Isaac—all with the light of adventure shining upon their faces. They were starting away to fight for their liberties, and we were greatly impressed."

Only two of George's uncles served in the Union Army, though. Officials thought that his Uncle Jacob, though a brawny man, was too old to enter the service, since he had a few white hairs. His Uncle Isaac, on the other hand, was considered too young to enlist. One of the uncles who served was killed in battle, but the other uncle fought throughout the war without being wounded. George said that white men were indignant because blacks were allowed to enlist. He recalled that slaveholder Stanton Buckner was forced to hide out in the woods for several months because he had tried to kill a slave, Frank Buckner. Frank, however, forgave the slaveholder and stated that he was at fault. Stanton then returned to active service.

George valued education and hoped that every American youth, black and white, would strive for higher education. His recollection of his own earliest educational experience was reciting the ABCs from McGuffy's blue speller to his sister, who served as his first teacher. In later years he attended a school conducted by the Freemen's Association [Freedmen's Bureau?]. He bought a grammar book from a white boy and studied it at home. When he was sixteen, he was employed to teach other black children and regretted how limited his ability must have been. George said, "When I taught those children, I boarded with an old man whose cabin was filled with his own family. I climbed a ladder leading from the cabin into a dark, uncomfortable loft, where a comfort and a straw bed were my only conveniences."

When George left Greensburg, he went to Indianapolis, where he became acquainted with the first educated black he had ever met: Robert Bruce Bagby, then principal of the only school for blacks in Indianapolis. George said, "The same old building is standing there today that housed Bagby's institution then." George recalled that when he left Bagby's school, he had so little money that he had to work in a private residence as a houseman. Later he also waited tables in hotels and restaurants. While waiting tables, he met Colonel Albert Johnson and his wife, both natives of Arkansas. They were pleased to learn that he wanted an education and advised him to enter Indiana State Normal School [now Indiana State University] in Terre Haute. The thought of attending Indiana State appealed to George, but he felt he might have trouble succeeding in advanced courses because of his limited background. Mrs. Johnson, however, assured him that he could do the work, so he left Indianapolis for Terre Haute.

After studying two years at Indiana State, George felt that at last he was prepared to teach, so he taught for a time at schools in Vincennes, Washington, and other Indiana communities. George said, "I was interested in the young people and anxious for their advancement, but the suffering endured by my invalid mother, who had passed into the great beyond, and the memory of little Dickie's lingering illness and untimely death would not desert my consciousness. I was determined to take up the study of medical practice and surgery, which I did." Accordingly, George entered the Indiana Eclectic Medical College, from which he was graduated in 1890. Since his services were needed in Indianapolis, he practiced medicine there for a year before finally locating in Evansville. According to George, "When I came to Evansville, there were seventy white physicians practicing in the area. They are now among the departed. Their task was strenuous. Roads were almost impossible to travel. Striding a horse and setting out through all kinds of weather, those brave men soon sacrificed their lives for the good of suffering humanity."

On the advice of influential citizens of Evansville, through the influence of Evansville businessman and civic leader John W. Boehne, Sr., and on the recommendation of Secretary of State Bryan, George was appointed minister to Liberia during Woodrow Wilson's presidency in 1913. George appreciated the confidence of his friends in recommending his appointment to this position and cherished the experience that he gained abroad. Leaving his family to fill his appointment in Liberia was a big sacrifice for George, for his wife remained in Evansville with their four children. She thought the long voyage to Liberia and the hot climate there would be unsafe. At that time his daughters, Stella and Helen, were fifteen and eight years old; his sons, George and Zachariah, were six and four.

George returned from Liberia with many concerns for blacks living there. He hoped for improvements in sanitation, which he said was virtually nonexistent in Monrovia and other Liberian cities. Many houses were built of brick and corrugated iron, and because the climate was so hot, many people spent most of their time outdoors or on verandas. George said that educational facilities also should be improved: "Schools and colleges are constructed of corrugated iron and are too hot for the comfort of students."

In addition, he said, "The colonists have neglected gardening and have developed slothful habits. At home, men wear only loincloths and women only the scantiest attire. Men follow the professions of fishermen and boatmen. Some few are painters, smiths, and carpenters, but the majority of the men and women despise labor. Being sons and daughters of slaves, they desire freedom from toil and desire only to loll in comfortable idleness—eating and drinking upon their verandas and not leaving their homes for days together. The emancipated slaves have always been gentlemen of leisure in Liberia. They aspire to serve in church or affairs of state. Their most appreciated attire consists of black suits made from cool cloth, a high collar, and a cane—much like their parents described owners of some southern plantations. May God bless them and protect them and give them knowledge!" George held Liberians as dear as the blacks he knew and administered to in Indiana. "I'm glad they were not all deported to Liberia," he said. "I believe they are much better off here."

George said that the citizens of Liberia were grateful for American aid and showed their appreciation by presenting him with gifts, such as mangoes and palm oil. He added, though, that at that time "a thoroughly civilized Negro state does not exist in Liberia nor do I believe in any part of West Africa. Superstition is the interpretation of their religion. Their political views are a hodgepodge of unconnected ideas. Strength overrules knowledge, and jealousy crowds out almost all hope of sympathetic achievement and adjustment. The most treacherous impulse of the human nature and the one to be most dreaded is jealousy. Jealousy protrudes itself into politics and religion and prevents educational achievement."

George said that jealousy was found not only in West Africa, for he observed it as well in Europe and Evansville. While traveling to Spain on board a Spanish ship, he saw a very refined and polite Jewish woman reduced to tears by a Spanish officer's remarks concerning her nationality. He gave the following example of what he called "jealousy" in Evansville: "During a political campaign I was compelled to pay a robust Negro man to follow me about my professional visits and my social evenings with my friends and family to prevent meeting physical violence to myself or family when political factions were virtually at war within the area of Evansville. The influence of political captains had brought about the dreadful condition, and ignorant Negroes responded to their political graft without realizing who had befriended them in need. The Negro youths are especially subject to propaganda of the four-flusher, for their home influence is, to say the least, negative. Their opportunities limited, their education neglected, they are easily aroused by the meddling influence of the vote-getter and the traitor. I would to God that their eyes might be opened to the light. Receivers of emancipation from slavery and enjoyers of emancipation from sin through the sacrifice of Abraham Lincoln and Jesus Christ, why should not the Negroes be exalted and happy?"

Asked about his own views on religion and politics, George responded: "I believe almost every story in the Bible is an allegory composed to illustrate some fundamental truth that could otherwise never have been clearly presented as only through the medium of an allegory." George said he was an ardent follower of Franklin D. Roosevelt, and he spoke of Woodrow Wilson with bated breath. "I'm a Democrat," George said.

According to the interviewer, George was a veritable encyclopedia of black lore, and during an interview he often told a story to illustrate a point. As one story George said he heard near the end of the Civil War goes, "Andrew Jackson owned an old Negro slave, Sammy, who stayed on at the old home when his beloved master went into politics . . . became an American soldier and statesman and finally the seventh president of the United States. The good slave still remained through the several years of the quiet, uneventful last years of his master and witnessed his death, which occurred at his home near Nashville, Tennessee. After the master had been placed under the sod, Uncle Sammy was seen each day visiting Jackson's grave. 'Do you think President Jackson is in heaven?' an acquaintance asked Uncle Sammy. 'If he wanted to go there, he's there now,' said the old man. 'If Mr. Andy wanted to do anything, all hell couldn't keep him from doing it.'"

George said that he enjoyed living with his family in Evansville: "It has been a sweet home to me."

21. GEORGE TAYLOR BURNS

Yes, I Know a Lot about Boats

The WPA fieldworker talked to George Taylor Burns several times in 1939 and provided six texts, though only four are dated. Apparently George died that same year. George was born in Missouri of slave parents, though he scarcely remembered his father. His earliest recollection was of a wood yard owned and operated by the Burns brothers at Gregory's Landing, Missouri. Many boats stopped at the landing to load wood, as most engines in those days were wood-fired. Slaves on the Burns plantation cut and piled the wood, and when George was only five, he worked all day with his mother in the wood yard. George said, "The colder the weather, the more hard work we had to do."

George remembered the winter that he was separated from his mother, Lucy Burns. Because of the ice, many boats were tied up to their moorings. The old slaveholder died that winter, and his heirs sold many slaves, including

George's mother. George said he clung to his mother as she was being taken away, but he was pulled from her and watched her, chained to a long line of departing slaves, cross a distant hill. George never saw her again, though his memory of her remained vivid. Left motherless and always hungry, he often cried himself to sleep at night, and each day he carried wood. He said that one cold winter morning when he failed to answer the horn that called the slaves to breakfast, "Old missus went to the slave quarters to see what was wrong. She was horrified when she found I was frozen to the bed." She carried George to her kitchen and placed him near a big oven. When the warmth thawed him, the toes fell from his feet. "Old missus told me I would never be strong enough to do hard work, and she had the neighborhood shoemaker fashion shoes too short for anybody's feet but mine."

After that, George remembered standing in the slave market at New Orleans and hearing the auctioneer's hammer when he was sold by Greene Taylor, the brother of his mistress. Taylor, however, had to refund the money and return George to his sister when George's crippled feet were discovered. "Greene Taylor was like many other people I have known. He was always ready to make life unhappy for a Negro." George said he was imprisoned in New Orleans and was badly treated as a slave but witnessed even worse treatment of other slaves. For example, he saw fellow slaves beaten into insensibility while chained to the whipping post in Congo Square at New Orleans. He also recalled his fear of the Ku Klux Klan, the patrol, and other groups that made life dangerous for newly emancipated blacks.

George did not remember why he left Missouri, but the sister of Greene Taylor brought him to Troy, Indiana. When she learned that she could not own a slave within the state of Indiana, she indentured George to a flatboat captain for $15 a month to wash dishes and wait on the crew. George was so small that the captain had a low table and stool made for him so that he could work more comfortably.

After gaining experience on the flatboats, George was hired as a cabin boy on a steamboat and spent most of his active days on the river as a steamboat man. "I know steamboats from woodbox to sternwheel. The life of a river man is a good life, and interesting things happen on the river." One interesting experience that he recalled was when a flatboat he was on sank near New Orleans. After clinging for many hours to the drifting wreckage, he finally was rescued, half-dead from exhaustion.

George worked on several steamboats. He said *The Eclipse* was a beautiful boat with gold lettering, bright lights, and polished rails. Measuring 365 feet in length, it was the longest steamboat ever built in the west. George said that "For speed she just up and hustled." Among other boats he worked on were *The Atlantic,* on which he was cabin boy, and *The Big Gray Eagle,* on which he performed several jobs. "Don't forget I knew Pilot Tom Ballard and Aaron

Ballard on *The Big Eagle* in 1858. We Negroes carried passes so we could save our skins if we were caught off the boats, but we had plenty of good food on the boats."

When asked if he knew any songs sung by boatmen in earlier days, George said that the songs varied, for different boatmen sang the same songs to different tunes. Many boat songs were set to the tune of "Dixie," and a number of songs mentioned the name of the captain of some craft. Thus, "Dixie" was sung on any craft where W. H. Daniels was captain. George offered the following version of "Dixie":

> Oh, I was a slave in the land of Dixie
> But Captain Daniels saw I was pert and frisky
> Now I'm glad I'm a steamboat man.
>
> Old missus called me fat and lazy
> But after I left her, she went plum crazy
> She missed me so from Dixie Land.
>
> A boatman's life is a life of pleasure
> Plenty to eat and money to treasure
> Oh, who would go back to Dixie Land?
>
> The rousters are always dancin' and singin'
> Boat horns a-blowin' and bells a-ringin'
> Oh, who would go back to Dixie Land?
>
> Pretty gals come crowdin' where boats are landin'
> Smile at the cap'n where he is standin'
> And smile at the darky from Dixie Land.
>
> Sometime its stormy winds keep blowin'
> Then it's hard to keep the steamboat goin'
> Still I wouldn't go back to Dixie Land.

George recalled the following steamboats that he frequently saw between the years 1847 and 1860, and he remembered that they were all Ohio River boats: *The Wisconsin, Hoosier State, Jacob Strader, Telegraph No. 3,* and *The Madison Belle.* He knew the following river men: Captain Thomas Wright, Tom January, Wilson H. Daniels, Pilot Humphrey Goodman, Pilot Christopher Pegg, Pilot Alfred Dunning, and Pilot Ben Taylor. Cardinal Byington worked as a clerk on a number of different boats as the occasion demanded.

Many soldiers returned to their homes on flatboats and steamboats when the Civil War ended, just as many recruits had been sent to battle on them during the war. Soon after peace was declared, George met Elizabeth (Liza) Slye, a young slave girl who had just been set free. "Liza would come to see her mother, who was working on a boat. People used to come down to the landings to see boats come in." George and Elizabeth, both free, married and made their home in New Albany until 1881, when they moved to Evansville. In New Albany, George worked for a firm that built boats. "Louisville," he said, "was one of the busiest towns in the Ohio Valley"; however, he remembered New Orleans as the place where most of the surplus products were marketed. George said he had many friends along the waterfront towns.

George recalled a few superstitions of the river men but claimed that he had little faith in them: "It was bad luck for a white cat to come aboard the boat. Horseshoes were carried for good luck. If rats left the boat, the crew was uneasy, for fear of a wreck." He also remembered that the roustabouts sang songs while loading boats with freight and provisions, but he could never work as a roustabout because of his crippled feet.

Though intelligent, George had no formal education. He said, "The Negroes were not allowed an education. It was dangerous for any person to be caught teaching a Negro, and several Negroes were put to death because they could read." When interviewed, George's hair and beard were snow-white, and he was lame. He drew no pension, but owned a building located at Canal and Evans streets that housed a number of black families. Here is his edited narrative, collected during several interviews.

I worked on many boats in the Ohio River. Even when I was such a little child that I had to stand up on a soapbox to wash dishes, I was a river rat. When I was about twelve years old my mistress's brother stole me from my mistress and took me to New Orleans and sold me from the slave block. On our way to New Orleans I met a slave who was a cousin to my own mother. His fingers were badly mangled, and he was scarred from burns received when he had been taken a captive at Cave-In Rock.

The slave man declared that three men who had been captured by an outlaw gang hiding at Cave-In Rock had been burned at the stake. His captain had been put to death by a knife thrust from a ruffian, and he alone of all the crew of a captured boat had escaped by swimming from the rocks. He believed that the pirates believed him to have committed suicide when he jumped from the rocks and therefore made no effort to recapture him.

When night came I was with my master and some of his white friends out on deck. They talked of pirates on the Ohio River and of a hotel at Cave-In Rock. They said a great many boats had been robbed and a great many crews murdered by unknown pirates. Some of the pirates lived in cabins along the river, and two of them lived at the tavern near the cave at Cave-In Rock.

These cruel men had no mercy on the helpless river men who carried produce, mail, and money on boats from port to port, but killed and robbed them without mercy. Many were the boats that had started to New Orleans and were never heard from again. Some people believed all the boats had been wrecked by storms, but I believe some ghost or demon lived at the cave at Cave-In Rock and destroyed the crafts and men.

Harry Smith, one of my master's companions, said one of his uncles was lost from his family on a voyage down the Ohio River. He had sold his farm products and had a large amount of money with him. He was never heard from again, and his family was left penniless.

People believed boats had been robbed when cargoes of produce believed to have been sunk were discovered at different ports, but the boatmen were never again located. I knew Captain Wilson Daniels, and he knew many men that had been taken by pirates on the Ohio River. My uncle that lived at the wood yards in Missouri when I was a little child once met a Negro roustabout that had been taken by pirates on the Ohio River. That man was taken to Cave-In Rock and enslaved to the leader of the pirate gang—a man named Wilson that lived at Wilson's tavern near the cave. The roustabout escaped by swimming away one night, leaving his clothes behind him.

I was born about 1836, and piracy was practiced on the Ohio River when I was working on Ohio River boats. River men were still in fear of pirates and afraid to pass Cave-In Rock, believing some of the old pirate crews were still hiding there. Finally the river business became safe, and boating became the best business followed by Negroes and white workers. The life of a river man was a happy life in spite of dangers of storm and piracy.

Such were the stories told about Cave-In Rock by steamboat captains and travelers in the years from about 1780 to 1852 at Tell City, Indiana, Newburg, Indiana, and other points; and some are living today and have reached advanced years who recall the stories that made the youths of that time tremble while hearing tales of adventure and bloodshed related. The Ohio River is a long stream. I know because I have followed its course from Pittsburgh throughout its winding way.

I was still a young child, possibly seven years of age, when we came to Indiana. That may have been in the year 1839 or 1840, but within one month after landing at Troy, I had been indentured to a flatboat captain, and my life for the next seventy years was spent on the different rivers.

I have visited shipyards where steamboats were being built in Madison, Jeffersonville, and New Albany. Years later I worked in the shipyard at Madison. A few years ago you could have interviewed Martin Frank, one of the officers of the steamer Eclipse, *and Mr. Frank could have told you a great deal about river life. Mr. Frank died in 1913 after many years of river service. He was in the Federal Gunboat service during the Civil War. I knew Captain E. T. Sturgeon of the steamer* Eclipse, *and he was one of the bravest men I ever met. He was a very fine-looking man, six feet tall and just heavy enough to look well. He was very careful about his personal appearance and was kindly disposed toward everybody.*

There were pirates on the rivers in those days, and because of danger from pirates, the boats went up and down the streams in fleets. Old river men were not only afraid of pirates but recall attacks made by Indians. The land lying southwest of the Ohio River as far south as to the mouth of the

Tennessee River had at one time belonged to the Six Nations, and members of the tribes proved hostile to the river men.

River traffic was heavy just before the Civil War period. People went to Pittsburgh by hundreds to spend their money. At the wharf at Pittsburgh you could meet people of Scotch and Irish descent as well as English, French, Canadian, Indian, and African.

Before the Civil War period, the deckhands and roustabouts were mostly white men—in fact, all were excepting Negro slaves who had been indentured to boatmen, as I had been. The white deckhands finally became pilots, mates, or captains of the boat they had been working on as deckhands, and their places on the decks were filled by Irish and German laborers, many of whom had come to the United States to work on the Wabash and Erie Canal. About the year the war started so many boats were in operation that Negroes were given jobs as roustabouts on nearly all the steamers. I imagine the places on the decks were left vacant because so many white boatmen enlisted for military service.

After leaving Pittsburgh, the next good town I remember was called Rochester. There was a splendid river wharf there and nice hotels where guests were entertained. Good farms were located near the town, and thriving business was done by the merchants of the place. Rochester was about twenty-five miles south of Pittsburgh. Another little town was called Beaver, but it was so near Rochester that the boats seldom stopped at Beaver unless passengers demanded to be put ashore there. There were great rocks, sandbars, and wood islands near these towns. One group of great rocks, called McKees Rocks, was situated on the right bank of the river. The town of St. Marys was founded just about the time the Civil War begun. It was settled by Catholic people and named for the Holy Mother.

During the war steamboats were used to carry soldiers to the scenes of battle and to carry wounded soldiers to hospitals. Some boats were made into hospitals to take care of wounded men. Any boat needed for a hospital boat, ferry boat, or for any military purpose was requisitioned without permission of the captain or any officer or owner of the craft.

Speaking of showboats, you should have seen The Banjo. It sure was a beautiful sight. I was working on The Gray Eagle when The Banjo used to pass up and down the river. The captain would keep the calliope playing, and the roustabouts, all of them Negroes, would be out on the deck dancing and shouting to the roustabouts on The Gray Eagle.

Some of the shows The Banjo staged were "East Lynn" and "Ten Nights in a Barroom." "Uncle Tom's Cabin" was staged on that boat during a period from 1857 to 1860 and maybe for a longer time. When the showboat— with its deck ablaze with kerosene lamps and with every kind of gay banners and flags strung around its texas and sides—passed up and down the streams, people, white and black, would come flocking to the river's banks.

The Banjo *showed at New Orleans and at Cairo regularly. I remember it lay near the old wharf boat at Evansville, July 18, 1860, and people from all over this part of the country went to the show.* The Gray Eagle *was due to leave the wharf the next afternoon at four o'clock. Captain W. H. Daniels was in command. Captain Daniels never put any hard work on me because I was crippled. I was an assistant on the boat and only had light work to do. That day the captain said I could go on* The Banjo *and help a while, if I cared to, and of course I did. The next time we saw* The Banjo *she was laid up at New Orleans for repairs of some sort, but crowds were flocking to her as fast as ever.*

Some of the steamboats I remember passing in the '60s were The Lue Evans, *an elegant passenger steamer. Captain McDonald was her master, and she made regular trips between South Carrollton, Kentucky, on the Green River, and Evansville, Indiana. Captain Pillsbury was master of* The Masonic Gem, *and Captain John McClain was master of* The Kate Sarchet. *All these boats carried passengers and freight on the Ohio River, loading from any point.*

I was at one time cabin boy on The Atlantic *and remember* The Bracelet, The Union, The General Pike, The Messenger, *and* The Prairie Rose. *All these steamboats traveled from St. Louis to Cincinnati. Those were glorious days. No people were happier than the boat workers. All had plenty of food and were treated with greater kindness than the Negroes had ever known on the southern plantations. All the boatmen belonged to the long, long ago when rivers were the only reliable avenues of travel for men of merchandise from Pittsburgh to New Orleans and points between.*

My first memories are filled with boats. My babyhood was passed in Missouri, where my master kept a wood yard. Boats of every kind stopped there, for no coal was used to fire the boilers. The slaves worked from morning until late at night piling and sawing and hauling wood to sell to the boatmen.

Boatmen of the early days sensed trouble on certain rivers during certain months of the year, and passengers avoided those streams like pestilence when river tragedies were regularly occurring. In the year 1860, the Arkansas River seemed hoodooed by Davy Jones. No boat from the Ohio River bound for the Arkansas River reached its destination, and not fewer than six Arkansas River boats were sunk within four months' time. The Tempest, The Masonic Gem, The Rose Douglas, Interchange, Ellen Gray, *and* South Bend *went down in the unlucky river. Pleasure seekers as well as business travelers soon heard reports of the missing crafts and refused to voyage on the ill-fated or ill-omened Arkansas River crafts.*

The Arkansas is a peculiar river. It is 2,000 miles in length and drains an area of nearly 200,000 square miles. It belongs to the Missouri-Mississippi system and rises high up in the Rocky Mountains. It flows through the

Grand Canyon of the Arkansas, which it had formed by its flow. Its shores are seldom found in the river bottom or on the banks of the stream. Its waters are constantly rising and falling. Its channels are always changing. There have always been two flood periods each year—one in the early spring and the other in the late spring. The swampy shores seem to take up the water, and new loops and curves are always forming in the sandy soil. These cutoffs cause a lack of regular flow. Navigation was more difficult on the Arkansas than on any other river I have ever known. At any time the boats were likely to strike a snag.

I have never been on the Arkansas River above Little Rock, but I have talked with rousters who were very familiar with the stream. They said that if the boat got caught on a sandbar all the captain did was order the crew to keep the boat clean and go along with their regular duties. Soon the sand would wash from under the craft, and the boat would move off the bar.

In the year 1873, the April showers turned to cloudbursts, and the Arkansas River shifted about, leaving its regular banks. That year the old Perkins graveyard was almost washed into the river. The graveyard was situated about fifteen miles from Little Rock, and on April 13, the old river rose to about its highest. The graves began caving into the river until the entire cemetery was washed into the stream.

The cemetery was located in a horseshoe bend between the river and a lake. The water had formed an eddy, and perhaps the graves had been undermined by an underground stream before they started caving into the river. Five hundred dead bodies were discharged into the water. Jasper Pillow, a white man living at Little Rock, told me that the body of his cousin, Seely Pillow, who had only been dead about six weeks, was recovered from the river. He said about forty-five bodies were recovered on Sunday near the graveyard. Bodies were picked up at Little Rock for several days. The stream was swollen, and caskets floated about like small boats. A justice of the peace at Little Rock commanded officers and plain citizens to get into skiffs and rescue bodies, which they gladly did. Some of the bodies had been buried about one hundred years. Others only a few days.

When the railways were completed in the vicinities near the Arkansas River, navigation of passenger boats became scarce. Most of the navigation was kept up for freight and heavy loads. I don't know how many boats run on the river now, but I guess the river is still a peculiar stream.

One of the many disasters I recall occurred on the ninth day of June in 1849. On that day the steamboat Embassy was destroyed in the Ohio River. A large sandbar extends nearly across the river from Three Mile Island. I did not see the accident, as I was cabin boy on The Sultana at that time, but I heard Captain Bennett tell about the tragedy many times afterwards.

Captain Bennett was badly scalded and had to spend several weeks under a doctor's care, but what hurt him worse than his own suffering was the *knowledge of the suffering of other people; for more than twenty dead bodies were taken from the wreck, and many more were seriously injured. Captain Bennett never did know what caused the disaster. The boilers were not carrying too much pressure. The engines were not working at full speed. The machinery had been cleaned and greased, and no amount of investigating pointed out a flaw in the management of the boat. But about noon two of her boilers exploded, and the result was a horrible calamity.*

Captain Bennett said the wounded and dying people screamed and ran about with their clothes dripping wet with boiling water until they would fall down on the promenade floor, where they would die. Captain Bennett said one mother held one little child in her arms and held to the hand of one a little larger until the three passed away within a few minutes of each other. The Embassy was only one of the many steamboats which went down on account of her boilers exploding.

In an inquest, Edmund Gray told about seeing Captain Bennett crawling up the stairway to the texas on his hands and knees and that his hands and face had been scalded. He said persons on the boat who were farthest from the engines were not so severely burned, and many of them were rescued before The Embassy sank.

Yes, I know a lot about boats.

22. BELLE BUTLER

A Mean Old Devil

When interviewed, Belle Butler was living with her daughters in Indianapolis. She said she had worked very hard "in her days," but had had to give up doing nearly everything in recent years because of failing eyesight. The fieldworker said Belle was very cheerful, though, and enjoyed telling tales about slavery that she learned from her mother.

Belle's mother, Chancy Mayer, told Belle of the hardships she endured during her days of slavery. Chancy was held by Jesse Coffer, "a mean old devil." Slaves on the Coffer plantation were treated inhumanely. They scarcely had enough to eat unless they stole it, and then they ran the risk of being caught and getting a severe beating. Coffer whipped his slaves for the slightest infraction, and often he whipped them for nothing at all. He just enjoyed seeing them suffer. Many times Coffer whipped slaves, threw them down, and gouged out their eyes.

Chancy's sister also was a slave on the Coffer plantation. One day their master decided to whip both of them. After whipping them very hard, he started to throw them down to gouge out their eyes. Chancy grabbed one of his hands, and her sister grabbed his other hand. Each girl bit a finger entirely off each of

Coffer's hands, which pained him so much that he stopped struggling with them. He never attempted to whip them again, but he told them he would "put them in his pocket" [sell them] if they ever tried anything like that again. Not long after the fight, Chancy was given to one of Coffer's daughters, and her sister was given to another of his daughters and taken to North Carolina.

On the farm next to the Coffer farm, the overseers tied the slaves to joists by their thumbs, whipped them unmercifully, and then salted their backs to heighten the pain. When slaves slowed down on corn hoeing, no matter if they were sick or just plain tired, they received many lashes and a salted back. When one woman left the plantation without a pass, the overseer caught her and whipped her to death.

Slaves were never allowed to look at a book, for fear they might learn to read. One day when an old mistress caught a slave boy with a book, she cursed him and asked him what he thought he could do with a book. She said he looked like "a black dog with a breast pin on" and forbade him to ever look into a book again.

23. JOSEPH WILLIAM CARTER

I Wish the Whole World Would Be Decent

Joseph William Carter was born into slavery prior to 1836. Though born and reared in bondage, Joseph said that he had lived a long and a happy life. His mother, Malvina Gardner, was a slave in the home of a man named Gardner until D. B. Smith saw her. Admiring Malvina's good looks, Smith purchased her from Gardner. Malvina was distressed at having to leave her old home and her young mistress, Puss Gardner, who was fond of Malvina.

Both the Gardner and Smith families lived near Gallatin, Tennessee, in Sumner County. The Smith plantation was situated on the Cumberland River. Although the view of the river and valley from the Smith plantation was beautiful, Malvina was very unhappy. She did not like the Smith family and longed for her old friends back at the Gardner home.

One night Malvina gathered her few personal belongings and started back to her old home. Afraid to travel the highway, she followed a familiar path through the forest. Near the path, an Indian hunting party was camped on the side of the Cumberland Mountains, and a young Native American named Buck captured Malvina and made her his property. She lived for almost a year with Buck, and during that time learned much about Indian customs.

When Malvina was missed from her new home, Mr. Smith went to the Gardner plantation to report his loss. When he did not find her there, a wide search was made for her, but the Indians kept her thoroughly hidden. Puss Gardner, however, kept up the search. She knew the Indians were camped on the mountain and believed she would find the girl with them. When the Indians finally broke camp, the Gardners watched them start on their journey, and Puss Gardner saw Malvina among the women.

The men of the Gardner plantation, both white and black, overtook the Indians and demanded that the girl be given to them. After the Indians reluctantly returned Malvina, Mr. Gardner paid Mr. Smith the original purchase price, and Malvina once more was established in her old home with Puss Gardner.

Malvina was not yet twelve when she was captured by the Indians, and she was scarcely thirteen when she gave birth to Buck's son, Joseph. Joseph was born in the Gardner home and remained there with his mother. Joseph and his mother were treated very well by the Gardner family. When Joseph was a young man, he met many Indians from the tribe that had held his mother captive. From them he learned many things about his father that his mother had never told him. Though he was a Gardner slave and could have been named Joseph Gardner, he took the name of Carter from a stepfather.

Puss Gardner married a man named Mooney, and Mr. Gardner allowed her to take Joseph to her new home. Joseph's most vivid memories of slavery came from this period of his life on the Mooney plantation: "The Civil War changed things at the Mooney plantation. Before the War Mr. Mooney never had been cruel to me. I was Missus Puss's property, and she would never have allowed me to be abused, but some of the other slaves endured the cruelest treatment and were worked nearly to death. When I was a little bitsy child and still lived with Mr. Gardner, I saw many of the slaves beaten to death. Marse Gardner didn't do any of the whippin', but every few months he sent to Mississippi for slave whippers to come to the plantation and whip all the slaves that hadn't obeyed the overseers. A big barrel lay near the barn, and that was always the whippin' place."

Joseph remembered two or three professional slave whippers and recalled the death of two of the Mississippi whippers: "Marse Gardner had one of the finest blacksmiths that I ever saw. His arms were strong; his muscles stood out on his breast and shoulders; and his legs were never tired. He stood there and shoed horses and repaired tools day after day, and there was no work ever made him tired. I don't know what he had done to rile up Marse Gardner, but all of us knew that the blacksmith was going to be flogged when the whippers from Mississippi got to the plantation. The blacksmith worked on day and night. All day he was shoein' horses, and all the spare time he had he was making a knife. When the whippers got there, all of us were brought out to watch the whippin', but the blacksmith, Jim Gardner, didn't wait to feel the lash. He jumped right into the bunch of overseers and slave whippers and knifed two whippers and one overseer to death. Then he stuck the sharp knife into his arm and bled to death."

Joseph recalled the beginning of the Civil War: "When the war started, we kept hearing about the soldiers, and finally they set up their camp in the forest near us. The corn was ready to bring into the barn, and the soldiers told Mr. Mooney to let the slaves gather it and put it into the barns. Some of the soldiers helped gather and crib the corn. I wanted to help, but Puss Gardner was afraid they would press me into service and made me hide in the cellar. There was a big keg of apple cider in the cellar, and every day Puss Gardner handed down a big plate of fresh gingersnaps right out of the oven, so I was well fixed."

Joseph said that after the corn was in the crib, the soldiers turned in their horses to eat what had fallen to the ground. Before the soldiers camped at the Mooney plantation, they had camped upon a hill, and some skirmishing had occurred. Joseph remembered seeing cannonballs come over the fields. The cannonballs were chained together, and the slave children would run after them. Sometimes the chains would cut down trees as the balls rolled through the forest.

One story that Joseph related was of an encounter with an eagle: "George Irish, a white boy near my own age, was the son of the miller. His father operated a sawmill on Bledsoe Creek near where it empties into the Cumberland River. George and I often went fishing together and had a good dog called Hector. Hector was as good a coon dog as there was to be found in that part of the country. That day we boys climbed up on the mill shed to watch the swans in Bledsoe Creek, and we soon noticed a great big fish hawk catching the goslings. It made us mad, and we decided to kill the hawk. I went back to the house and got an old flintlock rifle Marse Mooney had let me carry when we went hunting. When I got back where George was, the big bird was still busy catching goslings. The first shot fired broke its wing, and I decided I would catch it and take it home with me. The bird put up a terrible fight, cutting me with its bill and talons. Hector came running and tried to help me, but the bird cut him until his howls brought help from the field. Mr. Jacob Greene was passing along and came to us. He tore me away from the bird, but I couldn't walk, and the blood was running from my body in dozens of places. Poor old Hector was crippled and bleeding, for the bird was a big eagle and would have killed both of us if help had not come." Joseph still showed signs of his encounter with the eagle. He said it was captured and lived about four months in captivity, but its wing never healed. The body of the eagle was stuffed with wheat bran by Greene Harris and placed in the courtyard in Sumner County.

Joseph said he did not believe in witchcraft but once had assisted his cousin, who claimed he was a folk healer: "I had a cousin that was a full-blooded Indian and a voodoo doctor. He got me to help him with his voodoo work. A lot of people, both white and black, sent for the Indian when they were sick. I told him I would do the best I could if it would help sick people to get well. A woman was sick with rheumatism, and he was going to see her. He sent me into the woods to dig up poke roots to boil. He then took the brew to the house where the sick woman lived and had her to put both feet in a tub filled with warm water, into which he had placed the poke root brew. He told the woman she had lizards in her body, and he was going to wring them out of her. He covered the woman with a heavy blanket and made her sit for a long time, possibly an hour, with her feet in the tub of poke root brew and water. He had me slip a good many lizards into the tub, and when the woman removed her feet, there were the lizards. She was soon well and believed the lizards had come out of her legs. I was disgusted and wouldn't practice with my cousin again."

When asked if he had served in the Civil War, Joseph responded, "Of course I did. When I got old enough, I entered the service and barbecued meat until the war closed." Barbecuing had been Joseph's specialty during slavery days, so he followed the same work during his service with the Federal army. He was freed by the Emancipation Proclamation, and soon met and married Sadie Scott, former slave of Mr. Scott, a Tennessee planter. Sadie lived only a short time after her marriage. He later married Amy Doolins, whose father was a blacksmith named Carmuel. After Carmuel was free, some countrymen pursued him and shot him nine times, but he finally killed himself to prevent meeting death at the hands of the hangman.

Joseph was disabled. In 1933 he had fallen and broken his right thigh bone, and since then he had walked with a crutch. When he celebrated his 100th birthday, a large cake decorated with 100 candles was presented to him. The party was attended by children and grandchildren, friends and neighbors. Joseph said his "politics is my love for my country. I vote for the man, not the party." His religion, he said, was the religion of decency and virtue: "I don't want to be hard in my judgment, but I wish the whole world would be decent. When I was a young man, women wore more clothes in bed than they now wear on the street." He also stressed the value of work and was glad that his children were industrious citizens.

Joseph had seven daughters, who also recounted tales they had learned from their grandmother about her Indian captivity. One of his daughters, Della Smith, who was interviewed along with Joseph, said of her father, "Papa had no gray hairs until after Mama died [seven years before the interview]. His hair turned gray from grief at her loss." Another daughter reported, "Papa has always been a lover of horses, but he doesn't care for automobiles or aeroplanes."

24. ELLEN CAVE

Her Owner Was a Mean Man

The Rising Sun *Recorder* published a version of Ellen Cave's narrative on March 19, 1937, and published her obituary on August 24, 1939. According to the obituary,

Mrs. Cave spent the first 12 years of her life as a slave in Taylor county, Kentucky, but two years after the civil war came to Carrollton, Ky., where she was united with her mother, who had been "sold down the river" to Louisiana several years before. At Carrollton, she married James Cave, who, like herself, had been a slave in Taylor county. To them were born 13 children. She later moved to Switzerland county where she spent a good portion of her life. For the past 30 years, however, she has made her home in this county.

When Ellen was interviewed by the WPA fieldworker, she was living in a garage in back of the Rising Sun courthouse, having lost her home and all of her possessions in the 1937 flood. Before the flood, Ellen had lived for many years on a farm about two and a half miles south of Rising Sun.

Ellen was born on a plantation in Taylor County, Kentucky. Her father died when she was a baby, and her mother was sold to someone in Louisiana when Ellen was a year old. Ellen was the property of a man who did not live up to the stereotype of the southern gentleman whose slaves refused to leave him after their freedom was declared. She said her owner was a "mean man" who drank heavily. He had twenty slaves, whom he fed only now and then. He was a southern sympathizer but joined the Union Army and became a captain in charge of a Union commissary. When he was suspected of and charged with giving supplies to the rebels, he was court-martialed, imprisoned, and sentenced to death. He escaped, however, by bribing a black guard. Ellen said that her master's father was as bad as his son. The master's father had a number of children with his many young female slaves, and he sold his own children down the river to Louisiana, where the work was so hard that many slaves died.

Ellen recalled seeing wagonloads of slaves sold down the river. In fact, she was put on the block several times herself, but she never was sold. She said that she would have preferred being sold, though, to continually facing the ordeal of the auction block.

While in slavery, Ellen worked as a maid in the house until she grew older, and then she was forced to do all kinds of outdoor labor. She remembered sawing logs in the snow all day. In the summer she pitched hay and did other kinds of work in the field. She learned to carry three buckets of water at the same time—two in her hands and one on her head—and she said she could still do it. On the plantation the chief article of food for the slaves was bran-bread; however, the master's children were kind and often slipped them meat and other food. Ellen was in slavery for twelve years before she was freed by the Emancipation Proclamation. Even after the war, her owner reluctantly gave her her freedom. Ellen left the plantation two years after the war and went to Carrollton, Kentucky, where she was reunited with her mother in 1867 and soon married James Cave, a former slave on a plantation near hers in Taylor County. She had thirteen children.

Ellen remembered seeing General Woolford and General Morgan of the Southern forces when they made friendly visits to the plantation. She saw

General Grant twice during the war. She saw soldiers drilling near the plantation. Later she was caught and whipped by night riders, or patrollers, as she tried to slip out to black religious meetings.

25. HARRIET CHEATAM

And Did We Eat!

When interviewed, Harriet Cheatam lived with a daughter, Mrs. Jones, at 816 Darnell Street in Indianapolis. The fieldworker reported that Harriet was a small, pleasant woman with beautiful white hair, of which she was very proud. Harriet said that although she used to spend her time piecing quilts, her eyes "have gotten very dim," so she could not piece quilts anymore. Here is her story:

I was born, in 1843, in Gallatin, Tennessee, 94 years ago this coming Christmas Day. Our master, Martin Henley, a farmer, was hard on us slaves, but we were happy in spite of our luck. When I was a child, I didn't have it as hard as some of the children in the quarters. I always stayed in the big house and slept on the floor, right near the fireplace, with one quilt for my bed and one quilt to cover me. Then when I growed up, I was in the quarters.

After the Civil War, I went to Ohio to cook for General Payne. We had a nice life in the general's house. I remember one night way back before the Civil War, we wanted a goose. I went out to steal one, as that was the only way we slaves would have one. I crept very quiet-like, put my hand in where they was, and grabbed. And what do you suppose I had? A great big polecat! Well, I dropped him quick, went back, took off all my clothes, dug a hole, and buried them. The next night I went to the right place, grabbed me a nice big goose, held his neck and feet so he couldn't holler, put him under my arm, and ran with him. And did we eat!

We often had prayer meeting out in the quarters, and to keep the folks in the big house from hearing us, we would take pots, turn them down, and put something under them. That let the sound go in the pots. We put them in a row by the door. Then our voices would not go out, and we could sing and pray to our hearts' content.

At Thanksgiving time we would have pound cake. That was fine. We would take our hands and beat and beat our cake dough, put the dough in a skillet, cover it with the lid, and put it in the fireplace. The covered skillet would act as our ovens of today. It would take all day to bake, but it sure would be good—not like the cakes you have today.

When we cooked our regular meals, we would put our food in pots and slide them on an iron rod that hooked into the fireplace. They were called pothooks. The pots hung right over the open fire and would boil until the food was done.

We often made ash cake. That's made of biscuit dough. When the dough was ready, we swept a clean place on the floor of the fireplace, smoothed the dough out with our hands, took some ashes, put them on top of the dough, then put some hot coals on top of the ashes, and just left it. When it was done, we brushed off the coals, took out the bread, and brushed off the ashes. Child, that was bread!

When we roasted a chicken, we got it all nice and clean, stuffed him with dressing, greased him all over good, put a cabbage leaf on the floor of the fireplace, put the chicken on the cabbage leaf, then covered him good with another cabbage leaf, and put hot coals all over and around him, and left him to roast. That is the best way to cook chicken.

26. ROBERT J. CHEATHAM

Educated Slaves Forged Passes and Escaped to Northern States

Lauana Creel deposited five texts of her interview with Robert J. Cheatham in the the WPA files. Robert came to Indiana with his parents after they were freed. His mother had died around forty years before the interview, though his father lived to be quite old. At the time of the interview, Robert was living with his second wife in a small apartment at 415 South Linwood Avenue in Evansville. Although an invalid, he believed that he and his wife would not be left to suffer from either hunger or cold weather. His ill health, though, had brought them poverty. At one time he and his wife had owned a house on Linwood Avenue, but they lost it and had to move to the small apartment in the black Children's Day Nursery.

Robert was born in Henderson County, Kentucky, on the farm of Dr. Henry H. Farmer, and was known as Bobby Farmer in his childhood. After the war ended, his name was changed to Robert J. Cheatham, which also was the name of his father and his father's master. Slaveholder Cheatham had brought his slaves with him from Virginia when he settled in Kentucky. Robert's father, "a full-blooded Negro," was only four years old then, but he often told tales of the journey from Virginia. His father became overseer of slaves on the Cheatham place and married Mary Farmer, who was held by Dr. Farmer. He was allowed to spend some time with his wife on Farmer's farm, but he was not allowed to live with his family until after the close of the Civil War.

Robert said that his father was a tenderhearted overseer. In fact, he said, "My father was a bum overseer" and gave the following paraphrased account as illustration: Slaveholder Cheatham was a wealthy man who had accumulated his fortune through the sale of slaves. Each year he returned to Virginia and bought slaves to bring back to Henderson County, Kentucky. On one particular trip, he took a large wagon train along the rough wilderness road between Virginia and Kentucky. Six covered wagons carried provisions and furnished shelter for Cheatham and his party of slave dealers. On the return trip, they were accompanied by nearly a hundred black slaves, overseen by Robert's father. This was the first trip Robert's father had made along this route since his childhood, when he was brought with his parents to Kentucky in the same kind of wagon train. Now overseer of Robert Cheatham's slaves, he nearly was overcome by his feeling of importance, according to Robert.

Often long stretches of the rough road had to be improved by the slaves before the wagon train could continue, and the party of slaves and slave dealers camped many nights on the long trip. Every night when the train stopped to make camp, one slave, Kezziah, appeared restless. He dreaded what was in store for him in Kentucky. The last night they camped in Virginia, he seemed especially restless. The following night they camped in Kentucky near a white settler's cabin nestled on the side of a hill, and the white settler visited slaveholder Cheatham and his party. Since provisions had become scarce, the party stayed another day and night hunting and preparing food. Before leaving, Robert's father and some of the slaves were sent to divide meat with the white settler and purchase meal with which to make bread.

Several days after reaching Cheatham's farm, Robert's father, as overseer, was busy telling the new slaves what was expected of them and finding a place for them to live when he noticed that Kezziah, the man who had seemed reluctant to leave Virginia, was missing. After several days, an older slave told Robert's father that Kezziah, half-starved, was hiding in a big haystack in a nearby field. "Take him food and water," said Robert's father, which the old slave did for several days. Then Robert's father told the old slave to tell Kezziah that the owner intended to set fire to the haystack that night, and the old slave believed him. Late that night, after Robert's father had gone to bed in his room in the big house, there was a loud rap on the door. Opening the door, Robert's father found Kezziah standing beside the old slave. To spare Robert's father of any blame, Kezziah told the owner that on his way back to Virginia he had stopped to visit the white settler they had met on the trip to Kentucky, and there the old slave had caught up with him and brought him back. That night Kezziah and slaveholder Cheatham became better acquainted. "What did he care for the loss of a haystack? There was plenty hay in the barns," explained Robert.

Robert said that Dr. Farmer, his master, was good to his slaves. He claimed that "Not a stroke was given in anger by my master to any slave." Still, although Farmer was kind to him and his relatives, and although his childhood days were "passed amid laughter and singing of songs," he said he was glad that young blacks no longer had to look forward to a life of slavery. Some slaves, though, did not leave Farmer's farm after the war. For example, Robert said, "My grand-mother was set free by Dr. Farmer when she was sixty years old, but she never would leave her old home, preferring to stay there and do housework rather than leave her friends."

Slaveholder Farmer neither bought new slaves nor sold his slaves, because he did not want to separate families. He was proud that all of his slaves were descendants of his father's slaves and that all were pure black. Since Farmer was a practicing physician as well as a landowner, he provided his slaves with good medical care. He also educated them. According to Robert, Farmer said, "You colored boys and girls must learn to read and write no matter what powers object. Your parents and your grandparents were taught to read and write when they belonged to my forefathers, and you young children have to learn as much." Robert said, "We read the Bible until the pages became dog-eared and the leaves fell from their binding."

About religion and freedom, Robert said, "My relatives were religious and were never refused the privilege of serving God. The Negro preachers preached freedom into our ears, and our old men and women prophesied about it. We prayed, and our forefathers offered prayers for 275 years in American bondage that we might be given freedom. The white man and the Negro man need to be friends. Abraham Lincoln was the agent of the true and living God, and there have been many other agents given to a trusting people in their hours of need."

According to Robert, "Dr. Farmer wasn't treated exactly fair. After being so careful that all his slaves were taught to read and write, he was cheated out of their services on many occasions through their knowledge. The slaves were required to carry passes when outside of their owner's sight. These passes were signed by their masters." Many of Farmer's educated slaves, however, forged their passes and escaped to northern states. Robert said they got away with it because "so few slaves were good penmen." He claimed that is why so many slaves were denied an education: "They wanted freedom at any cost. Many of them lived to regret escaping, as they knew little about taking care of themselves or transacting business. They necessarily became the prey of swindlers and cheats."

Robert told the following story as an example of an educated slave who escaped: He said that everything was astir on Dr. Farmer's plantation one au-tumn morning in 1850, for Jim, a strong plowman and general laborer on the plantation, was missing. Jim was smart, too, for no other young slave in that part of the country could read the Bible, storybooks, and letters as well as Jim could, and his writing was as good as slaveholder Farmer's. What's more, Jim was al-ways a leader at the dances and other affairs held in the slave quarters.

Jim's parents grieved because they knew that Jim, who could copy his mas-ter's writing, had written his own pass and was on his way to Canada. They also feared because they knew the harsh punishment given to fugitive slaves if they were caught. For days and nights a posse of armed men, both whites and blacks, scoured the country searching for Jim, but they never found him. Only after the slaves were freed did they learn of his whereabouts. Robert explained that "After the Civil War, Jim came back to Kentucky and married one of his cousins. They spent some time at Evansville, but several years ago decided to go back to Canada, where Jim had entered land. His friends often gathered at his cottage while he was a resident of Evansville and enjoyed hearing him relate how he wrote his own pass into a land of freedom. Dr. Farmer lost many valuable Negroes through their ability to read and write, but was never sorry when he learned that they were doing well for themselves in a free state. His will made by himself and signed by his wife gave the promise of freedom to all slaves they possessed at the death of the master and mistress, but some of the Negroes just couldn't wait and passed themselves from one state into another by counterfeited passes."

Robert recalled an occasion when he escaped some swindlers around the close of the Civil War: "Several of my uncles and cousins had enlisted as Union soldiers and hadn't returned from the war. One day another slave boy whispered to me to 'Come down by the old cotton barn tonight.' Along with several of the young Negroes, I went to the place that night. A fine-looking white man was talking to the slaves when I got down there. He was telling them that a rich man in a northern state had put up a large amount of money to spend on educational material for the Negro youths. 'All you have to do is sign these papers, and the books will be sent to you.' While we went up to sign the papers, the stranger stood by his saddle. I said to my cousin, 'Hold the torch close, Johnnie; I want to read this paper.' Johnnie held the torch, and I read not an order for books, but a paper of indenture calculated to bind each of us to the services of some rascal. When we refused to sign the papers, the man galloped his horse away, and we never heard from him again. That partially explains our longing for books."

Dr. Farmer had an old Bible in which he kept the birth records of every member of his family and every black child born on his farm. The old Bible proved useful when Robert applied for an old-age pension. Robert was unable to prove the date of his birth, so his wife made a trip to Kentucky, where she found two of Dr. Farmer's daughters, Sarah Farmer and Honor Farmer Davies, still residing at the old Farmer home place. They still had the Bible and found the record of Robert's birth. The Bible, which for more than two hundred years had been in the Farmer family, was taken to the Vanderburgh County courthouse in Evansville to establish Robert's birth date. The copy made to accompany the application for pension was accidentally destroyed, though, and again Robert's wife had to go back to Kentucky to get proof of his birth. This time she brought back a notarized certificate signed and sworn to by Honor Davies; however, evidence from the Bible was required, so his wife had to make another trip to Kentucky to get the Bible.

Robert claimed that he was not superstitions and did not believe in spells or supernatural powers, but he had stories of such things told by other blacks.

Though he discounted the tales, he claimed he wanted to keep the folklore alive as long as possible. Robert especially kept alive family legends and recalled a number of stories told by his parents. For example, his father, overseer on the Cheatham plantation, told him the following story:

Father said he had made the rounds of the fields and had come back to the big house to tell Marse Bob that everything was in order: the children had been put to bed, the farm implements stored away for the night, the horses all fed, and not a slave was missing. Then he stood near the steps of the back veranda and talked to Marse Bob and the missus for a few minutes. A number of Union soldiers were camped about three miles from the Cheatham farm on the old fairgrounds.

It was father's duty to report to Marse Bob if any of the slaves were missing. There was some danger that they would run away to war or to freedom by the Underground Railroad. Father had a room to himself at the big house, where he was very comfortable when his work was finished. That night he asked for permission to visit Marse Cheatham's daughter, who had married and kept house with her husband several miles from the old Cheatham home. Marse Cheatham allowed him to make the visit, so he mounted his horse and started on his way.

The road he had to travel led him by the fairgrounds, and as he passed, he was hailed by one of Marse Cheatham's slaves that he had seen only a few hours earlier in the evening. "What are you doing here, Bert?" said Father. "We have joined the Union Army," Bert said, and then, "Bobby, I want you to steal Lucy for me tonight. She is my lawful wedded wife, and I can't go away and leave her in bondage." Father was afraid to steal Lucy. He knew Marse Cheatham would have no mercy if he ever found out the truth, but Bert begged and cried until Father said he would get her if possible. He turned his horse back toward Marse Bob's home and tethered him below the slave cabins.

Lucy was a pretty mulatto girl about twenty years old. She sewed for the Cheatham family and was allowed to visit her mother every evening at the slave quarters. Father went down to her mother's cabin. A candle was burning on the table inside, and he could see the old woman and Lucy at work on a patchwork quilt. He waited a long time before Lucy got up and started home. When she got out of sight of her mother's cabin, he grabbed her and ran to his horse. "Keep quiet, Lucy; I'm stealing you for Bert," he said. He took her down by the lane and told her to wait for him there. Soon he came back with one of Marse Cheatham's fastest mares saddled for the flight. Before long, Lucy was given over to her husband at the Union camp, and Bert was a happy man.

When Father started back home, he heard the thunder of galloping hoofs on the boardwalk that was built from the landing place on the Ohio River up Alvis's Hill and out to the fairgrounds at Henderson, Kentucky. Father knew then that Lucy had been missed, so he loosed her saddle and let it fall by the side of the road; and giving Lucy's horse a hard lick with the quirt, he turned his own horse toward young missus's home and galloped away. Young missus was always glad to see any of the slaves from home, so she and young marse set supper on the table and talked while he ate.

Father said he was sleepy and tired, so he was given a pallet in the bedroom with the master and mistress. He slept but little; he was so worried about stealing Lucy. A good slave who had been taught to sew and do housework was well worth a thousand dollars, and he knew who was guilty.

Early in the morning he went back to the Cheatham home. All the slaves, women and children, had gathered together in the yard. "They goin' hang you, Bobby," said one of the girls. "Why are they going to hang me?" asked Father. "For stealing Lucy!" several voices declared. "Is Lucy gone?" asked Father. He put the whip to his horse and hurried away. He soon overtook the searchers. "Where have you taken Lucy?" yelled the master, and my father saw he had a long rope slung across the pommel of his saddle.

Father said that he knew nothing about the affair and led the posse to the home of his young mistress. She, of course, testified that he had spent the night at her home, and he was allowed to join the searching party looking for Lucy. The horse had gone home without a saddle, and Father discovered the saddle and called the attention of the other searchers that Lucy's horse had surely come unsaddled. Father's horse was showing signs of fatigue, and that night Marse Bob Cheatham gave a fine horse to Father for his very own. Lucy made her way into the northern states after being concealed by the Union soldiers for several months, and after the Civil War ended, she and her husband returned to Henderson. They often visit friends at Evansville, but Father never divulged his part in the stealing of Lucy.

Family ties are held sacred to the Negro as to the white man. Husbands are loyal to their wives and children. Although for hundreds of years it had been the privilege of the masters to separate families, it was a cruel practice and caused much heartache among the slaves.

Another family story, actually a story within a story, involves the night that Robert was born. Robert swore that the story is true. He said that Dr. Farmer, the slaveholder, told him part of the story, and Vinson, the captive, told him the rest of it after the Civil War:

My parents said I was born on a very stormy night while rain and hail was falling, and thunder and lightning made everybody afraid to stick their heads outside the door. The Fisher boys and the Vinson boys had been given their freedom. They had worked in Indiana and several other states and had accumulated money enough to lease a farm near Anthoston in Henderson County, Kentucky. Their farm and cabin home was only three-fourths of a mile from Dr. Farmer's home, where I was born. When the old midwife and the nurse left our house, they told Dr. Farmer they heard running horses and believed some devilment was afoot. Early in the morning, Dr. Farmer sent some of the slaves over to the Vinson place, and they came back and reported that the door was standing open and everybody was gone. Also they said that the bolt had been broken.

Dr. Farmer was a leader among men, and he soon gathered up a searching party and started out in search of the slaves. They were traced to Tennessee, but there their trail was lost, and they were never heard of again until after the close of the Civil War. After the close of the war, Vinson came back and told the story of his kidnaping. It is, as I remember, like this:

My brother and I were reading and talking to Joe Fisher when somebody knocked at our door. When we opened the door the storm was so bad we could only see a few feet outside the cabin. We told the stranger to come in out of the storm. He walked in, and we saw he was a white man. Soon there was another knock. We was scared to open the door again, and in a few minutes the door was battered against by a big piece of log, and the wooden bolt gave way. There was three of us, all without guns or any other weapons, while the four white men were armed, so all we could do was to go with them. They took us to the traders' yard in Tennessee, where we were put up in a sort of barracks or slaves' pen to be sold also. "Who will buy this young man? He's as strong as an ox, healthy and smart. He's a left-handed fiddler!" Soon a purchaser came and bought me, then bought one of my brothers, but sold him within a few hours. I never met either my brother nor my friend again.

My new master started out with a wagon train toward the South. We had only struck camp one night when my new master met a number of Union soldiers. The captain of the Union encampment ordered his men into action. My new master was scared almost to death and ran away as fast as his horse could run, leaving wagons, provisions, and slaves to the Union soldiers. We slaves joined the Union forces, and I fought until I received my honorable discharge and was a free man again.

Vinson, the left-handed fiddler, fiddled in Tennessee and Kentucky for public dances, barbecues, and public gatherings for many years. His only sorrow was being separated from his companions. His lease had run out on his land in Henderson County, but the wide world has much to offer to the free man, and he lived to enjoy many years of freedom. Only by chance did he meet the Union soldiers; otherwise, he would have been taken to the South to become a bonded slave. His kidnapers profited by the adventure. They got the $900 that the captives brought at auction and went on their way unmolested. No amount of pleading, no proof of freedom, would have touched the hearts of the slave traders; only the accidental skirmish between the wagon train and the Union soldiers gave him back his manhood and his freedom. He always hoped that some similar occurrence had saved his companions, but he never learned about it if such was the case.

27. JAMES CHILDRESS

Slaves Always Prayed to God for Freedom

When interviewed, James Childress was living with John Bell at 312 Southeast 5th Street in Evansville. According to his obituary in the *Evansville Courier* (December 17, 1941), he died on December 16, 1941, leaving "no known survivors." Locally known as Uncle Jimmie, he never tired of telling stories of his childhood. Born in Nashville, Tennessee, in 1860, he remembered some exciting events of Civil War days as related to him by his own family and by the family of James Childress, his owner. He remembered sorrowful days when his Uncle Johnnie and Uncle Bob started off to war, but he also recalled happier days when the Cumberland Valley was beautifully carpeted with bluegrass and wildflowers.

Although James could not recall any occasion when his master was cruel to a slave, he remembered that the slaves always prayed to God for freedom, and that black preachers always preached about the day when the slaves would be free and happy. He sang a stanza of "Swing Low Sweet Chariot" and said that it related to God's setting the blacks free. James's story follows:

> When I was a child, my daddy and mama was slaves, and I was a slave. A beautiful view could always be enjoyed from the hillsides, and there were many pretty homes belonging to the rich citizens. Slaves kept the lawns smooth and tended the flowers for miles around Nashville when I was a child. We was all well fed, well clothed, and lived in good cabins. The slaves at Mr. Childress's place were allowed to learn as much as they could. Several of the young men could read and write. Our master was a good man and did no harm to anybody.
>
> I never got a cross word from Marse John in my life. When the slaves got their freedom, they rejoiced and stayed up many nights to sing, dance, and enjoy themselves. Although they still depended on old Marse John for food and bed, they felt too excited to work in the fields or care for the stock. They hated to leave their homes, but Mr. Childress told them to go out and make homes for themselves.
>
> Mother got work as a housekeeper and kept us all together. Uncle Bob got home from the war, and we lived well enough. I have lived at Evansville since 1881, have worked for a good many men, and John Bell will tell you I have had only friends in the city of Evansville.
>
> My people loved God; they sang sacred songs. "Swing Low Sweet Chariot" was one of the best songs they knew.

28. SARAH COLBERT

The Village Witch

When interviewed, Sarah Carpenter Colbert lived with her daughter in a very comfortable home at 1505 North Capitol Avenue in Indianapolis. She seemed happy, was glad to talk of her early days, and laughed when relating the experiences of her family. Sarah raised a large family and was very proud of her children.

Sarah was born in Allen County, Kentucky, in 1855. Her father, Isaac Carpenter, was the grandson of their master, Leige Carpenter, a kind farmer. Isaac worked on the farm until Carpenter's death, and then he was sold to Jim McFarland of Frankfort, Kentucky. McFarland's wife was mean to their slaves and whipped them regularly every morning just "to start the day right."

One morning after a severe beating, Isaac met an old slave who asked him why he let his missus beat him so much. Isaac laughed and asked what he could do about it. The old man told him to bite her feet the next time she knocked him down, and then maybe she would stop beating him and sell him. The next morning when Isaac was getting his regular beating, he fell to the floor, grabbed his mistress's foot, and bit her hard. She tried to pull away, but Isaac held on with his teeth. She ran around the room with Isaac holding on to her foot. Finally she stopped beating him, and she never struck him again. The next week he was put on the block, and since he was a strong man and a good worker, the bids were high. Leige Carpenter, Jr., son of his former owner, outbid everyone and bought him for $1,200.

Isaac's new mistress was mean to him, too, so again he went to his old friend for advice. His friend told him to get some yellow dust, sprinkle it around his missus's room, and, if possible, put some in her shoes. This he did, and shortly he was sold in the same county to Johnson Carpenter, who did not treat him any better. Tired of being mistreated, he remembered his former master, Leige Carpenter, telling him to never let anyone be mean to him, so he ran away to his old mistress and told her of his many hardships. Isaac told her what Leige Carpenter had told him, and she sent him back to Johnson Carpenter. She bought him at the next sale, though, and he lived with her until slavery was abolished.

Sarah's grandfather, Bat Carpenter, was an ambitious slave who dug ore and bought his freedom. Then he bought his wife, Matilda, by paying her master $50 a year. Matilda continued to live and work on the farm of her former owner for very small wages, and Bat, who lived close by, was allowed to visit her every Sunday. One Sunday, though, it looked like rain, and Bat's master told him to gather in the oats. Bat refused and was beaten with rawhide. He was so angry that he went to a witch doctor for a charm so he could fix his master. The witch doctor told him to get five new nails, as there were five members in his owner's family. He should walk to the barn, then take a few steps backward, stop, and pound one nail deep in the ground; then take a few more steps backward, stop, and pound in another nail, and so on, each time giving the nail the name of a member of the family, starting with the master, then the mistress, and so on. He did as instructed and was never beaten again.

Jane Garmon was the village witch. She tormented the slaves with her cat. At milking time the cat would always appear, and at night it would go from one cabin to another, putting out all the grease lamps with its paw. No matter what they tried, they could not kill that cat. An old witch doctor told them to melt a dime, form a bullet with the silver, and shoot the cat. He said a lead bullet would never kill a bewitched animal. The silver bullet fixed the cat, though. Jane also bewitched their chickens. The chickens were dying fast, and everything the slaves did to save them failed. Finally they built a big fire and threw the dead chickens into the fire. That broke the charm, and no more chickens died.

29. FRANK COOPER

Misery Days

Frank Cooper, an elderly man living at 715 Ott Street in Franklin when interviewed, talked about the mistreatment of slaves in Lincoln County, Kentucky. His information came from his mother, Mandy Cooper, who was 115 years old when she died. Mandy was held by three different families: the Goods, the Burtons, and the Coopers, all of Lincoln County, Kentucky. Frank told the following story, presented in part in his mother's words by the interviewer:

One day while my mother was washing her back, my sister noticed ugly, disfiguring scars on it. Inquiring about them, we found, much to our amazement, that they were Mammy's relics of the now gone, if not forgotten, slave days. This was her first reference to her "misery days" that she had ever made in my presence. Of course, we all thought she was tellin' us a big story, and we made fun of her. With eyes flashin' she stopped bathing, dried her back, and reached for the smelly ol' black whip that hung behind the kitchen door. Biddin' us to strip down to our waists, my little mother, with the bony bent-over back, struck each of us as hard as ever she could with that black-snake whip. Each stroke of the whip drew blood from our backs. "Now," she said to us, "you have a taste of slavery days."

With three of her children now having tasted some of her "misery days," she was in the mood to tell us more of her sufferings, still indelibly impressed in my mind: "My ol' back is bent over from the quick-tempered blows felled by the red-headed Miss Burton. At dinner time one day when the churnin' *wasn't finished for the noonday meal," she said with an angry look that must have been reborn in my mother's eyes—eyes that were dimmed by years and hard livin'—"three white women beat me from anger because they had no butter for their biscuits and cornbread. Miss Burton used a heavy board, while the missus used a whip. While I was on my knees beggin' them to quit, Miss Burton hit the small of my back with the heavy board. I know no more until kind Mr. Hamilton, who was staying with the white folks, brought me inside the cabin and brought me around with the cam-phor bottle. I'll always thank him, God bless him. He picked me up where they had left me like a dog to die in the blazin' noonday sun. After my back was broken, it was doubted whether I would ever be able to work again or not. I was placed on the auction block to be bidded for so my owner could see if I was worth anything or not. One man bid $1,700, after puttin' two dirty fingers in my mouth to see my teeth. I bit him, and his face showed anger. He then wanted to own me so he could punish me. Thinkin' his bid of $1,700 was official, he unstrapped his buggy whip to beat me, but my master saved me. My master declared the bid unofficial. At this auction my sister was sold for $1,900 and was never seen by us again."*

My mother also related some experiences she had with the paddy-rollers [patrollers], later called the Ku Klux. These paddy-rollers were a constant dread to the Negroes. They would whip the poor darkies unmercifully with-out any cause. One night while the Negroes were gathering for a big party and dance they got wind of the paddy-rollers approaching in large numbers on horseback. The Negro men didn't know what to do for protection, so they became desperate and decided to gather a quantity of grapevines and tied them fast at a dark place in the road. The paddy-rollers came thundering down the road bent on deviltry. Unaware of the trap set for them, they plunged head-on into these strong grapevines, and three of their number were killed and a score badly injured. Several horses had to be shot following injuries. When the news of this happening spread, it was many months be-fore the paddy-rollers were again heard of.

30. JOHN COOPER

I Got Religion

John Cooper—a seventy-six-year-old family man, member of the Baptist Church, and "good citizen"—was residing at 501 East 2nd Street in Muncie when he was interviewed about his father, Woodford Monroe, who was free-born on the Monroe plantation in Butler County, Kentucky. Woodford married

Sarah Phant, also freeborn but on the Cooper plantation. John inherited the name of his mother's owner rather than that of his father's owner because after his father married and arrived on the Cooper plantation, he was called Wood-ford Cooper. According to John, Woodford's master was kind to his workers and wanted them to be free. He paid them wages and gave them food from the plantation. John knew very little about his grandfather, who was a slave, for his grandfather had been sold and separated from his family.

Since Woodford was free, he was drafted into the Union Army, though he never served because the war ended before he left the plantation. After the war John moved with his family to Evansville, where his parents died and he was forced to face the world alone. Walking part of the way, John went to Anderson and worked there for a time before moving to Muncie in 1902.

Though born free, John grew up in an atmosphere of slavery and said he had to take out legal papers in order to vote. The fieldworker wrote that the "incidents of the past come to his mind more like a legend, with its lights and shadows, than the drama of a human reality" and attempted to record John's narrative "in his own idiom as near as we could gather it from his mental and verbal inflections":

> We is livin' in Evansville after I left the South. I got religion—come this here way: Our peoples was holdin' a big meetin' there. I go. One night the parson, he get he eye on me. He preach as if I had salvation. I answer him no, an' say on that I don't care to have it roun' 'cause it make one fool out of this free nigger. He ask then did I chance bide 'lone in Evansville. I say, lordy, Parson, worse'n that, I is a orphan an' 'lone in this world. Then he say, "Come, brother, the Lord am searchin' for the orphan an' the shorn lamb."
>
> There be a big lot of we's people at the altar an' makin' a big hallelujah noise. I hadn't more than hit the bench when the Lord says, says he, "Come in, John, I'm waitin.'"
>
> It was winter, then, an' the river was floatin' with ice. The parson, he announce all that got religion come down to the river next Lord's day at ten o'clock. The whole congregations was there, an' the train, it fetched a big load of lookers. Some colored brothers hefted some big chunks of ice out and make a hole at the edge of the water. Parson took us all in an chuck us under. Then we was loaded in a truck an' took home. The clothes, they freeze on our body, but we-uns all shout glory, hallelujah, we be chilluns of God. Every sin done be washed 'tirely 'way.
>
> I ain't never been nowhere only in the flock of the Lord since.

31. MARY CRANE

Almost Sold down the River

Mary Crane was living on Warren Street in Mitchell when she was interviewed. In the WPA files her narrative follows that of Thomas Ash (q.v.), in a single text called "Reminiscences of Two Ex-Slaves."

I was born on the farm of Wattie Williams in 1855 and am eighty-two years old. I came to Mitchell, Indiana, about fifty years ago with my husband, who is now dead, and four children and have lived here ever since. I was only a girl, about five or six years old, when the Civil War broke out, but I can remember very well happenings of that time.

My mother was owned by Wattie Williams, who had a large farm located in LaRue County, Kentucky. My father was a slave on the farm of a Mr. Duret nearby. In those days, slave owners, whenever one of their daughters would get married, would give her and her husband a slave as a wedding present, usually allowing the girl to pick the one she wished to accompany her to her new home. When Mr. Duret's eldest daughter married Zeke Samples, she chose my father to accompany them to their home.

Zeke Samples proved to be a man who loved his toddies far better than his bride, and before long he was broke. Everything he had or owned, including my father, was to be sold at auction to pay off his debts. In those days, there were men who made a business of buying up Negroes at auction sales and shipping them down to New Orleans to be sold to owners of cotton and sugar cane plantations, just as men today buy and ship cattle. These men were called "nigger-traders," and they would ship whole boatloads at a time, buying them up, two or three here, two or three there, and holding them in a jail until they had a boatload. This practice gave rise to the expression "sold down the river."

My father was to be sold at auction, along with all of the rest of Zeke Samples' property. Bob Cowherd, a neighbor of Matt Duret's, owned my grandfather, and the old man, my grandfather, begged Colonel Bob to buy my father from Zeke Samples to keep him from being "sold down the river." Colonel Bob offered what he thought was a fair price for my father, and a slave trader raised his bid $25. Colonel said he couldn't afford to pay that much, and father was about to be sold to the slave trader when his father told Colonel Bob that he had $25 saved up and that if he would buy my father from Samples and keep the slave trader from getting him he would give him the money. Colonel Bob Cowherd took my grandfather's $25 and offered to meet the slave trader's offer, and so my father was sold to him.

The Negroes in and around where I was raised were not treated badly, as a rule, by their masters. There was one slave owner, a Mr. Heady, who lived nearby, who treated his slaves worse than any of the other slave owners, but I never heard of anything so awfully bad happening to his slaves. He had one boy who used to come over to our place, and I can remember hearing Mr. Williams call to my grandmother to cook: "Christine, give Heady's Doc something to eat. He looks hungry." Mr. Williams always said "Heady's Doc" when speaking of him or any other slave—saying to call him, for instance, Doc Heady would sound as if he were Mr. Heady's own son, and he said that wouldn't sound right.

When President Lincoln issued his proclamation freeing the Negroes, I remember that my father and most all of the other younger slave men left the farm to join the Union Army. We had hard times then for a while and had lots of work to do. I don't remember just when I first regarded myself as "free," as many of the Negroes didn't understand just what it was all about.

32. CORNELIUS CROSS

Auctioned Off More Times Than He Had Fingers and Toes

Cornelius Cross said he had been auctioned off more times than he had fingers and toes, but that his mother was never separated from her family. His mother had seven sons (Granduson, Ben, Sonny, Philip, Cornelius, Solomon, and James) and five daughters (Dee, Mary Jane, Rachel, Nancy, and Addie). All of her children were born in the Indian Territory. Cornelius was born in a sorghum field, where his mother worked. He said he was happy in slavery because he always was allowed to stay near his mother during his childhood. When he was older, though, his white owners frequently punished him when he was disobedient.

After coming to Indiana, Cornelius worked on a canal boat on the Wabash and Erie Canal and traveled between Evansville and Terre Haute. He remembered two big locks at Lockport (Riley), but had forgotten the names of a number of locks and bridges. After leaving the canal boats, Cornelius settled in Evansville, where he lived for twenty years and worked for the Evansville branch of the Southern Indiana Gas and Electric Company.

On November 7, 1936, as he greased switches of the Southern Indiana Gas and Electric Company's streetcar tracks, Cornelius was struck by a drunken white man and was hospitalized for three months. While he was in the hospital, his wife died. Cornelius died on July 16, 1944, and his obituary was published in the *Evansville Courier* on July 17, 1944 (p. 23):

Cornelius Cross, 80, Negro, of 405 Southeast Fifth street, an employee of the Southern Indiana Gas and Electric company for more than 40 years, died yesterday. Mr. Cross, who went to work for the utility firm in 1902, recently retired.

Surviving are four daughters, Mrs. Elizabeth Riley and Mrs. Della Scott, Evansville; Mrs. Pearl Wilson, of Dayton, O., and Mrs. Estella Swancie, Indianapolis, and two sisters, Mrs. Dee Shipp, Hopkinsville, Ky., and Mrs. Rachel Weekly, Pembroke, Ky.

The body is at the Gaines funeral home.

At the time of the following interview, Cornelius was out of work and out of money.

I do not know the date of my birth, for I was born a way back. I do not know when. Evansville is a good place to live in, but I have not always lived in Indiana. I lived three years and six months at New Orleans. New Orleans was the first place I remember living at after the time my parents brought me from the Indian Territory, where we lived and where I was born. The Indian Territory had not been joined to the Oklahoma Territory. The surface of the area is level, but near the boundary in all directions you could see mountains in the distance.

My mother was named Henrietta and was a full-blooded Cherokee Indian. She was a loved and loving and honored mother and was faithful to her family and to her work. She had come across into Arkansas along with a band of her father's people. When the band had seen the area east of the Territory, they decided to stay and make their home in Arkansas. Soon they became restless and traveled farther east until they came to the Mississippi Valley, where hunting and fishing were profitable. While the party of Indians was staying in Arkansas, my mother met Ben [Boulton], a Negro slave of James Boulton, who was in the slave business at Little Rock, Arkansas. Ben joined the band of Indians and became the husband of Henrietta. Ben Boulton only became known as Ben Cross during the Civil War.

Ben and his Indian wife got along well together. Ben had escaped bondage, but he feared being recaptured. This fear caused the Indians to travel into the Indiana [Indian?] Territory, where many slaves had gained freedom. The Negroes received kindness in Indiana [Indian Territory?], but there was much Indian trouble, and soon the white settlers could no longer stand the Indians as neighbors. I have never heard it said that my people had trouble with white families, but all Indians suffered for the depredations of the uncivilized Indians.

I do not know whether my people were driven out of the Indian Territory following King Philip's War [1675–76?] or some Indian massacre, but I know my parents were driven back into the Indian Territory, lived there, and made the Territory their home. There they were well treated, well fed, and had few cares. The climate was delightful—the winters never severe, the summers not too warm for comfort and health. My mother was sorry to leave the Territory, but the old masters of slaves demanded that their property be returned to them, and all the half-breeds with slave parents were mustered out of the area and returned to their owners. My mother was not a slave, but she came with my father and brought seven sons and five daughters to be auctioned off from the slave block at New Orleans. We slave children did not wear pants, but a full, long shirt or dress made of coarse homespun cloth. When we were disobedient, the master or his wife made us raise the skirt high and take a sound whipping on our bared skin. It soon taught us to be obedient and to respect discipline.

I worked for several years on a boat on the the the Ohio River from New Orleans and Cincinnati. I knew Jim Howard . . . Red-Headed Jesse from St. Louis—the same Red-Headed Jesse was murdered at St. Louis by a deck hand. I knew Tom January, one of the best river men that sailed in the old river days.

The [Wabash and Erie] canal was a pretty sight. A great deal of masonry was used. A beautiful arch was erected over Burnett's Creek. High bridges were placed above trestles, and handrailings were built on each side of the bridges for safety.

Where that big chimney stands on the property of the Indiana Gas and Electric Company's property was a canal depot. The canal boats used to be run up on what is now Fifth Street and pass where the beautiful Central Library now stands. The New South *was one boat that carried a great deal of freight. These boats were double-decked boats and carried both freight and passengers.*

Many stories have been told of piracy on the Ohio River. A story of Cave-In Rock is partly true, as there was a large hotel at Cave-In Rock, and many things happened there. I do not know how many have been put in books and how much has been handed down from one person to another. Many things happened which we did not understand, but I never did believe in ghosts or haunts.

33. ETHEL DAUGHERTY

A Slaveholder Kept Many Black Women in His House

Ethel Daugherty told the fieldworker some unfortunate experiences of slavery that she had heard from older members of her family who had been slaves. She said her great-grandmother was a slave in Kentucky and was kept in the big house to help with the cooking. She received good food, but the slaves who worked in the fields were lined up and slopped like hogs. They had to eat from wooden troughs, into which all their food was poured.

At slave sales, women were forced to stand half-dressed for hours while a crowd of rough, drunken men bargained for them, frequently examining their teeth, heads, hands, and other body parts to determine their health and endurance. Sometimes owners of nearby plantations purchased children privately if they wanted them. If slave children attempted to return to their parents, usually they were severely beaten, and a closer watch was kept over them.

Four of Ethel's great-grandmother's children were sold, leaving her with only one son, her youngest. She lost all trace of her other children, partly because as soon as a child was sold, it took the name of the new master. Some children were sold several times, and each time their names were changed, making it extremely difficult to locate children who had been separated from their parents. Moreover, many children were shipped to different parts of the country and were not told who their parents were.

Ethel's great-grandmother said that once a mother and son were separated for years, and when the boy grew up, he began keeping company with his mother. When he happened to mention to his mother a small, nearly invisible scar he had, she realized who he was and told him he was her son. Ethel said there were many marriages of relatives before the Civil War closed.

She said that one slaveholder kept many black women in his house, similar to Mormonism. Ethel thought interracial marriages, which she blamed on slavery, were sinful, and at the time of the interview she thought there still were too many interracial marriages. She attributed them to lack of self-control or the "devil turned loose."

Ethel was sensitive about her family's mixed blood. Her stepfather was a mixture of three races, his mother being Native American. She said that when he was angry, he thought he was all Indian. Ethel's first husband's name was Grady. When people remarked that the name sounded Irish, they were told that the name had been in the family since slave days. Her husband's grandmother had been forced to live with her master, and Ethel claimed that as a result of that union, Mrs. Grady, Ethel's mother-in-law, had very long hair. Ethel said she had never told anyone about this before, because Mrs. Grady always felt very bad about her origin. Ethel's own eyes were blue, but she reasoned that was not her fault. She advised her own children to "stick to their color always." Her maiden name was Taylor, and she said there were blacks named Taylor in Kentucky—all "descendants of the white family who bestowed their name on the colored children years ago."

At the close of the war, her family was simply turned out to shift for themselves with no help from their master. Many of them came to Indiana, but Ethel was the only one to locate in Jefferson County.

34. JOHN DAUGHERTY

Ignorance of the Bible Caused All the Trouble

When interviewed, John Daugherty lived at 208 W. 6th Street in Madison. The fieldworker included part of his narrative (the last paragraph of this text) with that of his wife, Lizzie Daugherty (q.v.). As near as he could remember, he was about five years old when the Civil War ended. His family lived at Riddle Hill in Trimble County, Kentucky. He came to Indiana when he was sixteen or seventeen years old. He remembered a few instances of slavery.

One time his missus switched him with a peach limb because he had persisted in getting too near the heels of his master's horse when other children were picking burrs from the horse's tail. When soldiers passed through, he was frightened and cried until his grandmother hid him under the bed clothing at the foot of his missus's bed. He said his mother had a very hard time, as she had to cut corn, chop wood, and drive the oxen in the field. Many times her toenails were mashed off by the oxen stepping on her bare feet.

John said that now he and everyone else knew it was not right for his mother to wade in snow to her knees to get wood to cook meals while grown white men sat around the fire, but he did not seem to bear the slaveholders any ill will. He thought they had behaved as well as they could with the little knowledge they had. He thought ignorance of the Bible caused all the trouble; the slaveholders just had not read the Scriptures enough to know that it was wrong to hold human beings in bondage.

35. LIZZIE DAUGHERTY

One of the Saddest Events That Could Happen to a Mother

Lizzie Daugherty said that her mother had experienced one of the saddest events that could happen to a mother. While in slavery, she was ordered to clean a vacant house before her missus would move in. This house was located over a hill and about a half-mile from the slave cabin. There was no one to stay with her two babies, and it was out of the question to take them with her to a vacant house in the dead of winter; therefore, wanting to spare the children from getting out in the weather and taking cold, she fixed a fire, locked the door, and left them alone in her cabin.

When Lizzie's mother reached the top of the hill on her way home from her day's cleaning, she was shocked to see only a smoking mass where her cabin had stood. She hoped that someone had discovered the fire in time to save the children, but that had not happened.

Lizzie's mother was left childless, homeless, and with nothing but the clothing she was wearing. Lizzie said her mother felt as if her very heart had been crushed, and for weeks she did not want to talk to anyone. Lizzie regarded the tragedy as an accident, though, and not the fault of the woman who had ordered her mother to be away so long from her two children.

36. RACHAEL DUNCAN

Some of the Folks Was Mean to Me

When interviewed, Rachael Duncan, a former slave, was living at 46 Vincennes Street in New Albany, Indiana. The fieldworker mentioned that Rachael looked much younger than her age and that "she stepped quickly along through the yard to meet me, and I thought that I had the wrong person, so brisk was her walk."

Born in Breckinridge County, Kentucky, Rachael was about six or seven years old when freedom was declared, although she did not know her exact age. She could not read or write. She said that as a little girl she was "farmed out" to various white families until she hardly knew her own mother. One day when her mother came to see her, she ran and hid, as she did not recognize her and was afraid of her. Rachael's husband was nine years old during the Civil War and helped his father drive supplies to the soldiers.

Rachael lived with Emma Jenkins, the Nelson Walkers, and other white families. "Some of the folks was mean to me," she said. The nicest place she lived was near Doe Run. She remembered the old mill there, and how people from miles around used to bring their corn to the mill for grinding. At the time of the interview, the mill was still standing but was used as a summer hotel.

Rachael said that a year after the war there were so many snakes all over the country that everyone was afraid to venture out. One day as she was going down to the well, she almost stepped on a huge rattler, which rattled angrily and prepared to strike. She was too scared to run and stood as if turned to stone. Fortunately a black man came along and killed the rattler with his hoe. The snake was five feet long.

Rachael told a story about an old house in which her family lived in Kentucky. One day she heard something in the kitchen and went out to see what it was. When she got to the door, there sat a man without a head. Just as she started to run, he threw up his hands and vanished into thin air. After that, they always heard steps on the stairs, but they never saw anybody going up or down them. A man had been murdered and robbed near there during the Civil War, and it was said that this was his ghost seeking his murderers.

When asked about camp meetings, Rachael said, "Camp meetings? Yes, ma'am. They used to have some grand ones down in Breckinridge County. They was always held out in the woods in a clear space, away off to ourselves, under a big tree. And they was preachin' and singin' and folks got religion right. Yes, ma'am, they did. One man, I remember, got so took up with himself shoutin' and goin' on with the Lord that he run off into the woods and didn't come back for two days. Had got lost and was all chewed up by mosquitoes an' chiggers an' briers. The white folk didn't bother with us then. We always kept to ourselves when camp meetin' was on."

The interview ended when the fieldworker and Rachael smelled cabbage burning on the stove. The fieldworker concluded, "So I made a hurried departure, and the old woman went into the house to salvage her dinner, promising to think up some more stories for me next time."

37. H. H. EDMUNDS

They Poured Out Their Religious Feelings in Their Spirituals

H. H. Edmunds was born in Lynchburg, Virginia, in 1859, but several years after his birth, his master took him to Mississippi. Before moving to Elkhart, he lived in Nashville, Tennessee. Edmunds, who served as a minister for many years, was very religious, but he felt that religion had greatly changed from the "old time religion." He said that in slavery days, the blacks were so subjugated and uneducated that they were especially susceptible to religion, and they poured out their religious feelings in their spirituals.

Edmunds was convinced that the superstitions of the blacks, such as their belief in ghosts, were due to the fact that their emotions were worked upon by slave drivers to keep them in subjugation. He said white people often dressed as ghosts and frightened the blacks into doing many things, for ghosts were feared far more than slave drivers.

Edmunds could not remember the Civil War, but he clearly remembered the period of Reconstruction that followed. Blacks were very happy when they learned they were free. A few took advantage of their freedom immediately, but many, not knowing what else to do, remained with their former owners. Some remained on the plantations five years after they were free. Gradually they learned to care for themselves, often through instructions received from their former owners, and then they were glad to start out in the world for themselves. Of course, there were exceptions, for the slaves who had been abused by cruel slaveholders were only too glad to leave their former homes. Edmunds related the following account of his own freedom from slavery:

As a boy, I worked in Virginia for my master, a Mr. Farmer. He had two sons who served as bosses on the farm. An older sister was the hand boss.

After the war was over, the sister called the colored people together and told them that they were no longer slaves, that they might leave if they wished. The slaves had been watering cucumbers, which had been planted around barrels filled with soil. Holes had been bored in the barrels, and when water was poured in the barrels, it gradually seeped out through the holes, thus watering the cucumbers. After the speech, one son told the slaves to resume their work. Since I was free, I refused to do so, and as a result, I received a terrible kicking. I mentally resolved to get even someday. Years afterward, I went to the home of this man for the express purpose of seeking revenge. However, I was received so kindly and treated so well that all thoughts of revenge vanished. For years after, my former boss and I visited each other in our own homes.

38. JOHN EUBANKS

Most the Time We's Hungry, but We Win the War

The fieldworker submitted two texts of his interview with John Eubanks. One text is mainly a summary, and the other supposedly is in the informant's own words. At the time of the interview, John was living with his daughter, Mrs. Bertha Sloss, and several grandchildren at 2713 Harrison Boulevard, according to the WPA files; however, six months earlier he had been living with Mrs. Sloss at 2712 Van Buren Place in Gary, according to an article in the *Gary Post-Tribune* (March 29, 1937). A large man who said he had once weighed more than two hundred pounds, John was 98 years old when he was interviewed and said he hoped to live to be 100. Since his brother and mother both died at 98 and his paternal grandfather at 110, he thought he had a good chance to realize his ambition; however, he was badly crippled with rheumatism and had poor eyesight, and his memory was failing. Nevertheless, he recalled many details from his youth, though he was occasionally prompted by his daughter and grandchildren, who in recent years had taken notes on John's personal experience tales. John was proud of his fifty grandchildren, for most of them were high school graduates, and two were attending the University of Chicago.

John was Gary's only surviving Civil War veteran at the time of the interview. He said that in 1926 he was the only one of three surviving members of the Grand Army of the Republic in Gary, and he was extremely proud that he was the only one in a parade held that year. One of seven children, he was born a slave in Barren County, Kentucky, June 6, 1839. Though his father was a free man, his mother was a slave on the Everett plantation. As a child he was put to work hoeing, picking cotton, and doing other odd jobs.

Following the custom of the time, when children of the Everett family married, slaves were given to them as wedding presents. John was given to a daughter who married a man named "Eubanks," whose name John took. John was more fortunate than many slaves, for the Eubankses were kind to him. They lived in a state divided on the question of slavery and favored the North. His brothers and sisters were given to other members of the Everett family upon their marriage or sold down the river and did not see one another again until after the Civil War.

At the beginning of the Civil War, John was twenty-one. When the North seemed to be losing the war, black regiments were formed, and slaves joining the Union Army were granted freedom. The Eubankses told John that he could join the Union Army if he wished instead of running away, as other slaves were doing. John decided to join a black regiment located at Bowling Green, Kentucky. He said he walked the entire thirty-five miles to Bowling Green from Glasgow, where he was living. He served in the army as a member of Company K of the 108th Kentucky Infantry, a company of black volunteers. When General Morgan, the famous southern raider, crossed the Ohio on his raid across southern Indiana, John was one of the black soldiers who, after heavy fighting, forced Morgan to recross the river and retreat south. He also participated in several skirmishes with cavalry troops commanded by the Confederate general Nathan Bedford Forrest, and he was a member of a black garrison at Fort Pillow, which was located on the Mississippi. When the fort was captured, many black soldiers were massacred in the skirmish. John was in several other battles, too, but said he "never once got a skinhurt."

John could not remember all the units he was attached to, but he recalled that one of his units was part of General Sherman's army. He said he was with a regiment that started out with Sherman on his famous march through Georgia, but shortly after the campaign got under way, his regiment was sent elsewhere. His regiment was near Vicksburg, Mississippi, when Lee surrendered. John said that when Lee surrendered, there was much shouting among the troops. He remembered the exact date of his discharge, March 20, 1866, which his daughter verified by producing his discharge papers.

At the end of the war, John was one of many soldiers put to work loading cannons on boats to be shipped up the river. His company returned to Kentucky on the steamboat *Indiana*. Upon his return to Glasgow, he saw his mother and other members of his family, who were then free, for the first time in six years. Shortly after his return to Glasgow, he saw several blacks walking down the highway and was attracted to a young girl wearing a yellow dress. He said to himself, "If she ain't married, there goes my wife." Later they met, and they were married on Christmas Day in 1866. After their marriage, they lived on their own farm near Glasgow for several years before moving to Louisville, where John worked in a lumberyard. He came to Gary in 1923, two years after the death of his wife. They had twelve children, four of whom were still living in 1937—two in Gary and two in the South. In 1935 he returned for a brief visit to Glasgow, where he had been a slave. President Grant was the first president for whom John cast his vote, and he continued to vote until old age prevented him from walking to the polls. Although Lincoln was one of his heroes, Teddy Roosevelt topped his list of great men, and he said he never failed to vote for him. Of Lincoln's death, he said, "Sure, now, I remember that well. We all feelin' sad, and all the soldiers had wreaths on their guns."

John was featured in the *Gary Post-Tribune* on May 29, 1937, as the "Lone Civil War Survivor to Ride in Monday [Memorial Day] Parade." The following obituary was published in the same paper on January 24, 1938 (p. 6):

> John Eubanks, Negro veteran of the Civil war and last surviving member of the Grand Army of the Republic residing in Gary, died last night. He was 98 years old and succumbed to the infirmities of old age.
>
> He died in the home of his son, John Eubanks, Jr., at 2721 Harrison. His body was removed to Smith's funeral home pending completion of funeral arrangements. He is survived by his son; a daughter, Mrs. Bertha Sloss, also of 2721 Harrison, 15 grandchildren and five great great grandchildren.
>
> Death took "Grandpa" Eubanks before he was able to realize his ambition to live to be 110 years old, the age reached by his paternal grandfather. "Grandpa" was born June 6, 1839, in Glasgow, Ky., where he was one of seven children born to a chattel of the Everett family of Glasgow. He was the last of the slave family to pass on. . . .

Here is John's narrative from the WPA files:

> *I remember well, us younguns on the Everett plantation. I worked since I can remember—hoein', pickin' cotton, and other chores 'round the farm. We didn't have much clothes—never no underwear, no shoes—old overalls and a tattered shirt, winter and summer. Come the winter, it be so cold my feet were plumb numb most of the time, and many a time, when we got a chance, we drove the hogs from out of the bogs an' put our feet in the warm, wet mud. They was cracked, and the skin on the bottoms and in the toes were cracked and bleedin' most of time, with bloody scabs, but the summer healed them again.*
>
> *"Does you-all remember, Grandpap," his daughter asked, "your master? Did he treat you mean?" No, it were done thataway. Slaves were whipped and punished, and the younguns belonged to the master to work for him or to sell. When I were 'bout six years old, Marse Everett give me to Tony Eubanks as a weddin' present when he married Marse's daughter, Becky. Becky wouldn't let Tony whip her slaves who came from her father's plantation. "They are my property," she said, "an' you can't whip them." Tony whipped his other slaves, but not Becky's.*
>
> *I remember how they tied the slave 'round a post, with hands tied together 'round the post. Then a husky [man] lashed his back with a snake-*

skin lash till his back were cut and bloodened. The blood spattered an' his back all cut up. Then they'd pour saltwater on him. That dried and hardened and stuck to him. He never take it off till it healed. Sometimes I see Marse Everett hang a slave tiptoe. He tied him up so he stand tiptoe an' leave him thataway. Marse Everett whipped me once, and mother, she cried. Then Marse Everett say, "Why you-all cry? You cry, I whip another of these younguns." She try to stop. He whipped another. He say, "If'n you-all don't stop, you be whipped too!" And mother, she tried to stop, but tears roll out, so Marse Everett whip her too.

I wanted to visit Mother when I belong to Marse Eubanks, but Becky say, "You-all best not see your mother, or you want to go all the time." She want me to forget Mother, but I never could. When I come back from the army, I go home to Mother and say, "Don't you know me?" She say, "No, I don't know you." I say, "You don't know me?" She say, "No, I don't know you." I say, "I'se John." Then she cry and say how I'd growed, and she thought I'se dead this long time. I done explain how the many fights I'se in with no scratch, and she bein' happy.

I be twenty-one when war broke out. Marse Eubanks say to me, "You-all don't need to run 'way if'n you-all want to join up with the army." He say, "There would be a fine if'n slaves run off. You-all don't have to run off; go right on, and I don't pay that fine." He say, "Enlist in the army, but don't run off." Now I walk thirty-five mile from Glasgow to Bowling Green to this place, to the enlistin' place. From home, four mile to Glasgow; to Bowling Green, thirty-five mile. On the road I meet up with two boys, so we go on. They run 'way from Kentucky, and we go together. Then some bushwhackers come down the road. We's scared and run to the woods and hid. As we run through the woods, pretty soon we heard chickens crowing. We fill our pockets with stones. We goin' to kill chickens to eat. Pretty soon we heard a man holler, "You come 'round outta there," and I see a white man and come out. He say, "What you-all doin' here?" I turn 'round and say, "Well, boys, come on boys," an' the boys come out. The man say, "I'm Union soldier. What you-all doin' here?" I say, "We goin' to enlist in the army." He say, "That's fine," and he say, "Come 'long." He say, "Get right on white man's side." We go to station. Then he say, "You go right down to the station and give your information." We keep on walkin'. Then we come to a white house with stone steps in front, so we go in. An' we got to enlistin' place and join up with the army. Then we go trainin' in the camp, and we move on. Come to a little town . . . a little town. We come to Bowling Green, then to Louisville. We come to a river . . . a river, the Mississippi.

We were infantry, and pretty soon we gets in plenty fights, but not a scratch hit me. We chase them cavalry. We run them all night, and next mornin', the captain, he say, "They done broke down." When we rest, he say,

"See, they don't trick you." I say, "We got all the army men together. We hold them back till help come."

We don't have no tents. Sleep on naked ground in wet and cold and rain. Most the time we's hungry, but we win the war. And Marse Eubanks tell us we no more his property; we's free now.

39. JOHN W. FIELDS

Twelve Children Were Taken from My Mother in One Day

John W. Fields
(Courtesy of the Manuscript Division, Library of Congress)

When interviewed, John W. Fields lived at 2120 North 20th Street in Lafayette and was employed as a domestic in the home of Judge Barnett. He was born in 1848 on the plantation of David Hill near Owensburg, Kentucky. According to newspaper clippings about him in the files of the Tippecanoe County Historical Society, he died in Lafayette on February 7, 1953, and is buried in Springvale Cemetery. Despite adverse circumstances, John worked hard, saved his money, and became a respected property owner and a member of the Second Baptist Church in Lafayette. The WPA fieldworker speaks of John as "the owner of three properties, unmortgaged" and "a fine example of a man who has lived a morally and physically clean life." John said that black slaves were ardent believers in ghosts, supernatural powers, tokens, and signs and gave the field-

worker some beliefs, as well as a familiar folktale, during one of the two interviews with him. Here is John's story:

> My name is John W. Fields, and I'm eighty-nine years old. I was born
> March 27, 1848, in Owensburg, Kentucky. That's 115 miles below Louis-
> ville, Kentucky. There were eleven other children besides myself in my fam-
> ily. When I was six years old, all of us children were taken from my parents
> because my master died and his estate had to be settled. We slaves were di-
> vided by this method: Three disinterested persons were chosen to come to
> the plantation, and together they wrote the names of the different heirs on a
> few slips of paper. These slips were put in a hat and passed among us slaves.
> Each one took a slip, and the name on the slip was the new owner. I hap-
> pened to draw the name of a relative of my master who was a widow. I can't
> describe the heartbreak and horror of that separation. I was only six years
> old, and it was the last time I ever saw my mother for longer than one night.
> Twelve children were taken from my mother in one day! Five sisters and two
> brothers went to Charleston, [West?] Virginia; one brother and one sister
> went to Lexington, Kentucky; one sister went to Hartford, Kentucky; and
> one brother and myself stayed in Owensburg, Kentucky. My mother was
> later allowed to visit among us children for one week of each year, so she
> could only remain a short time at each place.
>
> My life prior to that time was filled with heartaches and despair. We
> arose from four to five o'clock in the morning, and parents and children
> were given hard work, lasting until nightfall gave us our respite. After a
> meager supper, we generally talked until we grew sleepy and had to go to
> bed. Some of us would read, if we were lucky enough to know how.
>
> In most of us colored folks was the great desire to able to read and write.
> We took advantage of every opportunity to educate ourselves. The greater
> part of the plantation owners were very harsh if we were caught trying to
> learn or write. It was the law that if a white man was caught trying to edu-
> cate a Negro slave, he was liable to prosecution entailing a fine of fifty dol-
> lars and a jail sentence. We were never allowed to go to town, and it was not
> until after I ran away that I knew that they sold anything but slaves, to-
> bacco, and whiskey. Our ignorance was the greatest hold the South had on
> us. We knew we could run away, but what then? An offender guilty of this
> crime was subjected to very harsh punishment.
>
> When my master's estate had been settled, I was to go with the widowed
> relative to her place. She swung me up on her horse behind her and prom-
> ised me all manner of sweet things if I would come peacefully. I didn't fully
> realize what was happening, and before I knew it, I was on my way to my
> new home. Upon arrival her manner changed very much, and she took me
> down to where there was a bunch of men burning brush. She said, "See these
> men?" I said, "Yes." "Well, help them," she replied. So at the age of six I start-

ed my life as an independent slave. From then on, my life as a slave was a repetition of hard work, poor quarters and board. We had no beds at that time; we just bunked on the floor. I had one blanket, and many's the night I sat by the fireplace during the long cold nights in the winter. My missus had separated me from all my family but one brother with sweet words, but that pose was dropped after she reached her place. Shortly after I had been there, she married a northern man by the name of David Hill. At first he was very nice to us, but he gradually acquired a mean and overbearing manner toward us. I remember one incident that I don't like to remember. One of the women slaves had been very sick, and she was unable to work just as fast as he thought she ought to. He had driven her all day with no results. That night after completing our work he called us all together. He made me hold a light while he whipped her and then made one of the slaves pour saltwater on her bleeding back. My innards turn yet at that sight.

A turkey gobbler mysteriously disappeared from one of the neighboring plantations, and the local slaves were accused of committing the fowl to a boiling pot. A slave convicted of theft was punished severely. As all of the slaves denied any knowledge of the turkey's whereabouts, they were instructed to make a search of the entire plantation. On one part of the place there was a large peach orchard. At the time, the trees were full of the green fruit. Under one of the trees was a large cabinet, or safe, as they were called. One of the slaves accidentally opened the safe, and, behold, there was Mr. Gobbler peacefully seated on a number of green peaches. The slave immediately ran back and notified his master of the discovery. The master returned to the orchard with the slave to find that the slave's wild tale was true. A turkey gobbler sitting on a nest of green peaches is a bad omen.

The slave owner had a son who had been seriously injured some time before by a runaway team, and a few days after this unusual occurrence with the turkey, the son died. After his death, the word of the turkey's nesting venture and the death of the slave owner's son spread to the four winds, and for some time after, this story was related wherever there was a public gathering with the white people or the slave population.

All through the South a horseshoe was considered an omen of good luck. Rare was the southern home that did not have one nailed over the door. This insured the household and all who entered of pleasant prospects while within the home. If while in the home you should perhaps get into a violent argument, never hit the other party with a broom, as it was a sure indication of bad luck. If Granddad had the rheumatics, he would be sure of relief if he carried a buckeye in his pocket.

When a 250-pound hog disappeared, the planter was certain that the culprit was among his group of slaves, so he decided to personally conduct a quiet investigation. One night shortly after the moon had risen in the sky, two of the slaves were seated at a table in one of the cabins talking of the *experiences of the day. A knock sounded on the door. Both slaves jumped up and cautiously peeked out of the window. Lo, there was the master patiently waiting for an answer. The visiting slave decided that the master must not see both of them, and he asked the other to conceal him while the master was there. The other slave told him to climb into the attic and be perfectly quiet. When this was done, the tenant of the cabin answered the door. The master strode in and gazed about the cabin. He then turned abruptly to the slave and growled, "All right, where is that hog you stoled?" "Massa," replied the slave, "I know nothing about no hog." The master was certain that the slave was lying and told him so in no uncertain terms. The terrified slave said, "Massa, I know nothing of any hog. I never seed him. The Good Man up above knows I never seed him. He knows everything, and He knows I didn't steal him!" The man in the attic by this time was aroused at the misunderstood conversation taking place below him. Disregarding all, he raised his voice and yelled, "He's a liar, Massa; he knows just as much about it as I do!"*

At the beginning of the Civil War I was still at this place as a slave. It looked at the first of the war as if the South would win, as most of the big battles were won by the South. This was because we slaves stayed at home and tended the farms and kept their families. To eliminate this solid support of the South, the Emancipation Act was passed, freeing all slaves. Most of the slaves were so ignorant they didn't realize they were free. The planters knew this, and as Kentucky never seceded from the Union, they would send slaves into Kentucky from other states in the South and hire them out to plantations. For these reasons I did not realize that I was free until 1864. I immediately resolved to run away and join the Union Army, and so my brother and I went to Owensburg, Kentucky, and tried to join. My brother was taken, but I was refused as being too young. I tried at Evansville, Terre Haute, and Indianapolis, but was unable to get in. I then tried to find work and was finally hired by a man at $7.00 a month. That was my first independent job. From then on I went from one job to another working as a general laborer.

I married at twenty-four years of age and had four children. My wife has been dead for twelve years and eight months. Always remember that "The brightest man, the prettiest flower, may be cut down and withered in an hour." Today, I am the only surviving member who helped organize the Second Baptist Church here in Lafayette, sixty-four years ago. I've tried to live according to the way the Lord would wish. God Bless you.

    The clock of life is wound but once.
    Today is yours, tomorrow is not.
    No one knows when the hands will stop.

40. GEORGE FORTMAN

Indian Slaves

When interviewed, George Fortman was blind and feeble. Though a former slave, he said that no black blood ran "through his veins." His mother was part Native American, and his white master, Ford George, was his mother's father as well as his father. According to the interviewer, "The face of George Fortman registered sorrow and pain; it had been hard for him to retell the story of the dark road to strange ears." Although the George family never sold slaves or separated black families, George remembered slave auctions where blacks were stripped of their clothing to exhibit their bodies. He recalled seeing many boats loaded with slaves on the way to slave markets, and some of the George slaves were employed as pilots on the boats. George himself held a number of positions on boats, including roustabout, cabin boy, cook, and pilot.

Too young to fight in the Civil War, George stayed home and worked during the war. He said there was plenty of wild game on the plantation, and the hunting season was always open. He recalled seeing many wolves, wild turkeys, catamounts, and deer near the Grand River. He said, "Pet deer loafed around the milking pens and ate the feed from the mangers."

At the time of the interview, George, a devout Christian, had lived in Evansville for thirty-five years, but he had had business connections there for sixty-two years. For eleven years he worked as a janitor at Lockyear Business College. He lived in a room at Bellemeade Avenue and Garvin Street and from there often walked to Lincoln High School, where he enjoyed watching and listening to students playing about the school. "They are free," he said. "They can build their own destinies; they did not arrive in this life by births of unsatisfactory circumstances. They have the world before them, and my grandsons and granddaughters are among them." Here is George's story, though apparently not verbatim:

> The story of my life I'll tell to you with sincerest respect to all and love to many, although reviewing my childhood and early youth causes me great pain. My story necessarily begins by relating events which occurred in 1838, when hundreds of Indians were rounded up like cattle and driven away from the Wabash Valley. It is a well-known fact recorded in the histories of Indiana that the long journey from the beautiful Wabash Valley was a horrible experience for the Indians, but I know the tradition as it relates to my own family. From this forced departure came the tragedy of my birth.
>
> My two ancestors, John Hawk, a Blackhawk brave, and Rachael, a Choctaw, had made themselves a home. He was a hunter and a fighter but professed faith in Christ through the influence of missionaries. My great-grand-

mother, Rachael, passed the facts on to her children, and they have been handed down for four generations. I, in turn, have given the traditions to my children and grandchildren. The Indians and the white settlers in the valley transacted business with each other and were friendly towards each other, as I have been told by my mother, Eliza, and my grandmother, Courtney Hawk.

The missionaries often called the Indian families together for the purpose of teaching them, and the Indians had been invited, prior to being driven from the valley, to a sort of festival in the woods. They had prepared much food for the occasion. The men had gone on a long hunt to provide meat, and the women had prepared much corn and other grain to be used at the feast. All the tribes had been invited to a council, and the poor people were happy, not knowing they were being deceived.

The decoy worked, for while the Indians were worshiping God, the meeting was rudely interrupted by orders of the governor of the state. The governor, whose duty it was to protect the poor souls, caused them to be taken captives and driven away at the point of swords and guns. My grandmother said the Indians prayed in vain to be allowed to return to their homes. Instead of giving the Indians their liberty, some several hundred horses and ponies were captured to be used in transporting the Indians from the valley. The homes of the Indians were reduced to ashes. Many of the older Indians and many children died on the long journey, and traditional stories speak of that journey as the "trail of death."

After long weeks on the trail, my great-grandfather and his wife became acquainted with a party of Indians going to the canebrakes of Alabama. They were not well-fed or well-clothed, and they were glad to travel south, believing the climate would be more favorable to their health. After a long and dreary journey, the Indians reached Alabama. Rachael had her youngest child strapped on her back, while John had cared for the older child, Lucy. Sometimes she walked beside her father, but often she became weary or sleepy, and he carried her, besides blankets and food, many miles of the journey. An older daughter, Courtney, also accompanied her parents.

When they approached the cane lands they heard the songs of Negro slaves working in the cane. Soon they were in sight of the slave quarters of Patent George's plantation. The Negroes made the Indians welcome, and the slave owner allowed them to occupy the cane house. Thus, the Indians became slaves of Patent George.

Worn out from the long journey, John Hawk became too ill to work in the sugar cane. Kindly Negroes helped care for him, but he lived only a few months. Rachael and her two children remained on the plantation, working with the slaves. She had nowhere to go, no home to call her own. She had become a slave, and her children had become chattel.

A year passed, and unhappiness came to Rachael, for her daughter, Courtney, became the mother of a daughter fathered by the slave owner's son, Ford George. The parents called the little girl "Eliza" and were very fond of her. Rachael became the mother of Patent George's son, Patent George, Jr.

Family tradition states that in spite of these unfortunate circumstances the people on the Georges' southern plantation were prosperous, happy, and lived in peace with each other. Patent George grew weary of the southern climate, though, and took his slaves to the iron ore region of western Kentucky, where their hard work amassed a fortune for the slave owner. Rachael Hawk and her daughters—Courtney, Lucy, and Rachael—came with the George family's wagon trains to Kentucky, but Rachael Hawk died on the journey from Alabama. The other full-blooded Indians entered Kentucky as slaves.

The male slaves soon became skilled workers in the Hillman Rolling Mills. A man named Trigg was owner of the vast iron works called the "Chimneys" in the region, but they were listed separately as the Hillman, Dixon, Boyer, Kelley, and Lyons Furnaces. For more than a half century these chimneys were the most valuable development in western Kentucky. Opened in 1810, these furnaces refined iron ore to supply the United States Navy with cannonballs and grapeshot, and the iron smelting industry continued here until after the close of the Civil War.

No slaves were beaten on the Georges' plantation, and old Missus Hester didn't allow any slave to be sold. She was a devoted friend to all.

As Eliza George, daughter of Ford George and Courtney Hawk, grew into young womanhood, Ford George went oftener and oftener to social functions. He was admired for his skill with firearms and for his horsemanship. While Courtney and his child remained at the plantation, Ford enjoyed the companionship of the beautiful women of the vicinity. At last, he brought home Loraine, his young bride. Courtney was stoical, showed no hurt, and helped Missus Hester and Missus Loraine with the housework.

Missus Loraine became mother of two sons and a daughter, and the big, white, two-story house facing the Cumberland River at Smiths Landing, Kentucky, became a place of laughter and happy occasions, so my mother told me many times. Suddenly sorrow settled over the home and the laughter turned into wailing, for Ford George's body was found pierced through the heart. Eliza was nowhere to be found. Ford's body lay in state many days. Friends and neighbors came bringing flowers. His mother, bowed with grief, looked on the still face of her son and understood—understood why death had come and why Eliza had gone away.

The beautiful home on the Cumberland River with its more than 600 acres of productive land was put into the hands of an administrator of es-

tates to be readjusted in the interest of the George heirs. It was only then Missus Hester went to Aunt Lucy and demanded of her to tell where Eliza could be found. Aunt Lucy told her, "She has gone to Alabama. Eliza was scared to stay here." A party of searchers was sent to look for Eliza and found her hiding in a canebrake in the lowlands of Alabama nursing a baby boy at her breast. They took Eliza and the baby back to Kentucky. I am that baby, that child of unfortunate birth. My white uncles told Missus Hester that if Eliza brought me back they were going to build a fire and put me in it since my birth was so improper to all of them, but Missus Hester always did what she believed was right, and I was brought up by my own mother. We lived in a cabin at the slave quarters, and Mother worked in the broom cane. Missus Hester named me Ford George, in contempt, but remained my friend. She was never angry with my mother. She knew a slave had to submit to her master, and, besides, at the time Eliza didn't know she was Ford George's daughter. Missus Hester believed I would be feeble either in mind or body because of my unfortunate birth, but I developed as other children did and was well treated by Missus Hester, Missus Lorainne, and her children. When Patent George died, Missus Hester married a man named Lam, and the slaves kept working at the rolling mills and making a fortune for the George families.

Five years before the outbreak of the Civil War, Missus Hester called all the slaves together and gave us our freedom. Courtney, my grandmother, kept house for Missus Lorainne and wanted to stay on, so I, too, was kept at the George home. There was a sincere friendship as great as the tie of blood between the white family and the slaves. My mother married one of Ford George's Negro ex-slaves and bore children for him. Her health failed, and when Missus Puss, the only daughter of Missus Lorainne, learned she was ill, she persuaded Eliza's husband to sell his property and bring Eliza back to live with her.

When the Freedmen started teaching school in Kentucky the census taker called to enlist me as a pupil. "What do you call this child?" he asked Missus Lorainne. "We call him the Little Captain because he carried himself like a soldier," said Missus Lorainne. "He is the son of my husband and a slave woman, but we are rearing him." Missus Lorainne told the stranger that I had been named Ford George, and he suggested she list me in the census as George Fordman, which she did, but she never allowed me to attend the Freedmen's School, desiring to keep me with her own children and let me be taught at home. My mother's half brother, Patent George, allowed his name to be reversed to George Patent when he enlisted in the Union Army at the outbreak of the Civil War.

It was customary to conduct a funeral differently than it is conduct-ed now. I remember I was only six years old when old Missus Hester Lam passed on to her eternal rest. She was kept out of her grave several days in order to allow time for relatives, friends, and ex-slaves to be notified of her death. The house and yard were full of grieving friends. Finally the lengthy procession started to the graveyard. Within the Georges' parlors there had been Bible passages read, prayers offered up, and hymns sung. Now, the casket was placed in a wagon drawn by two horses. The casket was covered with flowers, while the family and friends rode in ox-carts, horse-drawn wagons, or on horseback. With still many on foot, they made their way towards the river. When we reached the river there were many canoes busy putting the people across. Besides, the ferry boat was in use to ferry vehicles over the stream. The ex-slaves were crying and praying and telling how good Granny had been to all of them and explaining how they knew she had gone straight to Heaven because she was so kind and a Christian. There weren't nearly enough boats to take the crowd across if they crossed back and forth all day, so my mother, Eliza, improvised a boat or "gunnel," as the craft was called, by placing a wooden soap box on top of a long pole; then she pulled off her shoes, and, taking two of us small children in her arms, she paddled with her feet and put us safely across the stream. We crossed directly above Iuka, Livingston County, three miles below Grand River.

At the burying ground a great crowd had assembled from the neighborhood across the river, and there were more songs and prayers and much weeping. The casket was let down into the grave without the lid being put on, and everybody walked up and looked into the grave at the face of the dead woman. They called it the "last look," and everybody dropped flowers on Missus Hester as they passed by. A man then went down and nailed on the lid, and the earth was thrown in with shovels. The ex-slaves filled in the grave, taking turns with the shovel. Some of the men had worked at the smelting furnaces so long that their hands were twisted and hardened from contact with the heat. Their shoulders were warped and their bodies twisted, but they were strong as iron men from their years of hard work. When the funeral was over Mother put us across the river on the "gunnel," and we went home, all missing Missus Hester.

My cousin worked at Princeton, Kentucky, making shoes. He had never been notified that he was free by the emancipation Mrs. Hester had given to her slaves, and he came loaded with money to give to his white folks. Missus Lorainne told him it was his own money to keep or to use, as he had been a free man several months.

As our people, white and black and Indians, sat talking they related how they had been warned of approaching trouble. Jack said the dogs had been howling around the place for many nights, and that always presaged a death in the family. Jack had been compelled to take off his shoes and turn them soles-up near the hearth to prevent the howling of the dogs. Uncle Robert *told how he believed some of Missus Hester's enemies had planted a shrub near her door, and planted it with a curse so that when the shrub bloomed the old woman passed away. Then another man told how a friend had been seen carrying a spade into his cousin's cabin, and the cousin had said, "Daniel, what for you brung that weapon into my cabin? That very spade will dig my grave," and, sure enough, the cousin died and the same spade was used in digging his grave.*

I've never believed in witchcraft or spells, but I remember my Indian grandmother predicted a long, cold winter when she noticed the pelts of the coons and other furred creatures were exceedingly heavy. When the breast-bones of the fowls were strong and hard to cut with a knife it was a sign of a hard, cold, and snowy winter. Another superstition was "A green winter, a new graveyard; a white winter, a green graveyard."

More than any other superstition entertained by the slave Negroes, the most harmful was the belief in conjurers. One old Negro woman boiled a bunch of leaves in an iron pot, boiled it with a curse, and scattered the tea made from the leaves, and she firmly believed she was bringing destruction to her enemies. The old woman said, "Wherever that tea is poured there will be toil and troubles."

Things changed at the George homestead, as they change everywhere. When the Civil War broke out many slaves enlisted in hopes of receiving freedom. The George slaves were already free, but many thought it their duty to enlist and fight for the emancipation of their fellow slaves. My mother took her family and moved away from the plantation and worked in the broom cane. Soon she discovered she couldn't make enough to rear her children, and we were turned over to the court to be bound out.

I was bound out to David Varnell in Livingston County by order of Judge Busch, and I stayed there until I was fifteen years old. My sister learned that I was unhappy there and wanted to see my mother, so she influenced James Wilson to take me into his home. Soon good-hearted Jimmy Wilson took me to see Mother, and I went often to see her.

In 1883 I left the Wilson home and began working and trying to save some money. River trade was prosperous, and I became a roustabout. The life of the roustabout varied some with the habits of the roustabout and the disposition of the mate. We played cards, shot dice, and talked to the girls who always met the boats. The "Whistling Coon" was a popular song with the boatmen and a version of "Dixie Land." One song we often sang when nearing a port was worded "Hear the trumpet sound":

> Hear the trumpet sound,
> Stand up and don't sit down,
> Keep steppin' 'round and 'round,
> Come join this elegant band.
> If you don't step up and join the bout,

Old Missus sure will find it out,
She'll chop you in the head with a golden ax,
You never will have to pay the tax,
Come join the roustabout band.

I have always kept in touch with my white folks, the George family. Four years ago Missus Puss died, and I was sent for, but was not well enough to make the trip home.

I lived at Smiths Landing and remember the battle at Fort Donelson. It was twelve miles away, and a long cinder walk reached from the fort for nearly thirty miles. The cinders were brought from the iron ore mills, and my mother and I have walked the length of it many times. Boatloads of soldiers passed Smiths Landing by day and night, and the reports of cannon could be heard when battles were fought. We children collected cannonballs near the fort for a long time after the war.

I've always been befriended by three races of people, the Caucasian, the African, and the Negro [Indian?]. I've worked as a farmer, a river man, and been employed by the Illinois Central Railroad Company, and in every position I've held I've made loyal friends of my fellow workmen.

41. ALEX FOWLER

The First Black in Lake County

The fieldworker got her material on Alex Fowler from printed sources: the *Lake County Star* (January 5, 1934) and a history of Lake County, which she cites as volume 10, p. 137. Here is the fieldworker's report:

Lorenzo McGlason, a colonel in the northern army during the Civil War, came upon a Negro lad on a field of battle, while leading his troops in the southern states. He took the lad, named Alex Fowler, with him, and became greatly attached to him.

When President Lincoln issued the proclamation freeing the slaves, Col. McGlason sent the Negro lad up to his brother, W. G. McGlason, in Crown Point.

This young boy was among the first of the Negroes to cross the Mason and Dixon Line into the northern states, after the Emancipation Proclamation. He was the first Negro in Lake County.

Alex attended the public school in Crown Point and later operated the barber shop. The white boys were his companions, and he was held in high esteem by them, no color line barring their friendship.

On December 1934 F. E. Farley received a letter from Alex Fowler, who is now residing in Lansing, Michigan, and is past 85 years of age.

42. MATTIE FULLER

I Have Sang Myself to Death

Martha Susan Pierce Jacobs ("Mattie") Fuller was around eighty-two years old when she was interviewed. The next-to-the-youngest of eight children, she was born in Shelby County, Kentucky, of slave parents. In a two-part feature that appeared in the *Bloomington Daily-Telephone* shortly after Mattie's death, Zella Kinser Holland reported that Mattie had said that her father was "Andy Pierce and lived with a Shouse family in Boston, Ky." Her mother "was Cassie Young . . . and she lived with the Billy Grieg family at Simpsonville, Ky."

Following the Civil War, when she was six, Mattie crossed the Ohio River on a barge with her parents and seven brothers and sisters, and they settled in the Woodyard neighborhood northwest of Bloomington. Soon after their arrival, her mother died of a heart attack, and Mattie then lived briefly with General Morton Hunter and his wife on North Walnut Street until they found a permanent home for her with Dr. and Mrs. John J. Durand (also spelled Durant in the WPA files), who, according to Ms. Holland, "sent her to Louisville, Kentucky, to take a training course in hair dressing and also gave her music lessons from the best music teachers in Bloomington." On December 3, 1873, Mattie married Henry Clay Jacobs, a woodcutter, who along with their five children preceded her in death. In 1906 she married Levi Fuller, a cook on a Monon diner, but their unhappy marriage ended in separation, and he died around 1931. Mattie was living alone at 906 West Kirkwood Avenue when interviewed by the WPA fieldworker, who described her as "a very nice old lady, and very devout. She is just a town institution, something like the original plat. Everyone either knows her or knows who she is."

Mattie was well-known in the community because in the front of her home on West Kirkwood she operated Bloomington's earliest beauty shop for a number of years, and she also was active with her church and her music. She had a small folding organ, which she played while singing church songs and spirituals. According to Ms. Holland, "She often played and sang on the corner of the court house lawn for large appreciative crowds, who applauded and gave generously." Mattie told Ms. Holland, "I just believe what makes me like music so well is hearing a big harp as my folks come cross the Ohio river on the boat. That was the sweetest music I ever heard. A lady sat there and just kept playing on that great big harp."

According to her obituary in the *Bloomington Daily-Telephone* (August 23, 1940), "Though Mrs. Fuller had a difficult enough time providing for herself and the many who so frequently sought her aid, her greatest effort was in raising funds for the A.M.E. church of which she was a most staunch member. For 28 summers, Mattie served with her organ and favorite hymns at Bethany Park sessions and was able to collect some $7,000 all of which was devoted to the construction of the present church structure." Mattie would not accept a federal old-age pension when she became eligible, stating, "Honey, I was born a slave and now I'm going to stay free." Here is her story from the WPA files:

I was born in Kentucky. My father and mother were slaves. There were eight of us children. When we came to Indiana, we crossed the Ohio River. I have always enjoyed music, and on the boat when we came across, someone was picking a banjo. I have never forgotten it.

I was bound out to Dr. Durant. When I was fourteen, I married. The record of my binding out is in the courthouse. The people I was bound to gave me a dollar and told me to build a house. I have been building ever since. Nurre gave me that window because I am such a church worker. It is plate glass. Judge Wilson and Mrs. Wilson gave me that washstand. Lately I decided to build a rag house. When people asked me what I meant by a rag house, I said, "Never you mind; you'll see." I started last Saturday by papering this room.

I went to school in Louisville and learned how to make skin lotion and vanishing cream, which I sold for a living. When anyone asks me my age, I say, "Never you mind," and when they ask me how big a girl I was at the time of the Civil War, I say, "Never you mind."

Once I went to Kentucky to visit old missus. I was told to go to the back door, as colored people were not allowed at the front door. So when I got there, I went to the back door. A colored woman opened the door. She said to old missus, "Here is Mattie, Cassie's daughter, come to visit you." They invited me in, and we had the best dinner I ever tasted. We sat up half the night talking. They told me a lot of things about my father and mother that I never knew before. I stayed two weeks and had a fine time. When I came away, they gave me a lot of things.

I have lived in Bloomington forever. I have played and sang. I have sang myself to death. I have brought in $12,000 for my church. I would go places and play on my organ and sing. The white folks would crowd around and give me money for my church.

Here is my picture. There's my organ and my cup. There's my dress and my beads and my earrings and my slippers. That dress had a thousand beads on it. Some girls came one day and took my picture. I sell them for my church.

My brothers and sisters lived in Bloomington. They are all dead now. People are good to me. I can't bear to give up my home and liberty. My father and mother were slaves, and I was bound. So I want to stay in my home.

43. FRANCIS GAMMONS

Slaves Were Treated as Well as Could Be Expected

A brief summary of Francis Gammons's narrative was given to the field-worker by Francis Toney, who was living at 815 [South?] Ebright Street in Muncie at the time of the interview. Francis Gammons was born in 1835 on a tobacco plantation near Gallatin, Tennessee, and at the age of ninety-six she died at her home on East Jackson Street in Muncie. According to Ms. Toney, Francis Gammons said that "on the average" slaves were treated as well as could be expected on the plantation. Mrs. Gammons's husband, Wesley Gammons, ran away from the plantation and joined the Union Army during the Civil War. Ms. Toney said, "He wanted to be free and declared that he was willing to take his share in securing this freedom, which he did by fighting for the Union." When the Gammonses were set free, they walked to Gallatin, where they were remarried, for they feared they might lose their children if they were not legally married. Francis and Wesley Gammons lived in various southern communities until 1881, when they moved to Muncie. Wesley, a hod carrier, died a few months after the move.

44. JOHN HENRY GIBSON

He Liked Indianapolis So Well That He Decided to Stay

At the time of the interview, John Henry Gibson did not know his exact age, but according to the fieldworker, he was very old. Since he said he had fought in the Civil War, he could not have been a young man when the interview took place. His sight was nearly gone, as he could distinguish only light and dark. He claimed that he was proud of his name, having been named for his father's former master.

According to the WPA files, John was born a slave in Scott County, North Carolina. His owner, John Henry Bidding, was a wealthy farmer who also owned a hotel, or rooming house. When court was in session, officials stayed in the rooming house until the court affairs were settled. Bidding, who was kind to his slaves, died when John was very young. All of his slaves and property passed to his son, Joseph Bidding, who was as kind to his slaves as his father had been.

John's father was held first by General Lee Gibson, a neighboring farmer. His father met Elizabeth Bidding's maid, and they liked each other so much that Elizabeth Bidding bought John's father from General Gibson and let him marry her maid. John's mother lived only a short time, leaving one child.

After the Civil War, a white man by the name of Luster was moving to Ohio and took John with him. When they came to Indianapolis, John liked the city so well that he decided to stay. Luster told him if he ever became dissatisfied to come to Ohio, but John remained in Indianapolis until 1872, when he went back south and married. Later, he returned to Indianapolis, which he made his home.

After John's death in February 1939, first-page features on him appeared in both the *Indianapolis Star* (February 20, 1939) and the *Indianapolis Recorder* (February 25, 1939). The first of these articles, written by Edward L. Throm, reads in part:

> John [Gibson], weary of 112 years of life, died last week in his little shack at 1028 Colton street. A slave in North Carolina before the Civil War, he came to Indianapolis when he was 75 years old. He lived in this city 37 years.
>
> "I'se tired to death," he told a son a week before his death. He refused food or other nourishment to the end.
>
> At funeral services today, many friends, including a number of white persons he befriended, will pay homage to the former slave.
>
> Let one of them, Lee (Plez) Oliver, veteran Indianapolis policeman, tell the story of John Gibson:
>
> "Uncle John, whom I have known for years, must have helped more than 200 families during his life in Indianapolis," says Mr. Oliver. "A man of means in the poor community in the bottomlands around the City Hospital, he never refused a request for aid from struggling neighbors."
>
> Mr. Oliver explained that the former slave farmed a section of the bottomland[s] where the James Whitcomb Riley Hospital now stands.
>
> An old man even then, the diligent Negro raised corn and wheat, tended hogs and cattle, traded horses at his barn, and was successful most years. "When his neighbors, white and Negro alike, had bad years, Uncle John helped them. He gave them money and kept no books, as he could neither read nor write. 'They'll get around to it sometime,' was his only comment when he was asked how he would collect what was owed him," the policeman recalls.
>
> Several times there were hard winters for the Oliver family. On one of the first of these occasions, Mr. Oliver, then 12 years old, met Uncle John for the first time. He bore a note from his father to the Negro's house and found Uncle John sitting on his doorstep clad in his customary, spotlessly clean overalls.
>
> "What you got there, son?" asked the white-haired, white-mustached Negro.
>
> Told it was a note from Mr. Oliver, he said, "Read it to me." Then he brought out his old-fashioned leather snap purse and gave the boy money which meant that the Olivers could pay their rent.
>
> "On several occasions it has been told that he saw persons being evicted from their homes," Mr. Oliver said. "He'd walk up to the sheriff's deputies and say: 'How much do they owe?'"

"I think most of the people repaid Uncle John. He was respected too much for anyone to forget," Mr. Oliver said.

Uncle John, explaining once why he didn't worry about the money he loaned, told the boy, "I believe in the honesty of folks." Then the former slave smiled, "And I got a good memory too, son."

Opal L. Tandy's article on John in the *Recorder* agrees that his "little home at 1028 Colton street served as a refuge for under-privileged members of both races who came to him for advice, a loan, and sometimes a piece of bread," but says that John was around 115 years old when he died and was never a slave:

> During the last few years, Mr. Gibson had been doing plumbing work and about two years ago some acid leaked out of a pipe and caused his eyesight to be lost. Since then he had been on a steady decline and ate very little. John never was on the old folks' pension fund. He never wanted to be.
>
> Born in North Carolina about 115 years ago, he had lived in Indianapolis over 77 years. In his state, some Negroes were free men and Gibson never "tasted" slavery. John Gibson was a free, independent man and he acted it in every way, supporting himself until the end. He was the father of six children, was married twice. . . .

Tandy's article in the *Recorder* also provides information about John's last days:

> Gibson died early this week in his home alone and with no fire to keep him warm. But it was his wish that he went as he did. For days and days the veteran of 115 years had gone without fire and food. His son, John [George?], 873 Indiana avenue, heard about his self-inflicted fast and begged him to eat but to no avail.
>
> "I am just tired and want to rest," he murmured and refused to eat. The younger Gibson's wife sought to persuade him to take some food and he half-way promised to do so, but later declined.
>
> Sunday morning he was found dead by his son alone and unattended. The deputy coroner said he died from starvation.
>
> George said one time before this almost forty years ago, his father had gone on a fast for twelve days and locked himself up in a barn.
>
> His reply then was the same as it was several days ago, George said: "I am just tired and want to rest." George believes that his desire to fast periodically was the policy of some religious faith that his father harbored but never confessed to anyone.

45. PETER GOHAGEN

We Used to Have Some Fine Times

Peter Dunn
(Courtesy of the Manuscript Division, Library of Congress)

This photo is from the frontispiece of the Indiana interviews with
former slaves in the Library of Congress. Though identified as Peter
Dunn, who is mentioned in the Thomas Magruder interview, it
matches the description of Peter Gohagen, who was "big and strong of
physique," "revealed a grizzly, close-cropped head," and "wore a faded
blue heavy shirt and overalls and wool socks and thick brogans" as he
invited the fieldworker "to a chair on the porch."

When interviewed, Peter Gohagen was living at 648 West 6th Street in
New Albany. The fieldworker reported that "It was a very hot July day as I
trudged down the grassy path to Peter Gohagen's little clapboard house under
the mulberry tree. There he sat, with his old splint-bottomed chair tilted back
against the porch. It is hard to tell his age, but he must be nearly 90, although
he is big and strong of physique as yet. Taking off his battered felt hat, he
revealed a grizzly, close-cropped head, as he invited me to a chair on the
porch.... Hot as the day was, he wore a faded blue heavy shirt and overalls and
wool socks and thick brogans—all topped by the battered felt hat. I looked
around. His little house was neat and clean. Flowers grew in the yard. Chick-

ens pecked in the grass. Just inside the house door his wife sat and rocked as she 'jawed' with a visitor. Peter was very polite but distant until I told him what I wanted—some stories. Then he thawed out gradually and then completely when he discovered he knew my 'folks' in Kentucky." Here is Peter's story:

Yes, ma'am, I can remember well before freedom was declared. Indeed, I can. We lived with the Gohagen family just fourteen miles west of Elizabethtown in Kentucky near Rough Creek. My mother was Mary Gohagen. She wasn't really my mother. She just took me when I was little and raised me. She belonged to the Gohagens. I was about ten or twelve years old when freedom was declared. Some of the colored folks run off then, but we all had a good home, and some of us didn't leave for years.

You say your grandpappy lived near White Mills? Mr. George Cook, I remember him well. He was a little, heavyset Englishman. He had a great big place and a large family, too. He had a lot of niggers, but his favorites was always Aunt Barbara and Uncle Flem, an' when he died he left them a little farm on Nolin River. You say Aunt Barbara was your pa's nurse? Well, now, I sure am glad to see you, miss. Seems like folks from home. I ain't been back now for ten years. May never get back to the ol' homeplace again now. Yes, ma'am, ol' Aunt Barbara, what nursed your pa, was shore a mighty fine colored woman. She was low and heavyset and light-skinned. She nursed the Gohagen boys, too.

We used to have some fine times down in the valley. Used to have big barbecues down at White Mills on the different white folks' places. It was a white folks' affair, but we had just as good a time as they did. They'd roast whole sheep and beefs and pigs and chickens outdoors on spits over a big brick oven, and all the little ones would hang around for lickin's. We all got plenty to eat—sure enough, we did!

Then they used to be what they called beef shoots. The men all gathered at one place for a shootin' match. They all came for miles around. And the best shots would win a whole beef for a prize. They had plenty of eatin' then, too, and some drinkin'.

Do I remember the Big Dark [the total eclipse of the sun]? I sure does. About how long ago would that be now, ma'am? You say it was in the '60s? Well, it was right after the war. I was ridin' toward home on horseback, several of us. We noticed it kept gettin' darker and darker. We thought it was goin' to blow a storm and was anxious to get home before it hit. The women was all alone, and we knew they'd be scared.

We rode along as fast as we could, and every place we could see folks out lookin' at the sky and chickens runnin' and squawkin' and goin' to roost in the fence corner. Hogs hid under barns, and hosses got scared and kicked up their heels. Some of the fool chickens run against the rail fences and broke their necks. We could see dead chickens plumb till we got home.

There everybody was sure feared. Some of the colored folks was wringin' their hands and prayin' and some thought the end of the world had come. It kept gettin' darker, and the stars come out just same as it was night. Everybody went in their houses, 'cept the white folks, to wait till it quit doin' whatever it was doin'. Finally, it got light again, and everybody breathed easy again.

Yes, ma'am, I remember when Morgan and his soldiers went through Elizabethtown. The wagons and hosses was as long as from here, clear out of sight. A bunch of soldiers come through the place next to us. My Aunt Ceny lived on this place, and all the white folks and colored folks had hid their chickens 'cause they knew what would happen to them if they didn't. Aunt Ceny had hid hers under the porch. All was fine. The soldiers hunted around and didn't find much. Then Aunt Ceny's old Dominick rooster come out from under the porch and flapped his wings and crowed like it was Judgment Day. That fixed things. Of course, the soldiers found all her chickens, wrung their necks, and carried 'em off.

Yes, ma'am, I used to go huntin' with Bill and John Cook, Aunt Barbara's boys. Bill was tall and black, and John was in between. We sure had some times. I remember one night we was trying to shake a possum out of a tree, and the possum missed holt an' fell right on Bill Cook's head!

Did I ever see a ghost? Well, I should say I has. Seen plenty of 'em in my day. Why, one time I was a-ridin' one of Mr. Gohagen's fine hosses—Jessie her name was. We was a-goin' along through a woods, natural like. All at once I seen a possum in the road in front of us—walkin' along. Now, everybody knows that no possum that was ever born can go that fast. They are just naturally slow. And when I started Jessie up to catch that possum, he keeps goin' faster and faster, and here I was runnin' and still I couldn't catch that possum. He run along in the road ahead of me, just skimmin' the ground. And ever once in a while he would turn around and look at me. I knew right then that that weren't no natural possum 'cause possums ain't made that can outrun a hoss, let alone Jessie. She could run, that hoss. But I kept a-goin', and all of a sudden that possum just run up a hollow and disappeared. And I just kept on goin' until I got where I was goin'—yes, ma'am. That was a ghost, if I ever seed a ghost. And right after that my aunt died.

I remember when I was a little boy my ma used to send me to the store in White Mills. Sometimes I rode; sometimes I walked. I always liked to go there, for there was a hotel there for summer folks, and I could see the fine white ladies and men folks drivin' around in their carriages, and the storeman most always give me a lump of brown sugar.

Us folks used to have a mighty fine time down in the valley. After free-

dom come, I stayed around until I was about thirty and finally come on across the river into Indiana. I come here about fifty-five years ago. Some of my children was born here.

It sure is good to get to talk to you, ma'am. It's just like havin' a visit back home.

46. SIDNEY GRAHAM

Escaping from Ku Kluxers

When Hettie Watkins was interviewed about her father, Louis Watkins (q.v.), she also told a story about her uncle, Sidney Graham. As the fieldworker writes, "Miss Watkins, while giving the sketch of her father to this writer, related a story of one of her uncles which I regarded as a reflection of that courage with which the colored ex-slave was called upon, on various occasions, to defend his newly acquired rights as an American citizen. By such acts the ex-slave showed he appreciated his freedom, although it was not a point to be proven more than had already been proven by the many who had run away to join the Northern army, thus paying for their own freedom."

Ms. Watkins said that after the war, Sidney lived in Coltewah, Tennessee, and was employed in a powder mill on the farm of Peeler Parker. While working with some whites in the mill, Sidney accidentally splashed some hot water on a white man working near him. This caused some confusion, and at the close of the day some white men who were still incensed at Sidney told him that the Ku Kluxers would call on him that night. Knowing how the men felt, Sidney barricaded his house that night and prepared to take a firm stand.

In the middle of the night, sheeted forms approached the house, and a solemn voice called on Sidney to come out. Receiving no answer and growing impatient, the Ku Kluxers hurled themselves against the front door. It did not budge, so they attacked the rear door, which they broke through. The room was dark inside, and the Klansmen touched a torch to a big ball of cotton and threw the blazing ball into the middle of the room. Sidney shot and instantly killed the first man who tried to enter his house, so the Klansmen took the body and departed until dawn. In the meantime, Sidney slipped away, and later his family joined him in Nashville, Tennessee. He was never arrested.

47. MS. L. GREEN

If Anyone Got Paid for Her Family's History, She Wanted the Money

Ms. L. Green was the last of her immediate family. Both of her parents had been slaves. She said she knew "quite a bit" but wanted to wait awhile before telling any of her stories. She had been urged by a prominent Madison man to go back to Kentucky and pose for a picture by the old cabin where her father had been a slave. The man was to be paid for writing her family history, but Ms. Green said that if anyone got paid for her family's history, she wanted the money. She needed money badly because she had been on a WPA project that had been discontinued.

She told this much to the fieldworker, though. Her father was a carpenter and bellboy on the Preston farm in Kentucky near Bedford. He was always treated well. During the Civil War he fought under the name of Preston, but at the close of the war he took the name of Green again. He came to Madison at the close of the war. Ms. Green's mother was a slave near Milton, Kentucky; she did not know the exact location. Her mother's master was also her mother's father. The only punishment her mother ever received while in slavery was having one side of her hair clipped short for talking back to her mistress. The owner had come in just in time to hear her.

48. BETTY GUWN

Discipline Was Quite Stern

Betty Guwn was born a slave on March 25, 1832, on a large tobacco plantation near Canton, Kentucky. The plantation's second-largest product was corn. Betty was the personal attendant of the mistress. The house was a large Colonial mansion, and though she had many responsibilities, when she was caught up on her household duties, she was sent immediately to work in the fields. Discipline was stern on the plantation, and Betty was lined up for punishment with others on several occasions.

Betty was married while quite young by a method customary among slaves. If the slaves to be married were from different plantations, the slaveholders of the two estates bargained, and one slaveholder sold his rights to the other, on whose plantation the couple would then live. Betty's master bought her husband and set them up a log cabin, which was no more than a shack. Their cabin began to fill up with children, fifteen in all. The ventilation was ample, she said, and her husband could shoot a prowling dog from any of the four sides of the one-room cabin without opening the door. Cats could come into the cabin anywhere through the cracks between the logs. The slaves had "meetin'" some nights, and her mistress would call her and have her turn a tub against the mansion door to keep out the sound.

Her owner was very wealthy and also owned and managed a cotton farm of two thousand acres in Mississippi. Once a year he spent three months there picking and marketing his cotton. When he got ready to go to Mississippi, he called all his slaves around him and asked for volunteers to go with him. They had heard awful tales of the slave auction block at New Orleans, which was not far from the Mississippi plantation, but the owner would solemnly promise them that they would not be sold if they went down of their own accord. Betty continued her story:

> My missus called me to her and privately told me that when I was asked that question [about going to Mississippi] I should say to him, "I'll go." The master had to take a lot of money with him and was afraid of robbers. The day they were to start, my missus took me into a private room and had me remove most of my clothing. She then opened a strongbox and took out a great roll of money in bills. These she strapped to me in tight bundles, arranging them around my waist in the circle of my body. She put plenty of dresses over this belt, and when she was through I wore a bustle of money clear around my belt. I made a funny figure, but no one noticed my odd shape because I was a slave, and no one expected a slave to know better. We always got through safely, and I went down with my missus every year. Of course, my husband stayed at home to see after the family, and he took them to the fields when they were too young to work under the taskmaster, or overseer. Three months was a long time to be separated.

> When the Civil War came on there was great excitement among us slaves. We were watched sharply, especially for soldier timber for either army. My husband ran away early and helped Grant to take Fort Donaldson [Donelson]. He said he would free himself, which he did, and when we were finally set free, all our family prepared to leave. The master begged us to stay and offered us five pounds of meal and two pounds of pork jowl each week if we would stay and work. We all went to Burgard [Burkhart?], Kentucky, to live. At that time I was about 34 years old.

> My husband has been dead a long time, and I live with my children. If the good Lord spares me until next March the 25th, I will be 106 years old. I walk all about lively without crutches and eyeglasses, and I have never been sick until this year when a tooth gave me trouble, but I had it pulled.

49. JOSIE HARRELL

Buried Treasure on the Old Stephen Lee Place

An anonymous fieldworker interviewed Roy Monroe and Melvin Mering about Josie Harrell. They said that before the Civil War there was a very wealthy man by the name of Harrell who owned a large number of slaves in Louisiana. An epidemic of cholera swept through the South, and blacks were especially susceptible to the disease. Many of Harrell's slaves died, and he also caught the disease. Using Harrell's illness as an opportunity to escape, many of the slaves left; however, a beautiful mulatto slave woman named Josie steadfastly refused to leave her master. Through her devoted care and excellent nursing, Harrell finally recovered from the cholera.

Harrell then decided to free all his remaining slaves. He told Josie that if she would go with him to Ohio, he would marry her. After living in Ohio for a while, the couple decided to move to Indiana. A man by the name of Reed helped them with their barge down the Ohio River. They landed at New London in Saluda Township. When they landed, they rolled barrels of gold off the boat. They were so wealthy that Josie wore five-and ten-dollar gold pieces on her dresses for buttons and trimming.

About the time of the Civil War, the value of gold money was two and a half times that of greenbacks. Greenbacks were accepted as readily as gold where Harrell lived, though, so he traded in some of his gold. During the 1860s, someone broke into the Harrell home and stole many valuable jewels and a large sum of money. The suspect was a man named Wilson, who pretended to be a preacher and a doctor. A group of men captured him and strung him up on a tree in an attempt to force him to confess the crime. When they failed, they cut him down rather than murder him, but many people still thought he was guilty.

Later a treasure hunter arrived in this section of the country and told some men that he had heard that there was treasure buried on the old Stephen Lee place at the foot of a large wild cherry tree. The men became excited about finding the Harrell jewels and accompanied the treasure hunter to the Lee place. After the men dug a fairly deep hole and found nothing, the treasure hunter announced that he must have been wrong. Since there was nothing there, they might as well go home. The men left and never saw the treasure hunter again. Later, though, one of the men returned and found that the hole had been dug deeper. At the bottom of the hole there was a print left by a large iron kettle that had been removed.

No one ever learned whether the treasure hunter really found anything valuable. Some claimed he must have found the Harrell jewels; others thought that he had found money buried there by old Stephen Lee; and others thought that he found nothing of value.

50. MASTON HARRIS

Valued at $1,200, He Was Permitted to Buy His Freedom

Maston Harris reported that his father was a slave in Harrodsburg, Kentucky. Valued at $1,200, his father was permitted to work in an inn to buy his freedom; anything that he made over $13 a month was credited toward his freedom bill. It was his job to spy on card players and signal the "house cat" what cards the players held. Gambling for high stakes was customary, so when the house was winning, he received a large sum for his help. Thus, it did not take him long to save $1,200. His work was very risky, though, and if he had been caught, he probably would have been killed. His freedom papers, bearing the date 1833, were still in possession of the Harris family. At the time of the interview, the papers were in Cincinnati, but Maston had written to have them returned to him.

51. NEALY HARVEY

Many Times She Had Nothing to Eat

When interviewed about her grandmother, Nealy Harvey was living at 181 Geisendorff Street in Indianapolis. According to the fieldworker, "Nealy has not come very far. She was very untidy, her house and surroundings generally unkempt."

Nealy's grandmother was a slave, owned by a Mr. Stein in Byron, Mississippi. She was taken from her mother and sold when she was a very young child. Her master and his wife were mean to her, never allowing her any news of her parents and whipping her often and hard. Many times she had nothing to eat.

Her grandmother married one of the slaves on her master's farm and then went into the house as a cook. Her mistress was very hard to please. One day something went wrong in the house, and Mrs. Stein came to the kitchen to take her spite out on the cook, who was holding her new baby in her arms. Mrs. Stein started beating her and knocked the baby from her arms to the floor, fracturing the baby's skull. The baby died in a few days from the injury.

After slavery was abolished, Nealy's grandmother came to Indiana, got work as a cook, and worked until she was seventy-five years old.

52. JOSEPHINE HICKS

Her Master Was Also Her Father, so She Was Always Well Treated

Josephine Hicks, wife of Dr. Solomon Hicks (q.v.), was living on Poplar Street in Madison when she was interviewed about her grandmother, Mrs. Myers. Here is her narrative:

My grandmother, Mrs. Myers, was a slave near Danville, Kentucky. Her master was also her father, so she was always well treated. It was her work to do the spinning, so she had no outside work at all. When she was freed she *was given $500 in small denominations of paper money. When I was only six years of age she once called me to her, saying, "Josephine, I want to show you something." I can still see those little piles of paper money. These were kept intact for many years and later turned into the government for redemption in coins.*

My grandmother was one of the fortunate ones, if we can call anyone fortunate to be held in slavery. She couldn't realize why there was so many objecting to slavery, as she judged the custom by her own treatment.

53. DR. SOLOMON HICKS

All He Was Given Was a Three-Legged Horse to Start Life Anew

Dr. Solomon Hicks, husband of Josephine Hicks (q.v.), was living on Poplar Street in Madison when he was interviewed about his family's experiences in slavery.

My mother was a partial slave. By that I mean she was taken from her mother, who was a slave, while an infant and given to a family to raise. If she lived she would be a free girl when grown. She was given away in order that my grandmother would be of more value to her master if not burdened with the care of a baby. I have no idea who my real relatives were on my mother's side, but we always referred to the lady who raised her as "Grandmother."

My parents lived in Woodford County, Kentucky. I was in my fourth year before I knew my father. My three elder brothers and myself were trained by our mother's hand. She would put us to bed and cover up our heads, and if she caught us peeping out, it meant a whipping the next morning. But one time I heard someone enter our shack, and risking a whipping, I raised the covers a speck and saw the biggest, blackest man I had ever seen, my father. He had saddlebags and was giving out crusts of bread to my mother, who was putting it away in the old safe. Then to my delight, I saw him hand out a jug of milk. The next morning we little shavers did dance when we heard milk being poured out for our breakfast. In memory, I can plainly see us happily swaying to a rhythm all our own. My father wasn't allowed to come more than once a fortnight before the Emancipation Proclamation was issued. If it hadn't been for the kindness of Mr. David Mitchell, I don't see how my mother could have managed to keep us together. At this time we were living on his place. General Johnston had a camp in sight of our cabin, and it was our delight to fool around the soldiers. They planned to steal my brothers in two days and sell them down south. Mr. Mitchell heard of this and in his kindness sent word to my mother to keep her boys at home. Not satisfied with this, he sent two of his trusty slaves to guard our house until the danger was past.

There were large stone fences around, and I often saw the soldiers remove rocks and form a crude oven where they would store their food. If we were able to have a little pan of cornmeal to divide and gravy and meat, we considered it a feast in those times.

When the slaves became too numerous the old ones were sold down south in order to make room for the younger ones. I remember one gang that was sent south. Three owners brought their slaves together for a shipment. There must have been approximately seventy-five chained to a large cable. The line was about two blocks long, and as they marched off they were singing hymns that could be heard from here to the river, a distance of six blocks. In those days the true religion was manifest. No difference what happened, their faith never wavered. My uncle was in this gang, and so far as known he was the only one to return. He was sold three times, the last time purchasing his freedom. He was a minister and came back to Kentucky preaching.

After Father would cut one hundred pounds of hemp a day, he was allowed a very small pittance for all over that he could cut. My father was one of the unsung heroes as he labored this way for forty-seven long years to secure a little for his family. He was a basketmaker and would work far into the night in order to get a few baskets that he might sell at Clifton or Frankfort.

When my father was released after his forty-seven years of service, all he was given was a three-legged horse with which to start life anew. Our family remained in Woodford County, Kentucky, until 1869. Then we moved, and after several years we settled in Trimble County, Kentucky, near Milton. Here we were given a two-year lease on all the ground we could clear up, and we cleared forty acres and built a small log cabin. The man refused to renew the lease, so we then came to Indiana, settling near North Madison. Later we moved to Smyrna Township, Jefferson County, where my brothers and I purchased a small farm to provide a home for our parents. My mother died here. At this time I was in West Virginia working in order to meet the payment due on the farm. My father lived eight years longer, and he requested me to keep the younger children together. There were six small children. I kept them together until they grew old enough to want to leave the home nest. Then I bought the home farm and still own it, although I have been in Madison for many years.

Our name, Hicks, was taken from a white family who bore that name and passed it down to their slaves. It was customary for the slaves to take the name of their owner.

This story wouldn't be complete without a description of a family gathering. The only time I remember seeing my Aunt Lucinda and Uncle Jerry was *at a reunion at our house. We had coon for dinner, and Mother could sure cook coon. In honor of the occasion, she was using a new set of knives and forks. I can still see those white handles gleaming. Uncle Jerry was jabbing away at the coon when he broke his fork. Knowing a battle would be staged, he hid the fork under the tablecloth. Mother didn't find it until after he left and, of course, couldn't say anything to him.*

54. MRS. HOCKADAY

Northerners Would Not Trust Them

Mrs. Hockaday, the daughter of an ex-slave, was a large, pleasant, middle-aged woman living at 2581 Madison Street in Gary when interviewed. Like many other ex-slaves and children of ex-slaves, however, she did not want to discuss the cruel treatment that some slaves received, and she recounted in a general way only what she had heard former slaves discuss. The fieldworker paraphrased the interview.

Mrs. Hockaday said that after the Civil War many slaves, who for the most part were unskilled and uneducated, found it very difficult to adjust to their new way of life as free people. Formerly they had lived on the land of their masters, and although compelled to work long hours, their food and lodging were provided for them. After their emancipation, their lives changed. Not only were they free, but they had to make a living. Some former slaves found it difficult to secure employment, much as during the Depression. Fearful of not finding employment, many blacks never left the plantations, and many returned to the plantations to resume living much the same way they had before the war.

Mrs. Hockaday said that also as in the Depression years, relief stations were established in the North where blacks who were unable to find employment could obtain food and shelter. Since many blacks were experienced only in domestic service, when they came north they found it difficult to get jobs. The same was true during the Depression, when, driven by terrible living conditions in the South, blacks also came to Gary. Some slaveholders had schools for their slaves, and former slaves who could read and write were more successful in finding employment.

Another problem for blacks in the North was that they were not understood there as they were in the South. In the South they were trusted by their owners. During the Civil War, sometimes they were trusted with the family jewels and silver when the Northern army came marching by, whereas in the North, even though the North had freed the slaves, northerners would not trust them. For that reason many former slaves did not like northerners and remained on or returned to the southern plantations.

The Bible was the favorite book of former slaves, who were mainly Methodists and Baptists. Most slaves belonged to whatever church the slaveholder belonged to and generally continued in the same church after the war.

Since slaves took the name of their owners, children in the same family often would have different names. Mrs. Hockaday's father and his brothers and sisters all had different names. On the plantation they were called "Jones's Jim," "Brown's Jones," etc. Many on being freed left their old homes and adopted any name to which they took a fancy. One slave that Mrs. Hockaday remembered took the name of Green Johnson, and often he remarked that he surely had been green to adopt such a name. His grandson in Gary was an exact double for Clark Gable, except that he was black and Gable was white.

Many slaveholders gave their slaves small tracts of land that they could tend after working hours. Anything they raised belonged to them, and they could even sell the products and keep the money. Many slaves were able to save enough from these tracts to purchase their freedom long before emancipation.

Slaveholders thought that slavery was right and nothing was wrong about selling and buying human beings if they were black, much as a person would purchase a horse or automobile today. The owners who whipped their slaves usually stripped them to the waist and lashed them with a long leather whip, commonly called a blacksnake.

55. SAMANTHA HOUGH

I Believe a Little in Dreams

Samantha Hough, who was white, was ninety-three years old when she was interviewed by Velsie Tyler about slaves in Scott County.

Never were there many Negroes seen in the vicinity of Lexington. My Grandfather Pattison lived one and a half miles east of Lexington, where we lived later, and sometime about 1840 two very frightened runaway slaves came to his house. Grandfather hid them for a couple of days till something could be done with them. They were so nervous and afraid.

One finally decided to go back to his master, and Grandpa gave him a ticket so he could go. And he started the other one north, but the agents that hunted the escaped slaves surely heard about them, for Mother said they sneaked around our house all summer. Logs had been piled in the yard for a new barn. And at night they could be seen peeping and punching around in these. It was a shame a snake or something didn't jump out and scare them just a little.

A man in our neighborhood started to church at Concord one evening. As he walked along the creek, he saw a young girl walking ahead of him. He thought she was a stranger. He walked a little faster in order to overtake her. As he neared her, she arose and faded into the skies. He arrived at the church very pale and frightened. What it was we never knew, for he never drank or told lies. He really had seen something. Another man, rather wealthy, also told of seeing the vision of a woman—which looked very much like his wife, only she was so pale—as he crossed the same stream going to his farm.

I believe a little in dreams. To hear bells ringing in your ears is a sure sign of death. I have heard them so much this winter, and so many cousins and cousins by marriage have died—and last my own son. One time I dreamed my husband got his pension rejected, and everyone said that was impossible when I told it, but he did. Again I dreamed of a lost knife being in a certain place, and, sure enough, there it was.

56. ROBERT HOWARD

A Very Kind Old Man

At the time of his interview, Robert Howard was living in the Alpha Home for elderly African Americans at 1840 Boulevard Place in Indianapolis. He had no relatives, except a brother, and seemed satisfied living in the home. The fieldworker reported that Robert was a "very kind old man."

Robert was born in 1852 in Clark County, Kentucky. He said that his owner, Chelton Howard, was kind to him. His mother, with her five children, lived on the Howard farm in peace and harmony. His father, Beverly Howard, was held by Bill Anderson, who kept a saloon on the riverfront. Beverly was "hired out" in the house of Bill Anderson. He was allowed to go to the Howard farm every Saturday night to visit his wife and children. The family always looked forward to his visit with great joy, as they were devoted to him.

The Howard family, held first by Dr. Page in [Henry?] County, Kentucky, was sold only once. The family was not separated; the entire family was bought and kept together until slavery was abolished.

57. MATTHEW HUME

They Came to Indiana Homeless, Friendless, and Penniless

When interviewed, Matthew Hume and his wife had been married sixty-two years and had lived in the same community for fifty-five years. According to the fieldworker, they were highly respected by their neighbors. Matthew could not understand the attitude of former slaves who preferred to remain on the plantations, receiving only food and shelter, rather than to be free citizens with the right to develop as individuals.

Matthew told many interesting stories about the part that slavery had played in his family. He said that, on the whole, his family was fortunate in having a good master who would not keep an overseer who whipped his slaves.

His father, Luke Hume, lived in Trimble County, Kentucky, and was allowed to raise an acre of tobacco, an acre of corn, garden vegetables, and chickens for himself. He also could have the milk and butter from one cow. He was advised by the overseer to save his money, but Matthew said his father always drank it up. On this plantation all the slaves were free from Saturday noon until Monday morning, as well as on Christmas and the Fourth of July. A majority of them would go to Bedford or Milton and drink, gamble, and fight.

On the neighboring farm, the slaves were treated cruelly. Matthew had a brother-in-law, Steve Lewis, who carried marks on his back. For years he had a sore that would not heal where his owner had struck him with a blacksnake whip.

When Matthew was a small boy, he was placed in the fields to hoe. He was so small, and his hoe was in such bad shape, that he was unable to keep up with the other workers to hear what they were talking about. One day while bringing up the rear, he saw a large rock, which he carefully covered with dirt. Then he came down hard on the rock and broke his hoe. Instead of getting a whipping, he got a new hoe to replace the broken one. With the new hoe, he could keep close enough to the other workers to hear their conversations.

Another of his duties was to bring in the cattle. He had to walk around the road about a mile to get them, but was permitted to come back through the fields, which was only about a quarter of a mile. One afternoon his mistress told him to bring a load of wood when he came in. In the summer it was the custom to have the children carry wood from the fields. When he came up, he saw that the master's wife was angry. This annoyed him, so he stalked into the hall and slammed the wood into the box. She shoved him into a small closet and locked the door, but his howling soon brought his mother and father to the rescue.

As soon as children were old enough, they were sent to the fields to prepare the ground for setting out tobacco plants, which Matthew said was a very complicated procedure. First the ground was formed into large hills, each requiring about four feet of soil. Then children pulverized the clods and placed a foot in the center of each hill, leaving a track in the smoothed soil. The plants were set in the center of these hills. Woe to the youngster who failed to pulverize a hill, according to Matthew.

After one plowing, the tobacco was hand-tended. It was long, green, and divided into two grades. It was pressed by being weighted down in large hogsheads. On one occasion they were told their tobacco was so eaten up that worms were sitting on the fence waiting for the leaves to grow, but somehow his owner hid the defects and received the best price paid in the community.

The slaveholder's wife on a neighboring plantation was a devout Catholic, and she had all the children come each Sunday afternoon to study the catechism and repeat the Lord's Prayer. She was not very successful in training them in the Catholic faith, for when they grew up most of them became either Baptists or Methodists. Matthew said she did a lot of good in leading them to Christ, but he did not learn much of the catechism, as he attended only for the treats. He said that after the service they always had candy or a cup of sugar.

On the Preston place there was a big, strapping eighteen-year-old slave named Smith who was regularly whipped by an overseer. Smith went to Matthew's owner and asked for help, but was told that he would have to seek help elsewhere, which he did on the Payne farm. The next time Smith was tied to a tree and severely beaten, they were afraid to untie him. When the overseer finally dared to loosen the ropes, Smith kicked him as hard as he could and ran to the Payne estate and refused to return. He was a good worker on the Payne farm, where he received kind treatment.

A bad overseer was discharged once by Mr. Payne because of his cruelty to Luke Hume. The corncrib was so tiny that a man had to climb out one leg at a time. One morning, just as Matthew's father was climbing out with his feed, he was struck over the head with a large club. The next morning Luke broke the scoop off an iron shovel and fastened the handle to his body. This time he swung himself from the door of the crib, and seeing the overseer hiding to strike him, he threw the handle, which wounded the man's head, though it did not knock him out. As soon as Mr. Payne heard of the disturbance, the overseer was discharged and Mr. Mack was placed in charge of the slaves.

One way of exacting obedience was to threaten to send offenders south to work in the fields. The slaves around Lexington, Kentucky, came out ahead on one occasion. The slave collector was named Shrader. He had the slaves handcuffed to a large log chain and forced onto a flatboat. There were so many that the boat was grounded, so some of the slaves were released to push the boat off. Among the blacks was one who could read and write. Before Shrader could chain them up again, he was seized, chained, taken below Memphis, Tennessee, and forced to work in the cotton fields until he was able to get word from Richmond identifying him. In the meantime, the educated black issued freedom papers to his companions. Many of them came back to Lexington, Kentucky, where they were employed.

Matthew thought the Emancipation Proclamation was Abraham Lincoln's greatest achievement. The slaves on his plantation, however, did not learn of it until the following August. Then Mr. Payne and his sons offered to let them live on their ground under an agreement similar to renting and giving them a share of the crop. They remained there until January 1, 1865, when they crossed the Ohio at Madison. They had a cow that had been given to them before the Emancipation Proclamation, but it was taken away from them. So they came to Indiana homeless, friendless, and penniless.

58. LILLIAN HUNTER

Punishment Sent Direct from God

The fieldworker said that Lillian Hunter, a black woman living in Hanover at the time of the interview, spoke with a Scottish accent, so she was hard to understand. When asked if her grandparents had been in slavery, she said, "My ancestors were not in slavery, so far as I know, but my great-great-grandfather Copeland was a slave owner in or near Oberlin, Ohio." Lillian explained that she was not pureblood. Her father was a full-blooded African American, while her mother's people were mixed Scottish, Native American, and African American. She showed the fieldworker a picture of her slaveholding ancestor, who "looked like a typical Scotchman with his snowy hair and beard."

Copeland, her slaveholding ancestor, hated blacks. He was very cruel to them and cursed them with little provocation. Lillian said her mother often told her how the old slaveholder met his death:

> One bright, sunshiny day there wasn't a cloud in the sky, and my great-great-grandfather was standing by his dining room window when one of his slaves passed through the room. He immediately began cursing the man unmercifully, when a bolt of lightning struck him, killing him instantly. The slave was not injured, although he was in the same room. Our family always considered this as a punishment sent direct from God.

59. HENRIETTA JACKSON

Ironing White Folks' Collars and Cuffs

When interviewed, Henrietta Jackson was living in Fort Wayne with her daughter, who operated a restaurant. She had come to live with her daughter in 1917. According to the announcement of her funeral in the *Fort Wayne Journal Gazette* (April 30, 1940), they lived at 1220 S. Lafayette Street. Henrietta did not know exactly how old she was, but she thought she was about 105, though she looked much younger. Still, Henrietta was active and helped her daughter do some of the lighter work around the restaurant. At the time of the interview, on an August afternoon of over ninety degrees, Henrietta was busy sweeping the floor. Rather stooped, she moved slowly but without the aid of a cane or other support. She wore a long, dark cotton dress and a bandanna over her quite gray hair. She was intelligent, alert, cordial, and very much interested in everything going on around her. Her husband, Levy Jackson, had been dead fifty years.

They had nine children, two of whom were twins. Her youngest child was seventy-three, and only two were still living.

Born a slave in Virginia, Henrietta could not remember her father, for he was sold soon after her birth. When still a child she was taken from her mother and sold. She remembered the auction block and said that she brought a good price, for she was strong and healthy. Her new owner, Tom Robinson, treated her well and never beat her. At first she was a plowhand, working in the cotton fields, but then she was taken into the house to work as a maid. While she was there, the Civil War broke out, and Henrietta remembered the excitement.

Gradually the family lost its wealth, and the home was broken up. Everything was destroyed by the armies. When freedom came for the slaves, Henrietta stayed on with the master for a while. She then went to Alabama, where she obtained work in a laundry "ironing white folks' collars and cuffs." Henrietta said that she sometimes longed for her old home in Alabama, where her friends lived, but for the most part she was happy in Fort Wayne.

60. MATTIE JENKINS

Pins Were Stuck through Their Tongues

At the time of her interview, Mattie Jenkins, a ninety-six-year-old ex-slave, was living at 2nd and Ohio streets in Terre Haute. She described the Civil War as "dark days, and the world was on fire." Her owner in Georgia was Charles Morgan. There were eleven other slaves on his plantation. All "were kept all the time"; none were bought or sold, though one slave escaped. Mattie's brother tried to escape, but he drowned in the attempt. Mattie was born and raised on the Morgan plantation, was never sold, and never tried to escape. The slaves' main job was raising cotton, but they also washed, ironed, milked, tended stock, and raised feed for the stock.

She described extreme cruelty to slaves. Pins were stuck through their tongues; their tongues were burned; their hair was cut in unattractive ways; and often they were whipped. They were not supposed to know anything and were deprived of news and information. She said that Morgan's slaves were so uninformed that they knew nothing of the Emancipation Proclamation until a year after it was passed, and many were not freed when they should have been.

There were a number of slaves on a nearby estate, and their owner called them all together and explained to them how they had been given their freedom. He told them that they could go free or stay where they were and work for him. Some left, and others stayed because they liked the owner and hardly knew where to go anyway.

61. LIZZIE JOHNSON

They Wanted Most for Their Children to Learn to Read and Write

When interviewed about her father, Lizzie Johnson was living at 703 North Senate Avenue, Apartment 1, in Indianapolis. Deliberate in her delivery and sure of the facts of her early life, Lizzie was a very interesting old woman and remembered very well the things her parents had told her. She deplored the "loose living," as she called it, of the then current generation.

Her father, Arthur Locklear, was born in Wilmington, North Carolina, in 1822. He lived in the South and endured many hardships until 1852. He was fortunate in having a white man befriend him, for the white man taught him to read and write. Many nights after a hard day's work, he would lie on the floor in front of the fireplace, trying to study by the light of the blazing wood fire to improve his reading and writing.

Lizzie's father married very young, and as his family increased, he became ambitious for them, knowing that their future would be very dark if they remained in the South. He then started a movement to come north. Twenty-six or twenty-eight men and women who had the same thoughts about their children's future banded together, and in 1853 they headed somewhere north. The people selected had to be loyal to the cause of their children's future lives and morally clean, truthful, and hardworking. Some had oxen; some had carts. They pooled all of their scant belongings and started on their long, hard journey.

The women and children rode in the ox-carts; the men walked. They would travel a few days and then stop along the roadside to rest. The women would wash their few clothes and cook enough food to last a few days more, and then they would start out again. The trip took six weeks. Some settled in Madison, Indiana. Two brothers and their families went to Ohio, and the rest came to Indianapolis.

John Scott, a strong and thrifty member of the group, was a hod carrier, who earned $2.50 a day. He knew that his money would not accumulate very fast, so after working hard all day, he spent his evenings putting new bottoms in chairs and knitting gloves for anyone who wanted them. In the summer he planted a garden and sold vegetables. Working day and night, he was able to save some money. He could not read or write, but he taught his children the value of truthfulness, cleanliness of mind and body, loyalty, and thrift. He and his sons all worked together, bought some ground, and built a little house, in which the family lived many years. Before Mr. Scott died, he had saved enough money to give each son $200. His bank was tin cans hidden in various places inside his house. Will Scott, the artist, was a grandson of John Scott.

The thing these early settlers wanted most was for their children to learn to read and write. As slaves, many of them had been caught trying to learn to write and had had their thumbs smashed so that they would not be able to hold a pencil.

62. PETE JOHNSON

That's a Whipping House for the Likes of You

Pete Johnson lived on Broadway in Madison when he was interviewed. For twelve years he had been working as a houseman and groundskeeper for an elderly lady in Madison. His narrative follows:

Many a time I lay awake at night and think over those early days when I lived someplace in Kentucky. When I was just a tiny child, my mother left me with a family and went away. These people were so-called "rebels," but if they were, it is a pity there aren't more rebels in the country.

This family consisted of a brother and his sister. They were both very kind to us children, but I worked at various things, both indoors and out. The reason my feet are so large is because I jumped so many cows. My shoes were either heavy copper-toed affairs, or else I was almost barefooted. Many a time I would jump a cow in order to warm my feet in the warm straw where they had been lying.

When I was about ten or thirteen years of age, I was made dissatisfied with a good home by suggestions that I run away and cross the Ohio River to Indiana. Well do I remember the day I boarded the old ferryboat headed for Madison. I had my clothes tied up in a little bundle. The captain recognized me and said, "Pete, where are you going?" I answered, "Oh, just to Madison." When I arrived in Madison, I went to old Dr. Rogers. He was the only person I knew outside of Kentucky. I had met him when he came to see my old master and mistress. His first words to me were, "Well, Pete, you have left a mighty good home, but you can stay with me if you want to." I soon discovered he had told the truth.

I stayed there several months before I saw my old master. One Saturday evening, I saw him coming up the street. Not knowing what his attitude would be, I started to run and hide in a shed. However, he called me to him, and in his usual kind tone, he told me I could come back with him or stay with Mr. Rogers. I decided to stay in Indiana; but, my, I could scarcely keep back the tears as he walked slowly away.

Well, it was just about a year until I decided to go home. My old mistress and master were so nice to me, I don't see how I could have been misled into leaving them. My mistress tried to teach me to read on rainy days. I can still see the little yellow-backed reader. As soon as I learned my letters I wouldn't

pay any more attention to her, as I then felt so big I thought there was noth-
ing more for me to learn. I wish now I weren't so ignorant. For a time, my
uncle was the foreman on this farm. While he was here I didn't have such an
easy time, as he would commonly smack me over.

My mistress was so nice. When my mother and stepfather settled on a
farm a few miles down the river, she took me to see them. My mother begged
me to stay with her, but I wouldn't leave my mistress again. I stayed here
until I was married. My father-in-law heard of an opening for a young
couple near Louisville, Kentucky, on the Bardstown Road with a Widow
Ross. My wife and I arrived one cold, rainy night and were assigned to a
terrible old brick building for the night. The next morning about 4:00 A.M.,
I heard a bell jangling and got up to investigate. As soon as I poked my head
out, Mrs. Ross called, "That's for you, nigger!" Well, I complained about the
poor quarters, only to be told that "anything was good enough for nig-
gers." This was a terrible woman who kept pistols, guns, and other firearms
around in all rooms.

One night she ordered me to go about a block and a half to the post office.
There was shooting and carousing going on. I was afraid to venture out, but
the widow told me those were "only niggers shooting," and that's all I was.
There was a small, round house in the yard. I had never seen anything like
this, so looked into it. The widow saw me and called, "That's a whipping
house for the likes of you."

My wife and I put up with this sort of treatment for a week and couldn't
stand it any longer. Mrs. Ross wouldn't furnish any conveyance for our
trunk, which was all we had taken with us. I gathered one end and my
wife the other, and away we trudged with all our worldly goods. We finally
reached a settlement of good people who helped us back to our relatives by
paying our streetcar fare and taking our trunk for us. The widow refused to
pay us anything if we left, but all we wanted was to get away before we were
shot to death. I guess we made a record in staying an entire week at the
widow's.

63. ELIZABETH (BETTIE) JONES

Yes, Honey, I Was a Slave

Elizabeth "Bettie" Alvis Jones was living at 429 Oak Street, Evansville,
Indiana, when interviewed. Quite elderly, according to the fieldworker, she had
been cared for by her unmarried daughter since her husband's death. Often
alone because her daughter cleaned houses to provide for them, Bettie was

happy to talk to the fieldworker. Her obituary appeared in the *Evansville Courier* on July 25, 1946 (p. 12), under the heading "Negro Deaths":

> Mrs. Bettie Jones, 89, Negro, 429 Oak street, died yesterday at her residence.
>
> She is survived by two daughters, Mrs. Arnetta Letcher and Mrs. Gertrude Fagan, Evansville; a son, Horace, Evansville; six grandchildren, and three great-grandchildren.
>
> The body is at the Gaines funeral home. Funeral arrangements have not been completed.

The fieldworker paraphrased most of Bettie's narrative:

"Yes, Honey, I was a slave. I was born at Henderson, Kentucky, and my mother was born there. We were held by old John Alvis. Our home was on Alvis's Hill, and a long plank walk had been built from the bank of the Ohio River to the Alvis home. We all liked the long plank walk, and the big house on top of the hill was a pretty place."

Bettie said her master was a rich man who made his money by raising and selling slaves. She lived with her parents in a cabin near her master's home on the hill. She recalled no unkind treatment. "Our only sorrow was when a crowd of our slave friends would be sold off; then the mothers, brothers, sisters, and friends always cried a lot, and we children would grieve to see the grief of our parents."

Bettie's mother was a slave of John Alvis and married another slave of the same owner. The family lived at the slave quarters and never parted. "Mother kept us all together until we got set free after the war." Even then, many of the Alvis ex-slaves decided to make their homes at Henderson, Kentucky, since "It was a nice town, and work was plentiful."

Bettie was brought to Evansville by her parents; however, the climate did not agree with her mother, so she went to Princeton, Kentucky, to live with a married daughter and died there. In Evansville, Bettie married John R. Jones, a former slave of a Tennessee planter, John Jones. Her husband had been dead twelve years when Bettie was interviewed.

Bettie remembered when Evansville was a small town. She recalled when streetcars were mule-drawn and people rode on them for pleasure. "When boats came in at Evansville, all the girls used to go down to the bank wearing pretty ruffled dresses, and everybody would wave to the boatmen and stay down at the river's edge until the boat was out of sight." Bettie remembered when the new courthouse was started, and how glad the men of the city were to work on the building. She also recalled when the old frame buildings used for church services were razed and new structures were erected.

Bettie did not believe in evil spirits, ghosts, or charms, but she remembered hearing her friends express superstitions concerning black cats. Some former slaves believed that building a new kitchen onto a house was always followed by the death of a member of the immediate family, and if a bird flew into a window, some member of the family would die.

Bettie had not been scared when a recent flood came to within a block of her door, for she had lived through a flood while living at Lawrence Station in Marion County, Indiana. "We was all marooned in our homes for two weeks, and all the food we had was brought to our door by boats. White River was flooded then, and our home was in the White River flats. What God wills must happen to us, and we do not save ourselves by trying to run away. Just as well stay and face it as to try to get away. Of course, I'm a Christian. I'm a religious woman and hope to meet my friends in Heaven."

"I would like to go back to Henderson, Kentucky, once more, for I have not been there for more than twenty years. I'd like to walk the old plank walk again up to Mr. Alvis's home, but I'm afraid I'll never get to go. It costs too much."

64. IRA JONES

Ira's Family Was Mistreated by White People

Ira Jones was interviewed about his father, Ben Franklin Jones, who for eight years had been a slave on the Tandy farm in Kentucky, almost directly across the river from Ira's home in Hanover Township, Jefferson County.

When Union soldiers were marching through Kentucky, Tandy was so frightened that he hid in a dense thicket, and no one knew what had become of him. A few days after his disappearance, Ben was working in a field, and when he reached the end of a row, he thought he heard a voice saying, "Ben! Oh, Ben!" Ben continued his plowing, but again he heard the voice in a stage whisper, calling, "Ben! Ben!" Finally he decided to investigate the sound, and peering into the thicket he saw his master, who asked Ben to tell Mrs. Tandy where he was and fetch some food. Mrs. Tandy prepared a large package of food, and, concealing it within his shirt, Ben took it to his master, who was eagerly awaiting him.

One time some of the slaves were to be taken away to join the rebel army. Ben was among the group, but he escaped and ran barefooted over frozen ground. When he reached his home, his feet were so sore that he could hardly move. When freedom was declared, Ben crossed the Ohio and settled near Brooksburg, where he worked for a while before moving to Hanover Township, where Ira still resided at the time of the interview.

Ira said that his family was mistreated by white people. They punished his aunt by making her place her hands palms down on a barrel, and then they drove nails into her hands. As a result, she got lockjaw, causing her death.

Another aunt was told that she was to be shipped west. Instead she was placed on a boat and, with her small baby, sent to Mississippi. On the long journey, her constant prayer was "Don't take my baby away from me." She did not lose her child, and later she found her relatives in Kentucky by writing to her former church.

Ira's cousin Eliza Hotchkiss was whipped so hard that she carried a deep scar across her chest all her life; another cousin, Bill Hotchkiss, however, had such a good master that he was never much good at shifting for himself after receiving his freedom.

There was one young slave who always had an easy job as his owner's barber; but after the plantation failed, he was forced to do heavy farm work. A friend, Ike Williams, was so badly cowed by mistreatment that he was almost afraid to speak. One time a number of slaves were having a tussle with some heavy logs; after watching a while, Ike offered to move them into position with a team of oxen. When the logs seemed to go in place as if by magic, Ike's master said, "Ike, you should speak up when you know something."

Ira said that sometimes when slaves who had different owners married, they were forced to live apart. When his father was freed, he was turned out with nothing to start a new life on, but proved himself a good friend and neighbor to both white and black people in the community.

Ira mentioned the prejudices that some white people held against blacks, and he thought that blacks should receive much more consideration. As an example, he mentioned a ball game in which he was called safe on a close call. The baseman objected to a "damn black" getting a break in preference to a white person.

65. NATHAN JONES

A Very Cruel Way to Treat Human Beings

Nathan Jones was living at 409 Blake Street in Indianapolis when he was interviewed. He and his second wife were rooming with a family by the name of James. According to the fieldworker, the room was clean and comfortable, and the couple, members of the Free Will Baptist Church and living on a pension, were content and were doing "very well."

Nathan was born in Gibson County, Tennessee, in 1858, the son of Caroline Powell, one of Parker Crimm's slaves. Crimm was very abusive and cruel to his slaves. He would beat them for any offense, no matter how minor. He took pleasure in taking small children from their mothers and selling them, sending them as far away as possible.

Nathan's stepfather, Willis Jones, was a very strong man and a very good worker. Willis was resentful of his master's cruel treatment and decided to run away, living in the woods for days. His master sent out searchers for him, but they always came in without him. The day of a sale, Willis made his appearance and was the first slave to be put on the block. His new owner, a Mr. Jones of Tipton, Tennessee, was very kind to him. Willis said it was a real pleasure to work for Jones, as he had a kind heart and respected his slaves.

Nathan remembered seeing slaves, both men and women, face down with their hands and feet staked to the ground, giving them no chance to resist the overseers, who whipped them with cowhides until the blood gushed from their backs. Nathan said that was "a very cruel way to treat human beings."

Nathan married very young, worked very hard, and started to buy a small orchard, but he said that he was "figgered" out of it and lost everything he had put into it. He went to Missouri and stayed there until the death of his first wife. Then he came to Indiana, bringing his six children with him. Forty-five years before the interview, he married for the second time and with his second wife had four more children. Nathan was very proud of his ten children and one stepchild. He said they all helped him until times "got bad" and they could barely exist themselves.

66. RALPH KATES

I Came to the World a Year Too Late to Be Born a Slave

The fieldworker said that Ralph Kates spoke fluent English, "using no southern accent. His story was told in a straightforward way, expressing no prejudice toward race distinction." Until a year before the interview, Ralph was in good health and worked as a paperhanger and interior decorator, but by the time of the interview he had developed a bronchial cough and often was unable to work.

The fieldworker reported that Ralph "has never been a believer in ghosts, haunts, or spiritual visitations, and in his youth scoffed when other blacks told stories of goblins. He has no fear of graveyards, cats, nor rats and harbors no superstitions. His parents always told him that those things were only believed by ignorant persons."

Ralph said that he enjoyed hunting, "but I am always sorry to kill anything and kill only when it was necessary. I have gone hunting many times in Indiana. I caught rabbits, coons, foxes, and small game in Indiana and small game and deer in Tennessee."

Ralph was equally proud of his white father, Thomas Cates, "who was never his master," and his Guinean mother, who was "kindly disposed." He described his early childhood and youth as a time of complete happiness.

I came to the world a year too late to be born a slave. I wouldn't have been a slave even if I had been born several years earlier because my father bought my mother from an unkind master and soon gave her freedom. The former master of my mother was named "Fox." I've never heard his given name; my mother called him "Marse Fox." Thomas Cates was a white man of Indian and Spanish extraction, and he lived, studied, and practiced the habits of the white man. He saw Marse Fox abuse the slaves, so he bought my mother, Viney [Lavina], from him. They lived together and raised a family. Mother lived to be sixty-seven years old, or perhaps older. Her life was passed in Tennessee, and she always spoke with affection when talking of my father because he was always good to all of us.

I was born fourteen miles from Clarksville, Tennessee, on the farm of Thomas Cates, and while we were young children and needed his care, he never failed us. He was always willing to give me money to spend and provided the necessary things for all of us. After the Civil War, our family was broken up. That is, our father left us, but often visited us and brought gifts and money to the children. He was a smart man, working as a stonecutter or stone mason and interior decorator. He was also a good accountant and bookkeeper. He helped to build the new Vanderburgh County courthouse, working in stone and mortar. I was away from the city and didn't get to see him, but would have been happy to have talked with him again. The last time I heard from him, he was in California keeping books for a gold mining corporation. I am proud my people are free and glad my father gave his family freedom from a tyrannical master.

67. ALEXANDER KELLEY

A Mature Man-Slave of Good Physique
Was Worth as High as $3,000

When interviewed, Alexander Kelley was living with his wife, Bell Kelley (q.v.), at 1613 East Kirk Street in Muncie. His narrative follows:

My name is Alexander Kelley. I was born on the Wamoick plantation in Adkins [Anson] County, North Carolina, about 1855. My father's name was Alexander Wamoick, and he was sold from the plantation in 1859 to Joe Gray and Larkin Lynch. These men were slave traders, and they sold my father to a master who took him to Texas. I never saw him to remember him *clearly, for I was a child about four years of age when he was sold away from my mother. I was the last child in the family and the only one left, for my older brothers and sisters had been sold by Wamoick and taken away as fast as they became of profitable age. There were nine children in the family, but they were widely scattered and never saw each other again in slavery or after they became free. A mature man-slave of good physique and steady temper and average working ability and not disposed to run away was worth on the slave market as high as $3,000. That's why we slaves were always well fed.*

My mother's name was Margaret Kelley, but she was called Bell Kelley. [His wife's name also was Bell Kelley.] After Father was sold, Mother remained, and I was a baby by her side. Then Mother was sold, and I went with her to the new master's land whose name was Fitzgerald. This master then sold us to Jesse Wooten of North Carolina, and we went on his plantation. After Wooten bought us, he joined the army and went to the front. When he returned we were free, and I was now eight years old.

When Mother and I were freed, we were together but didn't remain on the Wooten plantation. We went from there to a log cabin on the farm of Dan Hutchings, where we were employed by him for some time. I grew to be a boy sixteen years of age, and Mother decided to take me farther west where I would have better advantages. In the year 1873 we left the Hutchings cabin and traveled out of Carolina on west to Indianapolis, Indiana. We found quarters to live in and both found work. I got some schooling, and meanwhile I picked up some knowledge in cooking. In the year 1883 I was employed as chef at the Grant Hotel in that city. I kept this position for three years when Mother and I and my wife heard of the gas boom at Muncie. We came on to Muncie, and I cooked in the different public stands and private families until 1894. I was then employed as chef in the Kirby House Hotel in Muncie, which place I held for a long period, or until I retired.

I was married while living in Indianapolis. Our family now consisted of my aged mother, my wife, and myself. My ex-slave mother has long since passed beyond. My wife and I now reside at our home, 1613 East Kirk Street, Muncie, Indiana.

68. BELL DEAM KELLEY

Bell's Parents Lived Together but Worked on Different Plantations

When interviewed, Bell Kelley (born Bell Deam) was eighty years old and residing with her husband, Alexander Kelley (q.v.), at 1613 East Kirk Street in Muncie. Around 1883, when she was about twenty-one, Bell married Alexander in Indianapolis. The gas boom attracted them to Muncie, where Bell was a housekeeper and Alexander was a chef in a leading hotel. Bell was born on December 25, 1857, on the King Deam plantation near Port Royal, Henry County, Kentucky. Her father, also named King Deam, was a slave born on the same plantation. She said that her father was quite a fiddler back in slave days and was called into white people's mansions to fiddle for their balls, dances, and apple peelings. These occasions, she said, brought the fashionable together.

Her mother, Susan Dickens, was born on the George Dickens plantation, which adjoined the King Deam plantation. That was where she and Bell's father were married. Both slaveholders consented to their marriage, but her mother remained George Dickens's property, and her father remained King Deam's property. They were given a shack on the Deam plantation, but they worked apart through the day. They were the parents of eight children, all born in slavery on the plantation, where they remained until they were freed. Only two of the children and a granddaughter were living at the time of the interview.

After freedom, Bell's parents gathered the family together and came to Indianapolis, where they found work and took advantage of local schools. Eventually the children married and moved to their own homes. Bell's aged parents died in Indianapolis several years before the interview.

69. ELVIRA LEE

God Washed Out Her Insides with Milk, Which Killed All Her Sins

When interviewed about her mother, Elvira Lee, Sarah Emery Merrill was living at 1710 Monon Avenue in New Albany. The fieldworker, Velsie Tyler, provided three texts, one dealing with songs and two with tales. Another fieldworker, Iris Cook, provided two nearly identical versions of another text collected from Sarah about her uncle, Lewis Barnett (q.v.).

According to Sarah, Elvira often talked of her experiences as a slave and as a free person in Kentucky. As soon as she was big enough, Elvira's main job was caring for her master's children. The slaveholder, whose name was Hall, was a well-educated man who often taught his children their lessons. Elvira studied with the white children and encouraged them to get their father to hear her lessons, too, each night. Consequently, when the white children were old enough to go away to school, Elvira had received a fair education in common school subjects.

Elvira was about sixteen years old when the Civil War began. Some men drilled in a large field belonging to Captain Hall, her owner, before they went into camp. During the war it was often very dangerous for officers to come home and visit their families. On one such visit home, Captain Hall spent most of the night in Elvira's cabin, for he had received word that soldiers were going to search his home for him. The following morning when Elvira's father, Ed, was working in the stables, he saw a man sneaking about the grounds and warned Captain Hall, who immediately left, taking Ed with him along a concealed trail along Green River.

On this particular occasion, the slaves soon learned that Captain Hall was visiting home, and all of them gathered around the big house to see him, not knowing that he already had slipped away. Soon soldiers came from every direction and searched the plantation. They questioned all the slaves, but learned nothing from them. They searched everywhere in the big house and the slave cabins; they fired shots into the trees and beat the shrubbery. Finally an officer said, "Old Aunty has told the truth; there's no man here," and they went away.

On another visit, Captain Hall was protected by his wife, who told the soldiers that she had a very sick child. When asked what the illness was, she said, "The doctor wasn't sure, but he thought that it was smallpox"—a disease feared so much by the soldiers that they soon left the plantation.

After the war, Captain Hall gave his slaves an acre of ground for a school and another acre for a church and cemetery. Elvira, one of the first black teachers, taught school in one of the cabins until the new school was built. Prejudice ran so high against the black school, however, that it was burned after a few weeks. Sarah said that the government soon settled the difficulties, and "Mother lived to see the Negroes getting an education as well as the white children." Elvira later married Edward Lee, who had been a Union soldier, and moved from Hart County, Kentucky, to New Albany, where she died six years before the interview with her daughter. Elvira helped organize one of the first black churches in New Albany and outlived all the other charter members.

Sarah said that her mother had taught her a couple of songs, and to her knowledge neither had ever been written down. Songs of blacks, she said, are different from those of whites. They are songs of experience. As blacks worked in the plantation fields, often for cruel slaveholders, their souls cried to be taken home to heaven or to be given the courage to continue. Sarah said that the "notes of our music are peculiarly shaped because the rhythm is not perfect." The songs were created "not according to a fixed rule but according to the rhythmical nature of our race." She said many of the old blacks could neither read nor write, but they knew that the entrance of the "Spirit of God" made a difference in their lives, though they could express it only orally.

Sister Ridley, an aged black woman, always confessed that God had split her open, scraped her just like a hog, and washed out her insides with milk, which killed all her sins. Then God healed her, and she was all pure and white inside. Aunt Reiny Thatcher, another old black woman, who lived to be 119 years old, said that when she had her "experience," the angels came right out of heaven and taught her the words and tune to the first spiritual. According to Sarah, "She

taught it to my mother, who taught it to me. She would say, 'Oh, Elvira, I saw them angels with these old eyes of mine, and I could hear them just as plain. And old Satan sure did howl when he found he couldn't have my spirit no more.'"
Here is Aunt Reiny Thatcher's song:

> One day, one day,
> Old Satan went abroad,
> And so my soul flew to God.
> Glory be to King Immanuel,
> To my King Immanuel,
> To my King Immanuel.
> Glory be to King Immanuel.
> Old Satan went a-howling,
> Just like a howling dog.
> Glory be to my King Immanuel.

Sarah described the other song as a black woman's "experience song":

> All around my house was walled with brick,
> And in the middle was steel.
> King Jesus arose and fought in blood,
> And conquered till he fell.
> Ah'm gwine to Glory, hallelujah!
> Oh, praise ye my Lord,
> Ah'm gwine to Glory, hallelujah!
> Love and serve the Lord.

Sarah also related a couple of tales that she had learned from her mother. According to one of them,

An old Negro slave on bended knees prayed, "Oh, God, my master's so mean to me, please take old Ephraim home. Please, Master, take old Ephraim home out of the miseries of this life." Over and over he prayed his earnest prayer. Some white boys passing by the cabin overheard the plea and thinking they would have some fun knocked on the door. "Who's there?" the colored man asked.

"It's the Lord come to take Ephraim home," called the boys.

"He's not here, Lord. He's gone. He's been gone from home for months," replied old Uncle Ephraim.

Sarah learned the following tale from her mother, too:

The old Negro slaves prayed that God would punish the mean slave owners, and this colored man's prayer was:

"Oh, Lord, my master's so mean to me. Please, Lord, rain down from heaven and kill all the mean white folks." As he pleaded with his Savior, he was overheard by a group of mischievous white boys who gathered a pile of stones and waited till they thought the old man would be asleep. They all

started throwing rocks on the cabin, the roof of which was very poor, and many of them went through.

Again the prayer was heard, "Oh, Lord, please stop raining rocks, for they is doin' as much bad as good."

70. ADELINE ROSE LENNOX

I've Seen and Done a Lot of Things That Most Folks Have Missed

There are two texts of interviews with Adeline Rose Lennox in the WPA files. One text, collected by Albert Strope, is dated September 7, 1937, on the copy in the WPA files, but is not dated in Rawick 1972. The other text, reproduced in Rawick 1977, lists the fieldworker as "unknown" and was filed on September 13, 1937, at the South Bend WPA office.

When interviewed, Adeline Rose Lennox was eighty-seven years old. She was living with the Richard Bailey family at 610 Wagner Avenue in Elkhart. Mrs. Bailey's first husband was Adeline's son, Johnny Steward, who had died in Tennessee about twenty years before the interview. The fieldworker said that Adeline did not know how to read or write, that she had never talked on a telephone, and that she had never seen a motion picture; however, Adeline said, "I've seen and done a lot of things that most folks have missed." She made no apologies for not having learned to read and write, because she said "none of us slaves was given any education." She said she had no desire to attend a movie, for "I used to attend circuses, but I quit going years ago. That was just after a circus came to town, down in Tennessee, and brought measles along. After that everybody for miles around had the measles."

Adeline was born on a tobacco and cotton plantation near Paris, Tennessee, on October 25, 1849. The daughter of slave parents, she spent the first sixteen years of her life as a slave. The plantation on which she was born was owned by Reuben Rose. Adeline told the fieldworker, "We all thought a great deal of Mr. Rose, for he was good to us." She said Rose's slaves were well taken care of and well fed, with plenty of corn, peas, beans, and pork to eat. She said she had more pork then than during the Depression. She explained that her parents took the name of Rose, which was her last name until she was married, because it was the custom of slaves to assume the names of their owners.

She remained with her parents on the Reuben Rose plantation until the plantation owner's son got married. Then, when she was seven years old, "I was carried away from my parents to the farm of the master's son, Henry Rose, and there I stayed until after the war." She recalled that she cried when she had to leave her parents, but Henry's wife told her that she had to go to a new home. At the age of fourteen, Adeline worked in the fields—driving a team, plowing, harrowing, and seeding.

Adeline said she was "treated tol'able" well when she was a slave and maintained, "I've worked a heap harder since I was freed than I did before. I was put to work when I was six years old, just like other slave children. We were never worked hard because of our age. We worked in the fields and in the houses. I had plenty to eat as a slave. We lived in little cabins, but we were comfortable, and I never saw one of us black'uns whipped. Our quarters, both on the Reuben Rose plantation and then later on the Henry Rose place, were in log cabins. The floors were dirt, and there were fireplaces built of mud and sticks." She said that the log houses were located a distance from the plantation owner's house.

She remembered the Civil War as "the War of the Secession" and recalled hearing the distant roar of cannons "when they were fighting up near Shiloh, Tennessee, and Beauregard was the leader of the Southern army." She admitted, though, that at the time she "didn't know what it was about, and it must have been months after the end of the war before I was freed. I never knew much about the war, for of course, our owners didn't tell us what it was about. I remember soldiers drilling in a field on the Henry Rose farm, and then later Henry's two sons, Dick and Ken, went away to war. Dick went into the Southern army, and Ken fought for the North." She said her owner, Henry Rose, had "laid out in the woods for several days one time when Southern soldiers were looking for him and then returned when he signed a pledge of allegiance."

She recalled that on many occasions Southern soldiers came to the farm with wagons and carried off all the food they could find to feed the Southern army. "I remember Mrs. Rose and how she attempted to prevent the soldiers from carrying away all we had. The war ended, and Dick and Ken Rose came home, both uninjured. It must have been months afterward that I was told my father was going to send for me. I remember that Mr. Rose said he wouldn't let me leave, and then Mrs. Rose interrupted, telling me, 'You're just as free as we are, and you can go.'"

Adeline said that she did not know she was a slave until the close of the Civil War. When the master's wife told her that she was free and could return to her father's home, she was reluctant to go. After gaining her freedom, she lived with her parents for about five years on the Reuben Rose plantation, and then the family moved to nearby Union City. She married a man named Steward, and they had one son, Johnny, who married young and died young. Her husband, Steward, died early in life, too, and Adeline then married George Lennox. After the death of her second husband, Adeline continued to live in the vicinity of Paris and Union City, Tennessee, until 1924, when she moved to Elkhart, Indiana, to live with her daughter-in-law, who had remarried.

At the time of her interview, Adeline's health had been failing for three years. With her daughter-in-law's help, she was able to live on a pension of around $13 a month. Called "Granny" by her neighbors, she enjoyed smoking tobacco and eating cornbread and boiled potatoes, but she did not eat sweets and did not like automobiles, which she said "are too bumpy, and they gather too much air." She said her "one ambition in life is to live so that I may claim Heaven as my home when I die."

Adeline died on October 6, 1938, according to her obituary in the *Elkhart Truth* (October 7, 1938), in which her name is spelled "Adline Lenox."

71. THOMAS LEWIS

There Was No Such Thing as Being Good to Slaves

When interviewed, Thomas Lewis was living on North Summit Street in Bloomington. He claimed that he had been born in 1857, but his obituary in the *Bloomington Herald-Telephone* (September 19, 1951) says he was ninety-nine when he died on September 19, 1951, which would make 1852 his year of birth. Thomas's well-developed narrative follows:

I was born in Spencer County, Kentucky, in 1857. I was born a slave. There was slavery all around on all the adjoining places. I was seven years old when I was set free. My father was killed in the Northern army. My mother, stepfather, and my mother's four living children came to Indiana when I was twelve years old. My grandfather was set free and given a little place of about sixteen acres. A gang of white men went to my grandmother's place and ordered the colored people out to work. The colored people had worked before for white men on shares. When the wheat was all in and the corn laid by, the white farmers would tell the colored people to get out and would give them nothing. The colored people didn't want to work that way and refused. This was the cause of the raids by white farmers. My mother recognized one of the men in the gang and reported him to the standing soldiers in Louisville. He was caught and made to tell who the others were until they had 360 men. All were fined and none allowed to leave until all the fines were paid. So the rich ones had to pay for the poor ones. Many of them left because all were made responsible if such an event ever occurred again.

Our family left because we didn't want to work that way. I was hired out to a family for $20 a year. I was sent for, and my mother put herself under the protection of the police until we could get away. We came in a wagon from our home to Louisville. I was anxious to see Louisville and thought it was wonderful. I wanted to stay there, but we came on across the Ohio River on a ferryboat and stayed all night in New Albany. Next morning the wagon returned home, and we came to Bloomington on the train. It took us from nine o'clock until three in the evening to get here. There were big slabs of wood on the sides of the track to hold the rails together. Strips of iron were bolted to the rails on the inside to brace them apart. There were no wires at the joints of the rails to carry electricity, as we have now, for there was no electricity in those days.

I have lived in Bloomington ever since I came here. I met a family named Dorsett after I came here. They came from Jefferson County, Kentucky. Two of their daughters had been sold before the war. After the war, when the black people were free, the daughters heard some way that their people were in Bloomington. It was a happy time when they met their parents.

Once when I was a little boy, I was sitting on the fence while my mother plowed to get the field ready to put in wheat. The white man who owned her was plowing, too. Some Yankee soldiers on horses came along. One rode up to the fence, and when my mother came to the end of the furrow, he said to her, "Lady, could you tell me where Jim Downs' stillhouse is?" My mother started to answer, but the man who owned her told her to move on. The soldiers told him to keep quiet, or they would make him sorry. After he went away, my mother told the soldiers where the stillhouse was. Her master didn't want her to tell where the stillhouse was because some of his rebel friends were hiding there. Spies had reported them to the Yankee soldiers. They went to the stillhouse and captured the rebels.

Next soldiers came walking. I had no cap, and one soldier asked me why I didn't wear a cap. I said I had no cap. The soldier said, "You tell your mistress I said to buy you a cap, or I'll come back and kill the whole family." They bought me a cap, the first one I ever had.

The soldiers passed for three days and a half. They were getting ready for a battle. The battle was close because we could hear the cannon. After it was over, a white man went to the battlefield. He said that for a mile and a half you could walk on dead men and dead horses. My mother wanted to go and see it, but they wouldn't let her because it was too awful.

I don't know what town we were near. The only town I know about had only about four or five houses and a mill. I think the name was Fairfield. That may not be the name, and the town may not be there anymore. Once they sent my mother there in the forenoon. She saw a flash, and something hit a big barn. The timbers flew every way and I suppose killed men and horses that were in the barn. There were rebels hidden in the barn and in the houses, and a Yankee spy had found out where they were. They bombed the barn and surrounded the town. No one was able to leave. The Yankees came and captured the rebels.

I had a cousin named Jerry. Just a little while before the barn was struck, a white man asked Jerry how he would like to be free. Jerry said that he would like it all right. The white men took him into the barn and were going *to put him over a barrel and beat him half to death. Just as they were about ready to beat him, the bomb struck the barn, and Jerry escaped. The man who owned us said for us to say that we were well enough off and didn't care to be free, just to avoid beatings. There was no such thing as being good to slaves. Many people were better than others, but a slave belonged to his master, and there was no way to get out of it. A strong man was hard to make work. He would fight so that the white men trying to hold him would be breathless. Then there was nothing to do but kill him. If a slave resisted and his master killed him, it was the same as self-defense today. If a cruel master whipped a slave to death, it put fear into the other slaves. The brother of the man who owned my mother had many slaves. He was too mean to live, but he made it. Once he was threshing wheat with a "groundhog" threshing machine run by horsepower. He called to a woman slave. She didn't hear him because of the noise of the machine and didn't answer. He leaped off the machine to whip her. He caught his foot in some cogs and injured it so that it had to be taken off.*

They tell me that today there is a place where there is a high fence. If someone gets near, he can hear the cries of the spirits of black people who were beaten to death. It is kept secret so that people won't find it out. Such places are always fenced to keep them secret. Once a man was out with a friend, hunting. The dog chased something back of a high fence. One man started to go in. The other said, "What are you going to do?" The other one said, "I want to see what the dog chased back in there." His friend told him, "You'd better stay out of there. That place is haunted by spirits of black people who were beaten to death."

72. LEVI LINZY

Salt and Pepper Put in Raw Wounds

The fieldworker provided only a summary of Haywood Patterson's account of African Americans living in Randolph County. Patterson said that he remembered some former slaves who had lived in his neighborhood, but they were all dead. He said that Levi Linzy had been a slave. His owner was so cruel to him that one day in anger Levi hit his owner on the head. As punishment, the owner gave him two hundred lashes and then put salt and pepper in the raw wounds. After Levi recovered from the severe whipping, he again hit his master on the head, but this time he escaped and went to Canada. When Levi heard about the Civil War, he returned to the United States with the intention of killing his former master, but Patterson did not know if Levi actually killed him. The entry on Levi Linzy in the *History of Randolph County* (1882) reads:

LEVI J. LINZY, farmer, P. O. Spartanburg, was born in South Carolina March 22, 1827. He is the son of Levi W. K. Linzy and Epsey Thompson, who were natives of the above State. When eleven years old, he was taken to Mississippi, where he was held in bondage for thirteen years, when he escaped and came to Shelby County, Ind., where he remained for one year. He then became a resident of this county, and was employed at farm work until 1853, when he went to Canada, where be remained until 1855, when he went into the lumbering districts of Michigan, and worked at saw-milling for one year; thence back to Canada. From there to Wisconsin, and was again engaged in saw-milling until July, 1858, when he returned to this county. He was married August 18, 1859, to Nancy Thompson, who was born in South Carolina July 19, 1844. She is the daughter of William Thompson, who was also a native of the above State. Mr. and Mrs. Linzy have had born to them ten children, six of whom are living, viz.: John F., born October 26, 1860; Charles B., September 30, 1862; Levi J., October 20, 1864; Cassius E., February 1, 1870; William A., October 24, 1874, and Mary J., April 15, 1877. Mr. Linzy enlisted in 1864 in Company G, Thirty-third Indiana Infantry. On his way South, he was taken sick, and remained in the hospital at Chattanooga for several months, joining his command again at Raleigh, N. C. From there, he marched with Gen. Sherman's command to Richmond, Va., where he was again taken sick. From there, he was sent to McDougle [McDougal?] Hospital, of New York, where he was discharged May 2, 1865. Mr. Linzy is a member of the M. E. Church, and highly respected by all who know him. He owns a farm of sixty-four acres in Section 12, on which he resides.

Patterson also reported that a full-blooded Irishman came to Randolph County from Mississippi and brought two black women with him. The Irishman built two houses, one for each woman, only a stone's throw apart and close to Patterson's house. He lived in one house one week and the other house the next week. He did not marry either woman, but had children by both. Patterson's wife was the Irishman's granddaughter.

73. SARAH H. LOCKE

An Intelligent Old Lady

Sarah H. Locke, the daughter of William A. and Priscilla Taylor, was born in Woodford County, Kentucky, in 1839. The fieldworker described her as "an intelligent old lady." She had been a good dressmaker and had sewn for a number of the "first families" of Indianapolis. She had been married twice. Her first husband died shortly after their marriage, and she was a widow for twenty-five years before she married again. When interviewed, she was living on a pension and appeared to be happy.

Sarah talked about her early days with great interest. Jacob Keephart, her master, was kind to his slaves and never sold them to slave traders. His family was very large, so they bought and sold slaves within the family or to neighbors. Sarah's father, brothers, and grandmother belonged to the same owner in Henry County, Kentucky. Her mother and two sisters belonged to another branch of the Keephart family, who lived about seven miles away.

Her father came to see her mother on Wednesday and Saturday nights, and they would have big dinners on these nights in their cabin. Her father cradled all the grain for the neighborhood. He was a very hot-tempered man and would not work when he was angry; therefore, every effort was made to keep him in a good humor when the workload was heavy. Sarah's mother died when the children were very young, and Sarah was given to the Keephart daughter as a wedding present and taken to a new home. She was always treated like the others in the family.

The women milked ten or twelve cows a day, knitted socks, and wove "linsey" for their dresses. Sarah said that Keephart sheared sheep right along with the slaves. After the abolition of slavery, Mr. Keephart gave her father a horse and rations to last for six months so the children would not starve.

Christmas was a joyous time for the Keephart slaves. They had a whole week to celebrate—eating, dancing, and making merry. Sarah remembered one night when the slaves were having a dance in one of their cabins. A band of Ku Kluxers came and took all the firearms they could find, but to the slaves' surprise no one was hurt. It did not take long for them to find out why no one was punished, because another night when the Kluxers were riding, the slaves recognized the voice of their young master among the riders. That was the reason why the Keephart slaves were not beaten when the firearms were found.

Sarah said that freeborn blacks were not allowed to associate with slaves because they were said "to have no sense" and would taint the slaves.

Charles and Lydia French, fellow workers with Sarah's family, went to Cincinnati and in 1857 sent for Sarah and her sister so that they could go to school, as there were no schools they could attend in Kentucky then. The girls stayed one year with the French family, and that was the longest time they ever went to school. After that, they attended school for only three months at different times. Sarah could read and write very well, though.

74. MARIA LOVE

Her Mother Had to Work Very Hard, Just Like a Man

Maria Love was living at 210 Geisendorff Street in Indianapolis when she was interviewed. The fieldworker said that Maria was living "in a little old worn shack, not very neat. She is very pleasant, with a sincere, open face, seeming quite out of place in her surroundings." Maria said that her mother, Elmira Polk, was a slave on the farm of Armstead Polk in Carters Creek, Tennessee. There her mother had to work very hard, "just like a man," plowing and working the crops in the fields from morning until night. After her mother's death, Maria was sent to her master's daughter in Alabama, where she lived until she was set free.

75. THOMAS MAGRUDER

A Possible Prototype for Harriet Beecher Stowe's Uncle Tom

Two fieldworkers deposited two separate texts, mostly from printed sources, about Tom Magruder in the WPA files. Allan Stranz's material came from the following sources: William G. Sullivan's writings on the Noble family, Genealogy Section, Indiana State Library; copy of the will of Noah Noble (1794–1844), fourth governor of Indiana (1831–37), Genealogy Section, Indiana State Library; and Jacob P. Dunn's history of *Greater Indianapolis* (Chicago: Lewis Publishing Company, 1910), pp. 242–244. In addition to these sources, Hazel Nixon consulted Anton Scherer, "Our Town," *Indianapolis Times,* May 26, 1936; William Wesley Woollen, *Biographical and Historical Sketches of Early Indiana* (Indianapolis: Hammond and Company, 1883), p. 61; John H. B. Nowland, *Sketches of Prominent Citizens of 1876* (Indianapolis: Tilford and Carlon, 1877); Charles Edward Stowe, *Life of Harriet Beecher Stowe* (Boston: Houghton, Mifflin and Company, 1889); Paxton Hibben, *Henry Ward Beecher: An American Portrait* (New York: George H. Doran Company, 1927); and Agnes M. Hanna's work on old houses in Indianapolis, which I have not been able to locate. She also interviewed Mr. Myers, the office manager of Crown Hill Cemetery; Philip Clements, Union Title Company, 1515 E. Market Street, Indianapolis; and Mr. Davis, then working in the Historical Room of the Indiana State House.

Thomas Magruder, known locally as "Uncle Tom," may have been the inspiration for the hero in Harriet Beecher Stowe's novel *Uncle Tom's Cabin.* Magruder, his wife, Sarah, and their two children, Louisa and Moses, were slaves of Thomas Noble, father of Noah Noble, former governor of Indiana. Thomas Noble lived first in Virginia and later in Belleview, Boone County, Kentucky.

When Thomas Noble died on February 14, 1817, he willed all of his real estate to his sons and all of his personal property, including a number of slaves, to his daughter, who freed Thomas and Sarah Magruder in 1831 and sent them to Indianapolis to work for her brother, Noah Noble. Governor Noble built a cabin for Tom and Sarah at the northeast corner of Market and Noble streets. Later, Louisa was brought to Indianapolis from Lawrenceburg and Moses was brought from Kentucky to care for their aged parents. Peter Dunn, former slave of Judge Isaac Dunn of Lawrenceburg, came to Indianapolis to live with the

Magruders, too. Louisa's daughter, Martha, commonly called "Topsy," also lived with the Magruders. Though free, as slavery was outlawed in Indiana in 1820, they worked as Noah Noble's servants.

Tom, Sarah, Louisa, Moses, Peter, and Topsy were living in the Magruder cabin in 1844 when Harriet Beecher Stowe, who was then living in Cincinnati, visited her brother, Henry Ward Beecher, who lived at East Market and New Jersey streets, just two blocks from Uncle Tom's cabin. The Beechers were friends of the Nobles, and it is said that they frequently visited the Magruders. Henry Ward Beecher especially enjoyed talking to Tom, who was around ninety-seven in 1844. During Tom's final years, both Henry Ward Beecher and Harriet Beecher Stowe were visitors to the cabin.

Many residents of Indianapolis believed that Stowe received her inspiration for the characters in *Uncle Tom's Cabin* while visiting Uncle Tom Magruder's cabin, for six characters in the novel correspond to members of the Magruder household: Tom, Sarah, Louisa, Moses, Peter, and Topsy. Tom Magruder, pious and religious, it is said, closely resembled the Uncle Tom of the novel.

Another of Noah Noble's black servants mentioned in Stowe's novel is Cuffie, also a former slave of the governor's father. Cuffie was brought to Indianapolis in 1841 to work for Governor Noble. Little is known about Cuffie, except that he was provided for in Noah Noble's will. Governor Noble also provided for the Magruders—Tom, Sarah, Louisa, and Moses—in his will, leaving them an acre of land and the cabin at Noble and Market streets as well as the income from the "canal farm," later known as Golden Hill.

Uncle Tom died in Indianapolis on February 22, 1857, and on February 24, 1857, the Indianapolis *Indiana State Journal* carried the following news item concerning him:

> To those unacquainted with "old Tom" the most interesting circumstance connected with him is the probability that he gave the name and the leading features of the character to Mrs. Stowe's celebrated hero. Of course no one knows that to be the case, but there are some circumstances which give it an air of probability. The coincidence of the character and the name are not much in themselves, but connected with the fact that Henry Ward Beecher, during his residence here, was a constant visitor of Uncle Tom's, well acquainted with his history, and a sincere admirer of his virtues, the coincidence becomes more suggestive. We have been told that Mrs. Stowe herself sometimes called to see the old man. "Uncle Tom's Cabin" too, was the name of his house among all his acquaintants, and was a familiar phrase here long before Mrs. Stowe immortalized it. At all events, we know that it is the impression with all the friends of Mrs. Stowe and her brother, in this city, that "Old Uncle Tom" was the original or at least the suggestion of the hero of the cabin.

There is no record of the present burial place of Thomas Magruder, but his daughter Louisa, who last lived at North 424 Highland Avenue, is buried at the foot of Catherine Noble Davidson's grave at Crown Hill Cemetery, Lot 13, Section 1. There is another mound near her grave, and the ground there has the appearance of two sunken graves. Perhaps when the body of Governor Noble was removed from Green Lawn, where Tom formerly was buried, Tom's body was also was removed and interred in Lot 13, Section 1, at Crown Hill.

Although Harriet Beecher Stowe said that the Uncle Tom of her book was a composite character drawn largely from the experiences of Josiah Henson, none of Henry Ward Beecher's friends denied that the fictional Uncle Tom was based on Uncle Tom Magruder. Fieldworker Nixon claims that "a perusal of *Uncle Tom's Cabin* shows a strong influence of Indiana characters. Names used are Indianapolis families: Fletcher (whose wife was a Bullard, cousin to Mrs. H. W. Beecher), Merrill (Sam), St. Claire (Noah Noble's mother was an Elizabeth Claire), and Sedgwick." She also says that the Baker farm, a half-mile west of Malott Park, was a station on the Underground Railroad. Baker hid slaves in his wheat bin, and at night he took them to Westfield, a Quaker settlement in Hamilton County. Mrs. Baker is mentioned in *Uncle Tom's Cabin* when Eliza is being helped by Quakers. Occasionally Henry Ward Beecher preached at Hammonds Park near the Baker farm.

Harriet Beecher Stowe's first observation of cruelty to slaves was during a visit from Cincinnati to Kentucky. Her brother Edward, of Boston, told her many sad accounts resulting from the fugitive slave law and urged Stowe to write something to counteract it. She started *Uncle Tom's Cabin* in Brunswick, Maine, and wrote a few chapters in Boston while visiting Edward. She told her children, however, that God wrote the book, that she saw Uncle Tom in a vision while at Communion at Bowdoin Chapel. She said her characters were universal types and that her work illustrated the fundamental principle of the Gospel as applied to the question of slavery. In her *Key to Uncle Tom's Cabin,* she does not give Tom Magruder and his family as the prototypes for the characters in her novel.

76. HETTIE McCLAIN

Slaves Were Held in Kentucky after the Civil War

Hettie McClain's story was told by her daughter-in-law, Adah Isabelle Suggs (q.v.), for Hettie and her husband, Thomas Suggs, were no longer living at the time of the interview. Hettie was the daughter of Hulda McClain, a slave, and William McClain, her white owner. She was born in Henderson County, Kentucky. Fearing that Hettie might be separated from her mother or fall into the hands of other slaveholders, William McClain took Hulda and Hettie to Newburgh, Indiana, and gave them papers of freedom. There McClain bought a cottage for them so they could live in comfort. Hettie said that they were happy in Newburgh, and her mother made many friends.

When Hettie was twelve, she and another young girl were in an orchard gathering apples for their mothers when they were approached by some young white men. The girls climbed to the ground and asked the strangers what they wanted. The men seized the girls, threw them into a wagon, and took them to Kentucky, where they entered bondage on William McClain's estate. The parents of the kidnaped girls thought they had drowned in the Ohio River. No one knows whether the girl picking apples with Hettie died or was sold after she was abducted and taken to a slave state.

McClain's estate was only a few miles from Archibald Dixon's plantation, on which Hettie's future husband, Benjamin Dixon, was a slave. Born in Caswell County, North Carolina, Archibald Dixon moved to Henderson County, Kentucky, with his father in 1805. A member of the bar, he practiced in Henderson County for many years. He was a member of the state house of representatives in 1830 and 1841, and in 1836 he was elected to the state senate. In 1843 he became lieutenant governor, and in 1849 he was elected as a Whig to the United States Senate to fill a vacancy created by the death of Henry Clay. In 1863 he a was delegate to the Frankfort Peace Commission.

Dixon did not object to Benjamin's marriage to Hettie. In fact, he allowed Benjamin to work for Hettie's owner part of the time so that the two could be together. Archibald Dixon had been a kind master and would have given liberty to Benjamin when the Thirteenth Amendment was adopted; however, young McClain, who inherited the McClain estate, continued to hold Hettie, so she and her husband remained in Henderson County until after the birth of their son, Thomas Dixon, who later took the name of Thomas Suggs. After years spent in Kentucky, Hettie, her husband, and their son moved to Evansville, where they made their home.

The fieldworker explained why slaves were held in Kentucky after the Civil War. Lee's surrender, she says, did not end slavery or slave recruiting. The Lexington *Observer and Reporter,* April 29, 1865, reported that although 72,000 blacks who served in the U.S. Army were freed, half the slaves in Kentucky still belonged to Confederate sympathizers and were not given freedom immediately at the end of the war. After the Thirteenth Amendment passed Congress, it was submitted to the states for ratification. Only a small group of Kentuckians were in favor of unconditional ratification. Some were in favor of rejecting the amendment altogether. Others favored ratification only on the condition that the United States pay Kentucky $36 million to compensate owners of slaves who had enlisted in the United States Army and were freed by the amendment. Governor Bramlette submitted the amendment to the Kentucky legislature on February 7, 1865, advising that it be ratified. He said that the institution of slavery was dead, but he wanted the federal government to compensate the state for the loss of slaves. This bickering delayed the freedom of a good many slaves in Kentucky.

77. ROBERT McKINLEY

Considered Rich, for They Could Eat Meat without Stealing It

Robert McKinley was born in Stanley County, North Carolina, in 1849, a slave of Arnold Parker. He and other members of his family living on Parker's farm were named Parker until after the Civil War, when they took the name of their father, who was John McKinley's slave. When interviewed, Robert lived in a small house at 1634 Columbia Avenue in Indianapolis. An herb doctor at the time, he was very glad to tell of his early life. He thought people in 1938 were living too fast "and don't remember there is a stopping place."

Parker, the slaveholder, was a very cruel man, but he always was kind to Robert because he had given him as a present to his favorite daughter, Jane Alice, and she would never permit anyone to mistreat Robert because she was fond of him. She even taught him to read and write. Though Parker owned a large farm, Jane Alice would not let Robert work on it. Instead, he helped Parker in the blacksmith shop.

Before whipping his slaves, Parker always drank a large glass of whiskey— to give him the strength to beat them, he said. Robert remembered seeing Parker beat Robert's mother until she fell to the ground, but, helpless to protect her, he could only stand and watch. Robert saw slaves tied to trees and beaten until Parker could no longer whip them. Then Parker would salt and pepper their backs.

Once when Confederate soldiers came to the farm, Robert told them where the liquor was kept and where the stock had been hidden. For this the soldiers gave him a handful of money, but Parker took it away from him.

A neighboring farmer, Jesse Hayden, was kind to his slaves. He gave them anything they wanted to eat because he said they worked hard and made it possible for him to have all he had, so it was partly theirs. Parker's slaves were not allowed to associate with Hayden's slaves, who were considered rich, for they could eat meat without stealing it. When slave traders came to the Parker farm, old Mrs. Parker would take meat skins and grease the mouths of the slave children to make it appear that she had given them meat to eat.

78. RICHARD MILLER

His Early Life Was a Nightmare

When interviewed, Richard Miller, "an old soldier," was living with his family in a comfortable home at 1109 North West Street in Indianapolis. He had only one good eye and wore a patch over the other one. He did not like to talk of his early life because it had been such a "nightmare," but he answered all the fieldworker's questions pleasantly.

According to the WPA files, Richard was born January 12, 1843, in Danville, Kentucky. His mother, an English subject, was born in Bombay, India, and was brought to North America by a group of people who did not want to be under English control. They landed in Canada, went to Detroit, where they stayed a short time, and then moved to Danville, Kentucky. There his mother married a slave named Miller, and they were the parents of five children. After slavery was abolished, they bought a little farm a few miles from Danville, Kentucky.

Richard's mother was very ambitious for her children and sent them to a country school. One day when the children came home from school, their mother was gone. When the whites learned that she was sending her children to school, which they did not want, she was taken to Texas, and nothing was heard from her until 1871. Then she wrote her brother that she was coming to visit to try to find her children, if any of them were left.

Richard, who was serving in the army, was anxious to see what his mother looked like. The last time he had seen her, she was wearing a blue cotton dress and washing clothes at the branch. All he could remember about her was her beautiful black hair and that cotton dress. When he saw her, he did not recognize her, but she told him things he remembered happening, and that made him think she was his mother. When Richard was told who had taken his mother from her children, he found the man and shot and killed him. Nothing was done to Richard.

Richard remembered a slave by the name of Brown in Texas who was chained hands and feet to a woodpile. Oil was thrown over him, fire was set to the wood, and he was burned to death. After the fire smoldered down, the white women and children took his ashes for souvenirs.

When slavery was abolished, a group of former slaves started down to the Far South to buy farms—to try to provide for themselves. They got as far as Madison County, Kentucky, and were told that if they went any farther south, they would be made slaves again. Not knowing if that was the truth or not, they stayed there and worked on Madison County farms for very small wages. This separated families, and family members never heard from each other again. Similarly, during slavery, the first Monday of the month was sale day, and slaves were chained together and sent to Mississippi, often separating mothers from children and husbands from wives, who never heard from each other again. Such separations are why so many blacks cannot trace their families back for as many generations as some whites can.

George Band was a very powerful slave who always was ready to fight. He always was able to defend himself and never lost a fight. One night a band of Ku Kluxers came to his house, took his wife, hung her from a tree, and hacked her to death with knives. Then they went to the house, got George, and took him to see what they had done to his wife. George asked them to let him go back to the house to get something to wrap his wife in. Thinking he was sincere, they allowed him to go. Instead of getting a wrap for his wife, however, he got his Winchester rifle and shot and killed fourteen of the Kluxers. Then he left immediately for the North. The county was never bothered by the Klan again.

Richard's obituary in the *Indianapolis Star* (August 19, 1946) says that he was born in Bombay, India, in 1840 instead of in Danville, Kentucky, in 1843 and focuses on his career as a cavalryman:

> A wrinkled, seasoned Civil War soldier who had fought American battles against the Indians in the West, with the Mexicans on the border, in the Boxer rebellion in China and in the Philippines in 1900, fought his last battle this week end.
>
> One of Indianapolis' oldest residents, 106-year-old Richard Miller died Saturday in his home, 1109 North West Street.
>
> Born Jan. 12, 1840, in Bombay, India, of Indian parentage, he came with his parents to the United States and settled at Detroit, later going to a farm near Danville, Ky.
>
> With his father and brother he entered the Fifth Kentucky Cavalry, the first colored unit of the Union Army, about 1862 and fought at Gettysburg and Vicksburg and in other famous battles under Gen. Ulysses S. Grant.
>
> After the war, he re-enlisted in the Fifth Cavalry, later farmed in Danville, Ky., and then entered the Ninth Cavalry. With the Ninth he fought Indians in the West, served on the Mexican border, helped put down the Boxer rebellion and fought in the Philippines.
>
> One of his proudest possessions was a certificate of merit signed by President Theodore Roosevelt in 1903. Although he kept few war souvenirs, he had an old blue cavalry uniform with a yellow stripe on the legs which he wore each Armistice Day.
>
> He closed his long military career as a cavalry instructor at Fort Riley, Kansas, retiring there in 1905. Since that time he had lived a quiet life in Indianapolis.
>
> Always active for his age, he was concerned when his 36-year-old son, George M. Miller, mortician, served during World War II with a medical detachment in the Philippines on some of the same battlefields where he had fought more than 40 years ago.
>
> He was an honorary member of the American Legion and was a member of Junction City No. 58, F. and A. M.
>
> The Rev. Robert Skelton, former chaplain, will conduct funeral services in the George M. Miller Mortuary at 1 o'clock Wednesday afternoon. Burial will be in Crown Hill Cemetery.
>
> Survivors besides the son are the widow, Mrs. Emma Miller 74; a sister, Mrs. Dillie Segar, 108, of St. Louis, Mo., and a half-brother, Will Miller of Danville, Ky., who is in his 80s.

79. BEN MOORE

Ben Was a Hoss

The fieldworker, Merton Knowles, wrote the following legendary account of Ben Moore from J. W. Whicker's "Sketches of the Wabash Valley" and from conversations he had with men in Fountain County who knew Ben, who allegedly was at the Alamo when it was stormed and captured on March 6, 1836. The sketch includes familiar folklore motifs of strong men, including Motifs F631, "Strong man carries giant load," and F615.01, "Death of strong man" (Thompson 1955–58). Here is Knowles's account of Ben Moore:

> Of the 180 inmates at the Alamo, three women, two white children and one Negro boy were spared. The boy was a servant of Colonel Crockett. His name was Ben Moore. After escaping from the Mexicans, he returned to Tennessee and lived there until just before the Civil War when he started with his family to Canada. When he reached the Negro settlement in the Bethel neighborhood east of Attica, he decided to go no farther and lived in Davis Township and Tippecanoe County the rest of his life.
>
> Ben, "Nigger Ben" as he was called, was, to use the vernacular, a "hoss." He stood six feet, four inches tall, was rawboned with little fat, and weighed 316 pounds. Ben was a peaceable, hardworking citizen when sober, but when he was drunk he was inclined to be quarrelsome, and more than once Attica was a bright crimson after one of Ben's sprees. Once in Attica he got boisterous, and Rube Beamer, whom the writer knew well, tried to arrest him with the help of several deputies. They succeeded after knocking him out with a brickbat.
>
> Moore was a railroad tie maker, and I have heard it said that he carried five ties at one time—one on his head and two under each arm. A green white oak railroad tie weighed considerably over a hundred pounds, so the feat was something remarkable.
>
> If a personal note may be pardoned, I had a conversation many years ago with Black Tom Brown, step-uncle of Mrs. Knowles. Brown was a big man, easily six feet tall, and very muscular. He could lift the back wheel of a grain separator, something considered quite a feat of strength. Tom was working in the tie woods with Ben when he heard old Ben calling him, "Oh, Mr. Brown!" He went to where Ben was working, and Ben asked him to help him carry a log for a short distance. Tom took one look at the log and expressed his convictions that it just couldn't be done. "Oh, yes, Mr. Brown, I take the big end." So Ben helped Tom up with the "little" end of the log, shouldered the big end with little effort, and marched away. But Tom said that his knees wobbled with every step he took.

Ben's vanity was his undoing. Late in life, he lifted a clay mixer from a wagon to the ground—a job for several men with skids. He succeeded, but the effort was fatal to the old fellow, and he died soon after.

Ben had four sons, and they were all powerful. Two died of consumption in the Bethel neighborhood. Elmer Brown, my brother-in-law, knew one of them very well. I think he was one of the consumption victims. Ben's youngest boy was inclined to be criminal and was the strongest man to enter the reformatory at Jeffersonville. Once he was placed in jail at Covington and accused of stealing twenty dollars. One day when an election was on in Covington, Ben's son decided to escape the bastille. Bob Miller, the sheriff, locked him in the cell, and being a politician (all the men in Covington are politicians) departed. At about two o'clock in the afternoon when he knew everybody would be interested in the election, Ben's son seized the iron door of the cell, broke the lock; and like a second Samson he broke both hinges, took up the heavy iron door, and smashed through the stone floor. Releasing the prisoners, he dropped into the cellar, tore out the cellar windows, and crossed the Big Four railroad bridge into Warren County. He, with his companions, was soon recaptured.

Such is the story of Ben Moore and his offspring. Years later the last survivor of the Negroes at the Underground Station at Bethel drove the hack to and from the Wabash Depot at Attica. I knew him well by sight and reputation. He was a respected, law-abiding citizen.

So far as I have learned at present, these are the only slaves or immediate descendants at present in the district—at least in Warren, Fountain, or Benton counties.

From his memory, fieldworker Knowles also recalled the following folksong, which he calls a "Negro Folk Song." He deposited the song in the WPA files on August 17, 1936. He said that Fountain County "received immigrants from at least three sources; from New England, Pennsylvania and Ohio, and the South. From the latter came Negro songs which became a part of our folklore. Some were also brought from the South by returning Federal soldiers."

"Run Nigger Run" (cf. White 1965: 168)

My ol' missus promise me
When she died she'd set me free,
But she done dead this many years ago,
And here I'm a-hoein' the same old row.

Oh, run, nigger, run, the paterollers ketch you;
Run, nigger, run, it's almost day.

Some folks say that a nigger won't steal,
But I caught one in my cornfield.
He run to the east, and he run to the west,
And he run his head in a hornet's nest.

80. JOHN MOORE

At the Wedding Both Bride and Groom
Jumped over a Broom Handle

One of nineteen children, John Moore was born in Rutherford County, Tennessee, between Murfreesboro and Nashville, on the first Sunday in February 1848. He was born a slave and remained a slave until he was seventeen. Son of Americus Moore and grandson of a slave woman and her white master, he adopted the name of Moore after his father's first owner, also named John Moore. John's grandfather was shot to death as he sat by his cabin door. Although he had been warned that the Ku Kluxers were coming after him and planned to defend himself, he fell asleep and was overtaken. The old man, son of a white master, had his gun across his knee when he was killed.

John's father and mother were married in the slave quarters of a Tennessee plantation. The wedding ceremony consisted of both groom and bride jumping over a broom handle. The broom was held by two guests at the ceremony, and jumping the broom was taken seriously. After jumping the broom, Americus and his slave wife remained true to their vows, though they later were remarried in a legal ceremony. Americus was given to Moore's daughter when she married Silas Tucker, so some of his children were named Tucker.

Memories of bondage remained vivid in John's mind throughout his life. For instance, he witnessed the brutal slaying of a fellow slave. "Marse Tucker just naturally had him killed to get rid of him," according to John, because the slave desired his freedom more than anything else and developed a habit of running away. Although the owner punished him and warned him not to try to escape again, the temptation for freedom overtook him, and he tried again.

The slaveholder had a hole dug just big enough to fit the body of the runaway slave and had him put into the hole. With his arms and legs pinioned to the earth and his body even with the top of the hole, the slave was beaten on his bare flesh by a blacksmith and his striker [blacksmith's helper] until he died. While he was still alive, his wounds were sponged with a mixture of vinegar, salt, and pepper, as the white slaveholder sat reading nearby. John recalled the sorrow of the other slaves who stood powerless to prevent this cruel treatment, and he remembered how the victim's family grieved his death.

John related a familiar folktale. He said his master was a prankster who enjoyed tormenting his slaves. Isam, one of the slaves, often prayed to the Lord to take him away from his situation and let him come on to heaven. His voice often reached outside his cabin, and other slaves often listened to him praying. One night the slaveholder climbed to the roof and heard the prayer, "Oh, Lord, please come take poor Isam to heaven." The slaveholder made an ominous sound on the shingles. "Who's there?" asked old Isam. "It is the Lord, come for Isam," said the slaveholder. "That nigger ain't home tonight," replied Isam, and that ended his prayers for deliverance for a long time. (Baughman J217.0.0.1.1, "Trickster overhears man praying for death to take him.")

The slaves, John said, were religious and always prayed for freedom. They enjoyed the sermons of black preachers because they preached from experiences and not from the Bible. The slaves praised and worshiped God because they believed that God would deliver them from bondage. John remembered that emancipation was a major theme of the sermons of black preachers.

John attended a school conducted by the Freedmen's Bureau. The teacher always kept his pistol on his desk because the white slaveholders objected to the education of blacks. Teaching blacks was a perilous occupation, according to John.

John remembered some folk traditions of his fellow slaves. "It rained blood one day," his grandfather told his father. Traditional accounts repeat the story of the Red Rain as follows: The slaves were forced to work in the fields on the Sabbath, which filled them with fear of God's wrath. When they prayed that they might be excused of this sinful practice, a storm broke the calm, and it rained blood. After that, the frightened slaveholder never again sent his slaves into the fields to work on the Sabbath; he always allowed them to rest and worship God on that day.

John also related a few folk beliefs that were handed down from parent to child and still existed in tradition: "If you don't want a visitor to come again, sprinkle salt in his tracks, and he won't come again. If a black cat crosses your path, go back home and start again; if he crosses your path again, go home and stay awhile and don't try to go where you had started out to go." John also recalled that slaves sprinkled chamber lye on their cabin steps at four o'clock in the morning to keep away evil spirits. Many slaves believed in the power to hex. If an enemy desired to hex you, all he or she had to do was to borrow or steal some object belonging to you and give it your name. For example, if an enemy wanted you to burn, he or she could place the object named for you in a hot fire, and your body would be tortured by the flames.

An old slave woman bent and twisted a poker she had borrowed from another slave woman, causing the hexed woman to bend nearly double from rheumatic pain. When winter came, a mild Tennessee winter though it was, the borrower put the poker outside the cabin, and it froze into the ground. The lender of the poker nearly froze to death that winter, but early in the spring a grandson of the cursed woman found the bent and twisted poker. He had it straightened by the blacksmith and returned it to his grandmother. Only then did they understand that she had been hexed, and after that they would not allow the hexer to enter their door. The sick woman was soon well and could stand in an upright position.

John was once imprisoned for stabbing to death a white man, Garret Jean. The stabbing was done in self-defense when the drunken white man attacked John. An angry mob surrounded the jail demanding John so that they could lynch him. The jailer protected John from the mob and moved him to safety. John received a fair trial, and his innocence was proven beyond a doubt. No one envied John his liberty after the truth was learned.

John was a good citizen of Evansville for many years and had many friends in his community. He died on February 4, 1929, and was buried at Locust Hill Cemetery on February 5, 1929.

81. HENRY CLAY MOORMAN

Slaves Seldom Married among Themselves on the Same Plantation

Henry Clay Moorman was born October 1, 1854, in slavery on the Moorman plantation in Breckinridge County, Kentucky. After slavery was abolished, his family remained on the plantation for a year. When they left, they boarded a boat at Cloverport and went to Evansville, Indiana. In 1903 Henry moved to Franklin to become pastor of the African Methodist Episcopal Church, which he served for twelve years. When interviewed, Henry was retired and living at 427 West King Street. He related his own personal experiences as well as stories handed down by his mother.

Henry was about twelve years old when freedom was declared. His father, Dorah Moorman, was a cooper who had a wife and seven children. They were held by James Moorman, who owned about twenty slaves. He was kind to his slaves and never whipped any of them. Henry claimed that the slaves loved their owner and were as loyal as family to him.

Henry said that as a boy he did small jobs around the plantation, such as planting tobacco and going to the mill. One day he was placed on a horse with a sack containing about two bushels of grain. After the sack was balanced on the back of the horse, he started to the mill, a distance of about five miles. About halfway there, the sack fell off the horse. Too small to lift the sack of grain, Henry could only cry over the misfortune, powerless to do anything about it. After about two hours, a white man riding by saw Henry's predicament, kindly lifted the sack up on the horse, and sent Henry on to the mill. As was the custom at the mill, Henry waited his turn and did his own grinding. After the miller had taken his toll, Henry returned to his owner and related his experience. Thereafter, they made sure the sack of grain was secure before sending Henry to the mill.

The slaveholders had so poisoned the minds of the slaves that the slaves were in constant fear of the soldiers. One day when the slaves were alone at the plantation, they sighted around two hundred Union soldiers approaching, and they all went to the woods and hid in the bushes. The smaller children were covered with leaves, and they remained there all night, as the soldiers camped nearby in a horse lot. The soldiers were very orderly but took all the food they could find. The slaveholders hid all their silverware and other valuable articles under the mattresses in the slaves' cabins for safekeeping when the soldiers were around.

There were three white children in the master's family. Wickliff was the oldest, and Bob was the middle child. Since the youngest child, Sally, was about the same age as Henry, Henry's mother served as a wet nurse for the white child, and often she nursed both children at the same time. Sometimes wives of white slaveholders served as midwives for black mothers.

There were two graveyards on the plantation—one for whites and one for blacks. Henry could not remember any deaths among the whites during the time he lived on the plantation. He did, however, recall a wedding of a female slave on the plantation just before slavery was abolished. He said in slavery days, slaves seldom married among themselves on the same plantation. Young men generally courted women on another plantation. It was customary for the young man to get the consent of three people before he was allowed to marry: the woman's mother, the woman's owner, and his own owner. When all had given their consent, the marriage would take place, usually on Saturday night. Slaves came from other plantations with a generous supply of fried chicken, hams, cakes, and pies to participate in a great feast, and everyone had a good time, generally with music and dancing. The new husband had to return to his owner after the wedding, but it was understood that he could visit his wife every Saturday night and stay until Monday morning. If by chance one of the two owners would buy the husband or wife, then the couple lived together. Otherwise, any children born to a wife in slavery would become the property of her master.

If a young man could not get consent to marry from all three parties, sometimes a couple attempted to elope, which caused a lot of trouble; in most cases, however, the owners encouraged young couples to marry. Henry could not recall any illegitimate children born on the Moorman plantation.

The slaves had other parties and dances. Slaves would gather from various plantations and hold parties that sometimes lasted all night. It was customary for slaves to get passes from their owners permitting them to attend these parties, but sometimes passes were not given for some reason. Patrollers, a bunch of young white men, would sneak up on defenseless blacks late at night and demand to see their passes. Slaves, both men and women, who could not show passes were whipped. Male slaves often would volunteer to take an extra flogging to protect their girlfriends. The patrollers were a mean bunch who reveled in the shameful practice of whipping blacks.

Henry died in March 1943, and according to the *Franklin Evening Star* (March 13, 1943), six pastors officiated at his funeral. His obituary appeared in the *Franklin Evening Star* on March 9, 1943:

> Born in slavery, the Rev. Henry Clay Moorman, age 88, retired colored Methodist minister, died early Tuesday afternoon at his home on West King street following an extended illness. The body has been taken to the Flinn mortuary, where the funeral and burial arrangements are to be completed later.
>
> The Rev. Mr. Moorman for years was a pastor of the African Methodist Church, having held pastorates throughout Indiana. He at one time served the local A.M.E. church, then returned to Franklin following his retirement several years ago to make his home. He had preached infrequently as a supply pastor on several occasions since that time.
>
> One of the fine old men of this community, the Rev. Mr. Moorman cast an influence which affected the lives of many. His fine, courteous disposition gained for him the friendship of many and his death comes as a severe shock to all.
>
> He was born in Breckinridge county, Kentucky, on October 1, 1854, and a member of a slave family. He entered the ministry following the Civil War. His survivors include the widow, Mrs. Lulu Carter Moorman, and a son, H. G. Moorman, Jr., who lives at Mount Vernon, Ind. Another son and a daughter have preceded their father in death.

82. AMERICA MORGAN

She Believed Firmly in Haunts

When interviewed, America Morgan was living at 816 Camp Street in Indianapolis with her son and his wife. She had married when she was seventeen and said she had had a good husband. They had ten children, but only a son and two daughters were still living in 1937. According to the fieldworker, "She is rather intelligent, reads and writes, and tries to do all she can to help those who are less fortunate than she." America was born in a log house daubed with dirt in Ballard County, Kentucky, in 1852, the daughter of Manda and Jordon Rudd. Manda Rudd was owned by Clark Rudd, and America said that the "devil has sure got him." Her father, Jordon, was owned by Mr. Willingham, who was very kind to his slaves. Jordon's last name became Rudd because he married Manda on the Rudd plantation. There were six children in the family, and everything went well until Clark Rudd whipped America's mother to death when America was five years old. Six small children were left motherless.

America remembered very clearly the happenings of her early life. She was given to her master's daughter, Meda, as a personal maid. She lived with her for one year before she was sold for $600 to Mr. and Mrs. Utterback, with whom she lived until the end of the Civil war. Mrs. Utterback was not as kind as Meda, though. Aware of Mrs. Utterback's reputation for mistreating slaves, Meda told her that if she abused America, she could come for her and she would lose the $600 she had paid for America. After that, America was treated very kindly by Mrs. Utterback.

Aunt Catherine, a slave who looked after all the children on the plantation, was very unruly, but no one could whip her. Once America was sent to get two men to come and tie Aunt Catherine. She fought so hard that it was all the men could do to tie her. They tied Catherine's hands, hung her to a joist, and lashed her with a cowhide. America said it "was awful to hear her screams."

She remembered one slave who had been given five hundred lashes on his back and thrown in his cabin to die. He lay on the floor all night. At dawn when he came to his senses, bloodhounds were licking his back. America said that when overseers lashed a slave to death, they turned the bloodhounds out to smell the blood so they would know black blood, which would help them track runaway slaves.

Aunt Jane Stringer was given five hundred lashes and thrown in her cabin. The next morning when the overseer came, he kicked her, told her to get up, and asked if she was going to sleep there all day. When she did not answer, he rolled her over; the poor woman was dead, leaving several motherless children.

When slaves were preparing to run away, they put hot pepper on their feet to throw the hounds off their trail. Aunt Margaret ran off, but the hounds tracked her to a tree. She stayed up in the tree for two days and would not come down until they promised not to whip her anymore. They kept their promise.

The mother of the slaveholder's wife was sick a long time, and little America had to keep the flies off her by waving a paper fly brush over her bed. She was so mean that America was afraid to go too near the bed for fear the woman might try to grab and shake her. After she died, she haunted America. Anytime America would go into the [bed]room, she could hear her knocking on the wall with her cane. Some nights they would hear her walking up and down the stairs for a long time. Aunt Catherine finally ran off because the old woman haunted her so much.

The old slaveholder came back after his death, too, and once every week he would ride his favorite horse, old Pomp, all night long. When a boy fed the horses the next morning, old Pomp would have his ears hanging down, worn out after his night ride. America believed firmly in haunts, and said she had lived in several haunted houses since coming up north.

In 1865 America's father came for her and took her to Paducah, Kentucky —"a land of freedom," according to America. At that time America was thirteen years old, and she "didn't know A from B," but "glory to God," a white man from the North came to Kentucky and opened a school for black children. That was America's first chance to learn, and she said that her teacher was very kind and sympathetic. She went to school for a very short time.

America's father was very poor and had nothing at all to give his children. Since Mrs. Utterback did not give America any clothes, all America had in this world was what she had on her back, so she was hired out for a dollar a week. The white people for whom she worked were very kind to her and continued to educate her after her work was done. They gave her an old-fashioned spelling book and a first reader, and she said she was "taught much and began to know life." America also was sent regularly to church and Sunday school. She said that was when she began to wake up to her duty as a free person. The Reverend D. W. Dupee was her Sunday school teacher, and she said she learned a lot from him.

83. GEORGE MORRISON

I Don't Really Believe in Ghosts, but You Know How It Is

George Morrison, called Uncle George by his neighbors, came to Indiana from Uniontown, Kentucky, and was living at 25 East 5th Street in New Albany when he was interviewed on separate occasions by two fieldworkers. George would not allow the female fieldworkers in his house, though, unless they were accompanied by a man. He said, "It just ain't the proper thing to do."

In his interview with Beulah Van Meter, George offered some information about popular entertainments. He said that the square dance was not popular in towns, but like the play party it was a great source of amusement in the country. At sundown in the summer and after dark in winter, whole families rode in wagons or buggies, set out on horseback, or walked to the house where the square dance was held. Babies went, too, and generally slept on the same bed where the visitors' coats were placed. In a room lighted by kerosene lamps, or sometimes by a lantern hanging on the wall, all the furnishings were removed. Music usually was provided by a single fiddler, who played on a platform in a convenient corner of the room. The fiddler had to be able to play good hoedowns and to call the sets. Sometimes another person called the sets and a banjo or guitar was added to the band, but usually the fiddler would be the band leader and the band.

Partners were chosen, which required no formalities or introductions since everyone knew one another and danced together. Often it was understood which couples would be partners. Dancing continued until about midnight, when everyone went home. The playing of "Old Dan Tucker" usually signaled the last dance.

George recalled a square dance that was held near Saint Joseph, Indiana, one summer afternoon. When interest began to lag and people seemed tired of dancing, George was invited to perform a dance from plantation days. The fiddler played a hoedown, which the audience had not anticipated, and George did his best to interpret a dance that slaves performed on the plantation. The audience's appreciation of his efforts pleased him: "Yes, ma'am," he told fieldworker Van Meter, "I had everybody laughin'. You could hear them for four miles."

Since George would not let unaccompanied women in his house, Iris Cook interviewed him at a neighbor's house, and got the following account:

I was born in Union County, Kentucky, near Morganfield. My master was Mr. Ray. He made me call him Mr. Ray, wouldn't let me call him Master. They was seven cabins of us. I was the oldest child in the family. Mr. Ray said that he didn't want me in the tobacco, so I stayed at the house and waited on the womenfolk and went after the cows when I was big enough. I carried my stick over my shoulder, for I was afraid of snakes.

Mr. Ray was always very good to me. He liked to play with me, 'cause I was so full of tricks and so mischievous. He give me a pair of boots with brass toes. I shined them up every day till you could see your face in 'em.

There was two ladies at the house, the missus and her daughter, who was old enough to keep company when I was a little boy. They used to have me to drive 'em to church. I'd drive the horses. They'd say, "George, you come in here to church." But I always slipped off with the other boys who was standing around outside waitin' for their folks and played marbles.

Yes, ma'am, the war sure did affect my family. My father, he fought for the North. He got shot in his side, but it finally got all right. He saved his money and came north after the war and got a good job. But I saw them fellows from the south take my uncle. They put his clothes on him right in the yard and took him with them to fight. And even the white folks, they all cried. But he came back. He wasn't hurt, but he wasn't happy in his mind like my pappy was.

Yes, ma'am, I would rather live in the North. The South's all right, but someways I just don't feel down there like I does up here.

No, ma'am, I was never married. I don't believe in getting married unless you got plenty of money. So many married folks don't do nothing but fuss and fight. Even my father and mother always spatted, and I never liked that, and so I says to myself, "What do I want to get married for? I'm happier just living by myself."

Yes, ma'am, I remember when people used to take wagonloads of corn to the market in Louisville, and they would bring back home lots of groceries and things. A colored man told me he had come north to the market in

Louisville with his master and was working hard unloading the corn when a white man walks up to him, shows him some money, and asks him if he wanted to be free. He said he stopped right then and went with the man, who hid him in his wagon under the provisions, and they crossed the Ohio River right on the ferry. That's the way lots of 'em got across here.

Did I ever hear of any ghosts? Yes, ma'am, I have. I heard noises and saw something once that I never could figure out. I was going through the woods one day and come up sudden in a clear patch of ground. There sat a little boy on a stump all by himself there in the woods. I asks him who he was and was he lost, and he never answered me. Just sat there looking at me. All of a sudden he ups and runs, and I took out after him. He run behind a big tree, and when I got up where I last saw him, he was gone. And there sits a great big brown man twice as big as me on another stump. He never says a word, just looks at me. And then I got away from there. Yes, ma'am, I really did!

A man I knew saw a ghost once, and he hit at it. He always said he wasn't afraid of no ghost, but that ghost hit him and hit him so hard it knocked his face to one side, and the last time I saw him it was still that way. No, ma'am, I don't really believe in ghosts, but you know how it is. I live by myself, and I don't like to talk about them, for you never can tell what they might do.

Lady, you ought to hear me rattle bones when I was young. I can't do it much now, for my wrists are too stiff. When they played "Turkey in the Straw," how we all used to dance and cut up. We'd cut the pigeon wing, and buck the wind, and all. But I got rheumatism in my feet now, ain't much good anymore, but I sure has done lots of things and had lots of fun in my time.

84. JOSEPH MOSLEY

Sometimes They Had Nothing but Garbage to Eat

When interviewed, Joseph Mosley and his daughter roomed with a Mrs. Turner at 2637 Boulevard Place in Indianapolis. He had lived in Indianapolis for thirty-five years and had been paralyzed for the last four years. The field-worker observed that Joseph's room was very clean and reported that Joseph was a pleasant man who was glad to talk of his past life. Joseph said it was not easy to get along on his small pension of $18 a month, and he wondered if the government was ever going to increase it.

One of twelve children, Joseph was born on March 15, 1853, fourteen miles from Hopkinsville, Kentucky. His owner, Tim Mosley, was a slave trader who supposedly had bought and sold ten thousand slaves. He went from one state to another buying slaves, bringing in as many as seventy-five or eighty at a time.

The slaves were handcuffed to a chain—each chain linking sixteen slaves. Some slaves walked from Virginia to Kentucky, and some walked from Mississippi to Virginia. In front of the chained slaves was an overseer on horseback with a gun and dogs, and in back of the chained slaves was another overseer, also with a gun and dogs. Their job was to make sure that no slave escaped.

Joseph's father was the shoemaker for all the adults and farmhands on the plantation. In September he began making shoes for the year. He made shoes first for the folks in the house, and next for the workers. Summer or winter, though, slave children never wore shoes.

Joseph's father and mother and all their children were slaves in the same family, though not all of his family lived in the same house. Some lived with the owner's daughters, some with the owner's sons, and so on. Brothers and sisters in a slave family were not allowed to visit one another.

After the death of Tim Mosley, Joseph, at seven years old, was given to Mosley's daughter. He had to pick up chips, tend the cows, and do small jobs around the house. The only clothing he wore was a shirt. After he was taken to the daughter's home, Joseph did not see his mother again until he was set free at the age of thirteen.

The owner was very unkind to the slaves. Sometimes they had nothing but garbage to eat. One Christmas morning, Joseph was told that he could go see his mother. He did not know that he was free, and he could not understand why he was given the first suit of clothes he had ever owned and a pair of shoes. Dressed in his new clothing, he started on the six-mile journey to visit his mother. He was so proud of his new shoes that after he was out of sight, he took them off because he did not want to get them dirty before his mother could see them. He walked the rest of the way in his bare feet.

After gaining freedom, his family came to Indiana, and his mother died in Indianapolis at the age of 105.

85. HENRY NEAL

You Are Just as Free as I or Anyone Else in This United States

Henry Neal was living on 5th Street in Madison when he was interviewed about his father, Peter Neal, and his own experiences as a slave. Henry was born in 1857 on the Fern farm in Hunters Bottom, Carroll County, Kentucky. According to his obituary in the *Madison Courier* (September 1, 1943), he worked on a farm as a young man and lived in Milton until around twenty years before his death. In Madison he worked as a drayman. Here is the WPA interview with Henry:

My father was a slave in the southern part of Carroll County, Kentucky, about twelve miles from Madison. I also was a slave until I was eleven years old, when we received our freedom. I was always treated kindly by my master, but had to work at choring around as soon as I was old enough.

Our master was a bachelor and one of the kindest men I ever knew. He was especially fond of all kinds of sports, such as fox and deer hunting. He always took my father with him on all of these parties. My father was the overseer on the plantation, and it was a common occurrence for him to hear the following call about the middle of the afternoon: "Oh, Pete! Come in and get ready to go on a deer hunt." Or "Come in by four o'clock. We're going fox hunting tonight."

Hounds were used to tree the foxes. These hunts often lasted nearly all night, and they would travel many miles in the chase. When a deer hunt was proposed, my father would row the skiff up or down the river as the master directed. They would go noiselessly through the water until they would come to the place where the deer were accustomed to come to drink. They would remain there quietly until the deer would arrive. As the deer lowered their heads into the water, they would strike them with the oar and kill them instantly.

When my father married, his master told him if he wanted to he could go to my mother's master, as he would probably be happier where his Maria was.

When the Emancipation Proclamation went into effect I will never forget my master's voice as he called my father to him and said, "Now, Peter, you are free, just as free as I or anyone else in this United States. It is now your privilege to decide where you want to live and what you wish to do. You may leave this plantation—your home—and start anew, or you may remain here and work for me. If you decide not to leave me, I will pay you wages in return for your help."

We remained for several years in the employ of this kind friend, and my mother was also employed as cook. While here my father was permitted to tend some ground for himself, and he raised chickens for market instead of stealing them, as so many do now. He was a thrifty sort and kept what money he earned until he was able to own a home and furnish it as he desired.

86. REVEREND OLIVER NELSON

Speak Those Greasy Words Again, Brother

As Richard M. Dorson points out in *American Negro Folktales,* "A stock situation in older European jokelore deals with a layman's literal and highly embarrassing retort to the pulpit message, and this verbal play is adopted with relish by Negro humorists" (1967: 363–364). In the following narrative, Reverend Nelson draws on two preacher anecdotes involving laymen taking a preacher's metaphors literally (in Thompson 1966, see Motif J2470, "Metaphors literally interpreted"; cf. Motifs J1738.5ff.).

> *As a young man I grew up in the services of a white, cultured lady. She had graduated from a university up east, and by paying strict attention to what she said, I had a better education than most of the slaves; therefore, I started on my ministerial life as soon as I was free.*
>
> *I was exhorting an older colored lady about Heaven, reading to her from Revelations. "Aunt Sarah," I says, "when we leave this world we'll go to a better world, one where there isn't work, and our food will be milk and honey." "Brother Nelson, is that all we're going to have to eat in Heaven? Milk gives me a pain in the stomach. Honey makes me sick, so I don't know whether I want to go to Heaven or not." After this experience it was decided that although milk and honey were mentioned as food in the Bible, this wouldn't appeal to the colored people, for few Negroes eat these foods.*
>
> *And I remembered what another old colored minister told me of an experience he had in trying to win souls. He preached, "Whenever you get to Heaven, I'll tell you, my brothers and sisters, what a good time we'll have. We all be eatin' cabbage and bacon and corn bread." One sister in the back of the church calls out, "Speak those greasy words again, brother."*

87. SARAH O'DONNELL

It Is Tiresome, but I Am Patiently Waiting the Call

Sarah O'Donnell died several years before the WPA interviews with exslaves were conducted, but the fieldworker included an account of her life written ten years earlier by Herman Rave and published in the Indiana Section of the *Louisville Times* on May 30, 1927. At the time of Rave's interview, Sarah was 107 years old. Her story, as told by Rave, follows:

> *Sarah O'Donnell was born May 4, 1820, on the place of William Thompson, Nelson County, Kentucky, near Bardstown, where her mother, Lucy, was a slave in the family of Mr. Thompson. When Thompson died, then Sarah, a young girl, was given to Miss Nancy Thompson, daughter of the old master. She later sold her young slave to Jack Mulligan, who gave her to his daughter, Mrs. Sallie O'Donnell, near Springfield, Kentucky. While in this family, she was married—the Reverend Father Kelly, Saint Rose Catholic Church, reading the ceremony.*
>
> *Meanwhile, the slaves had been liberated by Lincoln's proclamation, and*

the storm of the War between the States swept over the hitherto peaceful hills and valleys of the picturesque and historic section where Sarah O'Donnell lived, still in the services of the family for whose members she held a deep affection.

"I never had any education," said the old woman, whose face showed traces of considerable beauty in earlier days. She is very light in color. "I had to do hard work all my life, in the cornfields or wherever there was anything to do, but somehow I always had good masters until we were free, and I did not quit then. Oh, yes, some of the old family come over sometimes and visit me here, where I am lying helpless now with my daughter, Mrs. Clemens, who is taking care of me. During the last couple of years rheumatism has made me unable to stand on my feet, and I have to lie in bed. Of course, it is tiresome, but I am patiently waiting the call."

Mrs. O'Donnell has a remarkable memory, but her life has been an uneventful one, a humble one naturally. When asked whether she remembered Indians in her early youth, she said she saw a few once in a while in Bardstown. She remembered seeing Bishop Spalding there, and perhaps the greatest adventure of her life was the cooking of a meal for General Jefferson C. Davis and the company of soldiers who accompanied him and stopped at the O'Donnell estate. "He told me to get them something to eat. They were out on a scout in that neighborhood."

When asked whether they were Union or Confederate troops, she was not quite sure, but she was certain it was General Jefferson C. Davis, who was certainly in Kentucky at that time. "I hadn't much time to look and see who all they were. They were in a hurry and hungry, and you know it didn't pay to ask questions of soldiers, especially not of generals, as to who they were." She was quite right. General Davis was a member of a Clark County pioneer family.

"My husband and I had ten children, but only two of my daughters are still alive, Mrs. Susie Clemens here, and Mrs. Mattie Miller in Anderson, Indiana."

She is sure that the records of the Catholic Church in which she was baptized, confirmed, and married and the families of her owners can confirm her age. While her body has succumbed, at least partially, her mind is bright.

88. RUDOLPH D. O'HARA

Just Like the Ground Had Swallowed Him Up

Rudolph D. O'Hara was interviewed about his relatives' experiences as slaves on James W. O'Hara's plantation near Horse Cave, Kentucky. When Rudolph's grandfather ran away from the plantation, slaveholder O'Hara threatened to change his will: "If my slaves don't show a more helpful spirit hereafter, I'm going to change my will and not let Louisa free them at her death." Although O'Hara gathered a large number of men from his own and neighboring plantations to search for the runaway slave, their search was useless. Rudolph's grandmother, Cynthia O'Hara, house slave to Louisa O'Hara, said it was "just like the ground had swallowed him up." Cynthia was left with three small sons—James W., Willis, and Ruben—and a daughter, Florence. She knew Louisa O'Hara would take Florence into her home and teach her manners and how to be a valuable seamstress and housemaid, but the boys presented a different problem. She spent many days worrying about her sons and trying to control them. She never again heard from her husband.

After the deaths of James and Louisa O'Hara, their slaves, as promised, received their freedom. Cynthia came to Evansville with other liberated slaves, and there she worked harder to support her children than she had ever worked as a slave on the O'Hara plantation. She died before the Civil War started, and her sons and daughter remained at Evansville.

James W. O'Hara, her son, was a slave until the age of eleven, but he learned to read and write and became a prominent citizen. He was a member of the Evansville Light Infantry and a Christian who supported all movements to advance African Americans. His son, Rudolph, the informant, became a practicing attorney who served the black population of Evansville and Vanderburgh County. The fieldworker also interviewed Rudolph about George Washington Buckner (q.v.).

89. W. F. PARROTT

Slaveholders Showed a Different Face to Union Troops

W. F. Parrott was living at 202 Highland Avenue in Muncie when he was interviewed about his family's experiences in slavery. He graduated from Mitchell High School and Indiana University at Bloomington. He taught in black schools at Spencer for ten years, and he also taught at schools at Ghent and Carrollton, Kentucky. At the time of the interview, he had a daughter living in Washington, D.C., and a son finishing a degree at Ball State Teachers College in Muncie.

W. F. Parrott's grandfather, Amos Parrott, fought in the Revolutionary War under a Virginian, Colonel Richard Parrott, who also was Amos's master. Colonel Parrott led a detachment, of which Amos was a member, to defend a bridge against the advancing British. Although the British arrived in force, they were driven back by Colonel Parrott's detachment. After the war with England, Amos settled in Kentucky on another plantation owned by Colonel Parrott.

Amos's son, Richard, the informant's father, was born on the Richard Parrott plantation in Kentucky and was named, as was the custom, for Colonel Richard Parrott, whose personal slave he continued to be until he was fifteen years old. Then Richard married Sarah Smith, a slave from the Ben Smith plantation, on which she was born. They were married on the Smith plantation, and Colonel Parrott gave Richard to Ben Smith, which allowed Richard and Sarah to live together on the Smith plantation. Of their nine children, five were born in slavery. Since it was a rule among slaveholders that the children belonged to the mother who bore them, the Parrott children became the property of the Smith plantation.

On the plantation, husbands and wives worked apart during the week. On Saturday afternoon, though, the men sat with the women in a room of a big plantation building. There the women baked while the men cleaned cotton. Each man had to clean a specified amount of raw cotton, which was weighed and thrown on the floor at their feet. In the winter they were permitted to have a grate fire to keep off the chill. W. F. Parrott said that his father and the other slaves were amused at one slave's defiance, for he carefully picked out his allotment of cotton, tossed it in the fire, and went to sleep. When awakened by the toe of the overseer, who asked what he had done with his allowance of cotton, the slave frankly confessed that he had burned it. The overseer threatened to whip him to death, but the slave never was whipped. There was no separating machine on the Parrott plantation, so all the cotton was cleaned for the bale by hand.

Each fall when the ground began to freeze and this same slave was not given any shoes, he would get himself a bag, go to the hen roost, and fill the bag with enough chickens to trade for a pair of shoes. Although he was never whipped for stealing chickens, his experience in escaping punishment never prompted other slaves to take such liberties.

There was considerable support among the slaves on the plantation for the Union's cause. At every opportunity, they boldly befriended Union soldiers. Toward the end of the war, when the South realized that its cause was lost, Kentucky plantations were overrun with small units of Union soldiers. Slaveholders, to the amusement of the slaves, showed a different face to Union troops. For example, one time a slave woman fed a Union soldier, and the slaveholder stormed about it until the soldier appeared again. Then the slaveholder abruptly changed his tune and ordered the slave to feed the Union soldier: "Give him all he can eat, and be quick about it," he said. "He's hungry."

Another time the same slaveholder started to whip a slave, but when some Union soldiers came in view, he suddenly threw down the whip and told the slave to duck. Then in strong terms he ordered the black cook to prepare dinner for the soldiers. Once he displayed what appeared to be a Southern flag on a flagpole in his front yard. One day a mounted squad of Union soldiers came by looking for Johnny Rebs, spied the flag, and halted. Without dismounting, they called to the slaveholder for an explanation, and the plantation owner walked out into the front yard, smiled, and politely told the soldiers that what they saw was not a Southern flag but a rag that he had put on the pole to scare hawks away. The soldiers accepted his explanation and traveled on without harming him. Since the slaveholder appeared to sympathize with the North, he was drafted as a picket in the Union Army.

When the Parrott slaves were freed, the slaveholder ordered Sarah Parrott off his plantation. With the slaveholder's consent, her husband, Richard, had joined the Union Army and at that time was away. Sarah refused to go without her five children, for she knew that the slaveholder wanted her to leave so he could bind them to work for him until they were twenty-one. Then he would have to give her sons only $100 and a horse. Sarah kept the family together until Richard returned, and then the family left the plantation together and moved to Mitchell, Indiana. As soon as they could, they were married under civil law to protect their children from being considered orphaned and forced to be bound to their former slaveholder.

In her old age, Sarah visited her old slaveholder in Kentucky. He was in his declining years and much more feeble than Sarah, whom he had once considered his chattel. He greeted his former slave cordially, and they enjoyed talking about the old days in the South.

90. AMY ELIZABETH PATTERSON

She Became a Firm Believer
in Communication with Departed Ones

When interviewed, Amy Elizabeth Patterson lived with her daughter, Lula B. Morton, at 512 South Linwood Avenue near Cherry Street in Evansville. She was born on July 12, 1850, at Cadiz, Trigg County, Kentucky. In spite of her eighty-seven years, fifteen of which had been passed in slavery, she remained helpful in her daughter's home. The fieldworker said that Amy was a refined woman, gracious to every person she encountered and loved by her children and grandchildren. Amy hoped for better opportunities for blacks.

Amy's mother, Louisa Street, was held by John Street, a merchant of Cadiz. Louisa worked as a housemaid in the Street home, and Amy, her firstborn, was fair with gold-brown hair and amber eyes. John Street's wife knew that Amy was her husband's daughter, but she respected Louisa and her child, according to Amy. The Streets promised Louisa they would never sell her, since they did not want to part with Amy, so Louisa was given a small cabin near the big house. The

Streets had a child near Amy's age, and Louisa was wet nurse to both children in addition to her duties as Mrs. Street's maid.

Amy said that "John Street was never unkind to his slaves. Our sorrow began when slave traders came to Cadiz and bought any slaves they took a fancy to and separated us from our families." Separation from her mother and sisters at a slave auction was among Amy's earliest memories. John Street became wealthy dealing in slaves. He bought slaves and sold them yearly to other slave traders. Those he did not sell he hired out to other families. Some slaves were hired or indentured to farmers, stock raisers, merchants, and boat captains. Two years after the birth of Amy, Louisa gave birth to twin daughters, Fannie and Martha. About that time, John Street decided to sell all his slaves, as he was planning to move to another territory. His slaves were auctioned to the highest bidder, and Louisa and the twins were bought by a man living near Cadiz. Street, however, refused to sell Amy, for she showed promise of becoming an excellent house-maid and seamstress and was half-sister, playmate, and nurse to Street's son and daughter. Louisa grieved so much from the loss of her child that she was unable to perform her tasks, and Amy cried continually, so Street sold Amy to her mother's new owner.

Louisa gave birth to seventeen children, three almost white. Amy said, "That was the greatest crime ever visited on the United States. It was worse than the cruelty of the overseers, worse than hunger, for many slaves were well fed and well cared for; but when a father can sell his own child, humiliate his own daughter by auctioning her on the slave block, what good could be expected where such practices were allowed? Yes, slavery was a curse to this nation, a curse that still shows itself in hundreds of homes where mulatto faces are evidence of a heinous sin and proof that there has been a time when American fathers sold their children at the slave marts of America." She said she was glad the curse had been erased, even if by bloodshed.

Amy remembered superstitions of slavery days and recalled that many slaves were afraid of ghosts and evil spirits; however, she never believed in su-pernatural appearances until three years before the interview, when, through a medium, she received a message "from the spirit land." After that, she became a firm believer in communication with departed ones "who still love and long to protect those who remain on earth" but said that she did not believe in "ghosts and evil visitations."

Several years before the interview, her young grandson, Stokes Morton, had drowned. A good student, Stokes was well liked by his teachers and fellow stu-dents. After his death, his mother, Lula B. Morton, and Amy grieved so much that both declined in health and could not perform their regular duties. Suffer-ing from a dental ailment, Amy had to visit a dental surgeon, who suggested that she visit a medium to seek some comforting message from the drowned child. At once she visited a medium and received a message. According to Amy, "Stokes answered me. In fact, he was waiting to communicate with us. He said, 'Grandmother, you and Mother must stop staying at the cemetery and grieving for me. Send the flowers to your sick friends, and put in more time with the other children. I am happy here; I am in a beautiful field. The sky is blue, and the field is full of beautiful white lambs that play with me.'" The message comforted Amy, and she began spending more time with other members of her family and again visited her neighbors. Two years later she "felt a call" and again consulted the medium. That time she received a message from the child, his father, and a little girl who had died in infancy. Amy said she would not call again on the ones who had gone on to the land of promise. She said she was a Christian and a believer in the word of God. She admonished younger relatives to live in the fear and love of the Lord so that no evil would overtake them.

91. SPEAR PITMAN

Some Overseers Liked to See Blood and Whipped for Nothin' at All

The source of the narratives of Spear Pitman and Anthony Battle (q.v.) appears to be an article in the *Rockville Republican,* April 11, 1929, in which former slaves in Greencastle related their experiences. According to the interviewer, there were a few former slaves living in Greencastle in the 1930s, and G. E. Black interviewed them for the *Greencastle Banner.* Then quite old, these blacks were part of an exodus of six hundred former slaves who left the South in 1880. They scattered over several northern states, and those living in Putnam County said they "just happened" to come here.

Spear Pitman, who was ninety years old when interviewed, had been a slave in Edgecombe County, North Carolina. Spear said that until after the Civil War his last name was Bellamy, because he was held by Joseph Bellamy; when he registered to vote, however, there was some confusion about his name. He was told to get another name, and he selected Pitman. He and Carey Bellamy were on the same plantation. The following narrative came from Spear Pitman:

> *Alex Hunter had come over from the Hunter plantation and got into a fight with Noah Bellamy. Alex cut Noah in the belly so bad that his insides came out. Then John Savage, the overseer, came running up and whipped Alex until they quit fighting. They tied Alex up and sent word to Alex's master, old Hunter, and he sent word back to pretty near kill Alex, but not quite.*
>
> *So they whipped him, and then turned the dogs loose on him. They tore him pretty near to pieces, and I don't know but what the dogs ate some of what they pulled off. Then they took the dogs off Alex and poured raw alcohol on him. He had been screaming all the time the dogs were tearing him, but it was worse than ever when they put the alcohol onto him. I tried to get*

away from it, but old Savage told me if I didn't stay and see it he would give me some of the same thing. So I had to stay and see poor Alex try to get away from the dogs. He finally died, and old Hunter lost $1,000 on account of his death. That was on Joseph Bellamy's plantation, but Bellamy was a young fellow, and his guardians ran it for him.

I wasn't ever sold, but every year I was put up on the block and auctioned off to work for a year for some other plantation owner. Whoever bid the most got me for a year. They was all sorts, some good and some mean as they could be. The bad ones whipped for nothing at all lots of times. Whenever they would get on a strain about something, they would whip us to work it off. It made them feel better.

There was county officers that was called "paddle rollers" [patrollers] that rode around the county all the time stopping niggers and making them show their passes. Any slave that left his quarters had to have a pass from his overseer or the paddle rollers would catch him. If they caught a fellow, they whipped him before they took him back home. They sometimes whipped for nothing at all. I've got marks on my back that they put there—growed over by now but still plain. They'd tie us up and go to whipping with big leather whips. Some of the overseers whipped all the time. Some of them just liked to see blood, and they whipped for nothin' at all.

92. NELSON POLK

Dogs Couldn't Trail Runaway Slaves on a Stream Bed

The Reverend J. B. Polk, a local minister, had lived in Muncie less than a year at the time of the interview. His father, Nelson Polk, was born a slave on a plantation near Nashville, Tennessee, around 1830. According to family tradition, he was named for President Polk, rather than for his master, as was the custom. While yet a youth, he was sold to the Collins plantation near Greenwood, Mississippi. There he was married in a traditional slave ceremony to Amelia Ann Collins, a slave on the Collins plantation, and they had five children, also born in slavery.

Nelson lived with his family on the Collins plantation until they were freed in 1865. The family wanted to remain together on the Collins plantation and work for shares or wages, but the plantation owner did not want Nelson to stay on the plantation under any kind of arrangement. Nelson sadly left his family in Mississippi and, alone but a free man, returned to his former plantation near Nashville, Tennessee, where in a legal ceremony he married his second wife. His first wife remained in Mississippi, farmed for Collins on shares, and kept her children together until they grew up.

Reverend Polk related a few incidents that had occurred on the Collins' plantation in Mississippi, where he spent his childhood. The fieldworker reported "the substance of the story" as follows:

One evening the skies became overcast, and the clouds grew black. The thunder rolled, and a cloudburst was expected any moment. The family, with the mother, was sitting on the front porch. Appearing on the highway were two colored men—one leading a horse. Lashed on the horse was a runaway slave, bound hand and foot, who had been overtaken and was being returned to bondage by his overseer. Stopping at the house to escape the storm, the overseer pulled the bound slave off the horse and led him to the basement of the house, where he sat him down in the yard with his back to a wall. The overseer walked onto the porch under shelter. As the storm beat upon the bound slave, he sang and prayed that the master wouldn't whip him to death when the overseer got him home. After the storm was over, they traveled on, and the family never learned the fate of the captured slave.

When the slaves held a religious service in their quarters, they were required to turn a tub against the door to catch the sound and absorb it before it reached the mansion of the plantation owner. If they couldn't find a tub, they used a pot. This practice also was followed on plantations in Kentucky and Tennessee. No slave on the Collins plantation was permitted to pick up or open a book or get curious or anxious about any kind of education. A violation of these rules was certain to result in a whipping.

While working in the fields as a slave, Reverend Polk often heard shouts in the distance. Following that, one or more runaway slaves would dash in the fields among the hands and run around among them in an attempt to lose their scents in the midst of the field hands and, thus, confuse the dogs pursuing them. The runaway slaves would make loops, double back, and then hide themselves or run to the next plantation. When the frantic runaways were making their circles, the field hands would shout "Step long, jump high!" to distract the dogs. With the cooperation of the field hands, often they were successful. The master of the Collins plantation was not overly concerned if the search was abandoned and he was left with the runaways, for in such cases he put the runaways to work in his fields. If he had to surrender them, he charged a fee for food and lodging.

Slaves working in fields adjoining a river placed empty pots at intervals on the banks of the stream to be used by runaways who had to wade the stream. When a runaway arrived at the stream, he would put the pot over his head and wade into the water. The air in the pot around his head prevented the water from rising in the cavity and provided breathing space when the current closed over his head. Once across the stream, the runaway would leave the pot for the next runaway slave. Dogs couldn't trail runaway slaves on a stream bed.

Reverend Polk's mother was an ambitious woman who was too spirited to be whipped. She was efficient and rarely needed prompting. If she angered the master, she staved off punishment by telling him most emphatically to judge her by her work. By proving herself, she was spared the pain and humiliation of the whip for herself and her children, which gave them a sense of freedom while still living under slavery. Once freed, she gave her children all the educational and cultural advantages that hard work could provide.

93. NETTIE POMPEY

The Slave Children Were Treated as Well as the White Children

Nettie Pompey was living at 2021 Columbia Avenue, Indianapolis, when she was interviewed about her mother, Mary Jane Hampton, as well as about her own experiences as a slave. At the time, Nettie was ill and confined to bed because her doctor wanted her to have complete rest. The fieldworker reported that Nettie was "very pleasant and was very glad to tell about the kind treatment she had received." She was living on an old-age pension of $20 a month.

Mary Jane Hampton was born in New Orleans in 1820. She was a slave on the plantation of Noah Hampton. Hampton was kind to his slaves, never allowing any of them to be whipped or mistreated in any way. The slave children were treated as well as the white children in the big house.

As a child, Nettie was a favorite of the family, and she always wanted to sit near old Hampton. Although the white children objected, Hampton always told them to let her alone: "I can look after her just the same as I can you." After Hampton died, his wife, until her death, kept Nettie.

One day after freedom, Hampton's son, whom they had not seen for a long time, unexpectedly rode up to their cottage. With him he brought a book containing the birth dates of every one of the slave children. He gave it to the mother and told her to always keep it, as he wanted all of them to remember their ages.

94. MRS. PRESTON

Her Father's Farm Was Burned Out by the Ku Klux Klan

When interviewed, Mrs. Preston was eighty-three years old. The interviewer found her very charming and hospitable. She was the mother of ten children, but had lived alone on Elm Street in Madison since the death of her husband three years before the interview. Her neighbors in Madison said Mrs. Preston's house was so clean that one could almost eat off the floor.

Her first recollections of slavery were of sleeping at the foot of her mistress's bed so that she could get up during the night to feed the fire with chips she had gathered before dark, or to get a drink or something else her mistress might want during the night.

Her owner, a Mr. Brown, lived off the farm in Frankfort during the war. He had taken his best horses and hogs and left his farm and family in the care of an overseer. He left because he feared the Union soldiers would kill him, but he thought his wife would be safe on the farm, which proved to be true. Mrs. Preston said that the overseer called the slaves to work at four o'clock in the morning, and they worked until six in the evening.

When Mrs. Preston was a little older, she also had to drive about a dozen cows to and from the stable. Often she warmed her bare feet in the cattle bedding. She said that slaves did not always go barefoot; they sometimes wore old shoes or wrapped their feet in rags. Her next job was working in the fields hauling shocks of corn on a balky mule, which often bucked and threw her over its head. A little boy on another mule helped her haul the shocks. Men tied the shocks and placed them on the mules.

She remembered seeing Union and Confederate soldiers firing at one another across a river near her home. Her uncle fought two years and returned safely at the end of the war.

She did not feel that her master and his wife mistreated their slaves. At the close of the war, her father was given a house, land, a team, and enough provisions to start farming for himself; however, several years later the Ku Klux Klan gave the family ten days' notice to leave their farm. One member of the masked Klan, though, pointed out that they were quiet and peaceable and that a man with a crop and ten children could not possibly leave on such short notice, so the time was extended another ten days. Then they took what the Klan paid them for the farm and came north.

The family remained in Indiana until they had to buy their groceries "a little piece of this and a little piece of that, like they do now." Her father returned to Kentucky, but Mrs. Preston stayed in Indiana. In Kentucky, her father's farm was burned out by the Ku Klux Klan, but her family escaped into the woods in their nightclothes. Later they were befriended by a white neighbor, and their former owner built them a new house and provided them with provisions and guards for a few weeks until they were safe from the Klan.

95. WILLIAM M. QUINN

Gift Slaves

William M. Quinn, living at 431 Bright Street in Indianapolis when interviewed, was a slave until the age of ten. Then "the soldiers came back home, and the war was over, and we wasn't slaves anymore." He was born in Hardin County,

Kentucky, on a farm belonging to Steve Stone, also owner of his mother and brother. His father was held by a man named Quinn, who had an adjoining farm. When the family was freed, they took Quinn's name.

William said that they were "gift slaves," for they were never to be sold from the Stone farm. With that understanding, they were given to Stone's daughter as a gift. He said that the owner paid his brother and him ten cents a day for cutting and shucking corn, but it was unusual for a slave to receive money for working. His master had a son about his age who worked around the farm with William and his brother, and Mr. Stone also paid his son ten cents a day. When Stone found the boys playing when they were supposed to be working, he whipped them, "and that meant his own boy would get a licking too." William said that "Old Marse Stone was a good man to all us colored folks, and we loved him. He wasn't one of those mean devils that was always beating up his slaves like some of the rest of them." A black overseer once ran off and hid for two days "'cause he whipped one of old Marse Stone's slaves, and he heard that Marse Stone was mad and didn't like it."

William said, "We didn't know that we were slaves, hardly. Well, my brother and I didn't know anyhow 'cause we were too young to know, but we knew that we had been when we got older. After emancipation we stayed at the Stone family for some time 'cause they were good to us and we had no place to go." Emancipation came early for William and his mother and brother because Stone freed his slaves "a year before Lincoln did"; however, his father was not freed then because his master "didn't think the North would win the war."

William said that slaves on Stone's farm fared well and ate good food, and Stone's "own children didn't treat us like we were slaves"; however, some slaves on surrounding plantations and farms had it "awful hard and bad." He said that sometimes slaves ran away during the night, and "we would give them something to eat." His mother did the cooking for the Stone family, and she was good to runaway slaves.

96. CANDIES RICHARDSON

Jim Scott Beat Her Husband for Praying

Candies [spelled "Candus" in the WPA files and "Candies" in her obituaries] Richardson, living at 2710 Boulevard Place in Indianapolis when interviewed, was eighteen when the Civil War ended. She was born a slave on Jim Scott's plantation on the "Homer Chitter River" in Franklin County, Mississippi. Scott was the heir of "Old Jake Scott." He had about fifty slaves who raised crops, cotton, tobacco, and hogs. Candies cooked for Scott and his wife, Elizabeth. They were both cruel. She said that one time Scott struck her over the head with the butt of a cowhide whip because he had caught her giving a hungry slave something to eat at the back door of the big house. The blow made a hole in her head, and she still carried the scar.

The slaves had to call Scott and his wife "Master and Miss Elizabeth" or they were punished. There was no overseer to whip the slaves on the Scott plantation, because Scott did the whipping himself. Candies said he knocked her down once just before she gave birth to a daughter because she was not picking cotton as fast as he thought she should be. When slaves left the plantation, they were supposed to have a permit from Scott. If they were caught off the plantation without a permit, the "paddyrollers" [patrollers] would whip them. Scott beat her husband a lot of times because he caught him praying. Candies said the "beatings didn't stop my husband from praying. He just kept on praying. He'd steal off to the woods and pray, but he prayed so loud that anybody close around could hear 'cause he had such a loud voice. I prayed too, but I always prayed to myself." One time, Jim Scott beat her husband so hard for praying that his shirt was as red from blood "as if you'd painted it with a brush." Her husband was very religious, and she claimed that it was his prayers and "a whole lot of other slaves' [prayers] that caused you young folks to be free today."

Slaves did not have a Bible on the Scott plantation, for it meant a beating or even "a killing if you'd be caught with one. But there were a lot of good slaves who knew how to pray, and some of the white folks loved to hear them pray 'cause there was no put-on about it. That's why we folks know how to sing and pray 'cause we have gone through so much, but the Lord's with us. The Lord's with us, he is."

According to Candies, slaves who worked in the master's house ate the same food that the master and his family ate; those working on other parts of the plantation, however, did not fare so well. They ate fat meats and parts of the hog that people in the big house did not eat. A week's ration of food was given each slave, but if it was eaten before the week was up, the slave had to eat salt pork until the next ration. A person could not eat much of it, though, because it was too salty.

Candies said, "We had to make our own clothes out of a cloth, like you use, called canvas. We walked to church with our shoes on our arms to keep from wearing them out." Slaves attended a Baptist church that the Scotts belonged to and sat in the rear of the church. The sermon was never preached to the slaves: "They never preached the Lord to us. They would just tell us not to steal. Don't steal from your master!" They walked six miles to reach the church and had to wade across a stream. The women were carried across on the men's backs. Candies said they went through all that just to hear the minister tell them, "Don't steal from your master!"

Her husband went to the war to be "what you call a valet for Marse Jim's son, Sam." After the war, he "came to me and my daughter. Then in July—we could tell [it was July] by the crops and other things grown—old Marse Jim told us everyone was free, and that was almost a year after the other slaves on the other plantations around were freed." She said that in freeing them Scott said that "he didn't have to give us anything to eat and that he didn't have to give us a place to stay, but we could stay and work for him and he would pay us. But we left that night and walked for miles through the rain to my husband's brother and then told them that they all were free. Then we all came up to Kentucky in a wagon and lived there. Then I came up north when my husband died."

Candies said that she was "so happy to know that I have lived to see the day when you young people can serve God without slipping around to serve him like we old folks had to do. You see that pencil that you have in your hand there? Why, that would cost me my life if old Marse Jim would see me with a pencil in my hand. But I lived to see both him and Miss Elizabeth die a hard death. They both hated to die, although they belonged to church. Thank God for his mercy! Thank God! My mother prayed for me, and I am praying for you young folks." Although Candies was ninety years old when she was interviewed, she still walked a mile and a half to attend church.

Candies' obituary appeared in the *Indianapolis Star* on October 12, 1955, and in the *Indianapolis Recorder* on October 15, 1955. Nearly the same information appears in both obituaries, including a children's fict (a genre of folklore told to children to make them behave). The *Star* reports that Candies "recalled the days of the Civil War when a favorite threat used against children who misbehaved was that Abraham Lincoln would get them. 'They told us he was "a hairy man" and we would run and hide in fear of him,' she said." According to the notice in the *Recorder,*

> When Mrs. Candies Richardson was born, April 30, 1847, she had little reason to believe that her miserable condition as a chattel slave, along with that of four million other persons of her race, would end officially within 16 years, and that she would live the rich, full life of 108 years.
>
> The venerable matron was that age when she died Monday night at the home of her daughter, Mrs. Charlotte Tucker, 2335 N. Capitol avenue, and has the distinction of having been one of the few persons born in the onerous days of slavery yet living at [the] time of her death.
>
> Her obituary was read impressively at funeral services held at the Jacobs Funeral Home, Friday, Oct. 14. Burial was in Floral Park.
>
> Born a slave on the Jim Scott plantation at Brookhaven, Mississippi, [she] served faithfully until four years after President Lincoln had signed the Emancipation Proclamation, declaring slavery an involuntary servitude in the United States to be at an end, effective January 1, 1863.
>
> Mrs. Richardson often recalled that Negroes on her master's plantation did not learn of this historic and tremendously important act of Lincoln's until two years after the war.
>
> She also recalled the Civil War days when a favorite threat against children who misbehaved was that "Abraham Lincoln will get you if you don't be good."

Mrs. Richardson left the plantation and moved to Jackson, Miss., where she lived with her husband until his death in 1913. She moved here 37 years ago, and was a member of the West 10th Street Free Church of God.

Survivors besides the daughter Mrs. Tucker, are two other daughters, Mrs. Julia Hatter, Little Rock, Ark., and Mrs. Cora Sweeney, Los Angeles; three sons, Orentice [Prentice] Richardson, Little Rock, and Hughie Richardson, Jackson, Mich.; 22 grandchildren, five great-grandchildren, and 10 great-great-grandchildren.

97. JOE ROBINSON

Rube Black Beat His Slaves Severely for the Least Offense

When interviewed, Joe Robinson was living with his wife at 1132 Cornell Avenue in Indianapolis. He said the pension they received was barely enough for them to live on, and he hoped it would be increased. At the time of the interview, he was learning to read and write in a WPA class. The Robinsons had two children who were living in Chicago.

Joe was born in Mason County, Kentucky, in 1854. His owner, Gus Hargill, was kind to him and the other slaves. Hargill owned a large farm and raised a variety of crops. He always gave his slaves plenty to eat, so they never had to steal food. Hargill said his slaves worked hard to permit him to have plenty; therefore, they should have their share of the food.

Never sold, Joe, his mother, a brother, and a sister lived with the same owner until they were set free. Joe's father, however, was owned by Rube Black, who was very cruel to his slaves. He beat them severely for the least offense. One day he tried to beat Joe's father, who was a large, strong man; and Joe's father nearly killed the owner. After that, Black never tried to whip him again, but at the first opportunity, he sold him to someone in Louisiana. They never heard from him or of him again.

98. ROSALINE ROGERS

Slaves Couldn't Even Mix with Poor Whites

Rosaline Rogers, 110 years old when interviewed, lived at 910 North Capitol Avenue in Indianapolis with her granddaughters, of whom she was very fond. The interviewer described her as a "very pleasant" woman.

Rosaline was born in South Carolina in 1827, a slave of Dr. Rice Rogers. She said that Rogers, the youngest son of a family of eleven children, was very mean. When she was eleven, Rosaline was sold for $900 to a man named Carter and taken to Tennessee. Soon after arriving on the Carter plantation, she was sold again to Belby Moore, with whom she lived until the beginning of the Civil War.

The Moore slaves, both men and women, were herded into a single cabin, no matter how many there were. She remembered a time when there were twenty slaves in a small cabin. There were holes between the logs large enough for dogs and cats to crawl through. The only means of heat was a wood-burning fireplace, which also was used for cooking food. They ate corn cakes, side pork, and beans. Seldom did they have any sweets except molasses.

Slaves generally were given a pair of shoes at Christmastime, and if they wore the shoes out before summer, they had to go barefoot. Her second owner, though, would not buy shoes for his slaves. When they plowed, their feet cracked and bled from walking on hard clods. If they complained, they were whipped, so very few complained.

Slaves were allowed to go to their owner's church, but they had to sit on one of seven benches at the rear of the church. If those benches were full, they were not allowed to sit on any of the others. Her wealthy owner would not even allow his slaves to mix with poor whites, because he said the whites had been free all their lives and should be slaveholders themselves. Poor whites were hired by those who did not believe in slavery or could not afford slaves. Here is Rosaline's account:

> At the beginning of the Civil war, I had a family of fourteen children. At the close of the war, I was given my choice of staying on the same plantation, working on shares, or taking my family away, letting them out for their food and clothes. I decided to stay on; that way, I could have my children with me. They were not allowed to go to school; they were taught only to work.
>
> Slave mothers were allowed to stay in bed only two or three days after childbirth; they were forced to go into the fields to work, as if nothing had happened.
>
> The saddest moment of my life was when I was sold away from my family. I often wonder what happened to them; I haven't seen or heard from them since. I only hope God was as good to them as He has been to me.
>
> I am 110 years old; my birth is recorded in the slave book. I have good health, fairly good eyesight, and a good memory, all of which I say is because of my love for God.

99. PARTHENIA ROLLINS

Treated So Cruelly That It Would Make Your Hair Stand on Ends

At the time of the interview, Parthenia [spelled "Parthena" in the WPA files] Rollins was living at the rear of a house on Camp Street [843 Camp Street in the WPA files, 841 Camp Street in one obituary, 948 Camp Street in another obituary, and 848 Camp Street in a picture caption accompanying an obituary; see below] in Indianapolis with a daughter and grandson. She was in poor health, "all broken up with rheumatism." She said she could hardly talk about her early days because of the awful things that black people had had to go through.

Parthenia was born in Scott County, Kentucky, in 1845 [1833, according to the WPA files], a slave of Ed Duvalle, who was kind to his slaves. Parthenia said that he never whipped any adults but often whipped the children to correct them. She said he never really beat them, though. They all had to work, but they were never overworked. Duvalle's slaves always had plenty to eat.

She said that many slaves were not as fortunate as the ones on her plantation. Once when slave traders came through, they wanted a young woman, but they would not buy her because she had a baby. Her master removed the young mother from the sale, took the baby from her, and beat it to death right before her eyes. When they brought the woman back to the sale without the baby, she was bought immediately. Her new owner was pleased to get such a strong woman until she developed epilepsy—resulting, according to Parthenia, from the cruel way her baby had been killed, which she could not get out of her mind. The buyer then returned her to her former owner, who was forced to refund the money.

Another slave who displeased his owner was taken to the barn, killed, and buried in the barn. Until they were set free, the slaves who knew about it were afraid to talk for fear of the same thing happening to them.

Parthenia also remembered slaves being beaten until their backs were blistered. Then the overseers opened the blisters and sprinkled salt and pepper in them so that the wounds would hurt all the more. Many times slaves were beaten to death, thrown into sinkholes, and left for buzzards to feast on their bodies. Many of the slaves that she knew were half-fed and half-clothed and treated so cruelly that it "would make your hair stand on ends."

Obituaries of Parthenia Rollins were printed in the *Indianapolis Times* (October 24, 1952) and the *Indianapolis Recorder* (November 1, 1952). According to the *Times* obituary, Parthenia "often told her neighbors here of the greats of her day—of Jeff Davis and Lee, of hearing Lincoln speak and seeing the men march off to the Civil War. She was, to quote one neighbor: 'Like a history book come to life.'" The front page of the *Recorder* featured her picture, with the following caption: "Centenarian passes in city: Mrs. Parthenia Rollins, 848 Camp street, age 107, reputed to be the oldest person in Indianapolis or Marion County at the time of her death, died in her home Thursday, Oct. 23. She was born in Scottsboro[?], Ky., in 1845, and had lived here 48 years. . . ." The obituary in the *Recorder* continues:

> Mrs. Rollins lived in her native Kentucky during the Civil War and recalled many stirring events of the war. She also had heard Abraham Lincoln speak on several occasions.

Upon coming here to live, Mrs. Rollins became acquainted with the late Mme. C. J. Walker, founder of the nationally known cosmetics firm. Mrs. Rollins was employed by Mme. Walker as a personal aide and cook. Mrs. Rollins was famous for the delicacies she prepared and served during Mme. Walker's life time.

"Grandma" Rollins, as she was affectionately known, was one of the beneficiaries in the will of the late Mme. Walker. She received $14,500 from the trustees of the Mme. C. J. Walker estate during the last 33 years, drawing the sum in regular stipends. The funeral expenses for Mrs. Rollins were also borne by the trustees of the Walker estate.

Funeral services for Mrs. Rollins were held in the Stuart Mortuary Saturday, Oct. 25. The burial was in Floral Park cemetery. Survivors include a daughter, Mrs. Sarah Wagoner, and two grandchildren, Rollins and Rosie Wagoner.

100. KATIE ROSE

The Hant Began Coming to Our Cabin

Katie Rose, aged widow of Patrick Rose, was living at 412 Sumner Street in Evansville when interviewed. She said, "Evansville has been a pleasant place to live in, and I am certainly glad to call it home." According to Katie, however, Evansville was different when she was a young women. For example, she said that the courthouse was not located at Fourth Street between Vine and Division streets, as it was at the time of the interview, but stood at Main and Third streets. It was a two-story brick building, which, she said, looked very handsome. She especially admired the heavy columns that supported the portico. She recalled that the building of the new courthouse caused much comment in Evansville.

Katie told of other events that had taken place in Evansville. She remembered when Ben Sawyer was hanged for killing his wife with a smoothing iron. She said she had known Mrs. Sawyer very well. "We all called her Miss Lizzie, and she was a good woman. Ben Sawyer was hanged on Main Street, and a great crowd assembled from different parts of Indiana to see him strung up. I've got such a long remembrance. That's what's the matter with me," she said.

Katie recalled that at parties black youths played a game called "Rock Candy." She said the girls stood in two lines facing each other, and the boys stood at the foot of the two lines of girls. Facing one another, the girls placed their hands on each other's shoulders, and they kept time to the rhythm of the song (cf. White 1965: 162):

> A poor man, he sold me,
> And a rich man, he bought me,
> And sent me down to New Orleans,
> To learn how to rock candy.
> Rock candy, two and two.

Rock candy, two and two.
Rock candy, two and two.
For it's no harm to rock candy.

The song continued until all the boys had the opportunity to "rock candy" with the entire line of girls. The game was popular with both white and black youths, according to Katie; however, she said, "The preachers and church-going people hated for us to rock candy. They called it dancing, but that only made us more determined to play it." Katie also said, "We often saw lights off in the woods, near the river. We called them jack-o'-my-lanterns, and we always tried to see how fast we could run home when we saw them. I was always afraid to even try." Katie's story of slavery follows:

> Surest thing, you know, I was a slave in my girlhood, and I was smart and happy. I remember way back before the Civil War and know a heap about slavery. My master was John Holloway, one good man, and his wife was named Laurah. I was a little child when Mistress Laurah took a fancy to me. She always petted me, and I followed her around like a dog follows its master.
>
> Marse John lived in a fine white house about four miles from Henderson. Yes, I'm a Kentuckian. We lived on the old plank road, and I remember how us children used to stand out on the big front porch and listen to the sound of horses' hoofs as the hunters and horseback riders galloped over that old plank road. Miles and miles of plank road reached from the Ohio River to away up the Alvis Hill and out into the woods. We could hear horses for miles away, and often they would leave the plank road and take the dirt road, and we wouldn't see them as then they wouldn't pass our house, and we would watch and watch for them but not catch a glimpse of them.
>
> Young Marse Johnie and young Missus Nanny both were kind to us at home. Young Missus was sent away to school, and we only saw her twice a year. That was when she was home on a visit. We slave children would clap our hands when Old Missus called Mammy into the kitchen to bake ginger cake. Always she had her bake a big barrel full of the sweet cakes, and when Young Missus got home, Old Missus would blow a horn. She called it the farm horn. It was made from a cow's horn and could be heard all over the farm. When she sounded that horn, the slaves all knew to come to the house and stopped whatever work they had started to do. When Young Missus got home, the big barrel of ginger cakes was rolled out on the front porch. Old Missus sounded the horn, and all of the slaves would come up and kiss Young Missus' hand, and she would give us each a cake. She always smiled and stood there in her pretty dress all ruffled and clean, and she sure made a pretty picture. At night I slept in the cabin with my mother, but all day I followed Old Missus wherever she went.
>
> The slaves sang songs when the moon was bright, and the young slaves danced and played games.

My father died, and soon my mother was allowed to marry a slave named Joe, but we called him that man. When I was a very young girl my stepfather died, and then I saw my first hant, or ghost. My stepfather was a hunter and owned a pack of big-mouthed dogs. Soon after he died, the dogs all went away. Then the hant began coming to our cabin. Mother cooked on the open fire in the big chimney, and every night the cabin window would fly open and in would come my stepfather and his dogs. "Mammy, Mammy," I would call out, "That man's here again." He would go lift the lid from the dinner pot and eat. Then he would feed the pack of hungry dogs. A horn would blow far away, and the hunter and his dogs always left through the window. Next morning, I would tell my mother: "We will starve to death. I know because that man and his dogs will always eat up all our grub." But Old Missus always gave us plenty to eat. That man and his pack of dogs never stopped coming until after the war. They kept it up as long as my mother cooked on the open fire and left the pot of food on the crane.

Everything was happy and lovely at the Holloway home until the Civil War started. Then some of the slaves enlisted to fight, and Young Marse John went to the war. Old Missus and Young Missus never seemed happy again. Things went from worse to worse, and soon the young marse was brought home in a coffin.

When he was buried out in the orchard, the orchard was full of soldiers because young Captain Johnie was fetched home by his regiment. When he was let down into the earth, a volley of shots were fired by the soldiers. "What's them men a-shooting for?" I asked Old Missus, for I had stood clinging to her dress skirts, all the time enduring the funeral, and she said, "They're a-shooting the Devil, Katie." I went back to the house clapping my hands and yelling to the top of my voice, "Goody, goody, the Devil is dead!" A laugh went through the house. Even Old Missus laughed, but she was never happy again.

After the war was over, the slaves heard the old missus blow the farm horn for 'em to get to the house. When they got there, she said, "You are all free men and women." Some soon went away, but many stayed on the place. I never left until I was almost grown. I was called a young lady when I got to Evansville. The Negroes always invited me to their picnics and parties. I went to a party on the Newburgh Road, and while the party was going on, some Negroes walked into the house. They had come from across the river from Kentucky, and when they got inside they commenced shooting pistols. The party broke up, and when I left the house, I went into the barnyard and hid under the first thing I found. It was an old farm mule used for plowing that somebody had hitched to a post. When the old mule wouldn't stand still any longer, I started running down the road—and running and walking. I finally covered the road to Evansville.

I'm glad I've had so many years of freedom, although I can't recall a single unkindness shown to any slave of Old Marse and Old Mistress Holloway. Everybody was happy at the Holloway home.

101. JOHN RUDD

The Cries and Prayers of the Whipped Slaves Were Ignored

John Rudd sat in a rocking chair under a shade tree during the interview. His nose was straight and aquiline, according to the fieldworker, for his mother, Liza Rudd, was part Native American. At eighty-three [or eighty-six, according to his obituary below], he still held fond memories of his mother, and her misfortunes still grieved him. "Yes, I was a slave," he said, "and I'll say this to the whole world; slavery was the worst curse ever visited on the people of the United States."

John was born on Christmas Day in 1854 [or 1851 in the obituary below] in the home of Benjamin Simms at Springfield, Kentucky. His mother was the housemaid for Mrs. Simms, his godmother, and John remembered that he and his mother were treated kindly by all the members of the Simms family. When John was a small boy, Benjamin Simms died, and the Simms slaves were auctioned to the highest bidders. "If you want to know what unhappiness means," John said, "just you stand on the slave block and hear the auctioneer's voice selling you away from the folks you love." John explained how mothers and fathers were often separated from their dearly loved children at the auction block. John, his younger brother, Thomas, and his mother, however, were fortunate, as they were bought by the same master. An older brother, Henry, though, was separated from his family. He became the property of George Snyder and thereafter was called Henry Snyder.

Liza Rudd and her two small sons left the slave block as the property of Henry Moore, who lived a few miles from Springfield. John said that unhappiness met them at the threshold of Moore's estate. Liza was made cook, housemaid, and plowhand, while he and Thomas had to hoe, carry wood, and care for the Moores' small children.

John had been at the Moore home only a few months when he saw several slaves being badly beaten. Henry Moore kept a white overseer, and several white men were employed to whip slaves. John discovered that a large barrel standing near the slave quarters was used as a whipping post. Slaves were strapped across the side of the barrel, and two strong men wielded the "cat-o'-nine-tails" until blood flowed from the slaves' flesh. The cries and prayers of the whipped slaves were ignored; they were beaten until the floggers became exhausted.

One day when several slaves had just recovered from a beating, John was playing in the front yard of Moore's house and heard a soft voice calling him. The voice belonged to Shell Moore, one of his best friends on the Moore estate. Shell was one of those who had been severely beaten, and John had been grieving over his friend's misfortune. "Shell had been in the habit of whittling out whistles for me and pampering me. I went to see what he wanted with me, and he said, 'Johnnie, you'll never see Shellie alive after today.'" Shell made his way toward the cornfield, but John, watching him go, did not realize what Shell had on his mind. That night the owner announced that Shell had run away again, and the slaves were ordered to search the fields and woods. Three days later Rhoder McQuirk found Shell's body dangling from a rafter of Moore's corn-crib, where the unhappy slave had hanged himself with a leather halter.

Shell was a good worker and was well worth a thousand dollars. If he had been fairly treated, he would have been glad to work to repay the kindness. According to John, "Marse Henry would have been better to all of us, only Mistress Jane was always rilin' him up." Jane Moore was the daughter of "Old Thomas Rakin," one of the meanest of slaveholders, and she learned "the slave drivin' business from her daddy." John related the following story about his mother's experience with Jane Moore:

Mama had been workin' in the cornfield all day 'till time to cook supper. She was just standin' in the smokehouse that was built back of the big kitchen when Mistress walks in. She had a long whip hid under her apron and began whippin' Mama across the shoulders without tellin' her why. Mama wheeled around from where she was slicin' ham and started runnin' after Ol' Missus Jane. Ol' Missus run so fast Mama couldn't catch up with her, so she throwed the butcher knife and stuck it in the wall up to the hilt. I was scared. I was 'fraid when Marse Henry come in. I believed he would have Mama whipped to death.

"Where's Jane?" said Marse Henry. "She's upstairs with the door locked," said Mama. Then she told Ol' Marse Henry the truth about how Mistress Jane whipped her and showed him the marks of the whip. She showed him the butcher knife stickin' in the wall. "Get your clothes together," said Marse Henry.

John then had to be parted from his mother. Henry Moore believed that the slaves were going to be set free. War had been declared, and he wanted to send Liza deeper into the southern states, where the price of a good slave was higher than in Kentucky. When he reached Louisville, though, he was offered a good price for her services and hired her out to cook at a hotel. John grieved over the loss of his mother, but afterwards he learned that she had been well treated at Louisville. John continued to work for Henry Moore until the Civil War ended. Then his brother, Henry Snyder, came to the Moore home and demanded that his brothers be released to his charge.

Henry had enlisted in the Federal army and had fought throughout the war. He had leased seven acres of good farmland seven miles below Owensboro, Kentucky, and there in Daviess County Liza Rudd and her three sons were reunited. John had never seen a river until he made the trip to Owensboro with Henry. They made the trip on the big *Gray Eagle,* and John said, "I was sure thrilled to get that boat ride."

When John grew to manhood, he worked on farms in Daviess County near Owensboro for several years before working fifteen years as a porter for John Sporree, hotelkeeper at Owensboro. As porter, he met trains and boats arriving at Owensboro, and he recalled the *Morning Star* and *Guiding Star,* both excursion boats that carried people on pleasure trips up and down the Ohio River. For eight years he worked as janitor at the Boehne Tuberculosis Hospital. A fall he experienced while working there crippled him, and at the time of his interview he was walking with a cane. Nevertheless, he could still do a little work around his house and was able to visit friends.

John married Teena Queen, his first wife, at Owensboro, and they had one son, though John had not seen his son or heard from him for thirty years and believed that he was dead. His second wife, Minnie Dixon, still lived with John in Evansville at the time of the interview. They were living on an old-age pension of $14 a month.

When asked his political views, John claimed that his politics were his love for his government. A devout Catholic, he believed that religion and freedom were the two richest blessings ever given to human beings. John said he had had some trouble proving his age, so he had a friend write to the Catholic church at Springfield, Kentucky, where, thanks to his godmother, Mrs. Simms, his birth and christening were recorded in the church records.

John related other incidents of runaway slaves, remembered his fear of the Ku Kluxers, and recalled seeing seven ex-slaves hanging from one tree near the top of Grimes Hill just after the close of the war; however, the fieldworker did not record the details of any of these events.

John's obituary in the *Evansville Courier* (March 28, 1947) was brief: "John Rudd, 96, died at 7 o'clock last night at his home, 605 Oak street. He is survived by his wife, Minnie; and a nephew, Henry Taylor. The body is at the Thompson and Boatright funeral home."

102. ELIZABETH RUSSELL

I Hadn't Only Seen President Lincoln but Had Sat on His Knee

The fieldworker provided two texts of her interview with Elizabeth Russell—one in the fieldworker's words and the other allegedly in the informant's words—and the texts vary somewhat in their details. Elizabeth was born near

Atlanta, Georgia, on July, 4, 1856. Her mother was a slave, as was she, but they were lucky to have a good master for quite a while. When interviewed, Elizabeth was living with her youngest daughter, Alice Bassett, at 1015 North Lafountain Street in Kokomo. Elizabeth, according to the fieldworker, was one of the best-known African Americans living in Kokomo at that time.

Prior to the interview, Elizabeth had been in poor health for several years, but she still greeted everyone with a cheery smile and a kind word. A devout Christian, she had been a member of the Methodist Church since childhood. She was greatly interested in movements dedicated to the advancement of black people. Elizabeth had led an eventful life, one full of dramatic experiences centering on the Civil War.

As a child, Elizabeth was allowed to play with the master's daughter, and she shared the lifestyle of southern white children until her owner hired out her mother to cook for a next-door neighbor. One day when the neighbor had a large group of men for dinner, Elizabeth's mother burned the biscuits. The neighbor got mad and struck her, and she hit him on the head. Three men tried to restrain her, but she knocked all of them down and, leaving Elizabeth behind, ran to her master's home. The men caught Elizabeth, though, and locked her in a room of the neighbor's house until her mother's owner rescued her.

When Elizabeth was about six, her owner died, and, as usual, in the settlement of the estate, some of the slaves were sold. Elizabeth was separated from her mother and turned over to some people who operated a hotel in Atlanta. They, too, were very kind to Elizabeth and allowed her to participate in their own children's activities.

At this time, according to the fieldworker's paraphrased account, President Lincoln was making a tour through the south. One Saturday afternoon when Elizabeth was playing in the yard, she saw her owner coming up the road accompanied by a man dressed in overalls and wearing a red handkerchief around his neck. The stranger was President Lincoln, who picked her up in his arms and said, "Child, I hope you and your people will be free pretty soon." Lincoln stayed at the slaveholder's home for three days without any other southern people knowing it. According to the fieldworker, he was afraid he would be killed if anyone knew he was in town, so his visit was kept secret.

When the Civil War broke out, many southerners had to leave their slaves to join the fight. Elizabeth's owner, however, loaded his slaves in wagons and, with other slaveholders, headed for San Antonio, Texas, to escape the Yankees. On this wagon train, drawn by fifteen mule teams and fifteen yokes of oxen, Elizabeth was reunited with her mother. One evening about dusk, it was decided to camp near a large wooded area. Just as they started to pitch camp one of the children saw a white head rise out of the brush, and then another and another. It was a group of Ku Klux Klan, who immediately started chasing the slave children. All the children escaped except two, who were never heard of again.

The wagon train finally reached Roslin[?], Mississippi [perhaps Roseland, Louisiana], where they heard that some Yankees were coming from San Antonio to head them off. They could not turn back, since another group of Yankees was behind them, so they kept moving. One day they heard the Yankees' drums, so they draped their wagons in white, the sign of surrender. The Yankees told them that the war was over, that the slaves were free, and that all the slaves who wanted to could go back to their former owners. So Elizabeth and her mother returned to their former master in Atlanta and stayed there until Elizabeth was about seventeen.

Around that time Elizabeth had a supernatural experience. Two preachers were staying on the estate, and they kept talking about headless ghosts. They said to her, "Haven't you seen those two fellows with their heads cut off even with their shoulders?" This startled her, for she was afraid of ghosts, and she had to pass the spot where the two headless ghosts had been seen. One day as she was passing this place and carrying a baby, she saw the two ghosts standing there as plain as day. For a quarter of a mile she ran with the baby on her back. Just before she reached her destination, she had to cross a fence. Instead of climbing the fence, she simply fell over it and thought she had broken her arm. Soon after that eerie experience, the owner died, and she decided to move north to Kentucky.

Elizabeth took her belongings and started working her way northward by stage, which was very slow and expensive. By the time she was twenty she had reached Covington, Kentucky, where she stayed for a while before crossing over into Indiana. In 1877, when she was twenty-one, she met and married a young man named Russell, and they moved to a small farm furnished by the government. Here they lived happily, and one daughter was born to them—the one with whom Elizabeth was living at the time of the interview. Early in 1888, when her husband died, the family moved to Kokomo.

Elizabeth said that one of the greatest events of her life was meeting Abraham Lincoln on one of his trips through the South. She related another version of this family legend as well as variants of other experiences in her narrative below. For example, in the fieldworker's account reworked above, on the wagon train to Texas, Elizabeth learned from Yankees that the war was over, but in the following account, supposedly in her own words, she overhears whites in the big house talking about the North's victory and carries the news to her mother's cabin and hundreds of other slaves.

It was when the great president made his last trip to Little Rock, Arkansas, and stopped [in Atlanta] at the Anton House Hotel. The manager of the hotel, whose name was Mr. Palmer, took Mima, his little girl, and me up to the president's suite to see him, and the president sat Mima on one knee and me on the other, then trotted each of us on his foot with the nursery rhyme of "Trot, Trot to Boston." I will never forget how proud I felt to think I hadn't only seen President Lincoln but had sat on his knee. And when we left the room, he put his hand on my head and said, "God bless you, little one," and I truly believe that invocation has followed me through the years.

I was very small at the time of the Civil War, yet I served my people as a secret service agent. I was kept in the big house during the day to rock and attend the babies, and I would often pretend to be asleep and hear what the folks at the big house were saying about the battles and which side was winning or losing, and when the word came that the North had won and the slaves were free, it was I who carried the word to the hundreds of slaves in our section, having crawled to my mother's cabin to give the news, and though only a little child, God used me as a bearer of good news to my people.

During the war I was twice stolen, once by the Indians and once by the Ku Klux Klan. The latter was then traveling in a wagon train of thirty wagons, each drawn by eight mules, and we children were playing along the road when attacked by the Ku Klux Klan. My mother fought for me and saved me, but many of the poor little children were stolen on that trip.

Afterwards I was riding in a wagon that was filled with oil paintings, and it went in a rut and turned over and threw us out, pinning me between the wagon and the embankment, crushing my leg. They had to stop and strike camp. One of the old slaves gathered herbs and made what they called an ooze, and some of the men cut down a hickory tree and made splints for my crushed leg. The next day we went on our journey.

At this time some of the rebels were fleeing with their slaves and all their belongings to Texas from the Yankees and ran right into their hands. Those ahead of us were captured. So we turned back and returned home without being captured.

On the way back home I had another thrilling adventure. I was riding in the commissary wagon drawn by four carriage horses, and the horse in lead stepped into a yellow jackets' nest, and they all ran away, throwing me out on the side of the road. They all told my mother there was no use to look for me, as I was dead. No doubt the wild beasts had devoured me, as we were going through a dense woods. The four horses dashed their brains out against the trees or broke their legs in the thick underbrush, but my mother kept on going back along the road calling me, and about a mile and a half back she found me sitting on the side of the road. God had once more rescued me from a terrible fate.

The Indian chief that stole me was, I believe, the captain of a bunch of rebel Indian soldiers. They came to my master's house, and the folks gave them dinner. I don't remember how many there were, but I was old enough to help wait on the table. As they talked they said things we couldn't understand, only "papoose." And they got up and strolled out, the chief being the last to leave. He suddenly grabbed me, lifting me to his shoulder, and started *down the road. None of the folks realized that he meant to take me until he had gone some distance and didn't set me down. When they saw what was taking place, my master quickly raised a white flag above the housetop. In a few moments a number of men came on horseback and afoot, overtaking the Indians and rescuing me.*

I could go on relating many more thrilling events that I encountered up through my young life, such as when the dam broke and let forty feet of water overflow Hope Field, Arkansas, and I went across a cornfield on dry land to save an old blind lady who was alone in her cabin. And when I returned the water was up to my neck, and my husband had to swim to me to save me. This was in 1876–77.

One of the indelible sorrows of my life was the death of my mother, in whose footsteps I have endeavored to walk all my life. My mother is the only person I ever saw before or since who turned the other cheek when she was smitten on the right one. She was truly a saint. I had a stepfather who was very cruel, and the only mistreatment I ever had in all my life was from his hand. I have striven to do all I can to help suffering humanity and to be a real mother to all. It gives me much joy to have the many kind letters read to me from time to time sent to me from some dear one to whom I had given advice or comforted in time of sorrow.

Among my greatest treasures are my war letters from my boys overseas and my Mother's Day letters that I get each year. I have had quite an eventful life, seen much sorrow, many hardships, many adventures, thrills, and pleasures. I've seen the tallow dip, oil lamp, gas lamp, and electric lamps and have rode in about every riding contraption, except the airplane, from the ox-cart to the automobile.

The Fourth of July will be my seventy-ninth birthday, and I am proud to be spared to see the growth and progress of this city. I have been in Kokomo for thirty-five years and watched it grow from its mud roads to its asphalt pavements. It was forty years ago my two children and I left the South, along in April; the youngest of them is Mrs. [Alice] Bassett.

103. AMANDA ELIZABETH (LIZZIE) SAMUELS

Forced to Eat Chicken Heads, Fish Heads, Pig Tails, and Parsnips

When interviewed, Amanda Elizabeth (Lizzie) Samuels was living at 1721 [North?] Park Avenue in Indianapolis. The fieldworker said that Lizzie was "an amusing little woman" who must have been about eighty years old, but "holds to the age of sixty. Had she given her right age, the people for whom she works would have helped her to get her pension. They are amused, yet provoked, because Lizzie wants to be younger than she really is."

As a child, Lizzie lived in the home of the McMurrys, farmers in Robertson County, Tennessee. Her mother, a slave, worked on the McMurry farm until young Robert McMurry was married, and she was then sold to the Reverend Carter Plaster and taken to Logan County, Kentucky. Lizzie was given to young Robert McMurry, and she lived in the big house and helped his wife, who was not very kind to her. Lizzie was forced to eat chicken heads, fish heads, pig tails, and parsnips, which she very much disliked.

Although Lizzie was very unhappy living with the young McMurrys, she liked living with the old master because he treated the slave children just like his own children. They had plenty of good, substantial food and were protected in every way. The old master felt they were the hands of the next generation, and if they were strong and healthy, they would bring in a larger amount of money when sold. Lizzie's hardships did not last long, however, as the slaves were set free soon after young McMurry's marriage. Then the young master took her in a wagon to Keysburg, Kentucky, to be with her mother. Lizzie said she learned the following song from soldiers:

> Old Saul Crawford is dead,
>   And the last word is said.
> They were fond of looking back,
>   Till they heard the bushes crack,
> And sent them to their happy home
>   In Canaan.
> Some wears worsted,
> Some wears lawn.
> What they gonna do,
> When that's all gone?

104. MARY ELIZABETH SCARBER

Blacks Who Worked on the Donnell Farm Were Treated Kindly

The fieldworker talked with Mary Elizabeth Scarber about her grandmother, Harriet Herrington, and other family members in an interview at Mary Elizabeth's residence, 1116 East North Street in Indianapolis, where she lived with a son. Mary Elizabeth had worked very hard until about four years before the interview. She said she had quilted for a number of people, but since her eyes were "not so good," now she just did her housework.

Her grandmother, a slave in Alabama before she came north after freedom, served a very mean owner. She lived and worked on his farm for years. Mary

Elizabeth's grandfather was taken from her grandmother and sold to someone in Memphis, Tennessee. Her father was owned by old man Heron, who was very mean to him. Heron got tired of him, though, and sold him to a Mr. Lindsay. Her father was happy to be away from his former owner and found the situation somewhat better at the Lindsay home.

Mary Elizabeth's mother lived in middle Tennessee with a family by the name of Donnell who did not believe in slavery. The blacks who worked on the Donnell farm were treated kindly. Her father came to middle Tennessee and married her mother, and they had three children. The Donnells were very fond of them and would not permit the family to be separated.

The Donnell daughter married a man by the name of Phillips, who owned many slaves and wanted to make Mary Elizabeth's mother a slave, but old Mrs. Donnell would not consent. Before old Mrs. Donnell died, she made her daughter promise never to allow the Herrington family to be separated.

After the Civil War, Dutch Trice came north. He brought Mary Elizabeth's father with him, promising him a log cabin in which his family could live. Her father brought the family north, and they lived together in the log cabin on Spring Creek until one spring when there was a huge amount of rain. The water rose so high the children were put in the loft to keep from drowning. After the water receded, the family left the cabin because they were fearful of another flood.

Dave Young owned a farm, but he did not have enough help to run it; therefore, he offered to let Mary Elizabeth's father keep one-third of everything they raised if he would work for him. The family worked on the farm until they had saved enough to get to Indianapolis. "That was sixty-one years ago," according to Mary Elizabeth, who had the birth dates of all the blacks born on the Donnell place.

105. LULU SCOTT

'Course I Can See Spirits

When interviewed, Lulu Scott was living at 800 North California Street in Indianapolis. According to the fieldworker, she was "an elderly woman who refused to give her age, being very positive on that score. [She] has been a cook for years, is very garrulous, but was not definite concerning her early home. Her hair is kept dyed, and although she remembers things from far back she evidently overlooks the fact that such reminiscing rather establishes her age, which I judge to be at least seventy, if not more. Her complexion is dark; and she appears to be well preserved for one of her apparent years. She enjoys reminiscing and relates things in the most dramatic manner. She claims to be related to every person in the Norwood section but refuses 'to go runnin' out there 'cause they don't come runnin' over here to see me, so I just quit now.' Coming originally from Kentucky, she has lived in this city more years than she would confess, but a guess based on her conversation would place the date around thirty years or more. She is deeply religious and recalls with great pleasure that a bishop of her church once shook hands and chatted with her a moment." Lulu tells a lot about folklore and folklife in her narrative:

We was born about forty miles from Lexington, Kentucky, me and the others, eleven children altogether—about six and five, don't exactly remember which. [She did not recall the number of boys and the number of girls in her family.] Patrick Dood and Harriet—that's a pretty name, Harriet— they was my folks, my mother and father. They was slaves, but the children ain't never served, ain't never served, not nary lick they ever served. My father could read and write; don't know how he learn nor who teach him, but he know.

We lived on the plantation before the war. Then 'long come emancipation, and we moved off somewheres, and my father bought a farm, and we lived on that. We raised everything we used. Had hogs and chickens and geese and ducks and turkeys. And we kept the feathers from them for pillows. Little ol' frame house, didn't have but two doors and two windows and four rooms. The children fell asleep on the floor, like children will do, and my mother'd go roun' gatherin' 'em up and put 'em to bed. She laid some at the head and some at the foot of the bed. Five or six'd sleep in the bed, and she'd lay some at the head and some at the foot.

The children would go barefooted in the summer, but again fall would come, we'd get shoes. They'd send off in the fall for shoes for us, for winter shoes. My daddy'd get a fine pair of boots for ninety-eight cents, and reckon my mother pay roun' about the same for hers. A dressmaker'd come twice a year and make clothes for us. We'd come down the pike to meet her, a-swingin' on her, pesterin' her, carryin' bundles for her. All the suits for the little boys was made from the same cloth, all the suits just alike. All the scarfs, mittens, stockin's, socks, caps, and such like my mother'd knit. She knit everything; wasn't no store to be a-runnin' to ever' minute.

Potatoes and carrots and cabbage and apples'd be buried in the ground, but the apples'd sometime have a groun'y taste, so sometimes we wouldn't bury them. And we'd make a keg of sauerkraut; many's the hour I spent makin' sauerkraut. Why, just makin' it, like you make all sauerkraut.

Don't never sweep no dirt out'n doors after dark, and don't you empty no ashes after dark, neither, and when hosses kicked and neighed after dark, and late at night you know spirits was at 'em. They can see spirits the same as I can. 'Course I can see spirits. Seed one just before Christmas. I seed this'n and knowed they was something I done forgot to do, something she want me to do before she died. Like as not I done forgot to do it, and she done come back to see. I looked up from my work and see this person a-standin' by a table, head on one side like, and wearin' a blouse and skirt—just a-standin' there. And I quick turn my head and look off and look back, and she's done gone. That's the way to do. If you see a spirit and don't want to see it, just turn your head quick and back, and it'll be gone.

And back in those days, didn't have no almanac; we read the elements. We told rain by the moon and weather by the moon and by when the moon was goin' to change. Didn't' use no almanac—we could just go out and look up and tell just what the weather goin' be, tell by the elements.

Christmastime we'd hang up our stockin's and get a glass-headed doll. And we'd have black cake and plum puddin'. Black cake was like fruitcake except it didn't have no raisins or nothin' in it. We had turkey, chitlins, and everything—cook enough to last a week. And we'd go to church—the children in front and ol' folks behind.

A child born with a veil over its face, it can see spirits plain as day. They can just walk down the street and see 'em; they just step out the way and walk 'round 'em. You just watch, you'll see it happen time and again. 'Course they hardly ever say nothin' 'bout it, but that's just what they doin' —gettin' out of the way some spirit, and if you wasn't born with a veil, you can see spirits by lookin' over the left shoulder of anybody who was born with a veil.

A copper ring worn on the left ankle'll keep off rheumatism, and a little bag of asafetida worn roun' your neck on a string'll keep off certain diseases. They say, too, that a string tied to your ankle or wrist'll keep you from crampin' in water.

And when you got sick folks in the' house and you hear a dog howlin' and carryin' on, just get ready to give up that person 'cause it's a sure sign they'll die. If you never had rats in your house and one comes and gnaws and gnaws and can't catch 'em, it's a sure sign of death. Just like when you hear knockin' and you can't find it, it's death knocks.

And mark it down. When sick folks that been very low get suddenly better and want to eat a lot, just mark it down; it's death wantin' to be fed.

106. ARTHUR SHAFFER

They Moved at Least Two Hundred Slaves
over the Mason-Dixon Line

Arthur Shaffer was living at 813 South Mulberry Street in Muncie when he was interviewed about his grandfather, Hillery Chavious, whose ancestry was African American, Native American, and German. Freeborn in 1833, Hillery, one of fourteen children, lived near Richmond, Virginia. Knowing what freedom meant and seeing the misery of blacks held in slavery, Hillery, only seventeen, and his two older brothers helped slaves escape from southern plantations to freedom.

The Chavious brothers secretly went into the fields during the day and the slave quarters at night and offered to help slaves escape. They arranged to meet the runaway slaves on a particular night at a designated spot, from which the runaways were taken to a hiding place, perhaps a stable loft, a haystack, or, in emergencies, a place in the woods where they were covered with brush. They gave the runaways food and water and hid them until the roads were safe to travel. Then they took them to the next station on their flight across the Mason-Dixon Line.

The slaveholders generally organized a group of men with bloodhounds to chase the escaping slaves. The dogs were allowed to sniff shoes or pieces of clothing of the runaways to give them a scent to track. Rarely did the dogs leave a track until they were dragged from the heels of the terrified slaves. Sometimes when overtaken by dogs, escaping slaves climbed up trees or on buildings. They rarely were bitten if they had the courage to stand still. To throw the dogs off the scent, though, the Chavious brothers carried the runaways the last half-mile, for with the slaves' feet off the ground, the dogs could not pick up the scent.

The Chavious brothers moved from plantation to plantation helping slaves escape. They estimated that they moved at least 200 slaves over the Mason-Dixon Line into freedom.

107. JACK SIMMS

He Regretted Very Much That He Had Been Denied an Education

Jack Simms was living northwest of the hospital on Poplar Street in Madison when he was interviewed. The fieldworker said he was "a very interesting old man." Jack's daughter invited the fieldworker into the house, but Jack wanted to talk outside where he could "spit better." Jack finally decided that the interview could be conducted in the house, though, since the fieldworker "wouldn't be there long anyhow."

Once the fieldworker was in the house, Jack's daughter said that her father was very young at the time of the war. On hearing this, Jack remarked very testily, "If you're going to tell it, go ahead. Or am I going to tell it?" Born and raised on Mill Creek in Kentucky, Jack was, in fact, so young at the time of the Civil War that he did not remember very much about it or about how slaves were treated. He referred to the Civil War as the "Revolution War" and said he remembered seeing lines of soldiers on the Campbellsburg Road. He regretted very much that he had been denied an education.

108. BILLY SLAUGHTER

There Must Be Someone Left to Tell about Old Times

There are two reports of interviews with Billy Slaughter—the longer one focusing on personal experiences and local history, and the shorter one dealing with the "patty roll" [patrol]. From Billy Slaughter, George Thomas (q.v.), George Morrison (q.v.), and Colonel Lucien Beckner (Assistant State Director of the Federal Writers' Project in Louisville, Kentucky) the fieldworker obtained the following information about "patty roll": The term was derived from "patrol" and means the same thing. "Patty rolls" consisted of white men, usually slaveholders, whose duty it was to see that all black slaves were in their quarters by nine o'clock. Slaves who wished to remain out of their quarters later than the curfew had to get a pass or permit from their owners. Otherwise, the "patty roll" would chase them to their quarters, sometimes fastening wires across a road at about the same height as the escapees' chins. When blacks were caught without a pass, they were whipped. In some sections of the South, "patty rolls" even wore the same type of dress—white boots, black shirts, broad-brimmed white hats, and black breeches. The "patty roll" created a reign of terror among the slaves, though apparently some blacks enjoyed the thrill of being chased and of escaping.

Billy Slaughter was born on September 15, 1858, on the Lincoln farm near Hodgenville, Kentucky. When interviewed, he was living at 1123 Watt Street in Jeffersonville. At that time, descendants of the Slaughter family who had once owned him were still living near Hodgenville. According to the interviewer, they "lived between the Dixie Highway and Hodgenville on the right of the road driving toward Hodgenville about four miles off the state highway." Billy was sold once and was given away once before he was given his freedom.

Billy maintained that from a cliff on the Lincoln farm Indians threw settlers' children into a spring below. Unless the children could swim or the settlers rescued them, they drowned. Then the Indians gathered around the scene of the tragedy and rejoiced. Billy said he was thrown in the pool when he was a baby, but was rescued by white people. He remembered seeing several Indians, though not many. Abraham Lincoln was his hero, and he planned another trip to the Lincoln farm to once again see the cabin in which Lincoln was born.

Though ordinarily believed to have been fought over slavery, the Civil War, he maintained, really was not. He said the real reason for the war was that the South withdrew from the Union and elected Jefferson Davis president of the Confederacy. Southerners, or Democrats, he said, were called "rebels" and "secess," and Republicans were called "abolitionists." He said that firing on Harpers Ferry was firing on the United States, and there, through John Brown's raid, war was virtually declared. Billy explained that Brown was an abolitionist who was captured there and later killed. While Billy respected the federal government, he regarded John Brown as a martyr for the cause of freedom and included him among his heroes. Among his prized possessions was an old book written about John Brown's raid.

Another problem facing the North at that time was that the men taken from farms and factories to serve in the army could not be replaced by slaves. Not all blacks who wanted to join the Union forces were able to do so, because they were closely watched by their owners. Some slaves were made to fight in the Southern army whether they wanted to or not. This reduced the number of free blacks in the Northern army. As a result, he claimed, Lincoln decided to free all slaves. Billy recalled reading that Lincoln was walking the White House floor one night during the Civil War with a black man named Douglas, and that was when Lincoln made his decision to free the slaves. These events, according to Billy, led to the Emancipation Proclamation. The slaves were freed during the Civil War, but that was not why the war was fought.

At the beginning of the war, blacks who enlisted in the Union Army were given freedom, as were their wives and unmarried children. Billy's father joined the Union Army at the Taylor Barracks near Louisville, Kentucky, which was Camp Taylor during World War I; consequently, Billy's father and mother and their unmarried children were freed. Billy still had the papers declaring his freedom. He believed that black soldiers never fought in any decisive battles. He said there always had to be someone to clean and polish harness, care for horses, dig ditches, and construct parapets. Billy's father, however, was at Memphis during the battle there.

The Slaughter family migrated to Jeffersonville in 1865, when Billy was seven years old. At that time there was only one depot there—a freight and passenger depot at Court and Wall streets. What is now Eleventh Street was then a hickory grove, a paradise for squirrel hunters. On the ridge beginning at Seventh and Mechanic streets were persimmon trees. This was a favorite hunting ground of blacks for possum, and today the ridge is known as "Possum Ridge." The section east of St. Anthony's Cemetery was covered in woods. Since there were a number of beechnuts, many pigeons frequented the woods, and it was faster to catch pigeons there than to shoot them.

At this time there were two shipyards in Jeffersonville, Barmore's and Howard's. Barmore's shipyard was located on the site of a meatpacking company, which Billy called a "pork house." He had seen several boats launched from these yards, and large crowds gathered for the event. After the hull was completed in the docks, the boat was ready to launch. Several men were employed to launch the boat. Blocks serving as props were knocked down one at a time, with one man knocking down each prop. On its way to the river, the boat was christened with a bottle of champagne.

In his earlier days, Billy himself worked on a steamboat that traveled from Louisville to New Orleans. People then traveled on the river, for there were few railroads. First Billy cleaned the decks; then he cleaned the inside of the boat, including mopping the floors, and making the berths. Next he was ladies' cabin man, and later he took care of the quarters where the officials of the boat slept. Billy also worked as a second pantry man, which involved waiting on tables in the dining room. Since clothing had to be spotless, he sometimes had to change his shirt three times a day.

The meat on the boat's menu included pigeon, duck, turkey, chicken, quail, beef, pork, and mutton. Vegetables of the season were served, as well as desserts. It was nothing unusual for a half-dollar to be left under a plate as a tip for the waiter. Those who worked in the cabins never set a price for a shoe shine, but fifteen cents was the lowest they ever received.

During a yellow fever epidemic, before a quarantine could be declared, a boatload of three hundred people left Louisville at night to go to Memphis, Tennessee. The boat then went to New Orleans, where yellow fever was raging, and the captain warned them of it. Billy recalled how he had seen people fall over dead on two narrow streets. The streets were crowded, and there were no sidewalks, just room for a wagon. Here the victims sat in the doorways sleeping and falling over dead. When the boat returned, one of the crew was stricken with this disease, and Billy nursed him until they reached his home at Cairo, Illinois. No one else contracted yellow fever, and this man recovered.

Another job Billy held was helping to make the brick used in the U.S. Quartermaster Depot. Colonel James Keigwin operated a brick kiln in what is now a black settlement between Tenth and Fourteenth and Watt and Spring streets. The clay was obtained from this field. Billy's job was to off-bear the bricks after they were taken from the molds and to place them in the kilns to be burned. Wood was used as fuel.

Billy said he sometimes wondered why he was still left on earth when all his brothers, sisters, and friends were gone. Billy read the Bible quite often, and "the Bible," he said, "says that two shall be working in the field together, and one shall be taken, and the other left. I am the one who is left." He believed that he was still living because there must be someone left to tell about old times.

109. MOSES SLAUGHTER

A Cause That Had Both God and President Lincoln on Its Side

At the back door of the frame house occupied by Moses Slaughter and his daughter, who faithfully cared for the aged former slave, the fieldworker asked,

"May I arrange an interview with Mr. Moses Slaughter?" Moses's daughter replied, "If you won't talk too long or let him talk too fast, you may see Papa for a few minutes. He's so weak we don't allow him to exert himself. We want him to save his strength."

Inside the old-fashioned house, everything was clean and orderly. Moses, clad in white outing flannel pajamas, sat in his favorite easy chair. Beside his chair stood a bedside table, and on it was his favorite book, a well-worn Bible. Moses smiled as he welcomed the fieldworker and said that he was delighted to have callers because his daughter often was busy and he became lonely. Based on evidence that he considered reliable, Moses guessed that he was born before 1833. He remembered that he joined the Union Army when he was 30, so at the time of the interview he must have been more than 104 years old.

Moses believed that the southerners should have been remunerated for the loss of their slaves, and that if this policy had been ratified, the Thirteenth Amendment would have been accepted more gladly. He believed that northerners were as responsible for the existence of slavery as southerners.

Moses chuckled as he told the fieldworker how his mother had learned how to read from the slaveholder's children and passed the knowledge on to her own children. His mother would say to the slaveholder's daughter, "Come on here, Emily; Mama will keep your place for you." And while Emily read stories, dialogues, and poems, his mother, Emalina, followed each line until she was a fluent reader.

Moses, a professed Christian, was baptized in the Cumberland River while yet a slave. He was baptized again in the Ohio River when he joined the McFarland Baptist Church, which he helped to build, since at that time he was able to do carpenter work. At the time of the interview, he was not able to work, but the fieldworker said he "is pleasant and says he enjoys living. He is glad that the black children of today enjoy advantages unknown in his childhood. He is glad they are free."

A respected citizen, Moses was influential among local African Americans and had many white friends in Evansville and Vanderburgh County. He was commander of Fort Wagner Post No. 581 of the Grand Army of the Republic.

Moses had been a widower since March 4, 1892. Two of his six children died in childhood, and four were raised in Evansville. When the fieldworker remarked about "a beautiful walnut bedstead" in his house, Moses replied, "Yes, ma'am, money couldn't buy that bed. Every one of my babies was born in that bed. Virginia passed away there, and there's where I expect to die."

The fieldworker reported that Moses related the following narrative "with careful precision, using no noticeable southern accent. No slang phrases escaped his lips. His memories of the pioneer days and the war period are vivid."

I was born in Montgomery County, Tennessee, and my parents were the property of Joseph Fauntleroy, farmer and raiser of stock and slaves. Joseph

Fauntleroy was a very wealthy man, and he owned our entire family and had the right to sell, give away, and dispose of any or all of us as he saw fit.

My mother was the sweetest woman that God ever let live. She was gentle, loving, always smiling. She was the mother of ten children of her own, which she nursed and tended, and also was wet nurse of ten Fauntleroy children. All of us children, black and white, called my mother "Mama," and she never turned a deaf ear to a child.

She was housekeeper for the white family and slept in a room of the Fauntleroy home where she could care for the babies all night. Joseph Fauntleroy and his wife had so many friends and went about in society until they had no time to take care of their children, but they knew Mama would give them all the care they would ever need. She was a loyal slave, a Christian, and always ready to help the children pray.

When I was a good-sized little boy, Miss Emily Fauntleroy married G. H. Slaughter and Master Joseph gave me to Miss Emily for a bridal present. That was my first real sorrow, having to leave my mother and the other children. I have brothers named Fauntleroy that were never sold or given away, but I took the name of Slaughter when Miss Emily took me to her home.

When I was thirty years of age I enlisted at Clarksville, Tennessee, under Captain J. G. Parke. My second captain was Captain Bobbilts. We sang "Rally, Boys! Rally!" and all were enthused and hoping to win our freedom within a short time.

Army life is a hard life no matter how well the men are trained. It seems you are always meeting with some unexpected occurrence.

A policy of slave enlistment was proposed by General Lee. He suggested immediate freedom to all enlisted slaves, but the congress was not willing to sanction Lee's policy, and the big slave dealers argued against it because it would ruin their business. President Lincoln ordered a draft for 500,000 men, and about that time there was a great many Union sympathizers in the eastern section of Tennessee, so just as soon as the congress allowed the slaves to enlist, we enlisted.

I remember when our company was encamped at Johnsonville, Tennessee. We were in training, and our camp was near a wilderness. We had heard that John Bell Hood, lieutenant-general of the Confederate Army, was a natural born soldier. He had been given the command formerly held by J. E. Johnstone and had now been given command of the Army of the Tennessee. General Thomas called an army to oppose Hood, as he was planning a big battle at Nashville, Tennessee. So many Confederate soldiers were hiding in the wilderness our men couldn't march from Johnsonville to Nashville without surprising some party of Confederate skirmishers, so we were ordered to go by Clarksville—a much longer route than we would have had to travel— for our fear of the Confederate soldiers.

On that march we were afoot, carrying our packs. The roads were through the wilderness. We were in danger of becoming divided, and in that case many would have been lost. No maps or charts were given to us. We must just stay close together. Food was scarce, and we were unpaid, but one half of us guarded, while the other half worked, cutting our way through that awful wilderness. We went by way of the Cumberland River and through the Gap. The Gap was always a point well guarded. General Grant was commander of all the armies of the United States, and his plan was to crunch Lee's army and all the Confederate forces. General Thomas's command was made up of the Army of the Cumberland and the Army of the Ohio. Thomas was a thoughtful man, slow in all his ways of moving about. He was loved by all his men. When we reached Nashville, Hood's army was soon reduced to a handful. General Thomas commanded the Union corps, although the regiment had been put under a general corps commanded by Charles H. Ottensteen, colonel of the Thirteenth Regiment. Armies were divided into regiments. A regiment was a colonel's command and was a permanent association of soldiers. When regiments combined, brigades were formed. Combined brigades formed divisions, while divisions united to form armies. Each battalion was formed of two or more companies. A battalion was commanded by a field officer called "major."

Hood's army suffered severe losses in the Battle of Nashville on December 15th and 16th, 1864. Although our men were tired, the Union soldiers were fighting for a cause that had both God and President Lincoln on its side, and the Thirteenth Regiment fought for its own freedom.

No master was really good to his slaves. The very fact that he could separate a mother from her babes made him a tyrant. Each master demanded exact obedience from his slaves. Negro children were not allowed an education, and if they by any chance learned to read and write, they usually had to keep their knowledge a secret.

After the War ended I took to the river trade, steamboating on the R. C. Gray from Cincinnati to Fort Smith, Arkansas. On one trip the river froze into a solid sheet of ice. I lived at Paducah, Kentucky, but there was no way to get back home while the weather was so cold, so I got a job with a farmer who kept a corral for stock. I helped him care for the horses all that winter. Starting home in the early spring, I reached Lexington and worked near Lexington for a farmer, Mr. John Beaumont. While there I met Virginia Smith, ex-slave of a slave owner of Henley County, Kentucky. Virginia wanted me to stay in that part of the country. There was where we spent many happy days. We went to freedom celebrations, dances, picnics, and parties, and while working there I saved money to marry and make our wedding trip on. We moved to Evansville in 1867 and found it a good place to live in.

110. ALEX AND ELIZABETH (BETTY) SMITH
I Like to Talk and Meet People

According to her obituary in the *South Bend Tribune* (October 1, 1957), Elizabeth (Betty) Smith was born in McCracken County, Kentucky, on October 5, 1853, and died in South Bend on September 30, 1957. Her obituary says that she married Alex Smith "on a plantation in Kentucky" on the first Saturday of May in 1874, and that the couple came to South Bend from Hickman, Kentucky, around 1922. According to Alex Smith's obituary in the *South Bend Tribune* (May 13, 1942), he was ninety-seven when he died on May 12, 1942, though Mrs. Smith's obituary says he died at age eighty-eight. Other dates vary, too, in their obituaries, but the dates in Mrs. Smith's obituary are perhaps more accurate, because just before she died her family's Bible was discovered, and with the help of her pastor she "managed to piece together the important dates" in her life.

A biographical article on Alex and Elizabeth appeared in the *South Bend Tribune* on June 17, 1936. The reporter, John H. Magill, wrote that "Though Mrs. Smith can neither read or write and Mr. Smith claims only the barest knowledge of such things they both recounted happenings with a command of English that would do credit to one who had had the advantages of modern education. Without a day of school they have acquired through observation and natural aptitude the art of interesting conversation." The article points out that "Even after the slaves were freed they were not permitted to go to school; while in slavery they had no chance to see printed matter. Mrs. Smith told of an instance when she had picked up a book in which there were printed pictures. She was allowed to look at one of the illustrations but was not permitted to examine the print." The newspaper account also included information about life on the plantation:

> Both were born in Calloway county, Kentucky, on adjoining farms, Mrs. Smith in 1854 and Mr. Smith two years later. Mrs. Smith was fortunate in being born the property of a family who believed in treating slaves in a kindly manner but Mr. Smith remembers the sting of a whip wielded by the strong arm of the master. In those days, they both agreed, colored people were treated worse than dogs on some plantations. Children were torn from the arms of their mothers to be sold to a new master. Families often were widely scattered and almost never reunited.
>
> They lived in little log cabins chinked with mud without windows or ventilation except for the air admitted through the door. They were permitted the barest furnishings and food that was doled out to them from the "big house" was cooked in the open fireplace....
>
> Oftentimes they found themselves without sufficient clothing to protect their small bodies from the rigors of winter. Shoes were unheard of for the

colored people. While they both were too small to labor in the fields before the civil war they can remember tramping their ways through the corn and tobacco fields picking worms off the leaves and aiding in their small way. "There were about 50 slaves on each of the two farms," Mr. Smith said, "and while the adults and larger children had to work pretty hard the 'master' did not allow the very small children to labor. You see it would have stunted their growth and maybe ruined their market value."

When interviewed by the WPA fieldworker, Alex and Elizabeth Smith had been married sixty-four years and, according to Elizabeth, "never a cross word exchanged. Mr. Smith and I had no children." The elderly couple lived in a shack patched with tarpaper, tin, and wood at 217 South Lake Street on the west side of South Bend. The interview was conducted in their combination bedroom and living room. A large heating stove stood in the center of the small room, a bed was on one side, and a few chairs were scattered about. The floor was covered with an old patched rug. The only other room in the house was a very small kitchen.

Their shabby shack was situated in the center of a large lot, around which was planted a very nice vegetable garden. The property belonged to Harry Brazy. The old couple did not pay rent or taxes, and Brazy said they could stay there as long as they lived, "which is good enough for us," said Elizabeth. The only income the Smiths had was a government old-age pension, which amounted to about $14 a month.

Elizabeth, the talkative one, was a small, very wrinkled woman with a stocking cap pulled over her gray hair. She wore a print dress made of three different kinds of material: sleeves of one, collar of another, and body of a third. Her front teeth were brown stubs, suggesting that she chewed tobacco. When the interview concluded, Elizabeth said, "I like to talk and meet people. Come again."

Alex Smith was tall and probably well built at one time. When interviewed, he got around with a cane. Elizabeth said that he was not at all well, that he had been in the hospital for six weeks the winter before the interview. Alex remembered the Civil War, especially the marching of thousands of soldiers and the horse-drawn artillery wagons, though he had been a child of only five at the time. Alex's father rented a farm after the war, and Alex had been a farmer all his life.

As children, both Alex and Elizabeth Smith were slaves in Kentucky. The nearest town was Paris, Tennessee. Elizabeth, or Betty, as her husband called her, was a slave on the Peter Stubblefield (spelled "Studdlefield" in Alex Smith's obituary) plantation. She was named for Elizabeth Stubblefield, a relative of Peter Stubblefield. Alex was a slave on the nearby Robert Stubblefield plantation. On the Peter Stubblefield plantation, slaves were treated very well and had plenty to eat, but Alex said he went hungry many times on the Robert Stubblefield plantation: "Often, I would see a dog with a bit of bread, and I would have been willing to take it from him if I had not been afraid the dog would bite me."

As a child of five years or under, Elizabeth had to spin "long reels five cuts a day," pick seed from cotton and cockleburs from wool, and perform the duties of a housemaid. Young Alex had to chop wood, carry water, cut weeds, care for cows, and pick bugs from tobacco plants. He went barefoot both summer and winter and remembered the cracking of ice under his bare feet. The Stubblefields freed their slaves the first winter after the Civil War. Elizabeth's mother told her that the day the slaveholders came and told the slaves they were free to go any-place they desired, she was glad to be free, but she had no money and no place to go. Many slaves would not leave, and she said that she had never witnessed such crying as went on. Later Elizabeth was paid for working. First she worked in the fields for food and clothes. A few years later she nursed children for twenty-five cents a week and food, but after a time she received fifty cents a week, board, and two dresses.

111. MATTIE BROWN SMITH

There Was Lots of Colored Folks Crossed the River at This Point

Mattie Brown Smith was around age fifty-five when interviewed. She was well educated and had taught school at one time. Mattie's information came from her parents.

Yes, ma'am, I can tell you something interesting about the escape of slaves across the river, but I don't ever remember of hearing anything about any around here in New Albany. But we all came from Brandenburg, down in Meade County, Kentucky. My father was a slave and belonged to John Ditto. He didn't actually belong to him. John Ditto was a single man, and my father was hired out to him. My mother belonged to the Footes. I've heard them tell all this many a time till I could tell it in my sleep.

My uncle, Charles Woodford, was owned by Charlton Ditto, but was practically a free man. He was a blacksmith in Brandenburg and come and went as he pleased. But Uncle Charlie had heard so much about the escapes that he decided he wanted to be free, too. A white man, a Canadian named John Canada, worked in the blacksmith shop Uncle did; and when he found out Uncle wanted to go across, he got in touch with a certain man who ferried the runaways across the river. He was an old white man named Charles Bell who lived in Harrison County just below Corydon. He lived in a log house about five miles back from the river—with no road leading to the house from the river, just a bridle path. Mr. Bell had a skiff which he used to carry the slaves over. So this man, John Canada, in the shop with my uncle got in touch with Bell, and one dark night Uncle Charles got a few things together—in those days they carried what little they had in a tied-up handkerchief over a stick—and he sneaked around and told his wife and children good-bye, and they went down to the Ohio River—right at Moorman's place, almost to the salt well. They couldn't cross right at the town; that was too public, and the jail is right near the foot of Main Street, too, which leads right down to the river in Brandenburg. So they had to go up a piece.

Anyhow, Bell took Uncle Charlie across the river in the skiff and on back through the woods on a mule to his house, where he hid him a few weeks, and then took him on up through Corydon and across White River. And he went on up to Canada and finally got out to California. I've heard that sometimes they were taken up through Indianapolis.

After a while Uncle Charlie wrote to his wife, Aunt Marietta, and got her in the notion to try to get free, too, and join him. The plans were all laid for her to go, but she up and got scared and told the whole thing to Charlton Ditto, who had owned Uncle Charlie. So a bunch of white men around Brandenburg—Peter Fountain was the sheriff—him and some others got together, and one man who was fat and about the size of Aunt Marietta dressed up in her clothes, sunbonnet and all. And when Mr. Bell, the old man, came up in the skiff to get the colored folks, as had been arranged, this man got in the skiff, with another old colored man who was there waiting to get across, and he hit Bell over the head with a pair of brass knucks, and the men came out of hiding and took him to the Brandenburg jail—took the old colored man, too.

Mr. Bell laid there in jail a long time, and finally his daughter got word out to California to his sons who were there, and they came on back in a hurry. They went across the river in their skiff and shot up the Brandenburg jail and got their father out. Yes, ma'am! But the old colored man who was in jail with Bell wouldn't come; he was too scared. So they got Mr. Bell out and took him back on home.

But Uncle Charles came on back here from California when the war broke out and served in the army. Yes, ma'am, he sure did. My great-uncle, Horace Grigsby, he escaped by the same route. He belonged to John Ditto. There was lots of colored folks crossed the river at this point. I've heard my father and mother tell of it often. My father knew the Clark family, George Rogers Clark—yes, ma'am. I've got a platter now that belonged to them when they was down in Kentucky. And see that old safe in the kitchen? My father bought that in the auction sale of the Clark family.

My great-grandfather was in the Revolutionary War, and my great-grandmother, Hester Starks, served General Washington when she was only

eleven years old. She used to tell all they had to eat and said they had whole
pigs with apples in their mouths and all! That was back in Virginia.
But I don't know of any crossin' near here . . . never heard about any.

112. MRS. ROBERT SMITH

They Were Sorry to Leave Their Owners and Shift for Themselves

At the time of the interview with Mrs. Smith, there was a row of houses occupied by blacks in Hanover. The building lots had been purchased from Mr. Dunn, one of the original owners of the land where Hanover is now located. When the slaves were freed at the close of the Civil War, a group of Kentucky slaveholders purchased the land for a new home for their slaves and gave them enough money to build their houses. Mrs. Smith's uncle, a man named Sanders, was one of the former slaves who got land and some money to build a house here. She said that all of her relatives were treated so well while in slavery that they were sorry to leave their owners and shift for themselves.

113. SUSAN SMITH

The Presence of White People Still Seemed to Annoy Her

Susan Smith was held by Billy Carlisle, who lived near Campbellsville in Taylor County, Kentucky. She did not know her age or exactly how old she had been when the slaves were freed. As a slave, Susan had to raise and pick cotton, shear sheep, spin, thread looms, weave cloth, take the wool to the carding machine, mold candles, and go to the mill. She was especially interested in how food was stored for the winter. Some food, she said, was canned in tins and sealed with canning wax. Some fruit was made into preserves, some vegetables and apples were buried, and some fruits and vegetables were dried. Slaves attended the same church as whites, but there were no schools for slaves.

Several years after the Civil War, Susan came to Jeffersonville, where she worked in various homes. When she was unable to work, she was taken to the Clark County Poor Farm. She seemed embittered toward her former owners, recalling how hard she had to work and viewing them as taskmasters. The presence of white people still seemed to annoy her. She had the utmost regard for truth and would not tell anything unless she knew it was absolute fact; therefore, since she had no experience with play parties and square dances, she had nothing to report about them.

114. SYLVESTER SMITH

They Said the Civil War Would Be Only a "Breakfast Spell"

Sylvester Smith, who was eighty-six years old when interviewed, was born in 1852 at Goldsboro, Wayne County, North Carolina, about forty or fifty miles east of Raleigh, the state capital. His sister, her husband, and he were the only slaves on the estate of Richard Newsom. Newsom lived in a log house for some time, but later he built a frame dwelling. He had three girls and two boys. Sylvester, then quite young, lived with the Newsoms. His sister and her husband, however, lived in a shack that was no better than a coal shed. On Newsom's farm, Sylvester worked in the corn and cotton fields, cut wood, and gathered feed for the stock during the day. At night he was a house servant, keeping the fires and carrying water. Sylvester said he was treated well enough as a slave to convince him to stay with his former master a year without pay after gaining freedom. His sister, however, left immediately on gaining her freedom.

Sylvester recalled that soldiers leaving for the Civil War said it would be only a "breakfast spell." He was not old enough to serve in the war but saw a few light skirmishes. Several battles were fought within hearing distance. He said that for seven days and nights he heard the battle at Richmond. He could hear the heavy shooting plainly at night, and during the day he could hear it by placing an ear to the ground. He said that often slaves were stolen, so usually he was not allowed on the road. He was permitted, however, to go a short distance to a spot where trenches and rifle pits were dug. He said traces of these still could be seen.

According to his obituary in the *Terre Haute Tribune* (December 22, 1943), Sylvester died at the age of 91 in 1943 at his home on 1401 South 14th Street in Terre Haute and is buried in Grandview Cemetery.

115. MARY ANN STEWART

Eat Plain Foods, Take Reasonable Exercise, Refrain from Worry, and Read the Bible

Mary Ann Stewart of Harmony celebrated her 104th birthday on September 17, 1937. She had lived under the administrations of all but six presidents of the United States. Mary advised anyone desiring to live 104 years and still be active, as she was, to eat plain foods, take reasonable exercise, refrain from worry, and read the Bible. She had read the Bible seven times. She said that late in her life a rural carrier working out of Greencastle had taught her to read, stopping at her home each day to hear her recite her lesson. The fieldworker reported that Mary could still read and sew without glasses and was lively and happy.

Mary said she was born in Morgan County near Martinsville "when the county was wild, wooded, and living was very primitive." Her parents, Andrew and Liza Shular, apparently early settlers in Morgan County, died when she was young, leaving her with an uncle, who reared her. Mary, the only one of her family to marry, outlived three husbands. Her last husband was William Stewart, a Civil War veteran.

116. BARNEY STONE

Sixteen Years of Hell as a Slave on a Plantation

When interviewed, Barney Stone was nearly ninety-one, but the fieldworker reported that he was "in sound physical condition and still has a remarkable memory." Barney was a slave in Kentucky for more than sixteen years and a soldier in the Union Army for nearly two years. He learned to read and write while serving in the army and taught black children following the Civil War. Then for three years he studied in the home of a lawyer. When interviewed, he had been a Baptist preacher for sixty-nine years and had been instrumental in building seven churches. At the time of the interview, he was the only former slave living in Hamilton County and one of three living members of Hamilton County's Grand Army of the Republic—the other two members being white. He had been a member of three lodges: Knights of Pythias, Odd Fellows, and Freemasons.

Barney worked hard for the advancement of blacks in Tennessee and Kentucky as well as in Indiana. Besides preaching and lecturing, he also farmed. At the time of the interview, he still had a field of sweet corn and a large vegetable garden, which he plowed, planted, and tended himself. The fieldworker reported that "not a weed can be found in either."

Barney called his narrative "My Life's Story," in which he emphasized "sixteen years of hell as a slave on a plantation." The fieldworker commented that Barney's story "will convince the reader that, even though much blood was shed in our Civil War, the war was a Godsend to the American nation." According to the fieldworker, "This story is told just as given by Barney":

My name is Barney Stone. I was born in slavery May 17, 1847, in Spencer County, Kentucky. I was a slave on the plantation of Lemuel Stone for nearly seventeen years and was considered a leader among the young slaves on our plantation. My mammy gave birth to ten children, all slaves, and my father, Buck Grant, was a buck slave on the plantation of John Grant, his master. My father was used much as a male cow is used on the stock farm and was hired out to other plantation owners for that purpose and was regarded as a valuable slave. His master permitted him to visit my mammy each weekend on our plantation.

My master was a hard man when he was angry, drinking, or not feeling well. Then at times he was kind to us. I was compelled to pick cotton and do other work when I was a very small boy. He would never sell me because I was regarded as the best young slave on the plantation. Different from many other slaves, I was kept on the plantation from the day I was born until the day I ran away.

Slaves were sold in two ways, sometimes at private sale to a man who went about the Southland buying slaves until he had many in his possession. Then he would have a big auction sale and would re-sell them to the highest bidder, much in the same manner as our livestock are sold now in auction sales. Professional slave buyers in those days were called "nigger buyers." He came to the plantation with a doctor. He would point out two or three slaves which looked good to him and which could be spared by the owner and would have the doctor examine the slave's heart. If the doctor pronounced the slave as sound, then the nigger buyer would make an offer to the owner, and if the amount was satisfactory, the slave was sold. Some large plantation owners, having a large number of slaves, would hold public auction and dispose of some of them; then he would attend another sale and buy new slaves; this was done sometimes to get better slaves and sometimes to make money on the sale of them.

Many times, as I have said before, our treatment on our plantation was horrible. When I was just a small boy, I witnessed my sister sold and taken away. One day one of the horses came into the barn and Master noticed that she was crippled. He flew into a rage and thought I had hurt the horse—either that or that I knew who did it. I told him that I didn't do it, and he demanded that I tell him who did it, if I didn't. I didn't know, and when I told him so, he secured a whip, tied me to a post, and whipped me until I was covered with blood. I begged him, "Master, Master, please don't whip me, I don't know who did it." He then took out his pocket knife, and I would have been killed if Missus (his dear wife) had not made him quit. She untied me and cared for me.

Many has been the time I have seen my mammy beaten mercilessly and for no good reason. One day, not long before the outbreak of the Civil War, a nigger buyer came and I witnessed my dear mammy and my one-year-old baby brother sold. I seen her taken away, never to see her again until I found her twenty-seven years later at Clarksburg, Tennessee. My baby brother was with her, but I didn't know him until Mammy told me who he was. He had grown into a large man. That was a happy meeting. After those experiences *of sixteen long years in hell as a slave, I was very bitter against the white man, until after I ran away and joined the Union Army.*

At the outbreak of the Civil War and when the Northern army was marching into the Southland, hundreds of male slaves were shot down by the rebels, rather than see them join with the Yankees. One day when I learned that the Northern troops were very close to our plantation, I ran away and hid in a culvert, but was found, and I would have been shot had the Yankee troops not scattered them, and that saved me. I joined that Union Army and served one year, eight months, and twenty-two days, and fought with them in the Battle of Fort Wagner and also in the Battle of Millikins Bend. When I went into the army, I couldn't read or write. The white soldiers took an interest in me and taught me to write and read, and when the war was over I could write a very good letter. I taught what little I knew to colored children after the war.

I studied day and night for the next three years at the home of a lawyer, educating myself, and in 1868, I started preaching the gospel of Jesus Christ and have continued to do so for sixty-nine years. In that time I have been instrumental in the building of seven churches in Kentucky, Tennessee, and Indiana. I did this good work through gratefulness to God for my deliverance and my salvation. During my life, I have joined the K. of P. Lodge, and I.O.O.F. and Masonic Lodge. I have preached for the uplift and advancement of the colored race. I have accomplished much good in this life and have raised a family of eight children. I love and am loyal to my country and have received great compensation from my government for my services. I am in good health and still able to work, and I am thankful to my God and my country."

Under the headline "Rev. Barney Stone Dies at Ripe Old Age," his obituary appeared in the *Noblesville Daily Ledger* on November 21, 1942:

Rev. Barney Stone is dead, his death occurring Friday near the noon hour. He had not been in good health for three years, but kept busy with any engagements he had. He was in ill health since the death of Mrs. Stone, and gradually failed, but was able to attend Memorial services and offer prayer on special occasions, his prayers being helpful on any occasion.

He was not able to be present at the tribute paid to Aunt Nan Roberts in recent months, but he was there, upheld by friends, and made the address of the occasion. He was not able to vote the Republican ticket once more at the recent election, but he was carried to the polls and cast his last vote. He never failed in any duty of his life if he had a fair chance to perform it—he never had an opportunity in life, but he made them as the years went by and so became one of the best known and highly regarded men of Indiana.

Barney Stone came to Noblesville early in the Nineties and was the pastor of the Baptist church here for a time and then was an evangelist and in the late

Nineties he was appointed by the late Judge John F. Neal as Court Bailiff and was a most satisfactory public official.

Mr. Stone was a Civil War veteran, a member of the 108th Infantry, enlisting in Kentucky, in Company E of the Colored Infantry. And he was always faithful to his race, to his friends and to his country.

Rev. Mr. Stone was born in Kentucky on May 17, 1847, and the family was in slavery; but, the boy did the best he could and succeeded in becoming a teacher, a preacher, an evangelist, a great speaker on patriotic occasions and the head of a family which has added to the name of Stone in this community and country. . . .

117. MARY STONESTREET

They Had to Have Freedom Papers Before They Could Settle in Indiana

Mrs. Lewis still had the freedom papers of her grandmother, Mary Stonestreet. The papers—issued in Jessamine County, Kentucky, in 1853—described Mrs. Stonestreet as a "mulatto, aged 33 years." The old document was a prized possession of the family and was so worn that it was in about three pieces.

Signed by Mr. Sering, the document was recorded in Madison when the family entered Indiana. The family settled on State Road 29 near the present site of Bryantsburg. The freedom papers bore the Kentucky seal, and, according to Mrs. Lewis, as long as the papers were kept, blacks could not be sent back into slavery by slave chasers.

Mr. Stonestreet, Mrs. Lewis's grandfather, was a shoemaker by trade and made $500 worth of shoes to buy his freedom. When he married, his wife was given her freedom by her master, who was also her father. Their children, therefore, were born free, but had to have freedom papers before they could settle in Indiana.

118. ADAH ISABELLE SUGGS

One Night in a Dream Her Mother Received Directions for Escaping

Adah Isabelle McClain Suggs was born in slavery before January 22, 1852. Her owners were Colonel Jackson McClain and his wife, Louisa. Adah was raised and cared for by her mother in the slave quarters of the McClain plantation, a large estate in Henderson County, Kentucky, three and a half miles from the city of Henderson. She claimed that the McClains were good to their slaves and never beat them. Among her many childhood memories of the slave quarters, she recalled the slaves singing and dancing together after a day's hard work. She said their voices were strong, and their songs were sweet.

When Adah was not yet five years old, Louisa McClain visited the slave quarters to review the living conditions of the blacks. There she discovered that Adah had been taught by her mother to knit stockings, using wheat straws for knitting needles. Mrs. McClain at once took her from her mother's care and gave her a room in the McClains' house. Adah soon was borrowing books from the McClains' library and recalled receiving "words of praise and encouragement" for her efforts. Although Adah was happy in the big house, her mother knew that unhappiness was in store for her daughter if she remained on the plantation. Adah said it was a custom throughout the southern states that the firstborn of each female slave should be the child of her master, and young girls were forced into maternity at puberty. Slave mothers naturally resisted this appalling practice, and Adah's mother was determined to prevent her child from being victimized. According to the fieldworker, Adah's "escape from slavery planned and executed by her anxious mother, Harriott McClain, bears the earmarks of fiction, but the truth of all related occurrences has been established."

The first attempted escape was thwarted. When Adah was about twelve, Harriott tried to take her to a safe place, but they were overtaken on the road to a ferry that they had hoped would put them across the Ohio River. They were carried back to the plantation, and Harriott was punished and locked in an upstairs room. Adah knew her mother was imprisoned there and often climbed up to a window where the two could talk.

One night in a dream her mother received directions for escaping. She told Adah about the dream and instructed her how they might escape together. Adah got a large knife from Louisa McClain's pantry, and with it Harriott pried the lock from her door. Around midnight she went to a large tobacco barn and waited there for her daughter.

Adah had some trouble escaping, for as a useful member of the McClain household, her services were hourly in demand. The McClains' daughter, Annie, had been born with a cleft palate and later developed heart dropsy, which regularly required surgery in Louisville. Adah learned to care for Annie and drew the bandages for the surgeon. She vividly recalled one trip to Louisville when the McClain party stopped at the Gault House. Adah said, "It was a grand place," and described the handsome draperies, winding stairway, and other "artistic objects" she saw at the grand hotel. Adah loved Annie, who always wanted Adah near her, so Harriott McClain waited patiently for her daughter in the tobacco barn.

That night Adah and her mother traveled to Henderson, where they hid under Margaret Bentley's house until darkness fell. Frightened, they crept through the woods in constant fear of being recaptured. Federal soldiers put them across the Ohio River at Henderson, and from there they cautiously traveled to Evansville. Harriott's husband, Milton McClain, and her son, Jerome, were volunteers in a black regiment. Federal statute gave freedom to enlisted blacks as well as to their wives and children, so by statute Harriott McClain and her daughter should have been given their freedom anyway.

Arriving in Evansville, Adah and her mother were befriended by free blacks. Harriott obtained a position as a maid with the Parvine family. Adah said that "Miss Hallie and Miss Genevieve Parvine were real good folks." After working for the Parvines for about two years, Harriott had saved enough money to place her daughter in "pay school," where she learned rapidly.

On January 18, 1872, Adah married Thomas Suggs, who was deceased at the time of the interview. Though Thomas was held by Archibald Dixon and Bill McClain (*see* Hettie McClain), Adah and her daughter, Harriott Holloway, believed that he had adopted Suggs as his name because a man named Suggs had once befriended him in a time of trouble. Adah and Thomas had fifteen children—including twin daughters and a set of triplets, two sons and a daughter. Adah claimed she was happy in her belief in God and Christ and hoped for a glorious hereafter.

Ada died on February 20, 1938. Her obituary in the *Evansville Press* (February 21, 1938) reads, in part, "Mrs. Ada Suggs, 86, of 527 S. Linwood-av, died Sunday. She lived here over 63 years."

119. KATIE SUTTON

Yes, Ma'am, I Believe in Evil Spirits

It is not clear when Katie Sutton was interviewed, for the fieldworker said, "Three years ago Aunt Katie was called away on her last journey." Moreover, the fieldworker provided two texts of the interview with Katie, with both texts including a close version of the same song and some of the same folk beliefs. In both texts the fieldworker stressed that Katie believed in spirits and spells and reported several of her superstitions. "Yes, ma'am," Katie said, "I believe in evil spirits and that there are many folks that can put spells on you, and if'n you don't believe it, you had better be careful, for there are folks right here in this town that have the power to bewitch you, and then you will never be happy again. Evil spirits creep around all night long, and evil people are always able to hex you, so you had best be careful how you talk to strangers. Always spit on a coin before you give it to a beggar, and don't pass too close to a hunchbacked person unless you can rub the hump, or you will have bad luck as sure as anything."

According to Katie, the seventh son of a seventh son, or the seventh daughter of a seventh daughter, possesses the power to heal diseases, and a child born after the death of its father possesses "a strange and unknown power." Apparently Katie also had some kind of power, for she claimed that one time she had planted a tree and cursed her worst enemy, who then died that same year. She maintained that a rabbit's foot brought good luck only if the rabbit had been killed by a cross-eyed black person in a country graveyard in the dark of the moon, and she believed that kind of rabbit's foot could be found only once in a lifetime, or possibly once in a hundred years.

Katie said she scrubbed her back steps with chamber lye daily to keep away evil spirits and death. She also sprinkled salt in the footprints of departing guests "so they can leave no ill will behind 'em and can never come again without an invitation." During the interview, according to the fieldworker, a neighbor came in to borrow a shovel, but Katie said, "No, no, indeed, I never lend anything to nobody." After the neighbor left, Katie explained, "She just wanted that shovel so she could hex me. A woman borrowed a poker from my mama and hexed Mama by bending the poker, and Mama got all twisted up with rheumatism until her uncle straightened the poker, and then Mama got as straight as anybody. No, ma'am, nobody's going take anything of mine out'n this house."

According to Katie, "White folks are just naturally different from darkies. We are different in color, in talk, and in religion and beliefs. We are different in every way and can never be expected to think or to live alike. When I was a little girl I lived with my mother in an old log cabin. My mama was good to me, but she had to spend so much of her time at humoring the white babies and taking care of them that she hardly ever got to even sing her own babies to sleep. Old Missus and Young Missus told the little slave children that the stork brought the white babies to their mothers but that the slave children were all hatched out from buzzards' eggs, and we believed it was true."

The fieldworker reported that Katie's voice "was thin and wavering, but she recalled an old song she had heard in slavery days, and sang this lullaby":

A snow white stork flew down from the sky,
Rock-a-bye, my baby, bye,
To take a baby girl so fair,
To Young Missus, waitin' there,
When all was quiet as a mouse,
In Old Massa's big fine house.

Refrain:
That little girl was born rich and free,
She's the sap from out a sugar tree,
But you are just as sweet to me,
My little colored child,
Just lay your head upon my breast,
And rest, and rest, and rest, and rest,
My little colored child.

To a cabin in a woodland drear,
You've come, a mama's heart to cheer,
In this old slave's cabin,
Your hands my heartstrings grabbin',
Just lay your head upon my breast,
Just snuggle close and rest and rest,
My little colored child.

Your daddy ploughs old massa's corn, Your mama does the cookin',
She'll give dinner to her hungry child,
When nobody is lookin',
Don't be ashamed, my child, I beg,
'cause you was hatched from a buzzard's egg,
My little colored child.

120. MARY EMILY (MOLLIE) EATON TATE

These Are Scenes of My Childhood That I Can Never Forget

When interviewed, Mary Emily Eaton Tate, more familiarly known as Mollie, was the only former slave living in Jay County. She was born, as near as she knew, on June 30, 1859, on the old Mendenhall farm in Jefferson County, Tennessee, about five miles from Mossy Creek, now Jefferson City, and twenty-nine miles east of Knoxville, Tennessee. Mollie was one of eleven children, but only one brother was living when she was interviewed. Her husband, Preston Tate (q.v.), also had been a slave, held by Bill Tate, brother of Dave Tate, Mollie's owner. Mollie's mother before marriage was held by Larkin Johnson, who gave her to his daughter, "who married on the night the stars fell." Mollie's father was held by a man named Stiffy. Her mother was a cook, and her father worked on the East Tennessee, Virginia, and Georgia Railroad when it was being built. Their camp was at Purchess [Purchase?], now Chattanooga, Tennessee. Mollie's grandmother, Marciss Johnson, lived to be 115 years old and was the mother of nineteen children.

When interviewed, Mollie had lived in Portland more than fifty years and at the time was living at 657 2nd Street. The interviewer wrote that Mollie "is perhaps the only colored person in this part of the country living today who can recall the days just preceding the Civil War when a people were held in bondage and sold upon the auction block the same as other chattel, cattle, etc. Often mothers with babies in their arms were separated, perhaps never to see each other again. Only those who experienced these hardships they underwent in bondage can know and tell fully what it all meant." From firsthand knowledge, Mollie described slavery days:

My parents, Isaac and Nancy Eaton, lived in a little cabin on the plantation owned by Joe Eaton and wife, Sarah, and the name of Mary Emily Eaton was given the new babe, myself. When I was only a few weeks old, my parents moved to Grainger County, just across the Holston River, which winded its way through the plantation. Many were the happenings during the five or six years that followed.

I was too young to remember, but have heard my parents relate how once while they were about their tasks on the plantation I had been left alone in my cradle at the cabin. For some cause I became dissatisfied, and the master—perhaps making his usual visits around the cabins, I suppose—became annoyed at my crying and as punishment placed me in a fence corner. There was snow on the ground. Mother and Father discovered me still crying.

The North and South were waging battle. Mossy Creek and surrounding country was the scene of much warfare, and the little cabin of the Eatons was along the line of march. I, with the other children, was somewhat shy at first, but eventually we did come out, attracted by the music, and watched the soldiers go by with bayonets glistening in the sun.

The blue coats and the gray coats were as thick as hops, and as the fighting took place around Mossy Creek I could hear the cannon roar, and when the soldiers flanked they were on the next farm adjoining the Mendenhall farm. This farm belonged to Bill Tate, the master of Preston Tate.

Every day spies were making their rounds, and often soldiers, both Yankee and Rebel, visited our cabin, taking what they could find—bacon, molasses, meal, anything they wanted. They'd fill their canteens with water and be off. The cellar, a hole dug out under some boards of our cabin, contained our supplies, but the soldiers lost no time in searching until they found them. They did the same at the homes of the slave owners and all that were in their path. Father would take the horses, which belonged to the master, and hide them out in the woods and hills.

One regiment took my oldest brother, John, away, and we never heard from him for several years after the close of the war. Instead of Eaton, he had changed his name to John Crittendon and was in Detroit, Michigan.

When I was about five years old, I, with my parents, was sold to Dave and Mary Jane Parsley Tate, whose farm was in Hamilton County across the Holston River. When the ferryboat landed, Dave Tate carried me into the house. There were three older brothers and sisters, but the master, Joe Eaton, had them hired out on the Rankins' farm. Two younger brothers, Tolbert and Joe, were born on the Tate farm.

A short time before the war closed, the master, Dave Tate, was conscripted and had to go. Before leaving he charged Uncle Isom and Aunt Nancy to care for his wife, two sons, David and William, and daughter, Tennessee. He never returned alive. After several months his body was brought back to the old home and buried.

In making the clothing mother was one of the principal workers. Myself and other children helped pick and seed cotton. Mother carded and spun, then reeled and spooled it. Granny Parsley flayed and warped it. Then it was ready to put on the shuttles and weave. My older sister and mistress and her mother did most of the weaving. If some other color besides white was desired we gathered sumac bushes and berries and bark of oak trees, and mother used these to dye the goods. The mistress attended to the sewing. She would see that we would get a suit of clothes once in a while. Granny knit the stockings.

Father operated the cane mill and still house on the plantation. Many times have I rode the horse in grinding peaches, apples, corn, or whatever needed grinding. The master always kept his cellar well supplied with peach and apple brandy, corn whiskey, gin, rye, molasses, tree sugar, tobacco, and most anything you might mention. The supplies were barreled, sent down the river, and sold.

The washing was usually done at the spring or on the creek bank. On one occasion my older sister permitted me to accompany her. There had been a hard rain, and the water was carrying all kinds of debris downstream. The old foot log had been turned sideways. Heedless to the demand of my sister, I toed the log—of course, I was barefooted—to the other side of the creek to gather wild onions. But when I started back, and about halfway across, I lost my toehold, and off I went. The swift stream carried me under the log, and I bobbed up on the other side. I had presence of mind to grab the log and pulled myself out and crawled across.

At the time of the surrender, when the soldiers were on their way to Virginia, regiment after regiment passed by, and boys of the colored regiments who were acquainted with us would say, "Good-bye, Uncle Isom and Aunt Nancy," with bayonets on their shoulders, sabers at their sides, knapsacks and canteens on their backs. The tread of this vast number could be heard for miles. After the surrender, covered wagons and trainloads of artillery, guns, and everything that had been used in time of war passed by. These are scenes of my childhood that I can never forget.

Often I have carried on my head a piggin [small wooden pail] of water from the spring at the foot of the hill for Granny Parsley, mother of my mistress.

When emancipation was declared some rejoiced, while others seemed to think that they couldn't depend on themselves, refusing to leave the plantations, while others were driven away. After freedom we went to Hodgetown, Knox County, and lived there a year, then moved to the Mat Peck farm near my birthplace, the old Mendenhall farm. Here Father, assisted by others in his condition, built a big log house for his family: rough logs put together with chinking and mud, or rather clay, between them. One door was made of boards with wooden hinges. A hole was cut out in one side of the cabin for a window. Boards laid on the ground, sometimes very sparingly, served as the floor. The chimney was built of sticks and often would catch fire. It was nothing uncommon, however, to look out at cracks where the chinkin' would fall out and see snakes, lizards, and scorpions crawling or lying between the logs.

Father took up blacksmithing as a trade, and the children started to school at Mossy Creek, five miles, so I had to walk, not ride as nowadays, ten miles a day to attend school. Six weeks to three months was the limit of the session, part-time pay school and part-time free school. Before going I had to help carry water from the spring and gather bark off fence rails in the woods for mother's cooking. We would start for school about six o'clock in the morning through the woods, over gullies and rocks, up and down hills, over fences, and sometimes we would cry and say we heard or saw ghosts in the thickets. We always endeavored to get home before dark. Water and wood had to be brought in for the night. This was the regular routine.

In the meantime, the zinc mines opened at Mossy Creek. The owner, Mr. Sizer, wanted Father to work, and then we moved to Mossy Creek. Now I didn't have to walk quite so far to school. A Miss Josephine Denny from the north and a Mr. Yardley of Knoxville taught. I was about ten years old. After school hours I took care of Mrs. Tillson's baby. We were paid fifty cents every two or three weeks. I also was employed at Dr. Roten's, bringin' up the cows and the other chores around the house.

Eventually the mines went out, and we moved back to the Mary Jane Tate farm and remained a short time until we were again back to Mossy Creek. This wasn't for very long, as Father decided to buy a home three miles east at Rocktown, and the name was well chosen, for the roads were nothing, only rock—all sizes, little rocks, big rocks, boulders, flat, round, anything you care to mention.

Now I was walking six miles to school, and I'm sorry to say this was almost my last school days. I was permitted to go to two sessions, six free. What education I received in those days from my speller, reader, geography, arithmetic, and dictionary has never been regretted. My parents weren't able to continue my education, so the fourth grade was the end of my school days.

We moved back to Mossy Creek to what was called Branners' Old Red Store. I was old enough to be of some assistance to my parents now, as I earned fair wages cooking. Dr. Hood's was the first place at regular hire at one dollar per week, then Professor Brown's, principal of Mossy Creek high school and college. After they moved away I was at Professor Russell's and went with them to Knoxville and remained there for a time. The next place was lawyer John Yoe—was there until I returned home to Mossy Creek February 10, 1884.

Preston Tate, who first came to Portland in 1881, returned to Mossy Creek, and we were married on Thursday evening at eight o'clock on February 28, 1884, at my home. There were fifty or seventy-five guests. Bridesmaid was Mary Claven and best man John Kile. Tuesday, March 4, at 8 P.M., we left for Portland and arrived there after midnight, March 15, 1884.

It would seem peculiar nowadays to see children wearing tow sacks for clothing. But that was what the children on the plantation often wore, or at least that was the resemblance, just a hole on each side for the arms and one for the head.

Our meals at the cabin were cooked in the fireplace. Mother would make cakes of meal and water, sometimes a little salt, and cover them with ashes. Potatoes were baked likewise. With our menu of hoecakes and molasses, we thrived and grew stout and healthier than most children do today with all kinds of food and luxuries.

At about ten years of age while attending a revival meeting at an old cabin church in the charge of Uncle Benny Roper, I was converted. It was one night in February. I returned home with my parents and told my sister who was sick at the time, and she said, "Now, Mollie, you will have to give up your bad habits and be a good girl." My sister died soon afterwards, and her advice was indeed an inspiration to me at that time and has been all the days of my life to live up to my Christian profession.

121. PRESTON TATE

It Was Not Unusual for Boys and Girls to Dress Alike

Since Preston Tate had died on January 20, 1928, the fieldworker got his narrative from a story published in the *Portland Daily Sun.* Tate was born on December 15, 1854, in a cabin on the "old Bill Tate plantation" in Grainger County, Tennessee. He and Tolbert Bragg (q.v.) were held by the same person. One of the events of slavery and Civil War days related by Preston was a battle near Mossy Creek, Tennessee. He and other children were playing when they discovered that they were surrounded by soldiers. Frightened by shots "and shells flying thick and fast," they hid behind trees, crawled through thickets, and emerged from the battle unharmed.

Preston said that since not every boy in a family was fortunate enough to have a Sunday suit, one suit was rotated among them. When it came his turn, a boy was overjoyed on Sunday morning when he could dress up in a homespun suit and homemade shoes. The other boys in the family had to wear their everyday clothing, which consisted of only a long tow shirt. He said if you took a sack, cut an opening in the bottom for the head, and split each side for the arms, you would have something like a tow shirt. Sometimes it was difficult to distinguish a boy from a girl by their clothing, as it was not unusual for them to dress alike.

Preston made three trips to Indiana, the first in 1881, before settling permanently. He claimed that the climate made him ill on the first trip, so he returned south and did not return to Indiana until he had regained his health. His last trip south was to get married, and on March 5, 1884, Preston arrived in Portland with his bride, Mollie Eaton (*see* Mary Emily ["Mollie"] Eaton Tate). They stayed for a couple of days in the home of Mr. and Mrs. John Branner, who at that time lived on the corner of West 3rd and Ship streets east of the Lake Erie depot. Afterwards, they lived with Preston's stepfather, Tolbert Bragg, on West 2nd Street.

The following year, 1885, Preston bought a lot at the corner of South Western Avenue and 2nd Street, cleared the trees and underbrush, and built a three-room house, into which he moved his wife and infant daughter, Maude. At first, these rooms were covered only with laths. After working all day at a sawmill, Preston spent evenings putting paper on the laths. Only later were the walls plastered. As the years passed, additions were made to the small house to keep pace with other improvements in the community.

For thirty years Preston worked as a fireman at William North's sawmill in South Portland. After the mill burned down in 1914, he worked at Detamore's stone quarry. For his last twelve or thirteen years—in fact, up to the day of his death—he worked at Frands' greenhouse.

Preston's wife, also a former slave, was still living at 657 2nd Street in Portland when he died.

122. GEORGE THOMAS

Pioneer Industries and Amusements in Clark County

George Thomas was interviewed in the spring of 1936, when he was living at the Clark County Poor Farm. At that time the fieldworker was looking for "old songs," not narratives of former slaves, but she gathered the following information from George, thinking it might be needed "later on." It was fortunate that she asked him about his life, for after "the 1937 flood had subsided he was found drowned near his little shack in Jeffersonville." Most of the information she gathered was about early folklife in Clark County when George came there, and not about George's life as a slave. Supposedly, all this material came from George.

George was the slave of Jim Thomas, who gave him to George Thomas, his son. They lived near New Castle, Kentucky. George said that as a slave he helped turn the spinning wheel, and he knitted stockings after working all day. When his master caught slaves who had gone to sleep over their work, he whipped them, but George claimed that he never got a whipping he did not deserve. According to the fieldworker, George's attitude toward his former owners was kindly and respectful, as was his attitude toward all white people. George was about nine years old when the slaves were freed. Catching the spirit of many of the freed blacks, he ran away from home when he was around fourteen. Deciding to travel, he lived in seven different states, but most of the time he lived in Indiana.

When George came to Clark County, there were abundant forests, and many of the homes were log houses, which usually were erected at house raisings. At a house raising, families gathered at a designated place to construct a log house. The logs already had been hewn and dragged to the place where the house was to be built. While the men built the house, their wives cooked dinner, and everyone had a good time. The social function of the house raising was important, for there was no commercial entertainment then. Home building was carried on even more enthusiastically if the house was to be occupied by newlyweds. The pioneers were accustomed to hard work, and one day was all that was needed to build a log house.

Log rollings were still held in Clark County when George arrived, and George took part in some of them. When an owner of a plot of ground decided to cultivate the land, he first had to clear the trees. After the trees had been felled, a day would be scheduled for the men of the community to gather with their ox teams to drag away the logs. The logs usually were burned or rolled down a hill to rot. As with the custom of house raising, women came to the log rolling and cooked a big dinner.

At that time, some people still cooked food at a fireplace. Cornbread, for example, was baked at the fireplace and called ash bread. Cornmeal dough was made into a cake and placed on a clean hearthstone and covered with hot ashes until it was thoroughly baked. Cornmeal was ground on a gristmill that was driven by waterpower; it was not the sifted meal that one buys today. In the sifting process today, the husks of the grain are removed, but meal from the gristmill was ground whole, which required much sifting by housewives. George took corn to the Tunnel Mill near Charlestown to be ground.

Play parties were the usual form of amusement in Clark County. There were not any musical instruments at play parties. People sang songs to accompany the games they played. The guests in wagons or on horseback gathered at the host's home by sundown. Young men generally brought their sweethearts behind them on a plow horse, and husbands brought their wives and children in a wagon. Soon after arriving, the children went to sleep on the bed where the coats were laid. Then both young and old played "Skip to My Lou," "Weevily Wheat," and such games until about twelve o'clock, when it was time to go home. Later, in German Catholic settlements around St. Joe, square dances were held.

People had to preserve food for winter. Some fruit, such as apples and peaches, was dried. Corn also was dried. Cabbage, potatoes, turnips, and apples were buried in straw in the ground. Several shocks of fodder were placed over the mound of dirt covering the vegetables, and a ditch was dug around the mound. This kept the food from freezing even in the severest winter.

Making maple syrup was another pioneer industry in Clark County. In the spring of the year as the sap began to rise in the maple trees, a hole was bored through the bark and the cambium layer of the trees with an auger. The pith was removed from an alder stalk, and the stalk was placed in the hole in the maple tree to serve as a trough for the sap. Each morning the buckets of sap were gathered from the trees that were tapped, and the sap was boiled to a syrup.

Elliptically shaped iron griddles were used by Clark County housewives to fry chicken, but, according to George, that was not the use for which they were intended. He said that the griddles fit on top of the first step of a step stove after two lids were removed. Stove irons were set on the thin griddles, placing the irons closer to the fire.

123. GEORGE THOMPSON

I Have No Education; I Can Neither Read nor Write

George Thompson's obituary appeared in the *Franklin Evening Star* on December 8, 1941: "George Thompson, 87-year-old Franklin colored laborer and for many years a resident of this city died at 10 o'clock Sunday morning at his home on North Young street following an extended illness. . . . Mr. Thompson was born in Kentucky on October 8, 1854, the son of Joseph and Manda Thompson, both natives of that state. He is survived by his wife, Mrs. Edith Thompson." Here is George's narrative from the WPA manuscript files:

My name is George Thompson. I was born in Monroe County, Kentucky, near the Cumberland River on October 8, 1854, on the Manfred Furgerson plantation. Furgerson owned about fifty slaves. Mr. Furgerson was a preacher and had three daughters and was kind to his slaves. I was quite a small boy when our family, which included an older sister, was sold to Ed Thompson in Metcalfe County, Kentucky. Thompson owned about fifty other slaves, and as was the custom then, we were given the name of our new master, Thompson.

I was hardly twelve years old when slavery was abolished, yet I can remember at this late date most of the happenings as they existed at that time. I was so young and inexperienced when freed that I remained on the

Thompson plantation for four years after the war and worked for my board and clothes as coach boy and any other odd jobs around the plantation.

I have no education; I can neither read nor write. As a slave I was not allowed to have books. On Sundays I would go into the woods and gather ginseng, which I would sell to the doctors for from ten cents to fifteen cents a pound, and with this money I would buy a book that was called the Blue Back Speller. Our master wouldn't allow us to have any books, and when we were lucky enough to own a book we would have to keep it hid, for if our master would find us with a book he would whip us and take the book from us. After receiving three severe whippings I gave up and never again tried for any learning, and to this day I can neither read nor write.

As there were no oil lamps or candles, another black boy and myself were stationed at the dining table to hold grease lamps for the white folks to see to eat. And we would use brushes to shoo away the flies. Slaves were never allowed off of their plantation without a written pass, and if caught away from their plantation without a pass by the paddy-rollers [patrollers] or gorillars [guerrillas], who were a band of ruffians, they were whipped.

In 1869 I left the plantation to go on my own. I landed in Hart County, Kentucky, and went to work for George Parish in the tobacco fields at $25 per year and two suits of clothes. After working two years for Mr. Parish I left. I drifted from place to place in Alabama and Mississippi, working first at one place and then another, and finally drifted into Franklin in 1912 and went to work on the Fred Murry farm on Hurricane Road for ten years. I afterwards worked for Ashly Furgerson, a house mover.

I have lived at my present address, 651 North Young Street, since coming to Franklin.

124. JOE WADE

His Mother's Master Was Very Cruel to Her

Joe Wade, who lived at 821 North Senate Avenue in Indianapolis when interviewed, told about his mother, Mary Hays, who was a slave in Davidson County, Tennessee. Joe said his mother had a hard life because her master was very cruel to her. He tied her to a tree and beat her for anything that displeased him. If at any time she was unable to work, he locked her in a guardhouse with nothing to eat. Joe said that Mary could recall only one member of her family, her sister, but they were separated when they were children and did not know where each other was. After twenty years, they were reunited.

When slaves went to the fields to work, they had to form a line, and anyone getting out of line was tied to a tree and beaten unmercifully. According to the interviewer, "Joe was very serious and rather hard on the slave holders." He wished he could take the overseers to task for mistreating his mother.

125. REVEREND WAMBLE

His Mother Died from a Miscarriage Caused by a Whipping

Reverend Wamble was born a slave in Monroe County, Mississippi, in 1859. The Westbrook family there held many slaves, usually two hundred or more, who worked under the supervision of overseers—sometimes slaves themselves—who managed the farm. One of the Westbrooks' daughters married a wainwright named Wamble. The Westbrook family, as did the Wamble family, gave the newlyweds two slaves, including Reverend Wamble's grandfather. Since slaves took the name of their owners, Reverend Wamble's grandfather was named Wamble.

Families with moderate incomes tended to have only a few slaves and usually treated them kindly; as with a farmer with only a few horses, it was in their best interest to take good care of their slaves, because slaves were valuable, and most small slaveholders did not have the money to buy more. Many large slaveholders, however, were wealthy, and one slave more or less made little difference to them.

Reverend Wamble's father and his father's brothers, children of slaves born in Africa, were of the same age as slaveholder Wamble's boys, and they grew up together. Reverend Wamble's grandfather managed the farm, and the three white Wamble boys worked under him, just as the slaves did. Wamble never permitted any of his slaves to be whipped or otherwise mistreated.

Slaveholder Westbrook, a deacon in the Methodist Church, had two black overseers to manage the farm and the other slaves. Unlike slaveholder Wamble, he was strict with his slaves and did not permit them to leave the farm. A slave caught off the farm was whipped on the spot. On return to the farm, the slave was tied to a cedar tree and whipped again. Reverend Wamble's mother was a Westbrook slave, and when he was two years old, his mother died from a miscarriage caused by a whipping. When women slaves were in an advanced stage of pregnancy, they were made to lie face down in a specially dug hole in the ground and were whipped. Otherwise, they were treated like the men; their arms were tied around a cedar tree or post, and they were lashed.

The children of slaves usually became the property of the mother's owner, but since Reverend Wamble appeared to be a promising slave, both the Westbrooks and the Wambles wanted him, much as one would want a valuable colt. Although Reverend Wamble's grandmother was a Westbrook, she wanted her grandson to join his father as a Wamble slave, because the Wambles treated their slaves much better. So she hid him in a shed, which was more like a doghouse. Feeding him each night, she hid him from the Westbrooks until the war was over. If the South had won the war, though, Reverend Wamble would have been a Westbrook, since his mother had been a Westbrook slave; but after the

South lost, he lived with his father and took the name of his father, who was a Wamble slave.

Reverend Wamble recalled what happened to a Westbrook slave who ran away. One evening the slave showed up at Wamble's home and asked for some supper. After taking the slave into his home and feeding him, Wamble took a log chain that was hanging above the fireplace, tied it around the slave's waist, and left him to sleep on a bench in front of the fireplace. The next morning, after the slave had eaten breakfast provided by the Wambles, slaveholder Westbrook, his son, and an overseer appeared. Reverend Wamble recalled that from his hiding place in the shed he was awakened by the sound of the lash and the moaning of the slave. After the whipping, the slave was turned loose. When he had gone about a mile through the bottomland toward the river, Westbrook turned his hounds loose on the slave's tracks. Before the slave had gone another mile, the hounds had treed him, much as a dog trees a cat.

The Westbrooks pulled the slave down from the tree, and the dogs ripped his foot. They whipped the slave again, put long ropes around him, whipped him all the way back to the Wamble place, and there whipped him again. Then they drove him two miles to the Westbrook place, where he was whipped once more. No one knew what happened to the slave, whether he died or recovered. Ironically, Westbrook, a church deacon, permitted his slaves to be whipped, whereas Wamble, who never attended church, never whipped or mistreated his slaves.

Reverend Wamble said that except for the whippings they received, the slaves were well treated. They were well fed, and if injured or sick, were attended by a doctor, just as one would care for an injured horse or sick cow, since the slaveholder made more money if his slaves were able to work. The slaves generally received plenty of meat, potatoes, and whatever else was raised. If the slaveholder had plenty to eat, so did the slaves. If the slaveholder did not have much to eat, neither did the slaves.

The slaves' living quarters were made of logs covered with mud. The roof was made of coarse boards covered with about a foot of dirt. The floors also were dirt. The furniture included a small stove and beds made with two boards attached to two corner walls. The end that was not against a wall rested on a peg driven into the ground, forming, in a sense, a one-legged bed. Other boards were placed across the two boards, and the slaves slept on these boards or on the dirt floor. Blankets were not provided.

Only one of the three white Wamble boys joined the Southern army. Until the war was over, the other two boys, who refused to go to war, hid out in the surrounding woods and hills. The only time Reverend Wamble's father left the farm was to attend to his master, Billy Wamble, when he was in a hospital recovering from wounds received in battle.

Slaveholder Wamble was a practicing wainwright and made two or three wagons at a time, which usually took about six months. Then he hitched teams to them and went north to Missouri, Kansas, Arkansas, and other states until he had sold all but one of the wagons and teams, keeping one wagon and a team to return home. Sometimes he was gone from nine to twelve months, and during his absence, Reverend Wamble's grandfather was in charge of the farm.

Reverend Wamble's grandmother was a full-blooded African who was brought to this country as a slave when she was seventeen. She was a big, strong woman who was often hired out to do a man's work. Since slaves were forbidden to own or read books and newspapers, hardly any slaves were literate, but somehow Reverend Wamble's grandmother had learned to read and write. Reverend Wamble recalled that sometime during the Civil War his grandmother brought an old newspaper to his hideout late one night. From fried meat grease and a cord string, she made a candle, which made a very tiny light. She placed some old blankets over the walls so that the light could not be seen through the cracks in the shed, and then she placed the newspaper as close as possible to the light without burning it and read it. No one knew where or how she had learned to read and write, and it was not well known that she could read and write until after the Civil War.

If a young, good-looking, husky black man was considered trustworthy, the family might make him the driver of the family carriage. They dressed him in the best clothes, including a silk-finished beaver hat. The driver sat on a seat on the top and toward the front of the carriage. No matter how long he had to wait or the condition of the weather, he had to remain on the seat while waiting for any member of the family he was driving.

Mail was carried in the same kind of carriage, also with a black driver. In each village there was a designated mail stop, and upon nearing each mail stop on the route, the driver sounded a bugle that could be heard for miles around to summon people to come and get their mail. Reverend Wamble claimed that many times in winter when horses pulling a carriage stopped at a mail stand, the driver would be frozen to death. Men would take the dead driver from the carriage seat, carefully saving the beaver hat for the next driver. As Reverend Wamble recalled, in the South none of the white people worked at manual labor; they usually sat under a shade tree. They were usually clerks, bookkeepers, or tradesmen.

Since slaves could not vote, they had no knowledge of politics when they became free. They knew only that they were free and had a vote. Reverend Wamble remembered as a boy seeing white and black soldiers marching on election day. He said that politicians always told blacks that it was in their best interest to vote for them, no matter what hardships they were causing blacks to suffer. One time after blacks were forbidden to vote, they marched in a body to the polls, demanded a Democratic ballot, and then were permitted to vote.

After the war, Reverend Wamble lived with the Wambles until his father, in partnership with another man, purchased forty acres of land. He attended school first for a period of only two months in 1871. In 1872 the government built a school, taught by a missionary, on his father's farm, and he attended this school for seven years. The school term was three months each year. Reverend Wamble said that he was twenty-seven years old before he read his first newspaper.

In 1880 Reverend Wamble married for the first time, but his wife died in Memphis, Tennessee, in 1888. By this marriage there were four children. On February 1, 1892, Reverend Wamble and his two surviving children all entered school in Little Rock, Arkansas. One of his daughters died in the third year of school, but the other graduated from a normal school in Little Rock and was a teacher for several years. At the time of the interview, she was working as a nurse and married to a minister in Louisiana. The three oldest of her ten children had earned degrees, and the others were expected to do the same. Reverend Wamble married his second wife in 1894, and she died in 1907. By this marriage nine children were born. His youngest daughter by his second marriage graduated from a college in Pine Bluff, Arkansas, and taught in New York City.

Wanting to earn more money, two of his sons came to Gary in 1924. At the time of the interview, both were working in the post office. Two years later Reverend Wamble, also wanting to earn more money, followed his sons to Gary. After working two years in a coke plant, he was laid off during the Depression. He had been in the ministry for thirty-seven years. Though advanced in years, he was active and healthy when interviewed. He said he had a small pension and was just waiting until it was time to pass on to the next world. Six of his children and seventeen of his grandchildren were living.

126. LOUIS WATKINS

They Were Taught to Read, Write, and Figure

Apparently Louis Watkins's experiences were told by his daughter, Hettie Watkins, who at the time of the interview was living at 813 South Pershing Drive in Muncie, for in the fieldworker's account of Sidney Graham (q.v.) he writes that "Miss Watkins, while giving the sketch of her father to this writer, related a story of one of her uncles [Sidney Graham]." Louis Watkins was born in 1853 on Peeler Parker's plantation, which was located about fifteen miles from Chattanooga, Tennessee, near White Oak Mountain. Louis claimed that his owner was good to him and that his overseer never whipped him. He was permitted to go to church with his parents on Sunday, a day of rest for the slaves. He had a white tutor who came on Sunday afternoons and taught the slaves in a room in the big house. Louis said they were taught to read, write, and figure, and they could "go as far as they were capable." They were encouraged to read books and to look at pictures at certain times outside of work hours. He said all the slaves were well-read, well-clothed, and well-housed.

The slaveholder kept four grown slaves to work in the fields, and his wife kept two slaves to work in the big house. After the whites had eaten, the slaves were taken to a big kitchen, where they ate substantial meals together. An unmarried black woman was in charge, and she saw that all the slaves got all the food they wanted. No one had to leave the table hungry. Louis's family remained together, because none of the slaves was ever sold off the plantation.

His owner had a powder mill on the plantation, and he operated the mill as a separate business mainly with white help. Louis, a boy at the time, ran errands in and out of the mill under the watchful eye of the whites in charge. One time he failed to clean the powder off the soles of his bare feet, and at his parents' cottage, he sat down in front of the stove and stuck his feet too near the grate. A spark flew out of the stove and ignited the powder. Fire encircled his bare feet, and the calluses on his soles were so badly burned that he had to remain in bed until new flesh covered his feet. Powder around his ankles also ignited, leaving a generous patch of blisters. Louis recalled this experience as the outstanding event of his slave days.

When the slaveholder told the slaves that they were free, they were given a choice of leaving or remaining on the plantation to work for wages. None of the slaves left right away; all took time to relocate in adjoining villages, where they found work for wages. Louis was about twelve years old when his parents left the plantation to live in Coltewah, a small village. A number of years after the war, Louis found work and married. He, his wife, and their three children moved to Muncie in 1907. His wife was deceased at the time of the interview.

127. SAMUEL WATSON

Samuel Was Sent to the Poor House

Samuel Watson was born in Webster County, Kentucky, on February 14, 1862. His owner's home was located two and a half miles from Clay, Kentucky, on Crab Orchard Creek. When interviewed, he was living with William Crosby on Southeast 5th Street in Evansville. According to the fieldworker, Samuel possessed an unusually clear memory. In fact, he claimed that he remembered seeing soldiers and hearing cannons when he was only an infant.

One story from his childhood that Samuel told was about how the slaveholder's wife saved her husband's horses. She and a number of slaves were walking one morning when they were startled by the sound of galloping horses. In the distance they saw a large number of mounted soldiers riding over a hill. Samuel later was told that the soldiers were on their way to Fort Donelson and were pressing horses and enlisting blacks into service. Samuel's owner, Thomas Watson, had many able-bodied slaves and many good horses. Realizing the danger of losing their horses, Mrs. Watson opened a big gate that separated the corral from a forest and ran among the horses shouting and whacking them. The frightened horses ran into the forest toward the river. When the soldiers stopped at the Watson plantation they found only a few old work horses standing under a tree, and not wanting these, they went on their way. Samuel hid in a corner of the house by a large outside chimney, where his frightened mother later found him. He recalled that all the horses returned the following afternoon.

Samuel remembered when the war ended and the slaves were emancipated. He said that "some were happy" and "some were sad." Many dreaded leaving their old homes and their masters' families. When Samuel's mother and three children were told that they were free, the owner asked his mother to take her children and leave. She took her family to the plantation of Jourdain James, hoping to work there and keep her family together; however, the wages they received failed to support them, so she left James's plantation and worked from place to place until her children were half-starved, half-naked. The older children, Thomas and Laurah, remembering better and happier days, ran back to their former owner, Thomas Watson, who went to Dixon, Kentucky, and had an article of indenture drawn up binding them to his service for a number of years. Only Samuel remained with his mother, who took him to William Allen Price's plantation, which was located in Webster County, Kentucky, about halfway between Providence and Clay on Crab Orchard Creek. Price had Samuel indentured to his service for eighteen years, so Samuel lived and worked on Price's plantation for quite a while.

An indentured person was supposed to be given a fair education, a good horse with bridle and saddle, and a suit of clothes after years of hard work, but Price refused these things to Samuel because he said he did not deserve them. A lawyer friend sued on behalf of Samuel and received a judgment of $115. After paying the lawyer's fee, Samuel was left with $95 and his freedom.

In 1882 Evansville became Samuel's home. To get there he took the train to Henderson, Kentucky, then crossed the Ohio River on a transfer boat. Samuel was impressed by the boat and its crew and said he loved Evansville from the first glimpse. In 1890 he married an Evansville native who had experienced neither slavery nor indenture.

In Evansville, Samuel had several jobs. First, Dr. Bacon, a prominent citizen living at Chandler Avenue and 2nd Street, hired Samuel as a coachman. Next he was houseman for Levi Igleheart, who lived at 1010 Upper 2nd Street. Igleheart entrusted Samuel to care for his horses and manage some family business. Igleheart also recommended Samuel for a job at the Trinity Church, located at the corner of 3rd and Chestnut streets, and for six years this job paid him $30 a month. Then for several years a man named McKeely hired him as janitor for lodges and other organizations. Samuel also cleaned walls and hung paper and did pretty well, he claimed, until the Depression hit him, as it did others.

Samuel was entitled to an old-age pension, which he received from 1934 through 1935, but on January 15, 1936, the money was withheld for some reason and Samuel was sent to the poor house. Still, he said he was not unhappy and did what he could to make others happy. In 1936 he again applied for a pension and received $17 a month to pay for his upkeep. At the time of the interview, his only work was tending a little garden and doing light chores.

128. HENRY WEBB

Plans for the Escapes Were Hatched in a Black Masonic Lodge

Henry Webb was living at 638 West 7th Street in New Albany when interviewed. He said that his father, a slave, told him that runaway slaves used to come across the Ohio River from Portland, now a part of Louisville. Plans for the escapes were hatched in a black Masonic lodge located in Portland. Blacks crossed the Ohio River in a skiff supposedly operated by fishermen. If the coast was not clear on the Indiana side, they would go up the river for a short distance. Some went all the way up the river past Louisville and then crossed over, probably around Utica. Many blacks who crossed hid with friends in the hills back of New Albany, and then after all danger passed, they made their way north by way of Salem.

129. NANCY WHALLEN

Preaching and Shouting Sometimes Lasted All Day Sunday

Nancy Whallen was living at 924 Pearl Street in New Albany with her daughter when interviewed. She was around eighty years old, but she did not know her exact age. The fieldworker said Nancy was hard to talk to because her memory was failing and she could not hear very well.

Nancy was born and raised in Hart County, Kentucky, where she lived a typical life of a rural black person during the Civil War and just afterwards. She remembered soldiers coming through the farm and asking for food. Some of them camped on the farm and talked to her and teased her. She told about one big slave named Scott who could outwork all the others on the farm. He would hang his hat and shirt on a tree limb and work all day long in the blazing sun on the hottest day.

She said that blacks used to have revivals in the woods. They would some-times build a sort of brush shelter with leaves for a roof, and services were held there. Preaching and shouting sometimes lasted all day Sunday. Blacks came from miles around when they could get away. The revivals usually were held away from the whites, who seldom, if ever, saw these gatherings.

Nancy remembered a big eclipse of the sun, or the "day of dark," as she called it. The chickens all went to roost, and all the slaves thought the end of the world had come. The cattle lowed, and everyone was scared to death.

Nancy said she was about five years old when freedom was declared. She stayed in Kentucky after the war, coming to Indiana when she was a young woman.

130. ANDERSON WHITTED

They Often Took Babies from Their Mothers and Sold Them

Anderson Whitted
(Courtesy of the Manuscript Division, Library of Congress)

Anderson Whitted was born in 1848 in Orange County, North Carolina. At the time of the interview, he was a month away from his eighty-ninth birthday. Since his mother took care of the white children on the plantation, her own nine children were very well treated. The owner was from a family of Hickory Qua-kers and did not believe in mistreating his slaves. He always provided them with plenty to eat as well as with clothing to wear to church on Sunday. Despite a law that prohibited giving books to blacks, Anderson's family had a Bible and an elementary spelling book. Anderson said his uncle belonged to a mean owner, though. His slaves worked hard all day and were chained together at night. His uncle ran away during the early part of the war, and after two years broke through the lines and joined the Northern army. He returned to North Carolina after emancipation.

Anderson's father, held by Anderson's master's half-brother, lived fourteen miles away, but every two weeks he was loaned a horse to visit his family. His father could read and spell very well, and he taught his family on these visits. Anderson learned to read the Bible first and in later years learned to read other things. It was customary for the slaveholder to search the slaves' quarters, but Anderson's owner never did.

Anderson's owner was a physician, and Anderson's grandmother often assisted him on his rounds to care for the sick. When the war broke out, the owner's son joined the Southern army and was wounded, so the doctor took Anderson's grandmother with him to help in treating him and bringing him home. On the way home the doctor died, but his grandmother got the son home and nursed him back to health.

Life for the slaves was different after the son began running the place, for he was not good to them. Anderson was then sixteen years old, and his older brother was the overseer. The slaves had been allowed a share of the crops, but the new owner refused to give them anything to live on. In that region wheat was harvested in the middle of June. Although there was a big crop that year, before the harvest the entire family was turned out with nothing. Anderson left his older brother with his mother and the other children sitting by the road while he ran the fourteen miles to his father to find out what to do. His father borrowed two teams and wagons, rented a house on the edge of town, and moved the family in.

The slaves were freed about that time, and for the first time in their lives the entire family was together. After the war, the government was providing former slaves with hardtack and pickled beef, so his father went to a government office and received the family's allotment of food. Although the family was satisfied with the hardtack because they were free, Anderson said he had never seen any beef that looked like the pickled beef and thought it must have been horse meat. In 1865 his father started working in a mill and soon started bringing food home from there. In time, the family raised their own crops, too.

His older brother worked in the mornings and went to a Quaker Normal School in the afternoons. President Harrison appointed him to the revenue department, but later he was transferred to the post office department. He was retired on a pension at the age of seventy-five. At the time of the interview he was ninety-seven and still living in Washington, D.C.

During the war Anderson ran twelve miles away to a camp of some Northern soldiers. They gave him a horse to ride, and he stayed with them for two weeks gathering firewood. He said those were the happiest days he had ever known because they were his first taste of freedom.

Although Anderson was never sold, he often observed processions of slaves who had been. Following a sale, he would see a wagon loaded with provisions followed by the slaves all tied together. Slaveholders often took babies away from their mothers and sold them. Some old woman, too old to work, would then care for the children until they were old enough to work. At six they were put to work thinning corn, worming tobacco, and pulling weeds. At seven they were taught to use a hoe. At sixteen they were full hands, working along with the older slaves.

In April 1880 Anderson left Orange County because the land was too rough there to make a living. Leaving his wife and children behind, he started out in search of a better place to live. In November he sent for them, as he had found a job working at the brickyards in Rockville. At that time work was being completed on the courthouse. To make a living, Anderson often did the work of two men.

One child was born in Rockville, but his wife died soon after arriving there. Anderson stayed single for three years, but he married again when he found that he could not care for his family alone. After the death of his second wife a number of years before the interview, he spent winters with his three living daughters. During the summer months, a daughter came to Rockville to live with him.

131. ALFRED (PETE) WILSON

Ol' Boss Was Ordinarily Good to Us

According to *Shop Notes* (March 6, 1920), the house organ of the Showers Brothers factory in Bloomington, Pete Wilson was born in 1850 in Kentucky and moved to Bloomington in 1866. He began working for Showers Brothers in 1883. According to the feature on Pete in *Shop Notes*,

> Fully two-thirds of the working force of our company had not been born when "Pete" Wilson first hired himself out as a furniture worker. . . .
> He can tell many interesting tales of the early days of factory life. He has watched the working force grow from a handful of men to its present magnitude. Although having reached an age when most men are forced to retire he can always be depended on to be on the job. His health is good and his disposition fine. "Pete" can laugh as heartily as any man who works in the packing room. When the town went dry, "Pete" decided that Bloomington had lost all of its charm at least so far as he was concerned and he moved to Indianapo-

lis. But when the capital city fell in line by placing a ban on the sale of John Barleycorn "Pete" bought a ticket over the I.C. for Bloomington. He said "Indianapolis was no good no-how."

On December 30, 1875, Pete married Malinda Murphy. According to his obituary in the *Bloomington Telephone* (December 2, 1937), Malinda died in 1922, and Pete died on December 2, 1937. Pete's narrative follows:

> I was born in Shelby County, Kentucky, ninety-eight miles above Simpsonville. I have taken good care of myself and so don't look as old as I am. I am eighty-five years old. I was born a slave. I was twelve years old when I was freed. I saw soldiers lots of times during the war. I would be standing on the state road or on the farm and would see soldiers going by. Sometimes they would stop and talk to us and ask us how we were getting along and give us what consolation they could.

> Ol' Boss was ordinarily good to us. He never cursed or swore and never got rough with us. He was nice to his hands. There were ten or twelve of us boys on the farm. We were raised up to work. Of course, he never paid us wages.

> My mother and father and ten children came to Indiana two years after we were freed. Wagons took us from Simpsonville to Louisville and put us on the Monon train. We stayed overnight in New Albany and then came to Bloomington. I have lived here ever since. The only one of the family besides myself still living is my sister. She lives in the south part of town. She was over to see me the other day.

> I bought a horse and wagon when I came here. Later I was married. I farmed and raised a family of ten. Three of my boys are still living. I got sick about five years ago. I'm not able to do any work. I live here with my granddaughter.

132. GEORGE WINLOCK

The Entire War Was a Mistake

George Winlock was living with his daughter and her family at 418 Southeast 5th Street in Evansville when he was interviewed. The fieldworker said he was "bent from years of active living and honest toil" and that he "is a living link between the past and the present history of Indiana. He also is a lover of two states in the Union—Kentucky, the state of his nativity, and Indiana, the state of his adoption." Though in his early nineties, he still washed dishes three times a day and performed other tasks around the house.

According to the WPA manuscript files, George was born in Logan County,

Kentucky, on December 25, 1846; however, the details about his date and place of birth differ in his obituary in the *Evansville Courier and Press* (June 11, 1939):

> George Winlock, 91, Negro, last survivor of Wagner Post, Grand Army of the Republic, and one of the few remaining Civil War Veterans in Southern Indiana, died yesterday at the home of his daughter, Mrs. P. T. Miller, 418 South Fifth street.
>
> He had been ill since May 14 when he was overcome by heat.
>
> Born in Warren County, Kentucky, in 1847, he was a slave for Adam Winlock, wealthy planter, serving as a chore and house boy. He ran away to enter the Union army. He served with the federal forces two and a half years.
>
> He came to Evansville in 1884 and worked for the John and Clem Reitz saw mills until 1900. He then worked for Schminke's stove firm until 1915 and then a year for the I. T. Thiele Stove Company as repair and delivery man before he retired.
>
> Other survivors besides the daughter are two grandchildren, Miss Mary Miller, Lincoln High School dean of girls, and P. T. Miller, Jr. and several nieces and nephews.
>
> Funeral services will be held at 1:30 o'clock tomorrow afternoon at the Gaines funeral home. Burial will be in Locust Hill Cemetery.

George told the WPA fieldworker that he was a slave for sixteen years and that his master, Adam Winlock, was a wise, kind, and just man. After serving with the Union Army in the Civil War, George returned to Kentucky and worked for a doctor named Covington at Bowling Green. Before moving to Evansville, he worked for a farmer at Hillsboro, Illinois.

George recalled several incidents of the Civil War. He said that General Grant's courage, physical perfection, and high moral standards impressed him and remained vivid in his memory. Here is his narrative:

> When I was a little past sixteen years of age, I ran away from my master and joined the Union Army. My services were under General Ulysses S. Grant, and my colonel was named Robert J. Ernest, and no braver man commanded a regiment. All during the period of the Civil War, the State of Kentucky was overrun by guerrillas. The guerrillas were largely made up of the disorganized soldiers, traitors, and deserters from the Confederate armies. They were a murderous band, and their plundering had become a problem hard to deal with. These desperate outlaws were pilferers, robbers, and often murderers. In 1886 the Union military forces made desperate efforts to quell the guerrillas, but such stern military measures had to be put into force that the efforts were met by a great deal of resentment.
>
> All over Kentucky it had been made to appear that the Union, compelled to act against the guerrillas, was acting against the people and against the state. Even the governor, whose name was Bramlette, believed that the citizens of his state were being acted against. He heard it noised about that outlawry was being acted against. It was a fact that in many instances inno-

cent persons suffered outrages, and some were killed. That is the irony of enforced discipline—that many have to suffer for the sins of others. One man in our community was murdered in private vengeance, and the crime was laid on the militia.

Military camps had been established at Owensboro and Calhoun, Kentucky, to protect the citizens of those areas, while in the upper section of the state, Union military troops prevented the Confederate troops from taking possession of that section. Up to the middle of November 1861, all the Federal troops in Kentucky were in command of General Anderson and General Sherman.

General Buell was in command of the Department of Ohio. He had a force under General Thomas at Somerset. The Confederate forces had control of Kentucky from the Cumberland Gap to the Mississippi River, but after the Battle of Fort Donelson the Confederates fell back from Kentucky. Then General Buell concentrated his army at Nashville, Tennessee, and when General Grant's army moved up the Tennessee River to Pittsburgh Landing, General Buell marched with his troops to the Landing from Nashville. The march to Pittsburgh Landing was the most trying trip we ever endured.

Some of the Federal soldiers believed that the presence on the battlefield of Buell's army made the victory certain. At any rate, there was a fruitless assault delivered by Confederate brigades, but Buell's army came up bringing up 25,000 fresh recruits. All that General Grant and Buell accomplished was the reoccupation of a few abandoned camps. The Battle of Shiloh was a failure for the Confederates and only a victory in a small way for the Union armies.

After the Battle of Shiloh, both the Confederate and the Union troops had lost so many men and the troops had suffered such hardships that neither side was ready for an attack. The Union forces then became united under General Hallack and moved to Corinth. Soon the Confederates left the area, and the Union armies under control of General Grant moved down the Mississippi River, and the next battle we fought was at Vicksburg.

We heard little more about General Buell until the war was ended, only that he had been in a battle with General Bragg and had moved from one base to another, but after the war was over, General Buell was given a country estate at Paradise, and his home became one of the showplaces of that section of the country.

General John H. Morgan made two raids through Kentucky. His trail could be followed from Glasgow to Elizabethtown. He was routed at Elizabethtown and hurried out of the state by way of New Haven and Burkesville by infuriated Kentuckians led by General E. H. Hobson.

Always when we Negroes would hear about depredations in Kentucky we

*would all be sad, but Colonel Bob always encouraged us and said, "Every-
thing is all right at home, boys."*

*The entire war was a mistake. The fight was not altogether over the
emancipation of the Negroes, but resulted from the political quarrels and
misrepresented facts. Many Negroes were happy while they were slaves. I
never had any unkindness shown me from white people, either before or
after I received my freedom.*

*The saddest thing that occurred during these terrible times was five days
after General Lee surrendered at the Appomattox courthouse and the Union
soldiers were all so happy. President Lincoln was assassinated. Every Union
soldier that had volunteered with the Union Army grieved over the death of
Abraham Lincoln. He had given his life for the cause of freedom. The newly
freed Negroes had lost their friend and champion, and the nation mourned.*

133. ALEX WOODSON

I Don't Believe in Ghosts, but I Do in Spirits

When interviewed, Alex Woodson was between eighty and eighty-five. The
fieldworker visited Alex and his second wife in their small house at 905 East 4th
Street in New Albany, where they ran a grocery store in the front room. The
stock was low in their tiny store, but with the help of Alex's pension, the old
couple got along.

Alex was born at Woodsonville, Hart County, Kentucky, just across Green
River from Munfordville. He was around seven when "freedom was declared."
His owner, Sterrett, had about a 200-acre place, on which his son-in-law, Tom
Williams, ran a store. When Williams married Sterrett's daughter, he was given
Alex, his mother, and a brother as presents. Williams was then known as "Young
Master" to distinguish him from Sterrett, who was called "Old Master."

When the war came, Sterrett gave Alex's mother a big roll of bills, "greenbacks as big as your arm," to keep for him, and he was forced to leave the area.
After the war, the Woodsons returned all the money to him. Alex remembered
his mother taking him and other children and running down the river bank and
hiding in the woods all night when the soldiers came. They were Morgan's men
and took all the cattle and horses in the vicinity and beat the woods looking for
Yankee soldiers. Alex said he saw Morgan at a distance on his big horse and that
he "was shore a mighty fine looker." Sometimes the Yankee soldiers would come
riding along, and they "took things, too."

When the the war was over, Sterrett came back home and, except for a few
who wanted to go north, the former slaves continued to live at Sterrett's place.
Sterrett lived in a big house with all his family, and most of the blacks lived

together in another good-sized house. There were a few cabins, too. Alex's story follows:

> Barbecues! My, we sure used to have 'em. Yes, ma'am, we did! Folks would come for miles around, would roast whole hogs and cows; and folks would sing, and eat, and drink whiskey. The white folks had 'em, but we helped and had fun, too. Sometimes we would have one ourselves.
>
> Used to have rail splittin's and wood choppin's. The men would work all day and get a pile of wood as big as a house. At noon they'd stop and eat a big meal that the women folks had fixed up for 'em. Them was some times. I've went to many a one.
>
> I remember we used to go to revivals sometimes, down near Horse Avenue. Everybody got religion, and we sure had some times. We don't have them kind of times anymore. I remember I went back down to one of these revivals years afterwards. Most of the folks I used to know was dead or gone. The preacher made me sit up front with him, and he asked me to preach to the folks. But I says that "No, God hadn't made me thata way," and I wouldn't do it.
>
> I've saw Abraham Lincoln's cabin many a time when I was young. It set up on a high hill, and I've been to the spring under the hill lots of times. The house was on the Old National Road then. I hear they've fixed it all up now. I haven't been there for years.
>
> After the war I growed up. I married and settled on the old place. I remember the only time I got beat in a horse trade. A sneakin' nigger from down near Horse Cave sold me a mule. That mule was just naturally no count. He would lay right down in the plow. One day after I had worked with him and tried to get him to work right, I got mad. I says to my wife, "Belle, I'm goin' to get rid of that mule if I have to trade him for a cat." And I led him off. When I come back, I had another mule and $15 to boot. This mule, she was shore skinny, but when I fattened her up you wouldn't have known her.
>
> Finally I left the old place and we come north to Indiana. We settled here, and I've been here for fifty years about. I worked in the old rolling mill, and I've been an officer in the Baptist Church at Third and Main for forty-one years.
>
> Do I believe in ghosts? [Here his second wife gave a snort.] Well, ma'am, I don't believe in ghosts, but I do in spirits. [Another disgusted snort from his wife.] I remember one time just after my first wife died, I was a sittin' right in that chair you're sittin' in now. The front door opened, and in come a big old gray mule, and I didn't have no gray mule. In she come, just as easy like, put one foot down slow, and then the other, and then the other. I says "Mule get out of here. You is goin' through that floor, sure as you're born. Get out that door." Mule looked at me sad-like and then just disappeared. And in its

place was my first wife in the clothes she was buried in. She come up to me, and I put my arms around her, but I couldn't feel nothin' [another snort from the second wife], and I says, "Babe, what you want?"

Then she started to get littler and littler and lower and finally went right away through the floor. It was her spirit; that's what it was. ["Rats!" said the second wife]. Another time she come to me by three knocks and made me get up and sleep on another bed where it was better sleepin'.

I like to go back down in Kentucky on visits, as the folks there won't take a thing for bed and vittles. Here they are so selfish that they won't even give a drink of water away.

Yes, ma'am, the flood got us. Me and my wife here, we went away and stayed two months. Was five feet in this house, and if it ever gets in here again, we're goin down in Kentucky and never comin' back no more.

134. ANTHONY YOUNG

He Doesn't Dare Touch You; You're a Free Man

Anthony Young's story was related by Mrs. Oscar Evelyn Day, who was living at 522 East 2nd Street in Muncie when interviewed.

Anthony was born in slavery in 1833 on a tobacco plantation at Horse Cave, Kentucky. Although he was never sold, while quite young he saw his father and a brother sold and taken from the plantation, and he never saw or heard of them again. As a child, he was sent on many errands to distant points of the plantation and to other places more than a mile away. He was never given any shoes, though, and in winter when the frost was on, he had to run to keep his feet from freezing. If he passed any hog pens, he chased the hogs from their beds, and as long as he dared he stood on the warm straw to warm his feet. If his owner caught him or if Anthony complained, the owner would stand him on his head, take his feet in his left hand, set his toe against the boy's head, and whip him with his right hand.

Anthony never left the plantation until after the war, though, because he was too young to run away to the North or join either army; however, his master did not consider him too young to drive the ox teams and follow the plow. When the slaves were freed, Anthony was not told. One day when his overseer was going to whip him, Anthony hid in the home of a white neighbor, who told him he was free: "Anthony, why do you run from him? He doesn't dare touch you; you're a free man. If he whips you you can have him arrested for assault and battery. You are now a citizen of America. Go home and tell him this, and he won't touch you."

When Anthony demanded wages, the owner promised to pay him $10 if he would stay and work a year. He stayed, but at the end of the first year he did not get the money. Then the owner told him that if he would work another year, he would pay him $15 in addition to the ten he owed him. Twenty-five dollars for two years of labor seemed like a lot of money to Anthony, so he stayed and worked another year. At the end of the second year the owner still would not pay him, so finally he left the plantation and walked to Bowling Green, Kentucky. There he married Mary Young, a former slave from the same plantation. They raised a family and came to Muncie about thirty-seven years before the interview with Mrs. Day. At the age of 102, Anthony died in 1935 at his home at 710 East Main Street.

APPENDIX I. INFORMANTS

1. Joseph Allen (b. 1851); hometown: Muncie, Delaware County; slave state: Kentucky; interviewers: 1) Martha Freeman, 2) William W. Tuttle; date of interviews: [1937]; Rawick 1977: 1–4.

2. George W. Arnold (b. 1861); hometown: Evansville, Vanderburgh County; slave state: Tennessee; interviewer: Lauana Creel; date of interview: not given; Rawick 1972: 1–7.

3. Thomas Ash (b. 1856?); hometown: Mitchell, Lawrence County; slave state: Kentucky; interviewer: Emery Turner; date of interview: not given; Rawick 1972: 8.

4. Rosa Barber (b. 1861); hometown: Muncie, Delaware County; slave state: North Carolina; interviewer: William Webb Tuttle; date of interview: not given; Rawick 1972: 11–12.

5. Lewis Barnett (b. ?); [told by Sarah Emery Merrill]; hometown: New Albany, Floyd County; slave state: Kentucky; interviewer: Iris Cook; date of interview: not given; Rawick 1977: 5–6.

6. Robert Barton (b. 1849); hometown: Terre Haute, Vigo County; slave state: Kentucky; interviewer: Charles Willen; date of interview: not given; Rawick 1977: 7–8.

7. Anthony Battle (b. 1851?); hometown: Greencastle, Putnam County; slave state: North Carolina; interviewer: Emily Hobson (Parke County fieldworker); date of interview: from an article in the *Rockville Republican,* April 11, 1929; Rawick 1977: 160–163.

8. George Beatty (b. 1862, d. 1951); hometown: Madison, Jefferson County; slave state: Kentucky [but the informant was born in Indiana]; interviewer: Grace Monroe; date of interview: from an article in the *Madison Herald,* January 24, 1939; Rawick 1977: 9–10.

9. Samuel Bell (b. 1853); hometown: Evansville, Vanderburgh County; slave state: Kentucky; interviewer: Lauana Creel; date of interview: not given; not in Rawick.

10. Mittie Blakeley (b. 1858); hometown: Indianapolis, Marion County; slave state: Mississippi; interviewer: Anna Pritchett; date of interview: January 24, 1938; Rawick 1972: 13–14.

11. Patsy Jane Bland (b. 1830, d. 1938); hometown: Terre Haute, Vigo County; slave state: Kentucky; interviewer: Anna Bowles Wiley; date of interview: 1937; Rawick 1977: 11–15.

12. Lizzie Bolden (b. ?) [told by Mrs. William D. Perry]; hometown: Madison, Jefferson County; slave state: Kentucky; interviewer: Grace Monroe; date of interview: not given; Rawick 1977: 16.

13. Carl Boone (b. 1850); hometown: Anderson, Madison County; slave state: Kentucky; interviewer: Robert C. Irvin; date of interview: 1937; Rawick 1972: 15–18; 1977: 17–19.

14. Walter Borland (b. 1867, d. 1941) [not a former slave]; hometown: Bloomington, Monroe County; slave state: none; interviewer: Estella R. Dodson; date of interview: October 12, 1937; Rawick 1977: 252–253.

15. Julia Bowman (b. 1859); hometown: Indianapolis, Marion County; slave state: Kentucky; interviewer: Anna Pritchett; date of interview: January 10, 1938; Rawick 1972: 19–20.

16. Angie Moore Boyce (b. 1861, d. 1938); hometown: Franklin, Johnson County; slave state: Kentucky; interviewer: William R. Mays; date of interview: not given; Rawick 1972: 21.

17. Edna Boysaw (b. 1852, d. 1942); hometown: Brazil, Clay County; slave state: Virginia; interviewer: Walter R. Harris; date of interview: not given; Rawick 1972: 22–24.

18. Callie Bracey (b. ?); hometown: Indianapolis, Marion County; slave state: Mississippi; interviewer: Anna Pritchett; date of interview: December 10, 1937; Rawick 1972: 25–26.

19. Tolbert Bragg (b. 1836, d. 1922); hometown: Parker, Jay County; slave state: Tennessee; interviewer: Martha Freeman; date of interview: from an article in the *Portland Daily Sun,* September 21, 1936; Rawick 1977: 20–21.

20. George Washington Buckner (b. 1852, d. 1943); hometown: Evansville, Vanderburgh County; slave state: Kentucky; interviewer: Lauana Creel; date of interview: not given; Rawick 1972: 27–35; 1977: 22–26.

21. George Taylor Burns (b. 1836?); hometown: Evansville, Vanderburgh County; slave state: Missouri; interviewer: Lauana Creel; date of interview: May 16, May 29, June 13, July 13, 1939; date not given for two texts; Rawick 1972: 36–39; 1977: 27–42.

22. Belle Butler (b. ?); hometown: Indianapolis, Marion County; slave state: not given; interviewer: Anna Pritchett; date of interview: December 28, 1937; Rawick 1972: 40–42.

23. Joseph William Carter (b. 1836?); hometown: Evansville, Vanderburgh County; slave state: Tennessee; interviewer: Lauana Creel; date of interview: not given; Rawick 1972: 43–49.

24. Ellen Cave (b. 1844?); hometown: Rising Sun, Ohio County; slave state: Kentucky; interviewer: Grace Monroe; date of interview: March 19, 1937; Rawick 1972: 50–51.

25. Harriet Cheatam (b. 1843); hometown: Indianapolis, Marion County; slave state: Tennessee; interviewer: Anna Pritchett; date of interview: December 1, 1937; Rawick 1972: 52–54.

26. Robert J. Cheatham (b. ?); hometown: Evansville, Vanderburgh County; slave state: Kentucky; interviewer: Lauana Creel; date of interview: October 1937; Rawick 1977: 45–61.

27. James Childress (b. 1860, d. 1941); hometown: Evansville, Vanderburgh County; slave state: Tennessee; interviewer: Lauana Creel; date of interview: not given; Rawick 1972: 55–56.

28. Sarah Colbert (b. 1855); hometown: Indianapolis, Marion County; slave state: Kentucky; interviewer: Anna Pritchett; date of interview: December 1, 1937; Rawick 1972: 57–60.

29. Frank Cooper (b. ?); hometown: Franklin, Johnson County; slave state: Kentucky; interviewer: William R. Mays; date of interview: July 29, 1937; Rawick 1972: 61–63.

30. John Cooper (b. 1861?); hometown: Muncie, Delaware County; slave state: Kentucky; interviewer: William Webb Tuttle; date of interview: not given; Rawick 1977: 135–137.

31. Mary Crane (b. 1855); hometown: Mitchell, Lawrence County; slave state: Kentucky; interviewer: Emery Turner; date of interview: not given; Rawick 1972: 9–10.

32. Cornelius Cross (b. 1864?, d. 1944); hometown: Evansville, Vanderburgh County; slave state: Louisiana; interviewer: Lauana Creel; date of interview: not given; not in Rawick.

33. Ethel Daugherty (b. ?); hometown: Madison, Jefferson County; slave state: Kentucky; interviewer: Grace Monroe; date of interview: not given; Rawick 1977: 62–63.

34. John Daugherty (b. 1861, d. 1948); hometown: Madison, Jefferson County; slave state: Kentucky; interviewer: Grace Monroe; date of interview: not given; Rawick 1977: 64.

35. Lizzie Daugherty (b. ?); hometown: Madison, Jefferson County; slave state: [Kentucky]; interviewer: Grace Monroe; date of interview: not given; Rawick 1977: 65–66.

36. Rachael Duncan (b. 1858?); hometown: New Albany, Floyd County; slave state: Kentucky; interviewer: Iris L. Cook; date of interview: not given; Rawick 1977: 67–68.

37. H. H. Edmunds (b. 1859); hometown: Elkhart, Elkhart County; slave states: Virginia, Mississippi, Tennessee; interviewer: Albert Strope; date of interview: not given; Rawick 1972: 65–66.

38. John Eubanks (b. 1839, d. 1938); hometown: Gary, Lake County; slave state: Kentucky; interviewer: Archie Koritz; date of interview: October 25, 1937; Rawick 1972: 67–76.

39. John W. Fields (b. 1848, d. 1953); hometown: Lafayette, Tippecanoe County; slave state: Kentucky; interviewer: Cecil C. Miller; date of interview: September 17, 1937; Rawick 1972: 77–83.

40. George Fortman (b. ?); hometown: Evansville, Vanderburgh County; slave state: Kentucky; interviewer: Lauana Creel; date of interview: not given; Rawick 1972: 84–95.

41. Alex Fowler; hometown: Creston, Lake County; slave state: not given; interviewer: Ethel Vinnedge; date of interview: October 5, 1936; Rawick 1977: 70.

42. Mattie Fuller (b. 1856, d. 1940); hometown: Bloomington, Monroe County; slave state: Kentucky; interviewer: Estella R. Dodson; date of interview: September 29, 1937; not in Rawick.

43. Francis Gammons (b. 1835, d. 1931); hometown: Muncie, Delaware County; slave state: Tennessee; interviewer: William Webb Tuttle; date of interview: September 2, 1937; not in Rawick.

44. John Henry Gibson (b. 1827?, d. 1939); hometown: Indianapolis, Marion County; slave state: North Carolina; interviewer: Anna Pritchett; date of interview: January 24, 1938; Rawick 1972: 96–97.

45. Peter Gohagen (b. 1847?); hometown: New Albany, Floyd County; slave state: Kentucky; interviewer: Iris L. Cook; date of interview: July 14, 1937; Rawick 1977: 71–75.

46. Sidney Graham (b. 1850?); hometown: Muncie, Delaware County; slave state: Tennessee; interviewer: William Webb Tuttle; date of interview: not given; Rawick 1977: 76–77.

47. Ms. L. Green (b. ?); hometown: Madison, Jefferson County; slave state: Kentucky; interviewer: Grace Monroe; date of interview: not given; Rawick 1977: 78,

48. Betty Guwn (b. 1832); hometown: Muncie, Delaware County; slave state: Kentucky; interviewer: William Webb Tuttle; date of interview: not given; Rawick 1972: 98–100.

49. Josie Harrell (b?); hometown: Madison, Jefferson County; slave state: Louisiana; interviewer: not given; date of interview: not given; Rawick 1977: 133–34.

50. Maston Harris (b. ?); hometown: Hanover, Jefferson County; slave state: Kentucky; interviewer: Grace Monroe; date of interview: not given; Rawick 1977: 79.

51. Nealy Harvey (b. ?); hometown: Indianapolis, Marion County; slave state: Mississippi; interviewer: Anna Pritchett; date of interview: December 9, 1937; Rawick 1977: 80–81.

52. Josephine Hicks (b. ?); hometown: Madison, Jefferson County; slave state: Kentucky; interviewer: Grace Monroe; date of interview: not given; Rawick 1977: 88.

53. Dr. Solomon Hicks (b. ?); hometown: Madison, Jefferson County; slave state: Kentucky; interviewer: Grace Monroe; date of interview: not given; Rawick 1977: 84–87.

54. Mrs. Hockaday (b. ?); hometown: Gary, Lake County; slave state: not given; interviewer: Archie Koritz; date of interview: not given; Rawick 1972: 101–104.

55. Samantha Hough (b. 1843); hometown: Scottsburg, Scott County; slave state: not a slave; interviewer: Velsie Tyler; date of interview: not given; Rawick 1977: 92–93.

56. Robert Howard (b. 1852); hometown: Indianapolis, Marion County; slave state: Kentucky; interviewer: Anna Pritchett; date of interview: January 10, 1938; Rawick 1972: 105–106.

57. Matthew Hume (b. ?); hometown: Madison, Jefferson County; slave state: Kentucky; interviewer: Grace Monroe; date of interview: not given; Rawick 1972: 107–110.

58. Lillian Hunter (b. ?); hometown: Hanover, Jefferson County; slave state: not a slave; interviewer: Grace Monroe; date of interview: not given; Rawick 1977: 94.

59. Henrietta Jackson (b. 1832?, d. 1940); hometown: Fort Wayne, Allen County; slave state: Virginia; interviewer: Virginia Tulley; date of interview: not given; Rawick 1972: 111–112.

60. Mattie Jenkins (b. 1841); hometown: Terre Haute, Vigo County; slave state: Georgia; interviewer: Charles Willen; date of interview: not given; Rawick 1977: 95.

61. Lizzie Johnson (b. ?); hometown: Indianapolis, Marion County; slave state: North Carolina; interviewer: Anna Pritchett; date of interview: December 9, 1937; Rawick 1972: 113–114.

62. Pete Johnson (b. ?); hometown: Madison, Jefferson County; slave state: Kentucky; interviewer: Grace Monroe; date of interview: not given; Rawick 1977: 96–98.

63. Elizabeth (Bettie) Jones (b. 1857, d. 1946); hometown: Evansville, Vanderburgh County; slave state: Kentucky; interviewer: Lauana Creel; date of interview: not given; Rawick 1972: 116–117.

64. Ira Jones (b. ?); hometown: Hanover Township, Jefferson County; slave state: Kentucky; interviewer: Grace Monroe; date of interview: not given; Rawick 1972: 99–101.

65. Nathan Jones (b. 1858); hometown: Indianapolis, Marion County; slave state: Tennessee; interviewer: Anna Pritchett; date of interview: December 15, 1937; Rawick 1972: 118–119.

66. Ralph Kates (b. ?); hometown: Evansville, Vanderburgh County; slave state: Tennessee; interviewer: Lauana Creel; date of interview: not given; Rawick 1977: 102–103.

67. Alexander Kelley (b. 1855?); hometown: Muncie, Delaware County; slave state: North Carolina; interviewer: William Webb Tuttle; date of interview: not given; Rawick 1977: 104–105.

68. Bell Deam Kelley (b. 1857); hometown: Muncie, Delaware County; slave state: Kentucky; interviewer: William Webb Tuttle; date of interview: not given; Rawick 1977: 106–107.

69. Elvira Lee (b ?) [told by Sarah Emery Merrill]; hometown: New Albany, Floyd County; slave state: Kentucky; interviewer: Velsie Tyler; date of interview: not given; Rawick 1977: 126–130.

70. Adeline Rose Lennox (b. 1849, d. 1938); hometown: Elkhart, Elkhart County; slave state: Tennessee; interviewers: 1) Albert Strope, 2) not given; date of interviews: 1) September 7, 1937, 2) September 13, 1937; Rawick 1972: 120–22; 1977: 112–14.

71. Thomas Lewis (b. 1852?, d. 1951); hometown: Bloomington, Monroe County; slave state: Kentucky; interviewer: Estella R. Dodson; date of interview: October 4, 1937; Rawick 1972: 123–127.

72. Levi Linzy (b. 1827) [told by Haywood Patterson]; hometown: Spartanburg, Randolph County; slave state: South Carolina; interviewer: Martha Freeman; date of interview: not given; Rawick 1977: 159 (first paragraph); last paragraph in WPA files but not in Rawick.

73. Sarah H. Locke (b. 1839); hometown: Indianapolis, Marion County; slave state: Kentucky; interviewer: Anna Pritchett; date of interview: December 17, 1937; Rawick 1972: 128–130.

74. Maria Love (b. ?); hometown: Indianapolis, Marion County; slave states: Tennessee and Alabama; interviewer: Anna Pritchett; date of interview: December 8, 1937; Rawick 1977: 116.

75. Thomas Magruder (b. 1747?, d. 1857); hometown: Indianapolis, Marion County; slave state: Kentucky [servitude in Indiana]; interviewers: Allan M. Stranz and Hazel Nixon; date of interview: deposited December 29, 1937 (Stranz), but the texts are mainly from printed sources; Rawick 1977: 120–125.

76. Hettie McClain (b. ?); hometown: Evansville, Vanderburgh County; slave state: Kentucky; interviewer: Lauana Creel; date of interview: not given; Rawick 1977: 117–119.

77. Robert McKinley (b. 1849); hometown: Indianapolis, Marion County; slave state: North Carolina; interviewer: Anna Pritchett; date of interview: January 10, 1938; Rawick 1972: 131–133.

78. Richard Miller (b. 1840?, d. 1946); hometown: Indianapolis, Marion County; slave state: Kentucky; interviewer: Anna Pritchett; date of interview: December 9, 1937; Rawick 1972: 134–136.

79. Ben Moore (b. ?) [told by the fieldworker, Merton Knowles]; hometown: Attica, Fountain County; slave state: Tennessee; interviewer: Merton Knowles; date of interview: July 30, 1937; Rawick 1977: 138–140.

80. John Moore (b. 1848, d. 1929); hometown: Evansville, Vanderburgh County; slave state: Tennessee; interviewer: Lauana Creel; date of interview: not given; Rawick 1977: 141–145.

81. Henry Clay Moorman (b. 1854, d. 1943); hometown: Franklin, Johnson County; slave state: Kentucky; interviewer: William R. Mays; date of interview: 1937; Rawick 1972: 137–140.

82. America Morgan (b. 1852); hometown: Indianapolis, Marion County; slave state: Kentucky; interviewer: Anna Pritchett; date of interview: December 27, 1937; Rawick 1972: 141–144.

83. George Morrison (b. ?); hometown: New Albany, Floyd County; slave state: Kentucky; interviewers: Iris Cook and Beulah Van Meter; date of interviews: not given; Rawick 1972: 145–146A; 1977: 146–147.

84. Joseph Mosley (b. 1853); hometown: Indianapolis, Marion County; slave state: Kentucky; interviewer: Anna Pritchett; date of interview: December 1, 1937; Rawick 1972: 147–149.

85. Henry Neal (b. 1857, d. 1943); hometown: Madison, Jefferson County; slave state: Kentucky; interviewer: Grace Monroe; date of interview: not given; Rawick 1977: 148–149.

86. Reverend Oliver Nelson (b. ?); hometown: New Albany, Floyd County; slave state: not given; interviewer: Velsie Tyler; date of interview: not given; Rawick 1977: 150.

87. Sarah O'Donnell (b. 1820) [told by Herman Rave]; hometown: city not given, Clark County; slave state: Kentucky; interviewer: Beulah Van Meter; date of interview: From "County Jottings," Indiana Section of the *Louisville Times,* May 30, 1927; Rawick 1977: 151–152.

88. Rudolph D. O'Hara (b. ?); hometown: Evansville, Vanderburgh County; slave state: Kentucky; interviewer: Lauana Creel; date of interview: not given; Rawick 1977: 153–154.

89. W. F. Parrot (b. ?); hometown: Muncie, Delaware County; slave state: Kentucky; interviewer: William Webb Tuttle; date of interview: not given; Rawick 1977: 155–158.

90. Amy Elizabeth Patterson (b. 1850); hometown: Evansville, Vanderburgh County; slave state: Kentucky; interviewer: Lauana Creel; date of interview: 1937; Rawick 1972: 150–152.

91. Spear Pitman (b. 1839?); hometown: Greencastle, Putnam County; slave state: North Carolina; interviewer: Emily Hobson (Parke County fieldworker); date of interview: From an article in the *Rockville Republican,* April 11, 1929; Rawick 1977: 160–163.

92. Nelson Polk (b. 1830?) [told by Reverend J. B. Polk]; hometown: Muncie, Delaware County; slave states: Tennessee and Mississippi; interviewer: William Webb Tuttle; date of interview: not given; Rawick 1977: 165–168.

93. Nettie Pompey (b. 1820); hometown: Indianapolis, Marion County; slave state: Louisiana; interviewer: Anna Pritchett; date of interview: January 24, 1938; Rawick 1977: 169–170.

94. [Mrs.] Preston (b. 1854?); hometown: Madison, Jefferson County; slave state: Kentucky; interviewer: Grace Monroe; date of interview: not given; Rawick 1972: 153–154.

95. William M. Quinn (b. ?); hometown: Indianapolis, Marion County; slave state: Kentucky; interviewer: Harry Jackson; date of interview: September 9, 1937; Rawick 1972: 155–157.

96. Candies Richardson (b. 1847, d. 1955); hometown: Indianapolis, Marion County; slave state: Mississippi; interviewer: Harry W. Jackson; date of interview: August 31, 1937; Rawick 1972: 158–161.

97. Joe Robinson (b. 1854); hometown: Indianapolis, Marion County; slave state: Kentucky; interviewer: Anna Pritchett; date of interview: January 24, 1938; Rawick 1972: 162–163.

98. Rosaline Rogers (b. 1827); hometown: Indianapolis, Marion County; slave state: Tennessee; interviewer: Anna Pritchett; date of interview: December 29, 1937; Rawick 1972: 164–166.

99. Parthenia Rollins (b. 1845, d. 1952); hometown: Indianapolis, Marion County; slave state: Kentucky; interviewer: Anna Pritchett; date of interview: December 21, 1937; Rawick 1972: 167–168.

100. Katie Rose (b. ?); hometown: Evansville, Vanderburgh County; slave state: Kentucky; interviewer: Lauana Creel; date of interview: not given; Rawick 1977: 174–178.

101. John Rudd (b. 1851?, d. 1947); hometown: Evansville, Vanderburgh County; slave state: Kentucky; interviewer: Lauana Creel; date of interview: not given; Rawick 1977: 169–172.

102. Elizabeth Russell (b. 1856); hometown: Kokomo, Howard County; slave state: Georgia; interviewer: B. H. Stonecipher; date of interview: not given; Rawick 1977: 179–186.

103. Amanda Elizabeth (Lizzie) Samuels (b. 1857?); hometown: Indianapolis, Marion County; slave state: Tennessee; interviewer: Anna Pritchett; date of interview: December 1, 1937; Rawick 1972: 173–174.

104. Mary Elizabeth Scarber (b. ?); hometown: Indianapolis, Marion County; slave state: Alabama; interviewer: Anna Pritchett; date of interview: January 24, 1938; Rawick 1977: 82–83.

105. Lulu Scott (b. ?); hometown: Indianapolis, Marion County; slave state: Kentucky; interviewer: W. C. Hibbitt; date of interview: not given; Rawick 1977: 187–190.

106. Arthur Shaffer (b. ?); hometown: Muncie, Delaware County; slave state: Virginia; interviewer: William Webb Tuttle; date of interview: not given; Rawick 1977: 43–44.

107. Jack Simms (b. ?); hometown: Madison, Jefferson County; slave state: Kentucky; interviewer: Grace Monroe; date of interview: not given; Rawick 1972: 175.

108. Billy Slaughter (b. 1858); hometown: Jeffersonville, Clark County; slave state: Kentucky; interviewer: Beulah Van Meter; date of interview: not given; Rawick 1972: 176–180; 1977: 220–221.

109. Moses Slaughter (b. 1833?); hometown: Evansville, Vanderburgh County; slave state: Tennessee; interviewer: Lauana Creel; date of interview: not given; Rawick 1977: 193–199.

110. Alex Smith (b. 1854?, d. 1942) and Elizabeth (Betty) Smith (b. 1853, d. 1957); hometown: South Bend, St. Joseph County; slave state: Kentucky; interviewer: Henrietta Karwowski; date of interview: not given; Rawick 1972: 181–184.

111. Mattie Brown Smith (b. 1881?); hometown: New Albany, Floyd County; slave state: Kentucky; interviewer: Iris L. Cook; date of interview: May 12, 1936; two close versions not in Rawick.

112. Mrs. Robert Smith (b. ?); hometown: Hanover, Jefferson County; slave state: Kentucky; interviewer: Grace Monroe; date of interview: not given; Rawick 1977: 79.

113. Susan Smith (b. ?); hometown: Charlestown, Clark County; slave state: Kentucky; interviewer: Beulah Van Meter; date of interview: not given; Rawick 1977: 206.

114. Sylvester Smith (b. 1852, d. 1943); hometown: Terre Haute, Vigo County; slave state: North Carolina; interviewer: Charles Willen; date of interview: 1938?; Rawick 1977: 207–208.

115. Mary Ann Stewart (b. 1833); hometown: Harmony, Clay County; slave state: not given; interviewer: W. R. Harris; date of interview: not given; Rawick 1977: 209.

116. Barney Stone (b. 1847, d. 1942); hometown: Noblesville, Hamilton County; slave state: Kentucky; interviewer: Robert C. Irvin; date of interview: 1938?; Rawick 1972: 185–188.

117. Mary Stonestreet (b. 1820?) [told by Mrs. Edwin Lewis]; hometown: Bryantsburg, Jefferson County; slave state: Kentucky; interviewer: Grace Monroe; date of interview: not given; Rawick 1977: 115.

118. Adah Isabelle Suggs (b. 1852, d. 1938); hometown: Evansville, Vanderburgh County; slave state: Kentucky; interviewer: Lauana Creel; date of interview: not given; Rawick 1972: 189–192.

119. Katie Sutton (b. ?); hometown: Evansville, Vanderburgh County; slave state: not given; interviewer: Lauana Creel; date of interview: not given; Rawick 1972: 193–195; 1977: 210–211.

120. Mary Emily (Mollie) Eaton Tate (b. 1859); hometown: Portland, Jay County; slave state: Tennessee; interviewer: Martha Freeman; date of interview: from an article in the *Portland Daily Sun,* September 21, 1936; Rawick 1977: 212–219.

121. Preston Tate (b. 1854, d. 1928); hometown: Portland, Jay County; slave state: Tennessee; interviewer: Martha Freeman; date of interview: from an article in the *Portland Daily Sun,* September 21, 1936; Rawick 1977: 220–221.

122. George Thomas (b. 1876?, d. 1937); hometown: Charlestown, Clark County; slave state: Kentucky; interviewer: Beulah Van Meter; date of interview: 1936; Rawick 1977: 222–225.

123. George Thompson (b. 1854, d. 1941); hometown: Franklin, Johnson County; slave state: Kentucky; interviewer: William R. Mays; date of interview: August 2, 1937; Rawick 1972: 196–197.

124. Joe Wade (b. ?); hometown: Indianapolis, Marion County; slave state: Tennessee; interviewer: Anna Pritchett; date of interview: December 8, 1937; Rawick 1977: 229.

125. Reverend Wamble (b. 1859); hometown: Gary, Lake County; slave state: Mississippi; interviewer: Archie Koritz; date of interview: not given; Rawick 1972: 199–205.

126. Louis Watkins (b. 1853); hometown: Muncie, Delaware County; slave state: Tennessee; interviewer: William Webb Tuttle; date of interview: not given; Rawick 1977: 230–231.

127. Samuel Watson (b. 1862); hometown: Evansville, Vanderburgh County; slave state: Kentucky; interviewer: Lauana Creel; date of interview: not given; Rawick 1972: 206–208.

128. Henry Webb (b. ?); hometown: New Albany, Floyd County; slave state: Kentucky?; interviewer: Iris L. Cook; date of interview: not given; Rawick 1977: 232.

129. Nancy Whallen (b. 1860?); hometown: New Albany, Floyd County; slave state: Kentucky; interviewer: Iris L. Cook; date of interview: not given; Rawick 1972: 209–210.

130. Anderson Whitted (b. 1848); hometown: Rockville, Parke County; slave state: North Carolina; interviewer: Emily Hobson; date of interview: September 1937; Rawick 1972: 211–213.

131. Alfred (Pete) Wilson (b. 1850, d. 1875); hometown: Bloomington, Monroe County; slave state: Kentucky; interviewer: Estella R. Dodson; date of interview: October 6, 1937; not in Rawick.

132. George Winlock (b. 1846?, d. 1939); hometown: Evansville, Vanderburgh County; slave state: Kentucky; interviewer: Lauana Creel; date of interview: 1938?; Rawick 1977: 233–237.

133. Alex Woodson (b. ?); hometown: New Albany, Floyd County; slave state: Kentucky; interviewer: Iris Cook; date of interview: not given; Rawick 1972: 214–217.

134. Anthony Young (b. 1833, d. 1935) [told by Mrs. Oscar Evelyn Day]; hometown: Muncie, Delaware County; slave state: Kentucky; interviewer: William Webb Tuttle; date of interview: not given; Rawick 1977: 238–239.

APPENDIX II. SLAVE STATES OF INFORMANTS

ALABAMA
Elizabeth Scarber

GEORGIA
Mattie Jenkins
Elizabeth Russell

KENTUCKY
Joseph Allen
Thomas Ash
Lewis Barnett
Robert Barton
George Beatty
Samuel Bell
Patsy Jane Bland
Lizzie Bolden
Carl Boone
Julia Bowman
Angie Boyce
George W. Buckner
Ellen Cave
Robert J. Cheatham
Sarah Colbert
Frank Cooper
John Cooper
Mary Crane
Ethel Daugherty
John Daugherty
Lizzie Daugherty
Rachael Duncan
John Eubanks
John W. Fields
George Fortman
Mattie Fuller

Peter Gohagen
[Miss] L. Green
Betty Guwn
Maston Harris
Josephine Hicks
Solomon Hicks
Robert Howard
Matthew Hume
Pete Johnson
Elizabeth (Bettie) Jones
Ira Jones
Bell Deam Kelley
Elvira Lee
Thomas Lewis
Sarah H. Locke
Thomas Magruder
Hettie McClain
Richard Miller
Henry Clay Moorman
[Mrs.] America Morgan
George Morrison
 Joseph Mosley
Henry Neal
Sarah O'Donnell
Rudolph O'Hara
W. F. Parrott
Amy Elizabeth Patterson
[Mrs.] Preston
William M. Quinn
Joe Robinson
Parthenia Rollins
Katie Rose
John Rudd
Lulu Scott
Jack Simms
Billy Slaughter
Alex and Elizabeth Smith
Mattie Brown Smith
Mrs. Robert Smith
Susan Smith
Barney Stone
Mary Stonestreet

Adah Isabelle Suggs
George Thomas
George Thompson
Samuel Watson
Henry Webb
Nancy Whallen
Alfred (Pete) Wilson
George Winlock
Alex Woodson
Anthony Young

LOUISIANA

Cornelius Cross
Josie Harrell
Nettie Pompey

MISSISSIPPI

Mittie Blakeley
Callie Bracey
Nealy Harvey
Nelson Polk
Candies Richardson
Reverend Wamble

MISSOURI

George Taylor Burns

NORTH CAROLINA

Rosa Barber
Anthony Battle
John Henry Gibson
Lizzie Johnson
Alexander Kelley
Robert McKinley
Spear Pitman
Sylvester T. Smith
Anderson Whitted

SOUTH CAROLINA

Levi Linzy

TENNESSEE

George W. Arnold
Tolbert Bragg
Joseph William Carter
Harriet Cheatam
James Childress
Francis Gammons
Sidney Graham
Nathan Jones
Ralph Kates
Adeline Rose Lennox
Maria Love
Ben Moore
John Moore
Rosaline Rogers
Amanda Elizabeth Samuels
Moses Slaughter
Mary Emily Eaton Tate
Preston Tate
Joe Wade
Louis Watkins

VIRGINIA

Edna Boysaw
H. H. Edmunds
Henrietta Jackson
Arthur Shaffer

NOT A SLAVE

Walter Borland
Samantha Hough
Lillian Hunter

NOT GIVEN

Belle Butler
[Mrs.] Hockaday
Oliver Nelson
Mary Ann Stewart
Katie Sutton

APPENDIX III.
INDIANA TOWNS OF RESIDENCE OF INFORMANTS

ANDERSON
Carl Boone

ATTICA
Ben Moore

BLOOMINGTON
Walter Borland
Mattie Fuller
Thomas Lewis
Alfred (Pete) Wilson

BRAZIL
Edna Boysaw

BRYANTSBURG
Mary Stonestreet

CHARLESTOWN
Susan Smith
George Thomas

ELKHART
H. H. Edmunds
Adeline Rose Lennox

EVANSVILLE
George W. Arnold
Samuel Bell
George W. Buckner
George Taylor Burns
Joseph William Carter
Robert J. Cheatham
James Childress

Cornelius Cross
George Fortman
Elizabeth (Bettie) Jones
Ralph Kates
Hettie McClain
John Moore
Rudolph O'Hara
Amy Elizabeth Patterson
Katie Rose
John Rudd
Moses Slaughter
Adah Isabelle Suggs
Katie Sutton
Samuel Watson
George Winlock

FORT WAYNE
Henrietta Jackson

FRANKLIN
Angie Boyce
Frank Cooper
Henry Clay Moorman
George Thompson

GARY
John Eubanks
[Mrs.] Hockaday
Reverend Wamble

GREENCASTLE
Anthony Battle
Spear Pitman

HANOVER
Maston Harris
Lillian Hunter
Ira Jones
Mrs. Robert Smith

HARMONY
Mary Ann Stewart

INDIANAPOLIS
Mittie Blakeley
Julia Bowman
Callie Bracey
Belle Butler
Harriet Cheatam
Sarah Colbert
John Henry Gibson
Nealy Harvey
Robert Howard
Lizzie Johnson
Nathan Jones
Sarah H. Locke
Maria Love
Thomas Magruder
Robert McKinley
Richard Miller
[Mrs.] America Morgan
Joseph Mosley
Nettie Pompey
William M. Quinn
Candies Richardson
Joe Robinson
Rosaline Rogers
Parthenia Rollins
Amanda Elizabeth Samuels
Elizabeth Scarber
Lulu Scott
Joe Wade

JEFFERSONVILLE
Billy Slaughter

KOKOMO
Elizabeth Russell

LAFAYETTE
John W. Fields

MADISON
George Beatty
Lizzie Bolden

Ethel Daugherty
John Daugherty
Lizzie Daugherty
[Miss] L. Green
Josie Harrell
Josephine Hicks
Solomon Hicks
Matthew Hume
Pete Johnson
Henry Neal
[Mrs.] Preston
Jack Simms

MITCHELL

Thomas Ash
Mary Crane

MUNCIE

Joseph Allen
Rosa Barber
John Cooper
Francis Gammons
Sidney Graham
Betty Guwn
Alexander Kelley
Bell Deam Kelley
W. F. Parrott
Nelson Polk
Arthur Shaffer
Louis Watkins
Anthony Young

NEW ALBANY

Lewis Barnett
Rachael Duncan
Peter Gohagen
Elvira Lee
George Morrison
Oliver Nelson
Mattie Brown Smith
Henry Webb
Nancy Whallen
Alex Woodson

NOBLESVILLE
Barney Stone

PARKER
Tolbert Bragg

PORTLAND
Mary Emily Eaton Tate
Preston Tate

RISING SUN
Ellen Cave

ROCKVILLE
Anderson Whitted

SCOTTSBURG
Samantha Hough

SOUTH BEND
Alex and Elizabeth Smith

SPARTANBURG
Levi Linzy

TERRE HAUTE
Robert Barton
Patsy Jane Bland
Mattie Jenkins
Sylvester T. Smith

NOT GIVEN
Sarah O'Donnell

APPENDIX IV.
INDIANA COUNTIES OF RESIDENCE OF INFORMANTS

ALLEN
Henrietta Jackson

CLARK
Sarah O'Donnell
Billy Slaughter
Susan Smith
George Thomas

CLAY
Edna Boysaw
Mary Ann Stewart

DELAWARE
Joseph Allen
Rosa Barber
John Cooper
Francis Gammons
Sidney Graham
Betty Guwn
Alexander Kelley
Bell Deam Kelley
W. F. Parrott
Nelson Polk
Arthur Shaffer
Louis Watkins
Anthony Young

ELKHART
H. H. Edmunds
Adeline Rose Lennox

FLOYD

Lewis Barnett
Rachael Duncan
Peter Gohagen
Elvira Lee
George Morrison
Oliver Nelson
Mattie Brown Smith
Henry Webb
Nancy Whallen
Alex Woodson

FOUNTAIN

Ben Moore

HAMILTON

Barney Stone

HOWARD

Elizabeth Russell

JAY

Tolbert Bragg
Mary Emily Eaton Tate
Preston Tate

JEFFERSON

George Beatty
Lizzie Bolden
Ethel Daugherty
John Daugherty
Lizzie Daugherty
[Miss] L. Green
Josie Harrell
Maston Harris
Josephine Hicks
Solomon Hicks
Matthew Hume
Lillian Hunter
Pete Johnson
Ira Jones
Henry Neal

[Mrs.] Preston
Jack Simms
Mrs. Robert Smith
Mary Stonestreet

JOHNSON
Angie Boyce
Frank Cooper
Henry Clay Moorman
George Thompson

LAKE
John Eubanks
[Mrs.] Hockaday

LAKE/PORTER
Reverend Wamble

LAWRENCE
Thomas Ash
Mary Crane Madison
Carl Boone

MARION
Mittie Blakeley
Julia Bowman
Callie Bracey
Belle Butler
Harriet Cheatam
Sarah Colbert
John Henry Gibson
Nealy Harvey
Robert Howard
Lizzie Johnson
Nathan Jones
Sarah H. Locke
Maria Love
Thomas Magruder
Robert McKinley
Richard Miller
[Mrs.] America Morgan
Joseph Mosley

Nettie Pompey
William M. Quinn
Candies Richardson
Joe Robinson
Rosaline Rogers
Parthenia Rollins
Amanda Elizabeth Samuels
Elizabeth Scarber
Lulu Scott
Joe Wade

MONROE
Walter Borland
Mattie Fuller
Thomas Lewis
Alfred (Pete) Wilson

OHIO
Ellen Cave

PARKE
Anderson Whitted

PUTNAM
Anthony Battle
Spear Pitman

RANDOLPH
Levi Linzy

SCOTT
Samantha Hough

ST. JOSEPH
Alex and Elizabeth Smith

TIPPECANOE
John W. Fields

VANDERBURGH
George W. Arnold
Samuel Bell

George W. Buckner
George Taylor Burns
Joseph William Carter
Robert J. Cheatham
James Childress
Cornelius Cross
George Fortman
Elizabeth (Bettie) Jones
Ralph Kates
Hettie McClain
John Moore
Rudolph O'Hara
Amy Elizabeth Patterson
Katie Rose
John Rudd
Moses Slaughter
Adah Isabelle Suggs
Katie Sutton
Samuel Watson
George Winlock

VIGO

Robert Barton
Patsy Jane Bland
Mattie Jenkins
Sylvester T. Smith

APPENDIX V. UNALTERED VERSIONS OF PREVIOUSLY UNPUBLISHED INDIANA INTERVIEWS WITH FORMER SLAVES

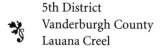

5th District
Vanderburgh County
Lauana Creel

A HIGHLY RESPECTED CITIZEN

From an Interview with Samuel Bell

That Samuel Bell is a highly respected citizen of Evansville, Indiana, is substantially proven by letters in his possession. These letters are from former employers for whom Samuel Bell has rendered perfect and obedient service.

Charles Leich states, that he has endorsed Uncle Samuel's checks for $200.00 and would have endorsed checks for a higher denomination without hesitating. Samuel Bell, the subject of this review, held the janitorship at the Citizen National Bank for a number of years, and when a man can hold the key to an institution where thousands of dollars has been entrusted, he is a trusted and trustworthy man. For sixty-two years Uncle Samuel was entrusted with important business: Mr. Jesse Weil and Aaron Weil endorsed his character in the following statement, "Where Samuel Bell acted as janitor he has always been faithful and trustworthy."

Dr. E. Conover certified [him] as a faithful, honest man. James Walker certifies that Samuel Bell has been known to him for forty years and recommends him for any kind of work and makes the following statement. "On one or two occasions, when there had been dishonesty from other persons in my office, he aided us materially in the recovery of a good portion of the stolen property." James Walker further states that he is "Glad to recommend him for any kind of work he would consider doing." James Walker is a Prominent attorney at law in the city of Evansville, as is his son, Henry Walker with offices in the Old National Bank Building, and Charles Leich is in the wholesale drug business, at 420 N.W. Fifth Street.

Another prominent man to compliment the character of Uncle Samuel Bell is Aaron Weil. His business is Insurance of all kinds with offices at 29 to 31 Main Street, in Evansville, Indiana.

Sidney L. Cumberts, 718 S.E. Sixth street, agent for Morton L. Ichenhauser United States Casualty Co., and the Sun Life Insurance Company, expresses his thanks to Uncle Samuel Bell for long and faithful service to his Uncle Mr. Alder, whom Samuel served thirty years.

Who is this man recommended for faithful service by prominent men of the city? He is a negro residing at no. 312 S. E. Fifth street, Evansville. Born a slave in 1853, both of Uncle Samuel's parents were full blooded negroes. His master was John Bell who owned a plantation in Kentucky and whom Samuel served as a slave serves his master until he had passed his twelfth year of life.

"Was your master good to his slaves?" was the question asked the old negro man. "Yes he was a good and a just man and fed his slaves well. He only used the lash when it was absolutely necessary. You know how it is in the court! Well it was the same way on the plantations in slavery days. A good slave was seldom punished but mean negroes had to be punished to prevent their taking advantage of their master and the other slaves." "Why do you compare the plantation slave rulers to our present day city courts, Uncle Samuel?" was the next question.

"Well it was like this: The negroes were not subject to the laws of the land and his punishment had to be governed by his deeds and errors. The Master's will was the only law he was compelled to obey. When a slave refused to work he was flogged until he was willing to work. The master had to feed and clothe him and expected him to repay with work."

When the Civil War came the negro was one of the central issues. The first pressing question was the treatment of fugitive slaves. Butler confiscated them as "Contraband of war" quoting the Encyclopedia Americana Vol. 20 p. 49. Large numbers of negroes became contraband goods and camps were established in which contraband negroes were housed. "Wherever these fugitives were massed, there grew up a system of controlled negro labor, under the guardianship of government officials." (p. 49)

A Contraband camp was located at Clarksville, Tennessee and to this camp Samuel Bell, accompanied by his parents, brothers and sisters, was taken when scarcely twelve years of age. His physical comforts were well cared for while housed at the contraband camp and he was taught to read and write.

His father lived only a short time after being placed in the camp and after his death the mother asked to be allowed to return to Kentucky. Her request was granted and she procured work in Hopkinsville, Kentucky. She later returned to the camp to reclaim her children, then leaving them with their grandparents she continued to work to support them. Within a few years she died and her children were returned to Clarksville, Tennessee.

"The government was not well founded and the Freedmen's Aid Society cared for the negroes. Colonel Eaton was in charge of the Freedman's Aid Society in

Tennessee and the contraband negroes were well treated in camp." The foregoing is the testimony of Samuel Bell. Samuel soon tired of camp life and asked for permission to start out in life depending on his own labor; he therefore, came out of camp and farmed in Dunbar's Hollow, a tract of farmland between two rivers; the Red River and the West Fork. I have gone through Dunbar's Cave many times. It is a great natural cave formed by God's own hand. A beautiful river forms a barrack, its music is beautiful to listen to: great pillars separate the cavern into many rooms. So, Uncle Samuel describes Dunbar's Cave. Samuel worked on Captain Perkins's cotton farm on the Cumberland River. He recalls the farm embraced 100 cabins and two cotton gins, after working in the cotton twelve months the negro youth traveled 20 miles to Brenton, situated ten miles out of Ashville, and found a pleasant home with Willie Newland's mother, there he worked as houseboy for two years. "The Newland family wanted to give me an education and make me fit for a lawyer, but I worked against my own interest and refused to obey their wishes." sorrowfully confessed the aged man of today.

"I have never been misused by the white man of America. He has always been my friend. I have been in bondage, orphaned by the death of my parents. I have lived in the contraband camps and toiled for both rich and poor, but I have never been given abuse."

"What is the happiest recollection of your entire life?" was asked the old man?"

"When Jesus saved my soul and gave me the hope of eternal life," answered he. "I was given the promise at a revival conducted by the Reverend W. H. Anderson in the Old McFarland Church at Evansville. Green McFarland baptized me and I have lived a Christian life since that day."

Samuel Bell is a Mason and has received the 32nd degree. He has enjoyed fraternizing with the order but he declares; "Religion is worth the greatest fortune. It explains why man must labor and suffer and his trying experiences makes him more worthy of the great reward promised by the kind Father. When his years of sorrow are fulfilled he will understand and appreciate the reward which is Heaven."

From reading letters in possession of Samuel Bell and from an interview with James Walker as well as an interview with Samuel Bell.

"Ex-Slave Stories."
District #5.
Vanderburgh County,
Lauana Creel.

"THE LIFE STORY OF CORNELIUS CROSS"

Bibliography:
Interviews with Cornelius Cross; 405 S.E. Fifth Street, Evansville, Indiana

"I do not know the date of my birth for I was born a way back, I do not know when."

These were the words of Cornelius Cross, ex-slave and for twenty years a resident of Evansville, Indiana and a laborer for the Evansville branch of the Southern Indiana Gas and Electric Company.

"Evansville is a good place to live in but I have not always lived in Indiana. I lived three years and six months at New Orleans. New Orleans was the first place I remember living at after the time my parents brought me from the Indian Territory, where we lived and where I was born."

When asked about his memories of the Indian Territory, Cornelius Cross said that his memories are not so vivid. He recalls wearing moccasins, a wig of long black hair, beaded gauntlets and bright colored shirts and playing with the other Indian lads.

"The Indian Territory had not been joined to Oklahoma Territory." He said. "The surface of the area is level but near the boundary in all directions you could see mountains in the distance."

"Why did your parents leave the Indian Territory?" was the necessary question to ask the old man.

"My mother was named Henrietta and was a full blooded cherokee Indian. She had come across into Arkansas along with a band of her father's people, when the band had seen the area East of the Territory, they decided to stay and make their home in Arkansas. Soon they became restless and traveled farther East until they came to the Mississippi Valley where hunting and fishing were profitable sports."

"While the party of Indians were staying in Arkansas my mother met Ben, a negro slave of James Boulton, who was in the slave business, at Little Rock, Arkansas. Ben joined himself to the band of Indians and became the husband of Henrietta. Ben Boulton only became known as Ben Cross during the Civil War."

"Ben and his Indian wife got along well together, Ben had escaped bondage but he feared being recaptured. The fear caused the Indians to travel into the Indiana Territory, where many slaves had gained freedom."

"The negroes received kindness in Indiana, but there was much Indian trouble and soon the white settlers could stand the Indians as neighbors no longer."

"I have never heard it said that my people had trouble with white families." said the aged negro, "but all Indians suffered for the depredations of the uncivilized Indians."

"I do not know whether my people were driven out of the Indiana Territory following King Phillips war or some Indian massacree, but I know my parents were driven back into the Indian Territory, lived there and made the territory their home. There they were well treated, well fed and had few cares."

"The climate was delightful, the winters never severe, the summers not too warm for comfort and health. My mother was sorry to leave the territory but the old masters of slaves demanded that their property be returned to them and all the half-breeds with slave parents were mustered out of the area and returned to their owners." "My mother was not a slave, but she came with my father and brought seven sons and five daughters to be auctioned off from the slave block at New Orleans."

Cornelius Cross declared that he has been auctioned off more times than he has fingers and toes, but his mother was never separated from her family. He said she lived to raise her sons and daughters. Her sons were: Granduson; Ben; Sonny; Philip; Cornelius; Solomon and James. Her daughters were: Dee; Mary Jane; Racheal; Nancy and Addie. All these were born in the Indian Territory. Cornelius was born out in the field, where his mother worked in the kafircorn, while his father followed the chase.

After coming from the Indian Territory, the sons of Ben and Henrietta soon grew large and strong and were given employment in public places. Cornelius worked on a canal boat in the Wabash Erie Canal. The boats traveled from Terre Haute to Evansville, a distance of 150 miles. Receiving stations were built along the canal and distributing points called depots.

"The canal was a pretty sight." said the aged half-breed, as he looks back on visions of the long ago. "A great deal of masonry was used. A beautiful arch was erected over Burnett's creek. High bridges were placed above tressels and hand railings were built on each side of the bridges for safety."

Cornelius Cross remembers the two big locks at Lockport, but he has forgotten the names of a number of locks and bridges.

"I worked for several years on a boat in the Ohio River from New Orleans, and Cincinnatti [sic]. I knew Jim Howard; Red Headed Jesse, from St. Louis, the same Red Headed Jesse was murdered at St. Louis by a deck hand. I knew Tom January, one of the best river men that sailed in the old river days."

"Tell me more about the Canal." said the interviewer. The old man answered the request by explaining several points of interest in the arrangements of the structures. "Where that big chimney stands on the property of the Indiana Gas and Electric Company's property, was a canal depot. The canal boats used to be run up on what is now Fifth street and pass where the beautiful Central Library now stands."

"The New South was one boat that carried a great deal of freight. There boats were double decked boats and carried both freight and passengers."

"Many stories have been told of piracy on the Ohio River. A story of Cave In Rock is partly true as there was a large hotel at Cave In Rock and many things happened there. I do not know how many has been put in books and how much has been handed from one person to another. Many things happened which we did not understand, but I never did believe in ghosts nor haunts."

Cornelius Cross, after leaving the boats, settled at Evansville. He said he was happy in slavery because he was allowed to stay near his mother during his childhood and youth. When he was older and was disobedient, his white master or mistress always punished him as the offense deserved. "We slave children did not wear pants, but a full long shirt or dress made of coarse home-spun cloth. When we were disobedient the master or mistress made us raise the skirt high and take a sound whipping on our bared skin. It soon taught us to be obedient and to respect discipline." Henrietta Cross made her home in Hopkinsville, Kentucky at the home of her daughter. She lived to be one hundred and twenty years of age and only for a few months was she unable to do light house work. "She was a loved and loving and honored mother and was faithful to her family and to her work." her son said.

Cornelius Cross recalls many kindnesses shown by his mother. The home of Cornelius Cross is a two storied frame building located at 405 South East Fifth street. He has toiled to pay the cost and upkeep of his property but on November the seventh, 1936, a drunken white man struck the negro as he worked at a street intersection where he greased the switches for the Southern Indiana Electric Company's street car tracks. The negro was carried to the Deaconness Annex, a hospital maintained for negroes. There he lay for three months. His wife, Elmer Cross, passed away while he was at the hospital. He has been unable to work since that time and is in embarrassing financial circumstances.

Carefully folded away in an old trunk upstairs Cornelius Cross keeps the costume worn by himself when he was a small lad: a black hair wig, a pair of moccasins, a beaded gauntlet and a gay colored shirt. These and his memories arc all that remain of that happy long ago, when an Indian mother sang to him in the free and beautiful days when he lived in the Indian Territory.

LAUANA CREEL,

1415 S. BARKER AVENUE,

EVANSVILLE, INDIANA.

Monroe County
District #11
September 29, 1937
Slave Data

Submitted by:
Estella R. Dodson
Bloomington, Ind.

INTERVIEW WITH HATTIE FULLER, COLORED

Reference:
Mrs. Hattie Fuller, 906 West Fifth Street, Bloomington, Indiana.

I was born in Kentucky. My father and mother were slaves. There were eight of us children. When we came to Indiana, we crossed the Ohio River. I have always enjoyed music. On the boat when we came across was someone picking a banjo. I have never forgotten it.

I was bound out to Dr. Durant. When I was fourteen, I married. The record of my binding out is in the court house. The people I was bound to gave me a dollar and told me to build a house. I have been building ever since. Nurre gave me that window because I am such a church worker. It is plate glass. Judge Wilson and Mrs. Wilson gave me that washstand. Lately I decided to build a rag house. When people asked me what I meant by a rag house, I said, "Never you mind; you'll see." I started last Saturday by papering this room.

I went to school in Louisville and learned how to make skin lotion and vanishing cream, which I sold for a living.

When anyone asks me my age, I say, "Never you mind," and when they ask me how big a girl I was at the time of the Civil War, I say, "Never you mind."

Once I went to Kentucky to visit old Mistress. I was told to go to the back door, as colored people were not allowed at the front door, so when I got there, I went to the back door. A colored woman opened the door. She said to old Mistress, "Here is Hattie, Cassie's daughter, come to visit you." They invited me in, and we had the best dinner I ever tasted. We sat up half the night, talking. They told me a lot of things about my father and mother that I never knew before. I stayed two weeks and had a fine time. When I came away, they gave me a lot of things.

I have lived in Bloomington forever. I have played and sang. I have sang myself to death. I have brought in $12,000 for my church. I would go places and play on my organ and sing. The white folks would crowd around and give me money for my church.

Here is my picture. There's my organ and my cup. There's my dress, and my beads, and my ear-rings and my slippers. That dress had a thousand beads on it. Some girls came one day and took my picture. I sell them for my church.

My brothers and sisters lived in Bloomington. They are all dead now. People are good to me. I can't bear to give up my home and liberty. My father and mother were slaves, and I was bound. So I want to stay in my home.

118 So. Clark St.,
Bloomington, Ind.,
Sept. 29, 1937

Mr. Doyle Joyce
Federal Writers' Project, WPA
Box 294, Vincennes, Indiana

Dear Mr. Joyce:

Mrs. Fuller is about 82 or 83 years old, I am told by Mr. William C. East, Monroe County Auditor. Her name was Pierce, then she married a man named Jacobs, and after his death a man named Fuller. She is now a widow, and lives alone. She is a very nice old lady, and very devout. She is just a town institution, something like the original plat. Everyone either knows her or knows who she is. She has a small folding organ, which she is glad to play, while she sings church songs and Negro spirituels [*sic*].

I went to the court house to see if I could find any record of her being bound out. I reasoned that if the entire family came at once, it must have been after the Civil War. No record could be found. Mr. W. C. East, the Auditor, says that either no record was made, or else it has been lost. Some of the county records are missing, and it is possible that the record I want might be among them. At any rate, Mr. East knows of no records concerning Mrs. Fuller. He has made a very thorough study of the records over a period of years, and would have noticed a record concerning Mrs. Fuller as he has known who she is all his life.

I am told that Mr. Paul Feltus, of the Bloomington Star, has some material on Mrs. Fuller. I will see him and try to get some information from him.

Very truly yours,

Estella R. Dodson
(Signed)

Submitted by:
William Webb Tuttle
District No. 2
Muncie, Indiana
September 2, 1937

NEGRO SLAVES IN DELAWARE COUNTY
MRS. FRANCIS GAMMONS

Reference: Francis Toney, 815 Ebright St., Muncie, Indiana

Mrs. Francis Gammons was born in 1835 on a tobacco plantation near Galliton, Tennessee. She died at the age of 96 at her home on east Jackson street, Muncie, Indiana. Mrs. Gammons while living and recalling her experiences as a slave stated that on the plantation of her master they were treated well on the average, as could be expected from the customs of the slave holders. When they were set free, she and her husband, Wesley Gammons, they walked off of the plantation and when they had located at Galliton they were married again under the law so that their children could be legally held in their union and not hazard the dangers of being claimed again by the slave customs under any ruse or scheme; or be persuaded to return. Wesley Gammons, the husband by slave marriage, ran away from the plantation and joined the army. He wanted to be free and declared that he was willing to take his share in securing this freedom, which he did by fighting for the Union. When the war was over the family resided a time at different more southern points until the year 1881 when they came to Muncie. Mr. Gammons was a hod carrier but died a few months after he came here.

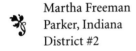

Martha Freeman
Parker, Indiana
District #2

SLAVE STORY
Randolph County

REFERENCE: Haywood Patterson who lives two and one half miles south of Baltonia, then turn east to the second house on the south side of the road (colored man).

A full-blooded Irishman who had lived in Mississippi, left the south and came to live in Randolph county. He brought with him two colored women whom he succeeded in getting this far without them being captured. He built two houses just a stone's throw apart, southeast across the field from where Mr. Patterson's home is now located and placed one of the colored women in each house. He would live in one house a week and then in the other house a week, having children by both women, but being married to neither. Some of his descendants are still living. P.M.B. Thompson was a son and Betsy Reynolds and Sarah Howland were two of his granddaughters. Mrs. Haywood Patterson is also a granddaughter.

Iris L. Cook   SLAVE STORY
District #4
Floyd Co.

A TRUE STORY OF A ROUTE OF UNDERGROUND RAILROAD AT BRANDENBURG, KY., AND ESCAPE OF SLAVES ACROSS THE RIVER THERE.

Reference: A. Mattie Brown Smith (colored), age about 55, 645 W. 5th St., New Albany, Ind.

Note: There are two texts of the following interview in the WPA files. Although typed on different typewriters and with variations in paragraphing, they are virtually identical, except one text gives the date of the interview, May 12, 1936, and includes the following headnote:

> **TRUE STORY OF AN ESCAPE related to me by Mattie Smith. (B)**
>
> And one route undoubtedly crossed the Ohio at or near Jeffersonville, and more than probably the late Dr. Nathaniel Field, who once defused an anti-abolitionist mob successfully, knew something about it. In New Albany there was a strong abolition feeling and it showed itself in an armed resistance against slave hunters at a very early day when Justice Woodruff, with a number of quickly gathered citizens, met a force at the ferry and drove them back. Those were hectic days. (C)

"Yes ma'am," said Mattie, "I can tell you something interesting about the escape of slaves across the river, but I don't ever remember of hearing anything about any around here in New Albany. But we all came from Brandenburg, down in Meade County, Kentucky. My father was a slave and belonged to John Ditto; he didn't exactly belong to him—John Ditto was a single man and my father was hired out to him. My mother belonged to the Foote's. I've heard them tell all this many a time, til I could tell it in my sleep."

"My uncle, Charles Woodford, was owned by Charlton Ditto, but was practically a free man, he was a blacksmith in Brandenburg, and come an' went as he pleased. But Uncle Charlie had heard so much about the "escapes" that he decided he wanted to be free, too. A white man, a Canadian, named John Canade [spelled "Canada" below], worked in the blacksmith shop Uncle did, and when he found out Uncle wanted to "go across," he got in touch with a certain man who ferried the runaways across the river. He was an old white man, named Charles Bell, living in Harrison County, just below Corydon—he lived in a log house about 5 miles back from the river—with no road leading to the house from the river—just a bridle path. Mr. Bell had a skiff which he used to carry the slaves over. So this man in the shop with my uncle, Mr. John Canada, got in touch with Bell and one dark night Uncle Charles got a few things together (in those days they carried what little they had in a tied-up handkerchief over a stick), and he sneaked around and told his wife and children goodbye, and they went down to the Ohio River, right at Moorman's place, almost to the Salt Well. They couldn't cross right at the town, that was too public, and the jail is right near the foot of Main Street, too, which leads right down to the river in Brandenburg—so they had to go up a piece.

Anyhow, Bell took Uncle Charlie across the river in the skiff, and on back through the woods on a mule to his house where he hid him a few weeks and then took him on up thru Corydon and across White river and he went on up to Canada and finally got out to California. I've heard that sometimes they were taken up through Indianapolis.

After a while Uncle Charlie wrote to his wife, Aunt Marietta, and got her in the notion to try to get "free" too, and [join] him. The plans were all laid for her to go, but she up and got scared and told the whole thing to Mr. Charlton Ditto, who had owned Uncle Charlie.

So, a bunch of white men from around Brandenburg, Peter Fountain was the sheriff, him and some others got together and one man who was fat and about the size of Aunt Marietta dresed up in her clothes—sunbonnet and all. And when Mr. Bell, the old man, came up in the skiff to get the colored folks, as had been arranged, this man got in the skiff, with another old colored man who was there, waiting to get across, and he hit Bell over the head with a pair of brass knucks and the men came out of hiding and took him to the Brandenburg jail, took the old colored man too. (D)

Mr. Bell laid there in jail a long time, and finally his daughter got word out to California to his sons who were there, and they came on back in a hurry. They went across the river in their skiff, and shot up the Brandenburg jail and got their father out. Yes maam! But the old colored man, who was in jail with Bell, wouldn't come, he was too scared. So they got Mr. Bell out and took him back on home. (D)

But Uncle Charles came on back here from California when the War broke out, and served in the army. Yes maam, he sure did. My great-uncle, Horace Grigsby, he escaped by the same route. He belonged to John Ditto. (D)

There was lots of colored folks crossed the river at this point. I've heard my father and mother tell of it often. My father knew the Clark family—George Rogers Clark—yes'm. I've got a platter now that belonged to them, when they was down in Kentucky. And see that old safe in the kitchen—my father bought that in the auction sale of the Clark family. (D)

My great-grandfather was in the Revolutionary War, and my great-grandmother, Hester Starks, served Gen. Washington when she was only 11 years old, she used to tell all they had to eat, and said they had whole pigs with apples in they mouths and all! That was back in Virginia. (D)

But I don't know of any "crossin" near here—never heard about any. (D)

I believe this story to be true because Mattie Smith is a well educated Negro, taught school at one time, and expresses herself in an excellent manner. Would have no reason to exaggerate to me.

(B—the writer)

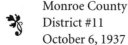

Monroe County
District #11
October 6, 1937

Submitted by:
Estella R. Dodson
Bloomington, Ind.

INTERVIEW WITH PETE WILSON, COLORED

Reference:
(A) Pete Wilson, West Fifth Street, Bloomington, Ind.

"I was born in Shelby County, Kentucky, ninety-eight miles above Simpsonville. I have taken good care of myself, and so do not look as old as I am. I am eighty-five years old. I was born a slave. I was twelve years old when I was freed.

I saw soldiers lots of times during the war. I would be standing on the state road or on the farm, and would see soldiers going by. Sometimes they would stop and talk to us, and ask us how we were getting along, and give us what consolation they could.

Old Boss was ordinarily good to us. He never cursed or swore, and never got rough with us. He was nice to his hands. He tried to give us the best he knew how. There were ten or twelve of us boys on the farm. We were raised up to work. Of course, he never paid us wages.

My mother and father and ten children came to Indiana two years after we were freed. Wagons took us from Simpsonville to Louisville and put us on the Monon train. We stayed overnight in New Albany and then came to Bloomington. I have lived here ever since. The only one of the family besides myself still living is my sister. She lives in the south part of town. She was over to see me the other day. I bought a horse and wagon when I came here. Later I was married. I farmed, and raised a family of ten. Three of my boys are still living.

I got sick about five years ago. I am not able to do any work. I live here with my granddaughter.

APPENDIX VI. THEMATIC INDEX

LIVING AND WORKING ON THE PLANTATION

Blakeley
Bland
Bowman
Bracey
Buckner
Burns
Cave
Cheatam, Harriet
Crane
Daugherty, John
Daugherty, Lizzie
Fields
Fortman
Gohagen
Guwn
Hicks, Josephine
Hicks, Solomon
Hockaday
Hume
Jackson
Jenkins
Kelley, Bell
Lennox
Locke
Love
McKinley
Moorman
Morrison
Mosley
Neal
O'Donnell
Parrott

Patterson
Preston
Quinn
Richardson
Rogers
Rose
Rudd
Slaughter, Moses
Smith, Alex and Elizabeth
Smith, Susan
Smith, Sylvester
Suggs
Tate, Mary
Tate, Preston
Thomas
Wamble
Watkins
Whitted
Young

THE TREATMENT OF SLAVES

Allen
Arnold
Ash
Barber
Barnett
Bell
Blakeley
Bolden
Boone
Bowman
Boyce
Boysaw
Bracey
Burns
Butler
Carter
Cave
Cheatam, Harriet
Cheatham, Robert
Childress

Colbert
Cooper, Frank
Crane
Cross
Daugherty, Ethel
Daugherty, John
Eubanks
Gammons
Gibson
Green
Guwn
Harvey
Hicks, Josephine
Hockaday
Howard
Hume
Hunter
Jackson
Jenkins
Johnson, Pete
Jones, Elizabeth
Jones, Ira
Jones, Nathan
Kates
Kelley, Alexander
Lennox
Lewis
Linzy
Locke
McKinley
Miller
Moore, John
Moorman
Morgan
Morrison
Mosley
Neal
Patterson
Pitman
Pompey
Preston
Quinn

Richardson
Robinson
Rogers
Rollins
Rose
Rudd
Russell
Samuels
Scarber
Slaughter, Moses
Smith, Alex and Elizabeth
Smith, Mrs. Robert
Smith, Susan
Smith, Sylvester
Stone
Suggs
Thomas
Thompson
Wade
Wamble
Watkins
Whitted
Wilson
Winlock
Young

ESCAPING FROM SLAVERY

Barnett
Barton
Battle
Beatty
Cheatham, Robert
Fields
Harris
Hough
Hume
Johnson, Lizzie
Johnson, Pete
Moore, Ben
Morrison
O'Hara
Polk

Quinn
Shaffer
Smith, Mattie
Suggs
Webb

EDUCATION

Allen
Barber
Barton
Buckner
Burns
Butler
Cheatham, Robert
Childress
Fields
Hockaday
Johnson, Lizzie
Johnson, Pete
Lee
Lennox
Locke
McKinley
Moore, John
Morgan
Nelson
O'Donnell
Polk
Robinson
Rogers
Scott
Simms
Slaughter, Moses
Smith, Susan
Stewart
Stone
Suggs
Tate, Mary
Thompson
Wamble
Watkins
Whitted

RELIGION

Bell
Boysaw
Bracey
Cheatam, Harriet
Cheatham, Robert
Childress
Cooper, John
Daugherty, John
Duncan
Edmunds
Gibson
Hockaday
Hume
Jones, Elizabeth
Lee
Lennox
Moore, John
Moorman
O'Donnell
Patterson
Polk
Richardson
Rogers
Rudd
Russell
Slaughter, Billy
Slaughter, Moses
Smith, Susan
Stewart
Stone
Tate, Mary
Watkins
Whallen
Woodson

FOLKLORE

Arnold
Barber
Beatty
Buckner

Burns
Carter
Cheatham, Robert
Colbert
Duncan
Edmunds
Fields
Fortman
Gohagen
Harrell
Hicks, Solomon
Hough
Hunter
Jones, Elizabeth
Kates
Lee
Lewis
Locke
McKinley
Moore, Ben
Moore, John
Moorman
Morgan
Morrison
Nelson
Patterson
Richardson
Rose
Russell
Samuels
Scott
Suggs
Sutton
Thomas
Woodson

RECOLLECTIONS OF THE CIVIL WAR

Ash
Barton
Beatty
Buckner

Carter
Eubanks
Fortman
Gammons
Guwn
Hicks, Solomon
Jones, Ira
Lee
Lennox
Lewis
Moorman
Morrison
O'Donnell
Parrott
Preston
Richardson
Rose
Russell
Simms
Slaughter, Billy
Slaughter, Moses
Smith, Alex and Elizabeth
Smith, Sylvester
Stone
Tate, Mary
Tate, Preston
Watkins
Watson
Whallen
Whitted
Wilson
Winlock
Woodson

LIVING AND WORKING AFTER THE CIVIL WAR

Allen
Arnold
Bell
Boone
Bowman
Boysaw

Bragg
Buckner
Burns
Cheatham, Robert
Childress
Cross
Daugherty, Ethel
Edmunds
Fortman
Fowler
Fuller
Gibson
Graham
Guwn
Hicks, Solomon
Hockaday
Hume
Jackson
Jenkins
Johnson, Lizzie
Jones, Elizabeth
Jones, Nathan
Kates
Kelley, Alexander
Kelley, Bell
Lennox
Lewis
Love
McClain
Miller
Moorman
Morgan
Mosley
Neal
Nelson
O'Hara
Parrott
Polk
Pompey
Quinn
Richardson
Robinson

Rogers
Rose
Rudd
Samuels
Scarber
Scott
Slaughter, Billy
Slaughter, Moses
Smith, Alex and Elizabeth
Smith, Susan
Smith, Sylvester
Stone
Stonestreet
Tate, Mary
Tate, Preston
Thomas
Thompson
Wamble
Watkins
Watson
Whitted
Wilson
Winlock
Woodson
Young

WORKS CONSULTED

Armstrong, Orland Kay. 1939. *Old Massa's People: The Old Slaves Tell Their Story.* Indianapolis: Bobbs-Merrill.

Baker, Ronald L. 1973. *Folklore in the Writings of Rowland E. Robinson.* Bowling Green, Ohio: Bowling Green University Popular Press.

Baker, T. Lindsay, and Julie P. Baker. 1996. *The WPA Oklahoma Slave Narratives.* Norman and London: University of Oklahoma Press.

Baughman, Ernest W. 1966. *Type and Motif Index of the Folktales of England and North America.* Indiana University Folklore Series no. 20. The Hague, The Netherlands: Mouton.

Berlin, Ira, Marc Favreau, and Steven F. Miller. 1998. *Remembering Slavery: African Americans Talk about Their Personal Experiences of Slavery and Freedom.* New York: The New Press.

Billington, Monroe. 1982. "Black Slavery in Indian Territory." *Chronicles of Oklahoma* 60 (Spring): 56–65.

Blassingame, John W. 1979. *The Slave Community: Plantation Life in the Antebellum South.* Rev. and enl. edition. New York: Oxford University Press.

Blassingame, John W. 1985. "Using the Testimony of Ex-Slaves: Approaches and Problems." In *The Slave's Narrative,* ed. Charles T. Davis and Henry Lewis Gates, Jr., 78–98. Oxford and New York: Oxford University Press. Reprinted from *Journal of Southern History* 41 (November 1975): 473–492.

Blassingame, John W., ed. 1977. *Slave Testimony: Two Centuries of Letters, Speeches, Interviews, and Autobiographies.* Baton Rouge: Louisiana State University Press.

Bontemps, Arna, ed. 1969. *Great Slave Narratives.* Boston: Beacon Press.

Botkin, B. A. 1944. "The Slave as His Own Interpreter." *Library of Congress Quarterly Journal of Current Accessions* 2 (July–Sept.): 37–63.

Botkin, B. A. [1945] 1989. *Lay My Burden Down: A Folk History of Slavery.* Reprint with foreword by Jerrold Hirsch. Athens and London: University of Georgia Press.

Cade, John B. 1935. "Out of the Mouths of Ex-Slaves." *Journal of Negro History* 20: 294–337.

Carter, Robert L., comp., and David E. Vancil, ed. 1992. *Indiana Federal Writers' Project/ Program Papers: A Guide to the Microfilm Edition at Indiana State University.* Terre Haute: Friends of the Cunningham Memorial Library.

Clayton, Ronnie W. 1990. *Mother Wit: The Ex-Slave Narratives of the Louisiana Writers' Project.* New York: P. Lang.

Dance, Daryl. 1977. "Wit and Humor in the Slave Narratives." *Journal of Afro-American Issues* 5 (Spring): 125–134.

Davis, Charles T., and Henry Louis Gates, Jr., eds. 1985. *The Slave's Narrative.* Oxford and New York: Oxford University Press.

Dorson, Richard M. 1959. *American Folklore.* Chicago: University of Chicago Press.

Dorson, Richard M. 1964. *Buying the Wind: Regional Folklore in the United States.* Chicago: University of Chicago Press.

Dorson, Richard M. 1967. *American Negro Folktales.* Greenwich, Conn.: Fawcett.

Dorson, Richard M. 1971. *American Folklore and the Historian.* Chicago: University of Chicago Press.

Dorson, Richard M., ed. 1983. *Handbook of American Folklore.* Bloomington: Indiana University Press.

Escott, Paul D. 1985a. *Slavery Remembered: A Record of Twentieth-Century Slave Narratives.* Chapel Hill: University of North Carolina Press.

Escott, Paul D. 1985b. "The Art and Science of Reading WPA Slave Narratives." In *The Slave's Narrative,* ed. Charles T. Davis and Henry Lewis Gates, Jr., 40–48. Oxford and New York: Oxford University Press.

Feldstein, Stanley. 1971. *Once a Slave: The Slaves' View of Slavery.* New York: William Morrow.

Fisk University. 1945a. *God Struck Me Dead: Religious Conversion Experiences and Autobiographies of Negro Ex-Slaves.* Social Science Source Documents no. 2. Nashville: Fisk University.

Fisk University. 1945b. *Unwritten History of Slavery: Autobiographical Account of Negro Ex-Slaves.* Social Science Source Documents no. 1 Nashville: Fisk University.

Franklin, John Hope. [1947] 1974. *From Slavery to Freedom: A History of Negro Americans.* New York: Alfred A. Knopf.

Georgia Writers' Project. [1946] 1984. *Drums and Shadows.* Athens: University of Georgia Press.

Gibbs, Wilma L., ed. 1993. *Indiana's African-American Heritage: Essays from "Black History News & Notes."* Indianapolis: Indiana Historical Society.

Hirsch, Jerrold. 1984. "Portrait of America: The Federal Writers' Project in an Intellectual and Cultural Context." Ph.D. diss., University of North Carolina.

Hurmence, Belinda. 1984. *My Folks Don't Want Me to Talk about Slavery: Twenty-one Oral Histories of Former North Carolina Slaves.* Winston-Salem: John F. Blair.

Hurmence, Belinda. 1989. *Before Freedom, When I Just Can Remember: Twenty-seven Oral Histories of Former South Carolina Slaves.* Winston-Salem: John F. Blair.

Johnson, Clifton H., ed. 1969. *God Struck Me Dead: Religious Conversion Experiences and Autobiographies of Ex-Slaves.* Philadelphia: Pilgrim Press.

Kelley, Robin D. G. 1998. Foreword to *Remembering Slavery: African Americans Talk about Their Personal Experiences of Slavery and Freedom,* ed. Ira Berlin, Marc Favreau, and Steven F. Miller, vii–viii. New York: The New Press.

Levine, Lawrence W. 1977. *Black Culture and Black Consciousness: Afro-American Folk Thought from Slavery to Freedom.* Oxford, London, and New York: Oxford University Press.

Lester, Julius, ed. 1968. *To Be a Slave.* New York: Dial.

Louisiana Writers' Project. 1945. *Gumbo Ya-Ya.* Boston: Houghton Mifflin.

Mangione, Jerre. 1972. *The Dream and the Deal: The Federal Writers' Project, 1935–1943.* Boston: Little, Brown and Co.

Nichols, Charles H. 1963. *Many Thousand Gone: The Ex-Slaves' Account of Their Bondage and Freedom.* Leiden, Netherlands: E. J. Brill.

Opie, Iona, and Peter Opie. 1955. *The Oxford Nursery Rhyme Book.* London: Oxford University Press.

Osofsky, Gilbert, ed. 1969. *Puttin' On Ole Massa.* New York: Harper and Row.

Penkower, Monty Noam. 1977. *The Federal Writers' Project: A Study in Government Patronage of the Arts.* Urbana: University of Illinois Press.

Perdue, Charles L., Jr., Thomas E. Barden, and Robert K. Phillips, eds. [1976] 1980. *Weevils in the Wheat: Interviews with Virginia Ex-Slaves.* Bloomington and London: Indiana University Press. Reprint, Charlottesville: University of Virginia Press, 1992.

Puckett, Newbell Niles. [1926] 1969. *The Magic and Folk Beliefs of the Southern Negro.* New York: Dover.

Rawick, George P., ed. 1972. *The American Slave: A Composite Autobiography.* 19 vols. Westport, Conn.: Greenwood Press. Vol. 6: *Alabama and Indiana Narratives.*

Rawick, George P., ed. 1977. *The American Slave: A Composite Autobiography.* Supplement, Series 1. 12 vols. Westport, Conn.: Greenwood Press. Vol. 5: *Indiana and Ohio Narratives.*

Rawick, George P., ed. 1979. *The American Slave: A Composite Autobiography.* Supplement, Series 2. 10 vols. Westport, Conn.: Greenwood Press.

Sekora, John, and Darwin T. Turner. 1982. *The Art of Slave Narrative: Original Essays in Criticism and Theory.* Macomb: Western Illinois University Press.

Slave Narratives: A Folk History of Slavery in the United States, from Interviews with Former Slaves. 1976. 17 vols. St. Clair Shores, Mich.: Scholarly Press.

Stowe, Harriet Beecher. [1853] 1968. *A Key to Uncle Tom's Cabin Presenting the Original Facts and Documents upon Which the Story Is Founded, Together with Corroborative Statements Verifying the Truth of the Work.* New York: Arno.

Thompson, Stith. 1966. *Motif-Index of Folk-Literature.* 6 vols. Bloomington and London: Indiana University Press.

Thornbrough, Emma Lou. [1985] 1993. *The Negro in Indiana before 1900: A Study of a Minority.* Bloomington and Indianapolis: Indiana University Press.

Vlach, John Michael. *Back of the Big House: The Architecture of Plantation Slavery.* Chapel Hill and London: University of North Carolina Press.

White, Newman I. [1928] 1965. *American Negro Folk-Songs.* Hatboro, Pa.: Folklore Associates.

Woodward, C. Vann. 1985. "History from Slave Sources." In *The Slave's Narrative,* ed. Charles T. Davis and Henry Lewis Gates, Jr., 49–59. Oxford and New York: Oxford University Press. Reprinted from *American Historical Review* 79 (April 1974): 470–481.

Writers' Program of the Work Projects Administration in the State of Indiana. 1941. *Indiana: A Guide to the Hoosier State.* New York: Oxford University Press.

Yetman, Norman R. 1967. "The Background of the Slave Narrative Collection." *American Quarterly* 19 (Fall): 534–553.

Yetman, Norman R. 1970. *Voices from Slavery: Selections from the Slave Narrative Collection of the Library of Congress.* Printed in paperback edition as *Life under the "Peculiar Institution": Selections from the Slave Narrative Collection.* New York: Holt, Rinehart and Winston.

Yetman, Norman R. 1984. "Ex-Slave Interviews and the Historiography of Slavery." *American Quarterly* 36 (Summer): 181–210.

INDEX

Page numbers in *italics* refer to illustrations.

African Methodist Episcopal Church, 33, 188, 190

Alamo, 184

alcohol use, 62

Allen, Eliza, 59

Allen, Joseph: biographical information, 275; education of slaves, 27; interview, 59–60; post–Civil War years, 51, 53; treatment of slaves, 21

Allen, Met, 60

Alpha Home for elderly African Americans, 153

Alsberg, Henry G., 5

Alvis, John, 161

American Negro Folktales (Dorson), 40, 196

The American Slave: A Composite Autobiography (Rawick), 9

Anderson, Bill, 153

Anderson, W. H., 69, 302

Anton House Hotel, 221

Arkansas River, 92–93

Arnold, George W.: biographical information, 275; interview, 60–64; post–Civil War years, 50, 54; slave folklore, 36, 41

Arnold, Oliver P., 60

Ash, Charles, 64

Ash, Thomas, 46, 64, 113, 275

ash cake, 101

Atlantic Monthly, 11

The Atlantic (steamship), 87, 92

auctions. *See* slave trade

B. S. Rhea (steamship), 63

Bagby, Robert Bruce, 28, 83–84

Bailey, Richard, 170

Ballard, Aaron, 87–88

Ballard, Tom, 87–88

Band, George, 182–183

The Banjo (steamship), 91–92

baptism, 32, 232

Baptists: Edna Boysaw, 78; John W. Fields, 128; Nathan Jones, 163; Candies Richardson, 209; Moses Slaughter, 232; Barney Stone, 241; Alex Woodson, 271

barbecues, 42–43, 47, 142

Barber, Rosa, 27, 41, 42, 64–65, 275

Barnett, Judge, 125

Barnett, Lewis, 25, 65–66, 167, 275

Barton, Robert, 26, 29, 48, 66, 275

basket-making, 150

Bassett, Alice, 220, 223

Battle, Anthony, 26, 67, 203, 275

Battle of Fort Donelson, 135, 269

Battle of Fort Wagner, 232, 243

Battle of Millikins Bend, 243

Battle of Shiloh, 269

Beal, Barney, 40

Beamer, Rube, 184

Beatty, George, 40, 67–68, 275

Beaumont, John, 234

beauty shop, 136

Beckner, Lucien, 229

Beecher, Henry Ward, 178

beef shoots, 142

Bell, Charles, 237, 310

Bell, John, 22, 68, 108, 301

Bell, Samuel: biographical information, 275; contraband camps, 22, 51; interview, 68–69, 300–302; religion of slaves, 32, 34

Bellamy, Joseph, 203–204

Bellamy, Noah, 203

Bethany Park, 137

Bible: in education, 28; importance of to former slaves, 152, 231, 240–241; slaves forbidden to own, 209

Bidding, Elizabeth, 138

Bidding, John Henry, 138

The Big Gray Eagle (steamship), 87–88, 91

Biographical and Historical Sketches of Early Indiana (Woollen), 177
Black, G. E., 203
Black, Rube, 21, 211
Blakeley, Mittie, 22, 70, 275
Bland, Patsy Jane, 14–16, 18, 70–72, 276
Blassingame, John W., 3
bloodhounds, 191
Bloomington Daily Telephone, 75, 136
Bloomington Herald-Telephone, 172
Bloomington Star, 307
Bloomington Telephone, 267
boatmen's songs, 41, 88
Boehne, John W., Sr., 84
Boehne Tuberculosis Hospital, 219
Bolden, Lizzie, 72–73, 276
Boone, Carl, 22, 33, 53, 73–74, 276
Boone, Miley (John), 73
Boone, Rachel, 73–74
Boone, Stephen, 73–74
Borland, Walter, 75–76, 276
Botkin, Benjamin A., 7–8, 35, 56
Boulton, Ben, 115, 303
Boulton, James, 115, 303
Bowman, Julia, 17, 55, 76, 276
Boxer Rebellion, 183
Boyce, Angie Moore, 52, 76–77, 276
Boyle, John, 71
Boysaw, Edna, 33, 52, 77–79
The Bracelet (steamship), 92
Bracey, Callie, 16, 17, 31, 79–80, 276
Bragg, Tolbert, 80–81, 252, 276
Branner, John, 253
Brazil Daily Times, 33, 77
Brazy, Harry, 236
Breeding, James, 76
Brown, Elmer, 185
Brown, George, 75–76
Brown, John, 48, 229–230
Brown, Sterling A., 5, 12
Brown, Tom, 184
Bryan, William Jennings, 84
Buckner, Dickie, 82
Buckner, Frank, 83
Buckner, George Washington, *81;* biographical information, 276; cabin, 14; education, 28, 52–53; family, 82–83; gift slaves, 15–16; interviews, 80–86; recollections of the Civil War, 46; slave folklore, 40
Buckner, Stanton, 81, 83

buried treasure, 147
Burns, George Taylor: background, 86–89; biographical information, 276; boatmen songs, 41; education of slaves, 27; indentured servitude of, 53–54; interview, 89–94; superstitions of rivermen, 36
Burns, Lucy, 86
Butler, Belle, 20–21, 27, 94–95, 276
Byington, Cardinal, 88

cabins, 14, 141–142, 171, 235, 254, 271. *See also* housing for slaves
Cade, John B., 4–5
Caldwell, Erskine, 12
camp meetings. *See* revivals
Canada, John, 237, 310
canals, 304
cane mills, 250
Carlisle, Billy, 239
Carpenter, Bat, 109
Carpenter, Isaac, 109
Carpenter, Leige, 109
Carpenter, Matilda, 109
carriage drivers, 259
Carter, Joseph William: biographical information, 276; folk healers, 39; interview, 95–98; military service of, 46–47; murder of slaves, 21
Cates, Lavina, 165
Cates, Thomas, 164–165
Catholicism, 33, 155, 219
Cave, Ellen, 15, 16, 23–24, 98–100, 277
Cave, James, 99
Cave-In Rock, 89–90, 116, 305
charity, 79, 139–140
Chavious, Hillery, 25, 227–228
Cheatam, Harriet, 15, 32, 100–101, 277
Cheatham, Robert J.: background, 101–105; biographical information, 277; education of slaves, 29; interview, 105–107; poverty in post–Civil War years, 54; religion of slaves, 31, 32; runaway slaves, 26; slave folklore, 36
children born into slavery, 43
children's fict (folklore), 42
Childress, James: background and interview, 108; biographical information, 277; education of slaves, 28; post–Civil War years, 51–52; religion of slaves, 32; treatment of slaves, 22

cholera, 146–147

Christmas season, 43, 176

churches: African Methodist Episcopal Church, 33, 188, 190; Baptist, 78, 128, 163, 232, 271; church attendance, 71, 73, 80; Colored Catholic Church, 33; Methodist Church, 220; Old McFarland Church, 302; organ music in, 307; slaves attending slaveholder's church, 152

circuses, 170

Citizen National Bank, 300

Civil War: George Arnold's recollections of, 61; battles of, 122, 135, 173, 207, 240, 243, 252, 269; causes of, 229–230; effect on South of, 96, 146, 157, 165, 193; end of, 250; Grand Army of the Republic, 121, 241, 268; military camps, 269; physicians in, 265; recollections of, 45–48, 83, 157, 167–168, 171, 207; Reconstruction, 120; referred to as the "Revolution War," 228; slavery as central issue of, 301; slaves held after, 49, 52, 132, 157, 180, 208, 272; slaves' support for Union, 200; soldiers stealing food from plantations, 143; spies during, 222. See also conscription; emancipation and Emancipation Proclamation; enlistment; military service of African Americans

Clark, George Rogers, 238, 311

Clark County Poor Farm, 239

Claven, Mary, 252

Clay, Henry, 180

Clemens, Susie, 198

Clements, Philip, 177

clothing for slaves: lack of shoes, 272; making, 250; Lulu Scott on, 226; Alex and Elizabeth Smith on, 235–236; varieties of, 17–18

Coffer, Jesse, 20–21, 94

Colbert, Sarah, 38, 109–110, 277

Collins, Amelia Ann, 204

Colored Catholic Church, 33

conjurers. See folklore; witches and witchcraft

Conover, E., 300

conscription, 46, 162, 201, 230, 249

contraband camps, 22, 51, 68–69, 301–302

conversion (religious), 32, 252. See also baptism; revivals

Cook, Bill, 143

Cook, George, 142

Cook, Iris, 16, 65, 167, 193, 310

Cook, John, 143

cooking, 15, 100–101, 252, 255. See also food

Cooper, Frank, 21, 23–24, 110–111, 277

Cooper, John, 32, 111–112, 277

Cooper, Mandy, 110

Cooper, Woodford, 111–112

cotton, 200

Cowherd, Bob, 113

Crane, Mary, 18, 19, 113–114, 277

Creel, Lauana, 101, 300, 303

Crimm, Parker, 163

Crockett, Davy, 40

Crosby, William, 261

Cross, Ben (Ben Boulton), 115, 303

Cross, Cornelius, 54, 114–116, 277, 303–305

Cross, Elmer, 305

Cross, Henrietta, 303, 305

Cuffie (character in Uncle Tom's Cabin), 178

Cumberland Gap, 234

Cumberland River, 234

Cumberts, Sidney L., 301

Cunningham Memorial Library, 3–4, 9, 13

Daniels, Wilson H., 88, 90, 92

Danvis Folks (Robinson), 11

Daugherty, Ethel, 20, 23, 51, 116–117, 277

Daugherty, John, 17, 34, 118, 277

Daugherty, Lizzie, 118–119, 277

Davies, Honor Farmer, 104

Davis, Jefferson C., 48, 198, 229

Day, Oscar Evelyn, 272

Deaconness Annex, 305

Deam, Bell, 53, 165–166, 166–167, 280

Denny, Josephine, 251

depression (economic), 51, 54, 55

dialects, challenges regarding, 11–12

Dickens, Susan, 167

Dillard, Carolyn P., 5

diseases, 146–147, 231

Ditto, Charlton, 237–238, 310

Ditto, John, 237–238, 310, 311

"Dixie" (song) as model for boatmen's songs, 88

Dixon, Archibald, 180, 246

Dixon, Benjamin, 180

Dixon, Minnie, 219

Dixon, Thomas. See Suggs, Thomas

Dodson, Estella R., 306, 307

Dood, Patrick, 226

Doolins, Amy, 98
Doolins, Carmuel, 98
Dorson, Richard M., 7, 56, 196
draft. *See* conscription
dreams, folk beliefs regarding, 37–38
Dunbar's Hollow, 302
Duncan, Rachael, 32, 119–120, 277
Dunlap family, 66
Dunn, Isaac, 177–178
Dunn, Jacob P., 177
Dunn, Peter, *141,* 177–178
Dunning, Alfred, 88
Dupee, D. W., 192
Durand (Durant), John J., 136, 306
Durr, John, 59

East, William C., 307
Eaton (Colonel), 69, 301–302
Eaton, Joe, 248–249
Eaton, Mary Emily. *See* Tate, Mary Emily
    (Mollie) Eaton
Eaton, Nancy, 248
eclipse, 142–143, 264
Eclipse (steamship), 87, 90
Edmunds, H. H., 33–34, 49–50, 120–121, 278
education for African Americans: Joseph
    Allen on, 59, 60; Robert Barton on, 66;
    Bible used in, 28; Patsy Jane Bland on, 71;
    Robert Cheatham on, 103–105; children
    of John Eubanks, 121; degrees, 260; John
    W. Fields on, 126; forbidden to slaves, 65,
    95, 159, 170, 205–206, 234, 259, 265;
    Oliver Nelson on, 197; schools, 68, 83–84,
    132, 168, 182, 192, 199, 260, 265; self-
    education, 243; Jack Simms on, 228; slaves
    learning from whites, 158, 159–160, 167,
    181, 232, 240–241; Mattie Brown Smith,
    237; Barney Stone, 241; Adah Isabelle
    Suggs on, 245; Mollie Tate on, 251;
    George Thompson on, 256; various
    accounts of, 27–30. *See also* schools for
    African Americans
Eldorado (steamship), 63
Ellen Gray (steamship), 92
Ellison, Fox, 64–65
emancipation and Emancipation Proclama-
    tion: Joseph William Carter on, 98; Ellen
    Cave on, 99; John W. Fields on, 128;
    freedom papers, 147–148, 244; Matthew
    Hume on, 51, 155; labor before and after,
    171; Peter Neal on, 196; preachers' ser-
    mons on, 187; Billy Slaughter on, 230;
    slaveholders' reactions to, 146; slaves held
    after, 49, 52, 132, 157, 208, 272; slaves
    purchasing their freedom, 76–77, 109,
    147–148, 152; slaves' reactions to, 121,
    151, 250; slaves remaining on plantations,
    153–154, 196; as theme of sermons, 187;
    Thirteenth Amendment, 49, 180, 232;
    George Winlock on, 270. *See also* escaping
    slavery
Embassy (steamship), 93
Emergency Relief Appropriations Act, 5
enlistment: Francis Gammons on, 308; Moses
    Slaughter on, 233–234; slaves enlisting in
    armies, 46, 64, 216; Mattie Brown Smith
    on, 311; Union Army, 230, 232; George
    Winlock on, 268. *See also* conscription
entertainment for slaves, 254–255
epidemics, 146–147, 231
Ernest, Robert J., 268
escaping slavery: accounts of, 25–26, 103,
    105–106; Lewis Barnett's escape, 65;
    Samuel Bell on, 301; bloodhounds to
    track, 191; John Canada's assistance with,
    237–238; capturing escaped slaves, 258,
    311; Robert Cheatham on, 105–106;
    forging passes, 103; Francis Gammons on,
    308; Samantha Hough on, 152; Pete
    Johnson on, 159–160; Masons assisting,
    263; America Morgan on, 191; Rudolph
    O'Hara on, 199; Nelson Polk on, 204–206;
    John Rudd on, 219; runaway slaves beat-
    en, 258; Arthur Shaffer on, 228; slaves
    purchasing their freedom, 76–77, 109,
    147–148, 152; Adah Isabelle Suggs on,
    245–246; George Thomas on, 254; Henry
    Webb on, 263; Anderson Whitted on,
    265–266; George Winlock on, 268. *See
    also* emancipation and Emancipation
    Proclamation; Underground Railroad
Eubanks, John, 46, 48, 121–125, 278
Evansville, Indiana, 61, 214, 303
Evansville Courier and Press, 108, 114–115,
    161, 219, 268
Evansville Light Infantry, 199
"experience songs," 169

Farley, F. E., 135
farm labor, 237

Farmer, Bobby, 101
Farmer, Henry, 101, 102–103
Farmer, Mary, 101
Farmer, Sarah, 104
Fauntleroy, Emily, 233
Fauntleroy, Joseph, 232–233
Federal Emergency Relief Administration, 5
Federal Writers' Project (FWP), 3–6
Feltus, Paul, 307
Fields, John W., *125;* background and inter-
    view, 125–128; biographical information,
    278; education of slaves, 27; life as slave,
    14; runway slaves, 26; separation from
    family, 19; slave folklore, 36, 41
Fields, Nathaniel, 310
Fifth Kentucky Cavalry, 183
First Baptist Church, 78
Fisher, Joe, 107
fishing, 303
floods, 162, 223, 225, 272
folklore: bad omens, 127; black cats, 161–162;
    George Washington Buckner on, 40, 82;
    buried treasure tale, 147; Robert Cheat-
    ham, 104–105; children's fict, 42; con-
    jurers, 133–134; of dreams, 37–38; John
    W. Fields on, 36, 41, 125–126; folk healers,
    39; "folk-say," 8; folk songs of slaves, 41–
    42; folk tales, 186–187; George Fortman
    on, 133–134; "hant," 216; Betty Jones on,
    161–162; Davy Jones, 92; on Abraham
    Lincoln, 210; *The Magic and Folk Beliefs
    of the Southern Negro* (Puckett), 36; of
    preachers, 196–197; riverboat men, 36, 63,
    89; "Rock Candy" (game), 42, 214–215;
    various accounts of, 35–44; voodoo, 97–
    98; will-o'-the-wisps, 39. *See also* ghosts
    and spirits; witches and witchcraft
food: advice on diet, 240; ash cake, 101; bar-
    becues, 42–43, 47, 142; cooking, 100–101,
    252, 255; eating conditions for slaves, 117;
    hardtack, 51, 265; at log rollings, 254;
    pickled beef, 51, 265; preparation and
    storage, 44, 239, 255; salt pork, 15; scarci-
    ty of, 15, 94, 149–150; slave diet, 209, 212,
    224, 226, 258; on steamships, 231; tales
    about, 151
Forrest, Nathan Bedford, 122
Fort Donelson, battle at, 135, 269
Fort Wagner, 232, 243
Fort Wayne Journal Gazette, 156

Fortman, George: biographical information,
    278; funerals, 44; interview, 129–135;
    recollections of the Civil War, 45; slave
    auctions, 19; slave folklore, 36, 41
Fountain, Peter, 238, 311
Fowler, Alex, 53, 135, 278
Frank, Martin, 90
Frankfort Peace Commission, 180
Franklin Evening Star, 190, 255
Free, W. O., 75
Free Will Baptist Church, 163
Freedmen's Aid Society, 69, 301–302
Freedmen's Bureau, 28, 30
Freedmen's School, 28, 30, 132
freedom granted to slaves. *See* emancipation
    and Emancipation Proclamation
freedom papers, 147–148, 244
Freeman, Martha, 59, 309
Freemasons, 241
Freemen's Association, 83. *See also* Freed-
    men's Bureau
French, Charles and Lydia, 176
*From Sundown to Sunup: The Making of the
    Black Community* (Rawick), 9
fugitive slaves. *See* escaping slavery; Under-
    ground Railroad
Fuller, Hattie, 306
Fuller, Levi, 136
Fuller, Mattie, 53, 136–137, 278
funerals, 44, 132–133, 139
Furgerson, Ashley, 256
Furgerson, Manfred, 255

Gable, Clark, 152
Gaines, Frances Foulkes, 77
Gammons, Francis: biographical information,
    278; interview, 138, 308; recollections of
    the Civil War, 46; treatment of slaves, 22
Gammons, Wesley, 138, 308
Gardner, Jim, 96
Gardner, Malvina, 95
Gardner, Puss, 95, 96, 97
Garmon, Jane, 38, 110
Gary Post Tribune, 121, 123
genealogy, 56
The General Pike (steamship), 92
George, Eliza, 131
George, Ford, 129, 131
George, Patent, 130, 132
Georgia Railroad, 248

Georgia Writers' Project, 5

ghosts and spirits: George Washington Buckner on, 82; Rachael Duncan on, 119; H. H. Edmunds on, 120; John W. Fields on, 125–126; Peter Gohagen on, 143; Samantha Hough on, 152–153; America Morgan on, 191; George Morrison on, 194; Amy Elizabeth Patterson on, 202; rivers and, 63; Elizabeth Russell on, 221; Lulu Scott on, 226–227; Katie Sutton on, 246–247; used as tool to frighten slaves, 120; various accounts of, 39; Alex Woodson on, 271–272. *See also* folklore

Gibson, John Henry, 53, 138–140, 278

Gibson, Lee, 138

gift slaves: George Washington Buckner on, 82; Mary Crane on, 113; John Eubanks on, 121–122; life of, 15, 19; Sarah Locke, 176; Americus Moore, 186; America Morgan, 190–191; William Quinn, 207–208; Moses Slaughter on, 233; Alex Woodson, 270

God Struck Me Dead: Religious Conversion Experiences and Autobiographies of Negro Ex-Slaves (Fisk University), 4, 9

Gohagen, Mary, 142

Gohagen, Peter: biographical information, 278; family of, 142; folk customs, 42; interview, 141–144

Gold Dust (steamship), 63–64

good luck charms, 37

Goodman, Humphrey, 88

Graham, Sidney, 52, 144, 260, 278

grain mills, 254

Grand Army of the Republic, 121, 241, 268

Grand Hotel, 166

Grandy, Charles, 11

Grant, Buck, 241

Grant, John, 241

Grant, Ulysses S., 100, 123, 183, 268

graveyards, 44, 189

Gray, Edmund, 94

Gray Eagle (steamship), 219

Greater Indianapolis (Dunn), 177

Green, Ms. L., 144–145, 278

Green River, 83

Greencastle Banner, 67, 203

Greene, Jacob, 97

Gregory's Landing, 86

Grieg, Billy, 136

Grigsby, Horace, 238, 311

guerrilla soldiers, 268

Guiding Star (steamship), 219

Guwn, Betty, 46, 51, 145–146, 278

Hammonds, Richard, 80

Hammonds family, 80

Hampton, Mary Jane, 206

Hampton, Noah, 206

Hanna, Agnes M., 177

hardtack, 51, 265

Hargill, Gus, 211

Harmony, Indiana, 78

Harrell, Josie, 40, 146–147, 278

Harris, Greene, 97

Harris, Joel Chandler, 11, 12

Harris, Maston, 26, 147–148, 279

Harrison, William Henry, 265

Harvey, Nealy, 148, 279

Hawk, John, 129–130

Hawk, Rachael, 129–130

Hayden, Jesse, 181

Hays, Mary, 256

Henley, Martin, 100

Henry Ward Beecher: An American Portrait (Hibben), 177

Henson, Josiah, 179

Herrington, Harriet, 224

hexes, 37, 187, 246–247. *See also* folklore

Hibben, Paxton, 177

Hickory Quakers, 264–265

Hicks, Josephine: biographical information, 279; interview, 148–149; jobs of slaves, 16; treatment of slaves, 22

Hicks, Solomon: biographical information, 279; interview, 149–151; payment of slaves, 17; post–Civil War years, 51; separation of slave families, 18; slave folklore, 36

Hill, David, 125, 127

Hillman Rolling Mills, 131

History of Randolph County, 174–175

history of slaves, 35–44

Hobson, E. H., 48, 269

Hockaday, Mrs., 30, 32, 50–51, 151–152, 279

Hoggard, David, 11

Holland, Zella Kinser, 136

Hood, John Bell, 233

Hope Field, Arkansas, 223

Hopkins, Harry L., 5
horse trading, 271
horseshoes, 127
Hotchkiss, Bill, 163
Hotchkiss, Eliza, 163
Hough, Samantha, 37, 152–153, 279
housing for slaves: construction of, 171, 235,
    250–251, 254, 258; descriptions of, 212,
    271; Hattie Fuller on, 306; Peter Goha-
    gen's cabin, 141–142; Betty Guwn on,
    145–146; living conditions of slaves, 14;
    Alex Woodson on, 271
Howard, Beverly, 153
Howard, Chelton, 153
Howard, Jim, 116, 304
Howard, Robert, 153, 279
Howland, Sarah, 309
Hume, Matthew, 17, 33, 51, 153–155, 279
Hunter, Alex, 203
Hunter, Lillian, 40, 156, 279
Hunter, Morton, 136
hunting, 164–165, 230, 303
Huntington, Albert, 66
Hurston, Zora Neale, 12
Hutchings, Dan, 166
Hutchinson, Dick, 75

Igleheart, Levi, 262–263
Illinois Central Railroad Company, 135
indentured servitude: freed slaves entering
    into, 50, 90, 104; lawsuit regarding, 262;
    terms of, 262
Indian Territory, 303
Indiana (steamship), 122
Indiana: A Guide to the Hoosier State (WPA),
    4
Indiana Eclectic Medical College, 28, 84
Indiana Federal Writers' Project, 3–4
Indiana State Journal, 178
Indiana State Normal School, 28, 84
Indiana University, 199
Indianapolis Recorder, 139, 140, 210, 213
Indianapolis Star, 42, 139, 183, 210
Indianapolis Times, 177, 213
Indians. See Native Americans
Interchange (steamship), 92
International Order of Odd Fellows
    (I.O.O.F.), 241, 243
interracial marriage, 117, 147
interviewing techniques, 6–7

Irish, George, 97
iron industry, 131

jack-o'-lanterns, 39, 215
Jackson, Andrew, 40, 86
Jackson, Henrietta, 15, 18–19, 54–55, 156–
    157, 279
Jackson, Levy, 156
Jacobs, Henry Clay, 136
jailbreaks, 311
James, Jourdain, 262
January, Tom, 88, 116, 304
Jean, Garret, 188
Jenkins, Emma, 119
Jenkins, Mattie: biographical information,
    279; interview, 157; post–Civil War years,
    49, 52; roles of slaves, 16; treatment of
    slaves, 21
John Brown's Raid, 48, 229–230
Johnson, Albert, 28, 84
Johnson, Charles S., 4
Johnson, Green, 152
Johnson, Lizzie, 27, 29, 158–159, 279
Johnson, Pete, 26, 30, 52, 159–160, 279
Johnstone, J. E., 233
jokes and pranks, 169–170, 186–187
Jones, Ben Franklin, 162
Jones, Elizabeth (Bettie), 22–23, 36, 55, 160–
    162, 280
Jones, Ira, 22, 45, 47, 162–163, 280
Jones, John R., 161
Jones, Lark, 38–39
Jones, Nathan, 23, 163–164, 280
Jones, Willis, 23, 164
Joyce, Doyle, 307

The Kate Sarchet (steamship), 92
Kates, Ralph, 36, 53, 164–165, 280
Keephart, Jacob, 175–176
Keigwin, James, 231
Kelley, Alexander, 53, 165–166, 166–167,
    280
Kelley, Bell Deam, 53, 165–166, 166–167,
    280
Kelley, Margaret, 165–166
Kelly, Robin D. G., 13
Kentucky, 3, 49
Kettering, William, 71
Kezziah (slave), 102
kidnapping freed slaves, 107

Kile, John, 252
King, Henry, 76–77
King, Margaret Breeding, 76–77
King Philip's War, 115, 304
Kirby House Hotel, 166
Knapp, Marie, 78
Knights of Pythias, 241, 243
Knowles, Merton, 40, 42, 184
Ku Klux Klan: abduction of African
    Americans, 220–221, 222; George Taylor
    Burns on, 87; Sarah Colbert on, 111; Sid-
    ney Graham on, 144; harassment of for-
    mer slaves, 23–24; Sarah Locke on, 176;
    murder of African Americans, 182–183,
    186; Mrs. Preston on, 206–207; retribu-
    tion against freed slaves, 52; John Rudd
    on, 219

labor tensions, 52, 78–79
Lay My Burden Down: A Folk History of
    Slavery (Botkin), 8, 35, 40
Lee, Edward, 168
Lee, Elvira: biographical information, 280;
    education of slaves, 29; interview, 167–
    170; recollections of the Civil War, 47;
    religious service of, 33; slave folklore, 40,
    41–42, 65
Lee, Robert E., 46, 122, 233
Lee, Stephen, 146–147
Leich, Charles, 300
Lennox, Adeline Rose: biographical informa-
    tion, 280; education of, 27; interview,
    170–172; labor of slaves, 16; log houses,
    14; post–Civil War years, 50, 55; recollec-
    tions of the Civil War, 47; religion of
    slaves, 34; separation from family, 18
Lennox, George, 171
Lewis, Steve, 154
Lewis, Thomas: biographical information,
    280; interview, 172–174; post–Civil War
    years, 52; recollections of the Civil War,
    47–48; slave folklore, 39
Liberia, 84–86
Library of Congress, 9, 13
Life of Harriet Beecher Stowe (Stowe), 177
Lincoln, Abraham: assassination of, 270;
    Robert Barton on, 66; George Washington
    Buckner on, 86; cabin of, 271; Robert
    Cheatham on, 103; enlistment of slaves,
    233; folklore regarding, 42, 210; Matthew

Hume on, 155; Parthenia Rollins on, 213–
    214; Elizabeth Russell on, 220–222; Billy
    Slaughter on, 230
Linzy, Levi, 21, 174–175, 280
living conditions of slaves, 14–15, 245
Locke, Sarah H., 16, 280; Christmas season,
    43; education of slaves, 29–30; interview,
    175–176; treatment of slaves, 19
Locklear, Arthur, 158
Lockyear Business College, 129
log cabins, 14, 171, 235, 254
log rollings, 254
Lomax, John, 6, 12, 35
Louisville Times, 197
Love, Maria, 16, 54, 176–177, 280
The Lue Evans (steamship), 92
Lulu Scott, 226–227
Lynch, Gray, 165
Lynch, Larkin, 165

Madison Courier, 67–68, 195
The Magic and Folk Beliefs of the Southern
    Negro (Puckett), 36
magic and spells, 37, 187, 246–247
Magill, John H., 235
Magruder, Louisa, 178
Magruder, Thomas, 177–179, 281
Magruder family, 177
mail delivery, 259
marriage between relatives, 117
The Masonic Gem (steamship), 92
Masons: assisting runaway slaves, 25, 263;
    Samuel Bell, 69, 302; Barney Stone, 243
Mayer, Chancy, 20, 94
McClain, Bill, 246
McClain, Harriott, 245
McClain, Hettie, 49, 179–180, 281
McClain, Hulda, 179
McClain, Jackson, 244
McClain, Jerome, 246
McClain, John, 92
McClain, Louisa, 244
McClain, Milton, 246
McClain, William, 179–180
McFarland, Green, 69
McFarland, Jim, 109
McFarland Baptist Church, 232
McGlason, Lorenzo, 135
McGlason, W. G., 135
McKees Rocks, 91

McKinley, John, 181

McKinley, Robert: biographical information, 281; education of slaves, 29; gift slaves, 15; interview, 181; slave folklore, 39; slave trade, 23; treatment of slaves, 21–22

McMurry, Robert, 224

McQuirk, Rhoder, 218

medicine, 38–39, 97–98, 103

mediums, 40. *See also* folklore; witches and witchcraft

Mering, Melvin, 146

Merrill, Sarah Emery: on Lewis Barnett, 65–66; runway slaves, 25; slave folklore, 40, 41–42; as source on Elvira Lee, 167

The Messenger (steamship), 92

Methodist Episcopal Church, 33, 188, 190

midwives, 189

military camps, 269

military service of African Americans: Joseph Allen on, 59; Joseph William Carter, 46–47, 98; Robert Cheatham on, 105; Mary Crane on, 114; John Eubanks on, 124–125; Francis Gammons on, 138; Levi Linzy on, 175; Richard Miller on, 182–183; James W. O'Hara, 199; Moses Slaughter on, 233–234; slaves enlisting in armies, 64, 216; slaves given freedom for serving, 46, 134; Mattie Brown Smith on, 238; Barney Stone on, 241, 243; George Winlock on, 268. *See* Civil War; conscription; enlistment

Miller, Bob, 185

Miller, George M., 183

Miller, Mary, 268

Miller, Mattie, 198

Miller, Richard, 52, 181–183, 281

Millikins Bend, 243

Million, Celia, 60

mine laborers, 52, 78–79

ministers and preachers: H. H. Edmunds, 33–34; on emancipation, 187; folklore on, 196–197; ; Solomon Hicks on, 150; Dick Hutchinson, 75; Henry Clay Moorman, 188–190; Barney Stone, 241–244; Reverend Wamble, 257–260

miscarriage caused by whipping, 257

mistrust of African Americans in the North, 151

Mitchell, David, 149

Mitchell High School, 199

mixed race slaves, 105, 117, 156, 202

Monroe, Roy, 146

Monroe, Woodford, 111–112

Monrovia, Liberia, 84–86

Moore, Americus, 186

Moore, Belby, 211

Moore, Ben, 40, 184–185, 281

Moore, Henry, 20, 217, 218

Moore, Jane, 218

Moore, John: biographical information, 281; education of, 30; interview, 186–188; religion of slaves, 32; slave folklore, 38, 40

Moore, Shell, 218

Moorman, Dorah, 188

Moorman, H. G., Jr., 190

Moorman, Henry Clay: biographical information, 281; folk customs, 42; graveyards on plantations, 44; interview, 188–190; labor of slaves, 16; post–Civil War years, 53; recollections of the Civil War, 45; religious service of, 33; slave folklore, 36; slave weddings, 43

Moorman, James, 188

Moorman, Lulu Carter, 190

Morgan, America, 30, 39, 190–192, 281

Morgan, Charles, 71, 157

Morgan, John Hunt, 48, 99, 122, 269

Mormonism, 117

Morning Star (steamship), 219

Morrison, George: background and interview, 192–194; biographical information, 281; "patty roll" term, 229; recollections of the Civil War, 47; runway slaves, 25; slave folklore, 39–40; square dances, 43

Morton, Lula B., 201–202

Morton, Stokes, 202

Mosley, Joseph, 18, 54, 194–195, 281

Mosley, Tim, 194–195

Mossy Creek, Tennessee, 252

mulatto slaves, 105, 117, 156, 202

Mulligan, Jack, 197

murder: of George Band's wife, 182; of Garret Jean, 188; of Klan Members, 183; Thomas Lewis on, 174; Parthenia Rollins on, 212–214; slaves whipped to death, 21, 96, 186, 191

Murphy, Malinda, 267

Murry, Fred, 256

music: church organ, 307; fiddlers, 167; George Morrison on, 194; square dances,

43, 192–193, 255; steamships, 61. *See also* songs

Native Americans: abduction of slaves, 95–96, 222–223; attacks on riverboats, 90–91; Six Nations, 91; as slaves, 115–116, 129–130
Neal, Henry, 49, 195–196, 281
Neal, John F., 244
Neal, Peter, 49, 195
Nelson, Oliver, 29, 41, 196–197, 281
New Orleans, Louisiana, 89, 146
New South (steamship), 116
Newland, Willie, 302
Newsom, Richard, 14, 240
Ninth Cavalry, 183
Nixon, Hazel, 177
Noble, Noah, 177
Noble, Thomas, 177
North, William, 253
Nowland, John H. B., 177

Observer and Reporter (Lexington), 180
Odd Fellows, 241, 243
O'Donnell, Sallie, 197
O'Donnell, Sarah, 33, 48, 197–198, 282
Odum, Howard, 12
O'Hara, Cynthia, 55, 199
O'Hara, James W., 199
O'Hara, Louisa, 199
O'Hara, Rudolph D., 26, 53, 80, 198–199, 282
Ohio River: George Beatty on, 67–68; George Taylor Burns on, 88, 89–90; piracy, 89, 116, 305
old age pensions. *See* pensions
"Old Dan Tucker" (song), 43, 192
Old McFarland Church, 302
Oliver, Lee, 139
oral history of slaves, 35–44
Ottensteen, Charles H., 234
"Out of the Mouths of Ex-Slaves" (Cade), 4–5
overseers, 155, 196

Page, Thomas Nelson, 12
Parish, George, 256
Parke, J. G., 233
Parker, Arnold, 181
Parker, Jane Alice, 181
Parker, Peeler, 260
Parrott, Amos, 199
Parrott, Richard, 199

Parrott, Sarah, 50, 55, 201
Parrott, W. F., 45–46, 53, 199–201, 282
parties, 189, 216
Parvine family, 246
Patent, George, 132
patrollers (paddle rollers): background of term, 229; Sarah Colbert on, 111; Henry Clay Moorman on, 189; Spear Pitman on, 204; Candies Richardson on, 209; George Thompson on, 256; treatment of slaves, 23–24. *See also* Ku Klux Klan
Patterson, Amy Elizabeth, 18, 40, 201–203, 282
Patterson, Haywood, 174, 309
Peck, Mat, 250
Pegg, Christopher, 88
pensions: of Robert Cheatham, 104; of Mattie Fuller, 136–137; of Adeline Rose Lennox, 171–172; of Joseph Mosley, 194; of Nettie Pompey, 206; of Joe Robinson, 211; of John Rudd, 219; of Alex and Elizabeth Smith, 236; various accounts of, 54; of Alex Woodson, 270; of Samuel Watson, 263
Perry, Mrs. William D., 72
Peterkin, Julia, 12
Phant, Sarah, 111–112
physicians during Civil War, 265
pickled beef, 51
picnics, 216
Pierce, Andy, 136
Pillow, Jasper, 93
Pillow, Seely, 93
piracy, 89–90, 116, 305
Pitman, Spear: biographical information, 282; interview, 203–204; Ku Klux Klan, 23–24; sources of material on, 67; treatment of slaves, 20, 21
Plaster, Carter, 224
play parties, 254–255
politics: in Liberia, 84–86; voting, 259
Polk, Armstead, 177
Polk, Elmira, 16, 177
Polk, J. B., 25, 27, 53, 204
Polk, Nelson, 32, 51, 204–206, 282
Pompey, Nettie, 54, 206, 282
Portland Daily Sun, 252
poverty, 54, 144–145, 239. *See also* pensions
powder mills, 261
Powell, Caroline, 163

The Prairie Rose (steamship), 92
pranks and jokes, 169–170, 186–187
preachers. *See* ministers and preachers
Preston, Mrs., 206–207, 282
Price, William Allen, 262
Pritchett, Anna, 7, 38
protests, 259

Quaker Normal School, 265
Quakers, 264–265
Queen, Teena, 219
Quinn, William M.: biographical informa-
    tion, 282; gift slaves, 15; interview, 207–
    208; payment of slaves, 17; post–Civil War
    years, 50; runway slaves, 25

R. C. Gray (steamship), 234
rabbit's feet, 37
Ramblet, Andy, 79
Rave, Herman, 197
Rawick, George P., 8–9, 13, 56
Ray, Wright, 68
Reconstruction, 120
Red-Headed Jesse, 116, 304
Reddick, Lawrence D., 5
Reitz, Clem, 268
Reitz, John, 268
relief stations, 51, 151
religion: angels, 168–169; baptism, 32, 112,
    232; Baptists, 78, 128, 163, 209, 232, 241,
    271; biblical stance on slavery, 118; camp
    meetings, 119–120; Catholicism, 33, 155,
    219; conversion, 32, 252; emancipation as
    theme of sermons, 187; freedom of slaves,
    103; Hickory Quakers, 264–265;
    importance of to slaves, 34, 111–112, 150,
    219, 226; importance of Bible, 152, 231,
    240–241; in Liberia, 85; Methodists, 33,
    188, 190, 220; missionaries, 129–130;
    Mormonism, 117; prayer, 31–32, 100–101,
    169, 187, 209; religious service of African
    Americans, 77–78; revivals, 32, 69, 119–
    120, 252, 264, 271, 302; songs, 136–137,
    168–169; spirituals, 120. *See also* churches;
    ministers and preachers
Remembering Slavery (Kelley), 13
revivals: Samuel Bell on, 69, 302; Rachael
    Duncan on, 119–120; Mollie Tate on, 252;
    various accounts of, 32; Nancy Whallen
    on, 264; Alex Woodson on, 271

Revolutionary War, 199, 311–312
Reynolds, Betsy, 309
Richardson, Candies: biographical informa-
    tion, 282; children's ficts, 42; clothing for
    slaves, 17; food for slaves, 15; interview,
    208–211; plantation life, 14; post–Civil
    War years, 51; recollections of the Civil
    War, 47; religion of slaves, 31, 33
riverboats. *See* steamships
Roberts Settlement, 4
Robinson, Joe, 21, 30, 54, 211, 282
Robinson, Rowland E., 11
Robinson, Tom, 157
"Rock Candy" (folk game), 42, 214–215
Rockville Republican, 67, 203
Rogers, Rice, 211
Rogers, Rosaline: biographical information,
    282; cabin of slaves, 14; education of
    slaves, 28; interview, 211–212; post–Civil
    War years, 50; religion of slaves, 31; shoes
    for slaves, 18
Rollins, Parthenia, 20, 212–214, 283
Rolliver H. Cook (steamship), 63
Roosevelt, Franklin D., 86
Roosevelt, Theodore, 59, 123, 183
Rose, Henry, 18, 170, 171
Rose, Katie: biographical information, 283;
    interview, 214–217; recollections of the
    Civil War, 45; slave folklore, 39, 41–42
Rose, Patrick, 214
Rose, Ruben, 170
The Rose Douglas (steamship), 92
roustabouts, 61, 63, 89, 91, 134–135
Rudd, Clark, 190
Rudd, John: biographical information, 283;
    interview, 217–219; Ku Klux Klan, 23–24;
    post–Civil War years, 53, 54; religion of
    slaves, 33; separation of slave families, 18;
    treatment of slaves, 20
Rudd, Liza, 217
Rudd, Manda and Jordan, 190
"Run Nigger Run" (folk song), 185
runaway slaves. *See* escaping slavery
Russell, Elizabeth: biographical information,
    283; children's ficts, 42; interview, 219–
    223; recollections of the Civil War, 45;
    slave folklore, 39

salt pork, 15
Samples, Zeke, 113

Samuels, Amanda Elizabeth (Lizzie), 20, 41, 223–224, 283

Savage, John, 203

Sawyer, Ben, 214

Scarber, Mary Elizabeth, 22, 53, 224–225, 283

Schaffer, Arthur, 25

Scherer, Anton, 177

Scholarly Press, 9

schools for African Americans: George Beatty on, 68; George Washington Buckner on, 83–85; country schools, 182; establishment of, 192, 259–260; Freedmen's Bureau schools, 28, 30, 132; Quaker Normal School, 265; teachers, 168, 199

Scott, Jake, 208

Scott, Jim, 208, 209

Scott, John, 158

Scott, Lulu: biographical information, 283; education of slaves, 29; interview, 225–227; post–Civil War years, 53; slave folklore, 36–37, 39

Scott, Sadie, 98

Scott, Will, 158

Second Baptist Church of Lafayette, Indiana, 128

Settle, Ophelia, 4

sexual exploitation of slaves, 26, 245

Shaffer, Arthur, 227–228, 283

Sherman, William Tecumseh, 122

shipyards, 230

shoes, 17–18, 272

Shop Notes, 266

Showers Brothers, 266

Shular, Andrew, 241

Shular, Liza, 241

Simms, Benjamin, 217

Simms, Jack, 28, 228, 283

Sims, John, 62–63

Sister Ridley, 40, 168

Six Nations, 91

Skelton, Robert, 183

Sketches of Prominent Citizens of 1876 (Nowland), 177

Slaughter, Billy: biographical information, 283; interview, 229–231; post–Civil War years, 54; recollections of the Civil War, 46, 48; religion of slaves, 34

Slaughter, G. H., 233

Slaughter, Moses: biographical information, 283; education of slaves, 29; interview, 231–234; post–Civil War years, 53; recollections of the Civil War, 46, 47; religion of slaves, 33

Slave Narrative Project, 6, 35

slave trade: auctions, 19, 23, 66, 117, 129, 146, 182, 242, 304; Robert Cheatham on, 102; Sarah Colbert on, 111; Mary Crane on, 113; families separated by, 18–19, 165–166, 202, 217; Solomon Hicks on, 150; Joseph Mosley on, 194–195; Amy Elizabeth Patterson on, 202; raising slaves for sale, 42, 161; sending slaves south, 155; slave traders, 23; slaveholders selling their own children, 99; Barney Stone on, 242; Anderson Whitted on, 266

Sloss, Bertha, 121

Slye, Elizabeth (Liza), 88

Smiley, Joe, 59, 60

Smiley, Mrs. Robert, 284

Smith, Alex: biographical information, 283; interview, 235–237; poverty in post–Civil War years, 54; treatment of slaves, 20

Smith, Ben, 200

Smith, D. B., 95

Smith, Della, 98

Smith, Elizabeth (Betty), 50, 54, 235–237

Smith, Harry, 89–90

Smith, Mattie Brown, 25, 237–239, 283, 310–312

Smith, Mrs. Robert, 22, 239

Smith, Sarah, 200

Smith, Susan: biographical information, 284; education of slaves, 28; interview, 239; post–Civil War years, 54; religion of slaves, 31; treatment of slaves, 20

Smith, Sylvester: biographical information, 284; food for slaves, 15; interview, 240; Newsom farm, 14; post–Civil War years, 49; recollections of the Civil War, 47

Smith, Virginia, 234

Smiths Landing, 135

Snyder, George, 217

Snyder, Henry, 217, 218

soldiers: attitudes toward slaves, 173; guerrillas, 268; Mrs. Preston on, 207; slaves' fears of, 188–189; slaves' support for Union, 200; song of, 224; use of plantations by, 171; Alfred (Pete) Wilson on, 267. See also Civil War; conscription; enlistment songs: "Dixie," 88, 134; "experience songs," 169; "Hear the Trumpet Sound," 134–135; hymns, 150; jubilee songs, 71; lullabies, 247–248; "Old Dan Tucker," 43, 192; at play parties, 254–255; "Run Nigger Run," 185; soldier's song, 224; spirituals, 120, 136–137, 307; "Swing Low Sweet Chariot," 32, 108; topics of slave songs, 168–169; "Turkey in the Straw," 194; "The Whistling Coon," 134–135

South Bend (steamship), 92

South Bend Tribune, 235

Southern Indiana Gas and Electric Company, 114–115, 303

Sporree, John, 219

spying during Civil War, 173, 222

square dances, 43, 192–193, 255

St. Marys (town), 91

Starks, Hester, 238–239, 312

steamships: *The Atlantic,* 87, 92; *B. S. Rhea,* 63; *The Banjo,* 91–92; *The Big Gray Eagle,* 87–88, 91; *The Bracelet,* 92; *Eclipse,* 87, 90; *Eldorado,* 63; *Ellen Gray,* 92; *Embassy,* 93; *The General Pike,* 92; *Gold Dust,* 63–64; *Gray Eagle,* 219; *Guiding Star,* 219; *Indiana,* 122; *Interchange,* 92; *The Kate Sarchet,* 92; *The Lue Evans,* 92; *The Masonic Gem,* 92; *The Messenger,* 92; *Morning Star,* 219; *New South,* 116; *The Prairie Rose,* 92; *R. C. Gray,* 234; *Rolliver H. Cook,* 63; *The Rose Douglas,* 92; *South Bend,* 92; *The Sultana,* 93; *Tempest,* 92; *The Union,* 92; George Taylor Burns on, 87–88; folklore of riverboat men, 36, 63, 89; food on, 231; music on, 61; roustabouts on, 63; Billy Slaughter on, 230

Sterrett (slaveholder), 270–271

Steward, Johnny, 170

Stewart, Mary Ann, 29, 240–241, 284

Stewart, William, 241

still houses, 250

Stiltz, Bill, 60

Stone, Barney: biographical information, 284; education of slaves, 29; interview, 241–244; recollections of the Civil War, 47; religious service of, 33; treatment of slaves, 23

Stone, Lemuel, 241

Stone, Steve, 208

Stonestreet, Mary, 244, 284

storage media for interviews, 6–7

stoves, 255, 268

Stowe, Charles Edward, 177

Stowe, Harriet Beecher, 177–179

Stranz, Allan, 177

Street, John, 201–202

Street, Louisa, 201

Stringer, Jane, 191

Strope, Albert, 170

Stubblefield, Elizabeth, 236

Stubblefield, Peter, 236

Stubblefield, Robert, 20

Sturgeon, E. T., 90

Suckow, Ruth, 12

Suggs, Adah Isabelle: biographical information, 284; education of slaves, 29; escaping slavery, 26; interview, 244–246; slave folklore, 37, 41; as source on Hettie McClain and Thomas Suggs, 179

Suggs, Thomas, 179, 180, 246

suicide, 218

Sullivan, William G., 177

The Sultana (steamship), 93

superstition. *See* folklore

Sutton, Katie, 37, 246–248, 284

"Swing Low Sweet Chariot," 32, 108

Tandy, Opal L., 140

Tate, Bill, 80, 249

Tate, Dave, 45, 249

Tate, Mary Emily (Mollie) Eaton: arrival in Portland, 253; biographical information, 284; clothing for slaves, 17; food of slaves, 15; interview, 248–252; recollections of the Civil War, 45, 47; religious conversion of, 32

Tate, Preston: background on, 248–249; biographical information, 284; clothing for slaves, 17; interview, 252–253; post–Civil War years, 53; recollections of the Civil War, 48

Taylor, Ben, 88

Taylor, Green, 87

Taylor, Priscilla, 175

Taylor, William A., 175

Taylor Barracks, 230

teachers, 168, 199. *See also* schools for African Americans

Tempest (steamship), 92

Terre Haute Tribune, 70, 240

Terrell, Louise, 16–17, 79
Thatcher, Reiny, 168–169
Thirteenth Amendment, 49, 180, 232
Thomas, Donald, 74
Thomas, Epsey, 175
Thomas, George, 16, 229, 253–255, 284
Thomas, Jim, 254
Thompson, Daniel, 74
Thompson, Ed, 255
Thompson, George, 28, 49, 255–256, 284
Thompson, Nancy, 175, 197
Thompson, P. M. B., 309
Thompson, William, 175, 197
Throm, Edward L., 139
Tippecanoe County Historical Society, 125
tobacco, 71, 154
Toney, Francis, 138
torture of slaves, 203–204
trains, 172–173
Trice, Dutch, 225
Tucker, Charlotte, 210
Tucker, Silas, 186
Tuttle, William W., 59, 308
Twyman, Joel W., 76
Tyler, Velsie, 65, 152, 167

Uncle Tom's Cabin (Stowe), 177–179
Underground Railroad: Robert Barton on, 66;
    Anthony Battle's description of, 26, 67;
    Walter Borland on, 75; Robert Cheatham
    on, 105; Thomas Magruder on, 179;
    Mattie Brown Smith on, 310–312
The Union (steamship), 92
Unwritten History of Slavery: Autobiographical
    Account of Negro Ex-Slaves (Fisk Univer-
    sity), 4, 9
U.S. Quartermaster Depot, 231

Van Cleve, Kay, 74
Van Meter, Beulah, 192
Vanderburgh County Courthouse, 165
Varnell, David, 134
voodoo, 97–98. See also folklore
Votaw, Jonas, 80
voting, 259

Wabash and Erie Canal, 114–115, 116, 304
Wade, Joe, 21, 256, 284
Wagner Post, 268
wainwrights, 258–259

Walker, C. J., 214
Walker, Henry, 300
Walker, James, 300, 302
Walker, Nelson, 119
Wamble, Reverend: biographical information,
    285; education of slaves, 29; interview,
    257–260; owners of, 14; treatment of
    slaves, 20, 22
Wamoick, Alexander, 165
Washington, George, 312
Watkins, Hettie, 144, 260
Watkins, Louis: biographical information,
    285; education of slaves, 29; interview,
    260–261; post–Civil War years, 49; re-
    ligion of slaves, 31; source of information
    on, 144
Watkins, Samuel, 50
Watson, Andrew P., 4
Watson, Samuel, 54, 261–263, 285
Watson, Thomas, 262
weather, 227
Webb, Henry, 25, 263, 285
weddings: Patsy Jane Bland on, 71–72; George
    Washington Buckner on, 82; John Moore
    on, 186; Henry Clay Moorman on, 43,
    189. See also gift slaves
Weil, Aaron, 300
Weil, Jesse, 300
Westbrook family, 257
wet nurses, 16, 202
Whallen, Nancy, 32, 47, 263–264, 285
Whicker, J. W., 184
whipping of slaves. See accounts under
    individual interviews
"The Whistling Coon" (song), 134–135
Whitted, Anderson, 264; biographical infor-
    mation, 285; education of slaves, 28; in-
    terview, 264–266; post–Civil War years,
    51, 53; recollections of the Civil War,
    46
will-o'-the-wisps, 39
Williams, Ike, 163
Williams, Tom, 270
Williams, Wattie, 113
Wilson, Alfred (Pete), 266–267, 285
Wilson, James, 134
Wilson, Johnny, 70
Wilson, Pete, 53, 312
Wilson, Woodrow, 53, 84–85
Winlock, Adam, 268

Winlock, George, 48, 267–270, 285
witches and witchcraft: Joseph William Carter on, 97; Sarah Colbert on, 109–110; George Fortman on, 133–134; Jane Garmon (witch), 38; John Moore on, 187. *See also* folklore
wood yards, 92
Woodford, Charles, 237, 310, 311
Woodruff, Justice, 310
Woodson, Alex: biographical information, 285; folk customs, 42–43; interview, 270–272; post–Civil War years, 54; recollections of the Civil War, 45, 48; work bees, 44
Woollen, William Wesley, 177

Wooten, Jesse, 166
work bees, 44
Works Progress Administration (WPA), 3, 5, 30
Wright, Thomas, 88
Writers' Unit of the Library of Congress Project, 7

yellow fever, 231
Yetman, Norman R., 8–9
Yoe, John, 251
Young, Anthony, 17, 49, 272–273, 285
Young, Cassie, 136
Young, Dave, 225
Young, Mary, 273

R ONALD L. BAKER, Chairperson and Professor of English at Indiana State University, is the author of *Folklore in the Writings of Rowland E. Robinson, Hoosier Folk Legends, Jokelore: Humorous Folktales from Indiana, French Folklife in Old Vincennes, From Needmore to Prosperity: Hoosier Place Names in Folklore and History,* and numerous articles in folklore journals. He is co-author of *Indiana Place Names* and editor of *The Folklore Historian,* journal of the Folklore and History Section of the American Folklore Society, and a monograph, *The Study of Place Names.*